Ways of Knowing

D1051121

Ways of Knowing

Competing Methodologies in Social and Political Research

Jonathon W. Moses and
Torbjørn L. Knutsen

Contents

List of Figures

List of Tables

Preface and Acknowledgements

Nearly a decade ago, your authors were enlisted to collaborate on a social science methods course for incoming graduate students. Because our research interests and backgrounds were quite different at the outset, this took some doing. Indeed, the book before you is the remarkable product of a long-running collaboration between students and faculty at the Department of Sociology and Political Science, at the Norwegian University of Science and Technology (NTNU). This journey travelled together has been an enjoyable one, and we hope our pleasure and enthusiasm is evident in the pages that follow.

In the beginning, the course that inspired this text aimed to introduce students to the methods and methodology of what is generally (if somewhat polemically) called 'positivist' social science. Although our students were already getting a strong introduction to statistical methods, the department felt it was necessary to provide more training for those students who would need to employ other research methods. Thus, the original focus of the course was on traditional philosophy of science issues, embroidered with comparative and case-study research methods.

Over the years, however, we began to realize that much of what our students were interested in did not fit very comfortably under the positivist rubric. Indeed, the term itself (positivism) began to grate on us. Worse, because of the strongly positivist orientation of their methods education, many of our students (not to mention our colleagues!) were often misinterpreting the way in which methods were being employed by influential contemporary social scientists. In response to these challenges, we began to expand the course to include alternative approaches to social science. Upon doing this, we started to recognize a need to distinguish between the different ways that particular methods are employed in varying methodological contexts.

The resulting product is *Ways of Knowing*. We have designed the book to cover and reflect upon what we understand to be the two main methodological traditions in contemporary social science: naturalism, which corresponds to what we called positivism, above; and constructivism, which, as you will see, corresponds to what many people call 'interpretivism'. These two methodologies are juxtaposed against one another to emphasize the underlying differences in how scholars from each tradition see and understand the world that they study. We then look at how particular methods are employed in different ways within each methodological tradition.

Given this book's remarkably long incubation period, it is difficult to acknowledge all the help and advice we have received. More than one late evening has been spent worrying that we may have forgotten to acknowledge an important source of inspiration or information. Perhaps our greatest partner has been time itself: we have benefited from being able to reflect back on the experiences of the last decade, changing and refining the arguments each time we taught our course anew. As one debt often leads to another, we would like to thank our respective families for putting up with all the time we have devoted to this project.

Obviously, our approach has been greatly influenced by the critical attention of several generations of students. Indeed, many students have been subjected to rough drafts of this book as we experimented with different ways to present the material. To all of our students: thank you for your patience, help and support.

As our university has a very liberal sabbatical programme, we have often found ourselves co-teaching the course with various colleagues. Through our collaboration, these colleagues have inevitably affected our thinking. As a result, and although they may not be aware of it, Jennifer Bailey, Espen Moe and Stephen Swindle have all contributed in their own way to the final product. Ola Listhaug, the patriarch of our department, has been instrumental in allowing us the freedom and time to pursue these interests (and many others). It is for this reason that we have dedicated our book to him.

We would be remiss if we didn't thank our publisher, Steven Kennedy, who – over several years – has both encouraged and badgered us about how this book should evolve. Steven is the model editor: well-informed, engaged and opinionated, with a well-trained eye for the market. There can be no doubt that our argument and this book have been greatly improved by his suggestions and the very useful and detailed comments of Palgrave's anonymous referees. To all these readers, we are thankful.

Despite all the time we have used, and the help we have incurred, we alone are responsible for any errors that remain. We do hope they are not many.

Jonathon W. Moses and Torbjørn L. Knutsen
Trondheim, Norway

The authors and publisher would like to thank the following who have kindly given permission for the use of copyright material:

Fagbokforlaget for Figure 3.1.
The American Statistical Association for Table 11.1 and Figure 11.1. Reprinted with permission from *The American Statistician*; Copyright 1973 by the American Statistical Association. All rights reserved.

Chapter 1

Introduction

> What we shall see is something like a battle of gods and giants going on
> between them over their quarrel about reality.
>
> Plato, *The Sophist*, 246

For as long as can be recalled, we have argued over different ways of
knowing. Gods, giants and even reasonable people cannot seem to agree
about the nature of reality and how we can understand it. There are –
quite simply – different ways of knowing, and students of social science
need to be aware of these differences and how they affect the methods
they choose to study social phenomena. Our book takes aim at this broad
target.

When the battles are between gods and giants over the nature of reality, we can expect sparks to fly. But the battles between mere mortals, or
even scientists, can also generate a great deal of heat. This heat was
clearly evident in a recent skirmish over the nature and extent of the
threat to our environment.

In 2001, Bjørn Lomborg – a former Greenpeace member and (then)
Associate Professor of Political Science at the University of Aarhus in
Denmark – published *The Skeptical Environmentalist*, a thick, dense,
astonishingly well-documented (1600 references and 2928 notes) critical
attack on the modern environmental movement. In return for his scepticism, Lomborg's book has been vilified; its author accused of fraud and
dishonesty, called the 'Antichrist', and even compared with Nazi defend-
ers.[1] If this was not enough, the Danish Committees on Scientific
Dishonesty (DCSD) judged the book 'clearly contrary to the standards of
good scientific practice' (DCSD, 2002, p. 9).[2]

Scientific American, one of the world's most popular science journals,
led the charge. Its 11-page editorial, subtitled 'Science defends itself
against the Skeptical Environmentalist', is remarkable if only because the
editor-in-chief of the world's most prominent journal of popular science
is willing to suggest that the scientific community speaks with a singular
voice. The editor invokes four 'leading experts' who were chosen to
speak on behalf of science. But these voices were hardly impartial,
autonomous or refereed; indeed, they were the voices of scientists that
Lomborg had criticized in his book. Worse, these critics did not grapple

1

with the facts in Lomborg's book, the sources he relied on, or even his reasoning; rather they attacked his novice credentials, (implicitly) juxtaposed against 'investigators who have devoted their lives' to natural science. Worse yet, when Lomborg (2002) tried to defend his reputation by publishing the text on his own website (with interspersed and detailed responses to every point raised by his critics), *Scientific American* threatened to sue Lomborg over copyright issues.

We do not wish to appear as supporters of Lomborg's provocative treatise. If for no other reason, he has earned our sympathy and admiration for simply surviving such a pounding from the scientific establishment. More to the point: we do not pretend expertise or insight into the issues that fuelled the Lomborg affair – indeed, we remain sceptical of any attempt (on either side) to simplify what must necessarily be a very complex problem. However, because Lomborg's book ruffled so many feathers, it provides a fascinating glimpse of the way in which modern science will have us understand the world. The nature of the skirmish demonstrates that the scientific process is not driven solely by the ideals of impartial and measured dialogue, drawing on empirical and rational support. Rather, it would appear that presuppositions or priors, aggressive rhetoric, economic and legal muscle, and authority all have a role to play in securing scientific knowledge.

To uncover this quarrel about reality we have to dig below the surface. Underneath any given research design and choice of methods lies a researcher's (often implicit) understanding of the nature of the world and how it should be studied. These underlying priors provide researchers with the philosophical ballast that is necessary to address important questions concerning the nature of truth, certainty and objectivity in a given project. These are very important issues, but they are receiving less and less of the attention they deserve from practising scientists. The reason for this is not difficult to discern. Contemporary social scientists enjoy a plethora of new and more sophisticated methods. As a consequence, social scientists are devoting more time and energy to mastering these new methods. The result is predictable, if unfortunate: much of contemporary social science is driven by a given researcher's familiarity with particular methods. This preoccupation often comes with very little reflection about how a given method corresponds (or doesn't) to the researcher's underlying methodology.

Our book aims to correct this unfortunate shortcoming by focusing on the important ways in which methodologies and methods relate to one another. Towards that end we use this chapter to introduce two central methodological perspectives: naturalism and constructivism. These two methodologies can be said to constitute the main camps in the battle over reality in today's social science research. For this reason, they provide the basic design of the book that follows: the first half is dedicated to how methods are employed in a naturalist methodology; the latter half looks at the same methods, as employed in a constructivist methodology.

Because these methodological traditions draw on different understandings of the nature of the social world, and on different ways of coming to understand that world, each of them employs common methods in different ways. For example, both naturalists and constructivists use comparisons, but they use them differently. Our primary objective is to highlight these differences so that students will better understand how their methodological priors affect the methods they choose and the way in which they use them. To underscore these differences, the closing part of this introductory chapter provides an overview of the book's design.

In the end, we hope to encourage students to become more aware of their own methodological positions and how these might affect their research. We also hope to make students more aware of the various ways in which methods can be employed in social science projects. Most of us study social phenomena because we are fascinated by their depth and complexity. With this book we wish to show how there is a corresponding degree of complexity and depth associated with the ways in which we can come to understand, and explain, these social phenomena.

Methodological Foundations

The Lomborg affair makes us realize that scientists disagree about some pretty fundamental issues. Indeed, this book will depict social scientists differing on a number of these. For example: How do we understand the nature of the world we study? How should we assess which methods, data and evidence are appropriate? What is the overall objective of scientific study? In the midst of all these differences, how do we assess competing claims? How do we know who is right? Is one side necessarily right, and the other wrong? How do we know?

To answer these difficult questions we must begin by simplifying. We do this by suggesting that most work in social science can be grouped under two methodological rubrics, which will be described in much greater detail below. These two different methodologies incorporate radically different views of the world and how we can come to understand it. As a consequence, each methodology employs similar methods in different ways – towards different objectives. It is our contention that many of the most significant differences and the major disagreements in social science can be traced back to these methodological differences.

Thus far, we have been using the word 'methodology' in a way that may be unfamiliar to students of social science. The reason for this will become clearer as this chapter proceeds. For now we might draw on Kenneth Waltz's depiction of 'methodologies' as something different – something more basic and comprehensive – than 'methods'. As such, he is worried that students,

> have been much concerned with methods and little concerned with the logic of their use. This reverses the proper priority of concern, for once a methodology is adopted, the choice of methods becomes merely a tactical matter. It makes no sense to start the journey that is to bring us to an understanding of a phenomenon without asking which method-ological routes might possibly lead there.   (Waltz, 1979, p. 13)

We concur. And we have written this book with an eye towards intro-ducing the student to the way in which methods and methodologies are related.

One useful way to consider this relationship is to think of methods as tools, and methodologies as well-equipped toolboxes.[3] With this anal-ogy, methods can be understood as problem-specific techniques. Thus, we can expect electricians to view the world differently than carpenters (that is, they aim to resolve different types of problems). Each tradesper-son relies on a different mixture of tools or approaches for solving the problems he encounters. This is a good thing: when inappropriate tools are employed, a tradesman can do great damage. Thus, we should not be surprised to find the electrician's toolbox filled with a different set of tools than those filling the carpenter's. On the other hand, we should not be surprised to find that the two people sometimes use the same tool.

Perhaps the toolbox analogy is too unwieldy in the hands of the build-ing trades. Instead, we might consider two different approaches to human health: one, the practice of 'the medical profession', the other that of 'homeopathic practitioners'. Without pretending to know all the differences that separate these two groups, we can recognize that their approaches imply different ways of understanding (and hence promot-ing) human health. Given these different approaches, we might expect a minor crisis should the medical bags of the scientific and homeopathic healers be inadvertently switched. Having said that, of course, there may be some tools that both healers share – yet the tools are used in different ways, and for different objectives.

If this analogy is useful, it is alarming for a number of social scientists who use the term 'methodology' as a fancy word for statistical methods. Thus, the central theme of John E. Jackson's (1996) overview of politi-cal methodology is the importation of econometric (read 'statistical') methods. For such scholars, it would seem, there is only one truly scientific method, and everything else is cold leftovers: having mastered the use of a hammer, the whole world around them can be understood in terms of nails. We hasten to note that this myopic affinity to a particular method is not restricted to statisticians: too many scholars, from a number of different methods backgrounds, are bound to a particular approach.

If we accept that methodologies imply real and important differences in understanding the world, then we can follow Hughes (1990, p. 11) in arguing that students should be aware of the methodological undergirdings of the social studies they read and (eventually will) produce:

> [For] every research tool or procedure is inextricably embedded in commitments to particular versions of the world and to knowing that world. To use a questionnaire, to use an attitude scale, to take the role of a participant observer, to select a random sample, to measure rates of population growth, and so on, is to be involved in conceptions of the world which allow these instruments to be used for the purposes conceived. No technique or method of investigation (and this is as true of the natural science as it is of the social) is self-validating: its effectiveness, i.e. its very status as a research instrument making the world tractable to investigation, is, from a philosophical point of view, ultimately dependent on epistemological justifications.

For the student of social science, however, this methodological diversity can be confusing. 'Methodology' often appears as one member in a trio from the philosophy of science, the two others being 'ontology' and 'epistemology'. These are the three musketeers of metaphysics – one of the more speculative fields of philosophy. *Ontology* is the most abstract of the three terms. It means the study of being – the study of the basic building blocks of existence. The fundamental question in the field of ontology is: 'What is the world really made of?' *Epistemology* is a more straightforward term; it denotes the philosophical study of knowledge. 'What is knowledge?' is the basic question of epistemology.

The third musketeer, *methodology*, is also a fairly straightforward term. It refers to the ways in which we acquire knowledge. 'How do we know?' is the basic question in methodology. Although methodology is a simple-enough term, it is commonly wrapped in ambiguity. The reason is that 'methodology' is sometimes used as a fancy synonym for 'method'. But these two terms are not synonyms. In this book, method refers to research techniques, or technical procedures of a discipline. Methodology, on the other hand, denotes an investigation of the concepts, theories and basic principles of reasoning on a subject. The methodology of the social sciences, then, is to be understood simply as philosophy of science applied to the social sciences.

Ancient philosophical ghosts, then, often frighten the new student who investigates conflicting ontological, epistemological and methodological clues. Worse, modern methods courses (and texts) often shelter students from their fears by assuming a single methodological, epistemological and ontological starting point. As we shall see in the chapters that follow, this often creates greater confusion later on, as students observe how the same method might be used in different guises towards different objectives – under different ontological presumptions. It is our experience that the beginning social science student can be helped by a clear overview of the different ways that methodology and method choices overlap.

This book aims to provide that broad overview. Our objective is to supply the larger context, into which more focused methods texts can be inserted and employed. In doing so, we hope to clarify some of the misunderstandings that students often encounter when they do not fully recognize the way in which one's choice of methods often (implicitly) reflects contentious methodological assumptions. Consequently, we hope to narrow the gap that now separates the implied ontologies and the methods employed by so many of today's social scientists (Hall, 2003).

In doing so, we raise some difficult and awkward questions about the relationship between the two main perspectives. Some authors, for example Marsh and Furlong (2002), argue that methodological perspectives are like skins – once you've got one, you're pretty much stuck with it. We are not convinced. We would rather liken methodologies to jackets that you can put on and take off. We think social science is better served by researchers who master several methodologies, who can self-consciously choose among concepts and theories, and who command many basic principles of reasoning. In the text that follows, we provide several illustrations of how it is possible to move between methodological traditions – often with great success. Our aim is to provide students with enough methodological awareness that they can become informed and careful consumers of social studies. Although we will touch on ontological and epistemological issues, we do so only lightly. Last, but not least: we intend to leave the ontological and epistemological proselytizations to others.

This way of thinking about the world is perhaps most familiar to students of International Relations (IR). For generations, IR students have been taught to interpret the world through three disparate ideological positions: liberalism, realism and radicalism (or Marxism). These students learn to recognize the different actors and levels of analysis associated with each ideology, and are taught to understand the world from the perspective of each. Many of us were taught to think of these different ideological perspectives in terms of 'different-coloured lenses', which implies that the thing being studied is the same for each viewer, while the thing being viewed might vary from lens to lens. The objective of this common practice was *not* to find the one ideology that 'best' fits the real world, but to emphasize the fact that the world can be perceived in different and contrasting ways.

This is roughly how we would like you to think about the different methodologies that we describe below. Different social scientists approach the world with different assumptions about how it actually is, and how they should appropriately study it. As a consequence, standard methods are used in different ways, when employed by scientists coming from different methodological perspectives. Although some of us will sympathize with one methodology more than another, all of us must be aware of the existence of these differences and how they affect the way in which methods are used.

Although we will spend a great deal more time in subsequent chapters (Chapters 2 and 8, in particular) describing the basic philosophical components to these two methodologies, we want to use this introduction to briefly lay out the methodological terrain as it appears to the practising social scientist. This terrain is dominated by two methodological traditions: naturalism and constructivism.

We are aware that philosophers of science may feel uncomfortable with such a simple depiction of the scientific world. But our intention is to help students understand the nature of contemporary social science research (not outline the nature of contemporary philosophical debate), and we contend that this research is still strongly characterized by this simple methodological dichotomy. Indeed, we think that this methodological divide is the most important cleavage separating contemporary social scientists.

We hasten to add that we have created these methodological traditions as ideal types – they do not exist independently in the world. As is often the case in science, we are imposing a simple model that divides the complicated world of social scientists into two competing camps. Worse, since they are ideal types, individual scientists might not feel comfortable in either camp; nor do the camps need to be seen as necessarily exclusionary or as opposites. For this reason, it may be more useful to think of these two methodologies as end points on an imaginary continuum, where individual authors find themselves at home some place between them. Indeed, both of us have subscribed to each methodological tradition at different times and in different places.

More recently, scholars have developed a new approach that attempts to bridge the gap that separates naturalism from constructivism. In contrast to the first two methodologies, scientific realism can be seen as a distinct movement, to which philosophers and practitioners of science actually claim allegiance. Because it has yet to make much of an explicit impact on the way in which social scientists conduct their research, we only refer to scientific realism in our introductory and concluding chapters, to show how it relates to the methodologies that still dominate the field.

Now that we have begun to throw out some pretty large and messy terms (naturalism, constructivism, realism), it is time to describe them in more detail.

Naturalism

How do we know? For most of the past century, the social scientist's answer to this question has been made with a nod to the natural sciences. In the push for scientific legitimacy, and the funding that follows in its wake, social scientists have quietly adopted a view of the world that was first articulated in the natural sciences. This view assumes that there is a Real World out there, independent of our experience of it, and that we can gain access to that World by thinking, observing and recording our experiences carefully. This process helps scientists reveal patterns that exist in nature but are often obscured by the complexities of life. Thus, we call this methodology *naturalism*, as it seeks to discover and explain patterns that are assumed to exist in nature.

In different academic contexts, naturalism is known by many different names. The most common of these is 'positivism', but 'empiricism' and 'behaviouralism' are also used to describe the same basic methodological position. As each of these terms, for a variety of reasons, has fallen into disrepute, or is used as a polemical epithet, we think it is useful to employ a more neutral and descriptive term to capture this methodology's essential characteristics.

Naturalists rely heavily on knowledge that is generated by sensual perception, such as observation and direct experience. For a naturalist, something is true when somebody has seen it to be true (and/or recorded it as such). As we shall see, naturalists also employ logic and reason. Ultimately, however, reason and logic need to be supported by direct experience if the naturalist is to rely on the knowledge that is produced.

From these core (ontological and epistemological) beliefs, naturalists have developed a rather narrow set of criteria for evaluating the reliability of the knowledge we produce. In particular, social scientists have increasingly turned to falsification and predictive capacity as the standards for evaluating their knowledge. From here, mainstream social science has developed a hierarchy of methods that can be used to test our knowledge under different circumstances.

Although it is not easy to summarize a methodological tradition – and we will examine the naturalist methodology in more detail in the chapter that follows (Chapter 2) – we might suggest that the naturalist's approach embraces the following five features:

- There exist regularities or patterns in nature that can be observed and described.
- Statements based on these regularities can be tested empirically according to a falsification principle and a correspondence theory of truth.
- It is possible to distinguish between value-laden and factual statements (and facts are, in principle, theoretically independent).
- The scientific project should be aimed at the general (nomothetic) at the expense of the particular (ideographic).
- Human knowledge is both singular and cumulative.

Perhaps the easiest way to understand the ambitious nature of the naturalist project is to recognize it in the influence and success of Edward O. Wilson's (2003) *Consilience*. Wilson, a biologist accustomed to working with ants, believes that all knowledge is intrinsically unified and interlocked by a small number of natural laws. Using the natural sciences as his model, Wilson sketches a project of unrivalled ambition: he aims to unify all the major branches of knowledge under the banner of (natural) science. Because there exists a Real World out there, independent of our experience of it; because we can know that World by careful thinking and observation in an objective and falsifiable manner; because such thinking and observations can uncover general patterns and laws that interact in a singular and cumulative project; then the scientific project is an enormous and singular one. This is a remarkably beautiful vision, but one which will require a great deal more synthesis and agreement among scientists than exists today, or ever has existed.

From this summary description of naturalist science we can return to examine the Lomborg affair, as described above. For social scientists, Lomborg is clearly employing a naturalist approach to his study of the environment: he uses sophisticated statistical techniques to try and uncover hidden patterns in the world, and he does so in a way that is falsifiable, cumulative and ostensibly objective. Thus, we might be surprised by the reaction to Lomborg's work by the broader naturalist community. For all parties agree on central ontological and epistemological features. All of them display the naturalist's firm commitment to truth. They all accept that there is a Real World out there independent of our experience, and claim that we can know that World by way of an objective and unfailing process. For naturalists, the rules of engagement are clear and the standards of evaluation are shared: Lomborg's research must be either true or false. In short, naturalists leave themselves little room for disagreement.

As a consequence of the methodological tradition in which it is anchored, you might think that a heated debate among naturalists would be a struggle about facts alone. But this is clearly not the case in the Lomborg affair. There is apparently more to science than observation, facts and proper procedural designs. Because the lessons from his research appear to conflict with the consensus among (natural) scientists, *The Skeptical Environmentalist* is perceived as not only false, but heretical.

Constructivism

Although the naturalist view has dominated modern social science, it has not escaped criticism, nor does it stand alone. Many social scientists are leery of accepting the naturalist's view of the world, as many of the patterns that interest them are seen to be ephemeral and contingent on human agency. For these social scientists, the patterns of interest are not firmly rooted in nature but are a product of our own making. Each of us sees different things, and what we see is determined by a complicated mix of social and contextual influences and/or presuppositions. It is for this reason that we refer to our second methodology as *constructivist*: it recognizes the important role of the observer and society in constructing the patterns that we study as social scientists.

As with other methodological positions, constructivists are known by a variety of names, many of which are not particularly endearing. The most common of these is probably 'interpretivism', but constructivism also corresponds to 'Gadamer's hermeneutics, Habermas's Critical Theory . . . French deconstructionists, post-structuralists, and other similarly suspicious continental characters . . .' (Ball, 1987, p. 2)! This methodology is described in more detail in Chapter 8, and the latter part of the book shows how constructivists employ traditional methods. For now, we wish to briefly introduce constructivism so that you can better understand how it differs from naturalism and why we use it as its methodological counterweight in the overall design of the book.

At the bottom of the differences separating naturalists from constructivists is the recognition that people are intelligent, reflective and wilful, and that these characteristics matter for how we understand the world. Constructivists recognize that we do not just 'experience' the world objectively or directly: our experiences are channelled through the human mind – in often elusive ways. It is in this short channel between the eye and the brain – between sense perception and the experience of the mind – that we find many challenges to naturalism. When our scientific investigation is aimed at perceptions of the world, rather than the world 'as it is', we open the possibility for multiple worlds (or, more accurately, multiple perceptions).

Consequently, constructivists recognize that people may look at the same thing and perceive it differently. Individual characteristics (such as age, gender or race) or social characteristics (such as era, culture and language) can facilitate or obscure a given perception of the world. Recognizing the wilfulness of human agency complicates any attempt to try and capture it in simple, law-like terms (as is common in the naturalist world). Once a social 'law' is known to human actors, they turn to exploit it in ways that can undermine its law-like features (Popper, 2002).

To make matters even more complicated, human agency creates things that have a different ontological status than the objects studied by natural scientists. As Max Weber (1949, p. 81) noted: 'We are cultural beings, endowed with the capacity and the will to take a deliberate attitude towards the world and to lend it significance.' This capacity gives rise to a class of facts that do not exist in the physical object world: social facts (such as money, property rights, sovereignty) depend on human agreement, and typically require human institutions, for their very existence (Searle, 1995, p. 2).

Because they recognize such ontological diversity and complexity, constructivists tend to draw on more and different types of evidence and proof. While constructivists recognize experience and reason as useful epistemological devices, they also realize that both of these can be influenced by the above-mentioned contextual factors – undermining any claims to their being objective transmitters of truth. Because social contexts are filled with meaning, constructivists find utility in a much broader set of epistemological tools, including empathy, authority, myths and so on.

Given the fact that constructivists focus on the reflective and idiosyncratic nature of knowledge, the overall objective of constructivist science is quite different from its naturalist counterpart. Following Quentin Skinner (1975, p. 216), we might say that constructivists try to understand action 'not in causal and positivist terms as a precipitate of its context, but rather in circular and hermeneutic terms as a meaningful item within a wider context of conventions and assumptions, a context which serves to endow its constituent parts with meaning while attaining its own meaning from the combination of its constituent parts'. Rather than uncovering a true account, constructivists seek to capture and understand the meaning of a social action for the agent performing it (as well as for the scholar studying it). If something appears meaningful or real to a social agent, then it may affect his behaviour and have real consequences for the society around him.

While naturalists try to uncover singular truths in a falsifiable manner that corresponds to one true reality, constructivists embrace the particular and use their knowledge to expand our moral sympathies and political understandings. For the constructivist, truth lies in the eyes of the observer, and in the constellation of power and force that supports that truth. As even our descriptions of events are not free from the biases that surround us, constructivists have little hope of securing an absolute truth: the best we can do is to be honest and open about the way in which our contexts (and those of our subject matter) frame the way in which we come to understand. This is not to say that constructivists are all relativists: there can be better and worse constructivist accounts. Rather, constructivists are more hesitant and careful to claim truth as their own.

How, then, would constructivists interpret the Lomborg affair? First of all, constructivists would tend to approach a study of environmental crises from an entirely different perspective. While naturalists prefer experimental and statistical studies, the constructivist would argue that a better understanding of environmental crises might be gleaned by a more detailed examination of a particular event, in light of larger (global) developments.

More to the point, constructivists would distance themselves from Lomborg's attempt to try and capture a singular truth about the state of the world's environment: they have little need to argue for the predominance of one truth over the other. Instead, the constructivist's focus would turn from trying to document truth to establishing the other relevant factors that explain why one view of the world becomes 'true', at the expense of others. For the constructivist the battle is not so much about truth as it is about the power, interests and identities of those involved. Consequently, the Lomborg affair can be used to illustrate how attempts to describe scientific discovery in neutral terms (in terms of their reliance on empirical support, a firm distinction between empirical and normative knowledge, and so on) are misleading. Instead, constructivists encourage us to look closely at the potential role of power, ideas and authority in explaining reality and scientific progress.

Scientific Realism

Over the past several decades a new philosophy of science has risen to challenge the dominance of naturalism. In stark contrast to both naturalism and constructivism, scientific realism constitutes a self-conscious school, where scholars pride themselves in membership (although the name of the club tends to vary somewhat). Although they are known by many different names – including 'transcendental realists', 'relational realists', 'critical realists', and 'empirical realists' – scientific realists are philosophers of science on a mission: they offer a fully fledged metaphysical position by blending some of the most attractive features of both the naturalist and constructivist approaches.

Because of its relative youth, and because it was born in the thin and rarified air of metaphysics, scientific realism has yet to make a noticeable impact on the everyday practice of social science. For this reason we have not incorporated it into the basic framework of our book, or provided it with a more detailed philosophy-of-science account in a subsequent chapter, as we do with naturalism and constructivism.[4] This, we fear, would undermine the symmetry of the argument that follows, as scientific realism cuts across our methodological divide in a number of different ways. Still, scientific realism is an approach with much promise, and for that reason it is important to introduce it to the reader. Doing so allows us to reflect on how scientific realism differs from both naturalism and constructivism, and the more pluralist methodological approach we are advocating in the chapters that follow.

In a practical sense, scientific realism straddles the ontological positions of naturalism and constructivism. This, in itself, is worth some reflection, as it helps us to understand the nature of the difference that separates our two main methodological positions. At its ontological core, scientific realism comes closest to naturalism. Scientific realists recognize that there exists a Real World independent of our experience. At the same time they embrace Weber's famous constructivist maxim, that man is an animal suspended in webs of meaning that he himself has spun. Scientific realists realize that there can be many layers to the reality that they study, and that their access to the one 'Real World' is highly complicated. The more complicated the picture, the closer scientific realists come to the constructivist's point of view. Yet, they never let go of naturalism.

The constructivists' position is akin to the famous Eastern guru who tells his disciples that the world rests on the back of a tiger, and that the tiger is supported by an elephant, who stands on a giant turtle. When one of the disciples timidly asks what the giant turtle, in turn, stands on, the guru quickly replies: 'Ah, after that there is turtles all the way down!' In a sense, scientific realism provides a convenient way of avoiding the problem of two different and irreconcilable ontologies. After all, we doubt there are many constructivists who are willing to reject outright the possibility that a Real World might exist out there, buried deep, deep, deep, down. The relevant (and practical) questions to ask are: How deeply buried is this Real World? Does it make sense to employ research methods that assume it lies just beneath the surface?

While scientific realists recognize many layers of truth, and share with constructivists a realization that the social world is filled with complexity, they believe that the best way to uncover these buried truths is by way of scientific (read naturalist) approaches. Thus, Ian Shapiro (2005, pp. 8–9) has summarized the core commitment of scientific realism as the 'twofold conviction that the world consists of causal mechanisms that exist independently of our study – or even awareness – of them, and that the methods of science hold out the best possibility of our grasping their true character'.

But the similarities with naturalism tend to stop there. Scientific realists avoid references to 'universal laws' and hypothetic–deductive approaches to explanation; they are critical of those who use falsifiability as a means to distinguish between science and nonsense; and scientific realists even question the neutrality of the scientist (and his language!).

In short, scientific realists focus on 'necessity and contingency rather than regularity, on open rather than closed systems, on the ways in which causal processes could produce quite different results in different contexts . . .' (Sayer, 2000, p. 5). Compared to naturalists, scientific realists are willing to open up the scientific project by recognizing the possibility that powers can (and do) exist unexercised. In other words, scientific realists recognize and appreciate the open-ended nature of human exchange.

Where does this discussion lead us? As you will soon discover, we share much in common with scientific realists. This is especially true with respect to the role of methods in science. We concur with scientific realists in recognizing that good science should be driven by questions or problems, not by methods.

> Compared to positivism [naturalism] and interpretivism [constructivism], critical realism endorses or is compatible with a relatively wide range of research methods, but it implies that the particular choices should depend on the nature of the object of study and what one wants to learn about it. For example, ethnographic and quantitative approaches are radically different but each can be appropriate for different and legitimate tasks – the former perhaps for researching, say, a group's norms and customs, the latter for researching world trade flows. Perhaps more importantly, realists reject cookbook prescriptions of method which allow one to imagine that one can do research by simply applying them without having a scholarly knowledge of the object of study in question.   (Sayer, 2000, p. 19)

We agree completely with this. As a result, we have written this book to try and help students recognize how methods and methodologies relate, and, consequently, how methods can be employed in a number of different ways. More importantly, we hope that this recognition will help students realize the importance of tailoring their choice of methods to the problems that interest them (rather than tailoring their problems to the methods they have learned).

Where we differ from scientific realists is in the perceived need to define a new unifying scientific tradition. Scientific realism introduces itself as an approach for those constructivists who feel a need to enter into the scientific fold. Following Lane (1996, p. 364): 'it has now become possible to qualify as a scientist without being a positivist'. In short, scientific realism offers a new universal approach – one that can straddle the natural and social sciences, as well as the naturalist and constructivist traditions. It is a great synthesis of the two main methodological traditions in contemporary science, as described above.

We are leery of such ambitions. By contrast, we wish to encourage students to be sensitive to the methodological priors of social scientists, and to become more conscious and aware of how these priors affect our work (and how it should be evaluated). In short, we are sceptical of universal narratives. We do not proselytize for any given methodological position, or claim that one position provides better answers to all of life's difficult questions. Ours is a call for methodological pluralism, not methodological conformity.

Chapter Outline and Logic

This book aims to provide an approachable introduction to the main methodologies and methods currently employed in the social sciences. In contrast to existing methods textbooks, which aim to provide cookbook-like sketches of particular methods under a single methodological rubric, we aim to survey the broad horizons of contemporary social science research. To do this, we employ a simple, symmetrical outline that allows the student to compare and contrast the way in which methods are employed in different methodological contexts.

The body of the book is divided into two methodological alternatives: one naturalist, the other constructivist. The ontological and epistemological backgrounds to each methodology are presented as an introductory chapter for each section. Thus, Chapter 2 provides an introduction to the naturalist methodology, while Chapter 8 provides an introduction to the constructivist methodology. Because of the material covered in these two chapters, they are necessarily denser than the others. For this reason, we ask the reader's indulgence and patience when reading them. We believe that this investment in time and energy will pay off when we begin the methods chapters that follow.

By organizing our presentation in terms of two methodological alternatives, we do not intend to suggest that students and authors cannot (or should not) swap epistemological and ontological positions. We are simply proposing two ideal types for the purpose of clarifying different ontological and epistemological approaches (and their relationship to methods). Also, we think that a simplified (two-pronged) approach to methodology provides some pedagogic utility in that it can be used to deliver a relatively symmetrical depiction of the methods available to social scientists. In this way, we hope that the student will find it easier to remember the various ways in which methods are applied under different methodological contexts. In particular, we argue that each methodology appears to have its own hierarchy, or pantheon, of methods.

This hierarchy is clear (and most explicit) when we discuss the naturalist methodology. From this methodological perspective, the scholar expects to find natural patterns in the world, and careful applications of methods are used to uncover these patterns. This ontology lends itself to an empiricist[5] epistemology, where the collection of empirical evidence is used to persuade and predict.

From this point of departure, naturalists have developed a clear hierarchy of methods. At the top of this hierarchy lies the experimental method. This is the ideal method for naturalist explanations because of its ability to control and order causal and temporal relationships. When the experimental method is not a realistic alternative (and this proves to be relatively often), then naturalist social scientists prefer statistical approaches. Beneath statistical approaches lies the third best alternative (when there are too few observations to run reliable statistical queries): few-N comparative approaches. Finally, at the bottom of the naturalist's hierarchy of methods lies case study or historical approaches. Social scientists with a naturalist inclination are expected to employ this method only when faced with a paucity of data or relative comparisons.

In contrast, constructivist scholars tend to see the world as socially constructed. For this reason, they do not expect to see objective (and verifiable) patterns of social phenomena existing naturally in the social world. For the constructivist, motivations and presuppositions play a central role in accessing this world, and the objective of social study is to interpret and understand, not to predict. As a result, the constructivist can draw from a much broader epistemological stable.

Given these ontological and epistemological starting points, we should not be surprised to find that constructivists have little faith and find little utility in the naturalist's hierarchy of methods. They advocate an alternative hierarchy, a flatter and less clear ranking than that of the naturalists – but a hierarchy nonetheless. As constructivist scholars depend on maintaining the 'constitutive' context of a given phenomenon, they abhor methods that manipulate, dissect or reconstitute the setting in which relevant 'data' are embedded. Given this point of departure, a narrative approach is the constructivist's method of choice. Narrative approaches allow constructivists to dwell on the particulars and context that provide them with understanding and insight.

This is not to suggest that constructivists do not rely on comparative methods. Indeed, comparisons are just as important to constructivists as they are to naturalists. After all, comparisons play a central (if often implicit) part of the hermeneutic tradition. But constructivists use comparisons in a radically different way. Rather than trying to uncover nature's underlying patterns, constructivists use comparisons to develop associations which can increase our understanding over particular events.

These opposing hierarchies are used to structure our presentation of the most common methods in social science. Thus, after an introduction to the philosophy of naturalist social science in Chapter 2, we use the subsequent chapters to introduce the hierarchy of naturalist methods in preferred order: at the top is experimental (Chapter 3); followed by statistical (Chapter 4); then comparative (Chapter 5); and finally, in Chapter 6, case-study methods, in light of the ontological and epistemological suppositions of the naturalist approach.

At this point we reach the book's fulcrum, in Chapter 7, where we pause to examine the problems of naturalism and the utility of an alternative methodological approach. In particular, we question the assumption that methodological holism serves the social sciences – in other words, the notion that there is a Real World beyond our senses, and that observation and language can be used to depict that Real World objectively. These shortcomings are used to introduce different methodological approaches to social phenomena – one of which is constructivist in nature.

The second part of the book describes the constructivist approach. Chapter 8 mimics Chapter 2, in that it provides the ontological, epistemological and methodological counterweights to the mainstream (naturalist) tradition. From the constructivist perspective, the human world is seen as socially constructed; motivations and presuppositions play a central role in accessing this world; and the objective of social science is to interpret and explain, rather than to predict. As a result, the subsequent chapters illustrate the utility and application of different methods, in the context of constructivism. Thus, we begin with an introduction to narrative methods (Chapter 9), and follow it with a sketch of comparative (Chapter 10), statistical (Chapter 11) and experimental methods (Chapter 12). In this second part of the book we see how constructivists can employ the same set of methods as do naturalists, but how these methods are now prioritized and used in different ways, toward different ends.

By organizing the book in this symmetrical fashion we are emphasizing the utility of *balancing* these two approaches. We begin with the naturalist approach because it is the dominant and the most familiar methodological approach in contemporary social science. By concluding with a description of constructivist approaches we are not suggesting that the latter supersedes the former. Indeed, we think that the best scholarship in social science draws from both methodological wells: good work in the naturalist tradition is sensitive to constructivist concerns, and vice versa. Our aim is to encourage methodological pluralism, not to advocate one approach at the expense of the other.

Given this design, it occurs to us that there are several different ways that the reader might approach the text. We have designed the book in a way that emphasizes the two distinct methodological traditions, so that each particular method can be understood in light of an author's particular methodological commitments. But it is entirely possible for the reader to jump around the book by comparing approaches on a particular method. For example, those with an interest in philosophy-of-science issues might begin by reading (and comparing) Chapters 2 and 8. Alternatively, those readers who have a soft spot for comparative approaches might begin by reading and comparing Chapters 5 and 10. In short, we hope that the book's logic and symmetry make this sort of individual reading both accessible and useful.

We conclude the book by emphasizing the different roles/objectives of each methodology, and argue for a pragmatic approach that balances both. Students of social phenomena need to be aware of the different methodologies that underlie particular applications of method. This awareness is essential for constructing appropriate research designs as well as for critically consuming the social science work of others.

Chapter 2

Philosophy of Naturalist Science

The origins of modern science can be traced back to the early spring of 1610, with a slim book entitled *The Starry Messenger*. Today's readers would have to search long and hard for excitement or provocation in this book, as it largely describes the night sky. Yet, in the early 1600s, *The Starry Messenger* was capable of triggering condemnations, angry reactions and even calls for its author to be burnt at the stake.

The author was Galileo Galilei (1564–1642). His controversial observations were enhanced by a new instrument, the telescope, which enabled him to describe and draw pictures of configurations in the night sky. The telescope also enabled Galileo to see things that traditional science had not prepared him to expect – including mountains on the moon (which orthodox churchmen considered impossible) and three moons or satellites that circled Jupiter in a steady orbit. The latter was not only impossible, it was clearly in violation of church doctrine, which held that the earth was handmade by God and placed at the centre of an equally divinely crafted universe. The earth was encased in eight perfectly circular crystal spheres, to which the sun, the moon, the planets and the stars were attached (and pushed across the sky by angels). If moons orbited Jupiter, as Galileo said, this would break the crystal sphere to which Jupiter was attached.

The Church was in a quandary over what to do with the book (and with its author). In a sense, Galileo made things easier for them by blatantly stating that any discrepancy between his observations and those of Aristotle's must be the result of Aristotle's shortcomings. As church scholarship rested entirely on Aristotle's authority, Galileo's rumblings could not be ignored. If Aristotle had been wrong, then a thousand years of established knowledge would tumble down around the ears of scholars everywhere.

The Starry Messenger is a milestone in the history of science. It is often seen as the first true application of the scientific method – of a process that involves systematic observation, scrupulous note taking of the things and patterns observed, and thoughtful efforts to make sense of it all. The book represents a different approach to knowledge than that advocated by Aristotle and the Church. According to Galileo, the traditional approach did not further the cause of knowledge; rather, it inhibited new discoveries. The traditional approach to knowledge was weighed down by excessive reliance on established authorities and it hampered man's observation of nature. In Galileo's view, only free and independent scholars could observe nature impartially and gain new insights about its regularities.

This view gained Galileo many opponents among clerics who argued that he was rejecting tradition and authority – including the authority of God and the Church. The situation was untenable and uneven: in one corner was Aristotle, the Church, God and 2000 years of accumulated knowledge; in the other was Galileo. The situation was also dangerous: because Galileo persisted in his observations, his speculations and his disrespectful comments, the Inquisition charged him with heresy in 1633. Faced with a possible death sentence, Galileo agreed that cosmic questions were not 'legitimate problems of science' and publicly withdrew some of his claims. The Church, on its part, commuted his sentence to life imprisonment.

About the same time, Galileo's fellow stargazer, Johannes Kepler (1571–1630), found himself in a similar situation. He, too, broke with traditional science and struck out on his own. Like Galileo, he spent years observing planets and stars and accumulated vast piles of notes (both his and those of the great Danish astronomer Tycho Brahe). After a long and careful analysis of these notes, Kepler also drew conclusions that clashed with the established knowledge of the Church. First, he suggested that Aristotle was wrong (Aristotle had claimed that each planet travels in a perfect circle around the earth, whereas Kepler proposed that they orbit the sun in an elliptical pattern and that the speed of each planet is not uniform throughout the orbit; rather, planets travel fastest when their orbits are closest to the sun). Kepler expressed this orbit, including its curious variance, in the precise language of mathematics.

Isaac Newton (1642–1727) would later draw on the observations of both Galileo and Kepler to take the next great leap in human knowledge. He identified regularities in the sky and on earth, and argued that bodies attract each other according to a constant principle. Newton's supreme achievement was to bring Galileo and Kepler together, and to demonstrate that Galileo's laws of motion on earth and Kepler's law of planetary motion in the heavens were, in fact, two aspects of the same great regularity. Newton's *Mathematical Principles of Natural Philosophy* [1687] explained persuasively why the universe behaved according to clockwork-precise patterns of perfectly repeated movements in space.

The Birth of the Philosophy of Science

The above sketches, from the history of astronomy, provide a common story of the birth of modern science. It is a story of individual risk takers who relied on empirical observation to combat the myths of the past and liberate themselves from the faulty paradigms of their time. Related to this story is another, which provides us with the epistemological support needed to understand Galileo's, Kepler's and Newton's success. Sir Francis Bacon (1561–1626) – lawyer, politician and scientist – played a central part in this story.

Galileo had openly criticized Aristotle's *Physica*, thereby triggering a controversy with the Church that produced a new methodology – a controversy that very nearly cost him his life. Bacon objected to another of Aristotle's big books, the *Organon*, and ignited a similar revolution in ontology and epistemology. In the same way that Galileo's work was followed up by astronomers like Kepler and Newton, Bacon's work was followed up by philosophers of science – men like John Locke and David Hume.

Galileo and Bacon were both part of a critical movement which contributed to the secularization of human knowledge about the world. They both questioned traditional ways of knowing. They both challenged the Church-sanctioned idea that God had granted man 'natural reason', which could be accessed to understand the world. And they both ended up in conflict with the established church authorities – although Galileo suffered more seriously than did Bacon.

Francis Bacon and the Method of Induction

By trade, Francis Bacon was a lawyer and a politician – ending up as Lord Chancellor under King James I of England. By inclination, he was a tinkering jack-of-all-trades. One might even say that Bacon was more of a handyman than a scientist – indeed, he had more respect for handymen than for scientists, whom he referred to as 'spiders who make cobwebs out of their own substance' (Bacon, 1994 [1620], p. 105).

Bacon admired the skills of craftsmen. By watching them work he came to grasp a new way of obtaining knowledge about the world. In contrast to the sterile debates of Aristotelian philosophers of science, Bacon argued that the practical methods of craftsmen could generate new knowledge, informed by nature. When he sat down to write a book to introduce his new method, he began with a head-on attack on Aristotle's method (and with it, the method of Church scientists). His ambition was to write a book which superseded Aristotle's authoritative *Organon*; so Bacon called his book *Novum Orangum*.

Novum Orangum introduced an approach to acquiring knowledge that differed greatly from the approach used by traditional scientists. Traditional scientists would stick to Aristotle's advice and start with a general proposition. They would begin with generally accepted truths or axioms and would then use these truths to illuminate particular observations. By doing this, Bacon explained disparagingly, traditional scientists were unable to produce new knowledge; the approach simply drafted observations to serve already established truths. For science to proceed, Bacon continued, it was necessary to follow a different procedure – one that combined induction and experiment; a procedure that was a matter of routine among skilled craftsmen.

Unlike the scientists of the day, craftsmen did not start with general truths. They began by assessing the particular object or situation at hand. Craftsmen were employed to produce different things under different circumstances – a carpenter was ordered to fix a roof by one patron, build a table by another, and fix a hay-loft or a stable by a third. This variety of tasks necessitated an active, improvising, experimental approach, harnessed by inductive procedure. From his observation of craftsmen in action, Bacon argued that the scientist must begin with systematic observation. He must then build his argument from a large number of single observations towards more and more general truths. The craftsman and the scientist both begin with the particular and '[call] forth axioms from the senses and particulars by a gradual and continuous ascent, to arrive at the most general axioms last of all' (Bacon, 1994, p. 47f.).

This active way of engaging the objects of the world stood in stark contrast to the passive contemplation of church philosophers, who, in their observations of objects, plants and animals, too readily relied on preconceived notions and on the facts that supported them. The philosopher begins at the wrong end, Bacon charged; he begins with axioms or general truths, and seeks to understand the particulars in light of them. These different approaches are described in Figure 2.1

Bacon is seconding a critical point that Galileo had already hurled against traditional Church scientists: their main problem was that they engaged in deductive exercises based on authoritative texts. But craftsmen

Figure 2.1   *Classic deduction and induction*

Deduction builds on true and accepted claims (axioms). Deduction starts with general truths and proceeds through established rules of reasoning, towards explanation of single events.

Induction builds on sensual observations (sight, smell, touch, etc.). Induction starts with empirical particulars and generates more general truths.

were not without their own shortcomings, and Bacon noted that the main problem with the crafts was that they had no texts. The experience of craftsmen was handed down orally and practically from master to apprentice. The substantial knowledge and the pragmatic methods of a craft were kept alive as praxis, but they remained largely unrecorded. For Bacon, hope lay in combining experience with record keeping: when 'experience has learned to read and write, better things may be hoped' (Bacon, in Mason, 1962, p. 142). Craftsmen, in other words, must learn to record their observations. Their notes could then be checked and tested in a way that would provide an empirical basis from which new knowledge could be generated.

When Bacon explained this procedure, he justified it by two important claims: (1) only direct observations supply us with statements about the world; and (2) true knowledge is derived from observation statements. In other words, Bacon not only rejected the deductive method of the old philosophers; he protested the faith in God-given insights and made himself the champion of sense perception. In effect (if a little unjustly), Bacon became history's spokesman for the inductive method.

The old logic of deduction relied on reason alone and was applied by philosophers who followed the way of the spider. No new knowledge could come from such men who endlessly 'spin webs out of themselves'. Against this method of the spider Bacon contrasted the logic of induction – the logic of craftsmen who relied on trials and experiments and their faculties of observation. Craftsmen followed the way of the ant by collecting material in the world and using it. They could produce new knowledge. This was a great advantage, but it had to be tempered by the realization that such inductively produced knowledge was not necessarily true.

Although Galileo and Bacon agreed that systematic observation of the world could produce new knowledge, Bacon's argument had a darker edge to it. He saw that the human senses could not always be trusted, and that things of the world may not always be what they seem. An observer could not trust his senses blindly; he must also rely on 'common sense' and reason. In the end, then, Bacon recommended that science could not rely exclusively on either the 'way of the spider' or the 'way of the ant'. Science must rely on both, or 'the middle way':

> The middle way is that of the bee, which gathers its material from the flowers of the garden and field, but then transforms and digests it by a power of its own. And the true business of philosophy is much the same, for it does not rely only or chiefly on the powers of the mind. Nor does it store the material supplied by natural history and practical experiments untouched in its memory, but lays it up in the understanding

changed and refined. Thus from a closer and purer alliance of the two faculties – the experimental and the rational, such as has never yet been made – we have good reason for hope.   (Bacon, 1994, p. 105)

Locke, Hume and the Modern Philosophy of Knowledge

At the end of the seventeenth century, John Locke (1632–1704) elaborated on Bacon's empiricist foundations in an *Essay Concerning Human Understanding* [1690]. Locke set out to discuss the 'extent of *human knowledge*, together with the grounds and degrees of *belief, opinion* and *assent*' (Locke, 1984, p. 63, italics in original). He repeats Bacon's argument that all knowledge relies on sense perception, and defends it in a way that has since played a decisive role in modern science. This discussion had an enormous influence on subsequent British philosophy and has furnished the modern notion of empiricism with its basic claim that all knowledge is empirical in origin.

Locke did not deny the Christian axiom that man is God's creation, fashioned in God's image. However, he did deny the medieval notion that God had endowed man with innate (or *a priori*) ideas. For Locke, man was born with a mind that resembles a blank slate (a *tabula rasa*): there is no such thing as *a priori* knowledge. For this reason, knowledge of the world cannot be gained by turning our attention inward in an introspective search for a 'natural reason', divinely endowed by an omniscient God. For Locke, all knowledge is *a posteriori* – in other words, it can only be derived from sense experience. Knowledge enters the human mind through the organs of sense in the form of sense impressions; these are stored in the memory as single ideas and may be retrieved and recombined by the imagination.

Even fanciful ideas that have no correspondence to the Real World – a unicorn, for example – are arrived at through simple sense perceptions. Thus, we perceive simple phenomena, such as a horse and a rhinoceros, and we store these in our mind in the forms of simple ideas. By rearranging and recombining these simple ideas, the mind can form new, more complex ideas. Out of the single idea of a horse and the single idea of a rhinoceros, the mind can produce the complex idea of a unicorn.

In order to gain knowledge about the world, then, we must first gain impressions about the world – through our senses – and store these in our minds. We can then process these sense impressions in systematic ways, according to established rules of logic, 'justified by a sufficient and wary induction of particulars' (Locke, 2004, §13).

Locke's concrete and commonsensical style, his practical tone and his warnings against unverifiable speculations, combined to secure him a wide circle of readers and followers. As a result, his book was immensely influential. Indeed, when David Hume (1711–76) resolved to write an epistemological essay of his own half century a later, he could confidently assume that his audience was already familiar with Locke's argument.

Hume begins his *Inquiry Concerning Human Understanding* [1748] where Locke had left off. Like Locke, Hume agreed that all human knowledge comes from sense experience, and that the mind preserves sense impressions in the form of simple ideas. But Hume refined Locke's argument by probing his two faculties of the human mind (memory and imagination) in greater detail. Through this discussion, Hume refined some of Bacon's troubling insights about the fallibility of the human senses and things not being what they seem. From this scepticism Hume fashioned one of the most consequential arguments in modern epistemology: he began to doubt the universal validity of induction. This led him to wonder whether causal analysis was in fact possible at all – a doubt which shook the very foundations of the modern philosophy of science.

Hume the Empiricist: the Philosophy of Human Understanding

Like Locke, Hume claimed that we use *memory* to preserve and arrange the simple ideas we have stored in our mind. In fact, he held that we preserve these ideas in the exact order by which they entered the mind. He then suggested that we use *imagination* to rearrange and recombine these simple ideas into complex ideas. This delegation of responsibilities within the brain raises an important point: since ideas are sequenced by the order they entered the mind, simple ideas cannot be rearranged in any manner desired. In other words, the mind doesn't function in some random way: human imagination arranges ideas in ordered clusters or sequences. Thus, Hume believed that ideas are strung together by a principle of association or attraction. While this focus on associations is common to all scientific endeavours, Hume goes one step further by elaborating on their relationship to the concept of causation.

Whenever we see two events that appear together, we resort to the notions of cause and effect. This raises a dilemma for empiricists, as causality itself cannot actually be perceived. We can only perceive that A and B occur concomitantly, or simultaneously. It is our imagination, not our perception, which provides the actual (causal) link between A and B. Our imagination does this, suggests Hume, because it is our custom to associate events, and because the imaginative properties of our mind are capable of providing logical explanations for why B must occur in the aftermath of A. In other words, our mind is capable of devising theories, which we then impose upon the world. At this point, Hume's training as a sceptic comes in, full force.

Hume the Sceptic I: Doubting the Inductive Road to Knowledge

Hume sympathized with Bacon's two ideas that observations supply us with statements about the world, and that scientific knowledge could be derived from such observation statements. He also shared with Bacon some nagging doubts about man's frail faculties of observation. The more he turned these doubts around in his mind, the more sceptical he became of the primitive way that scientists often used observation statements as springboards for bold and unwarranted conclusions. He concluded that no number of observation statements, be it ever so large, can produce reliable generalizations. Whereas Bacon had considered general statements to be the reliable children of reason, Hume revealed them as bastards of custom and imagination.

Human knowledge is a flimsy phenomenon. Because of its flimsiness, Hume argues, science needs to treat causal claims with great caution. Strictly speaking, science should not try to explain facts; it should be content with describing them and demonstrating their regular appearance. The reason is obvious: patterns and regularities can be observed, causality cannot! We can observe facts. We can observe that first one fact (A) appears and that another fact (B) then appears. We can observe that the two facts always appear together. But our senses cannot observe any mechanism by which one causes the other. Our imagination, however, can easily enough conjure up some such mechanism, and our reason can make a causal connection credible. When push comes to shove, we must recognize that such causal explanations are all imaginary: they are made up.

This is not to suggest that all observation is relative: a Real World does exist. Rather, our perception of this Real World is held together by imaginary notions. John Passmore (1987) provides an example of how we can understand Hume's argument when he asks us to imagine a baby – an exceptionally bright child – whose parents have always given him soft cotton toys to play with. The baby has often dropped these toys out of his crib and they have fallen to the floor with a soft thud. One day his uncle comes to visit and gives the baby a rubber ball. The baby smells it, tastes it, feels it, and then drops it out of his crib. Instead of landing softly on the floor, the ball bounces around. The baby is surprised and confused, and begins to cry. For all his careful investigation, the baby's experience with toys is limited to those that land softly on the floor when dropped; he has no possible way of predicting the bouncing behaviour of the ball. This example serves to illustrate Hume's first point: that just by examining a thing, we can never tell what effects it may produce. Only as a result of experience can we determine its consequences.

To illustrate Hume's second point, Passmore changes focus from the baby to the uncle. When he sees that the baby throws the ball, the uncle expects the ball to bounce. If you ask him what caused the ball to bounce, the uncle might reply: 'Balls bounce. Rubber balls have the power to bounce when tossed. My nephew tossed the ball and caused it to bounce!' Asked to elaborate, the uncle might say: 'There is a necessary connection between a ball's being dropped and its bouncing . . .'! It is at this point that Hume asks his profound question:

> What experience has the uncle had that the child lacks? The uncle makes use of such general concepts as 'cause', 'power', 'necessary connection'. If these are not just empty words, they must somehow refer back to experience. Well, then, what, in the present case, is his experience? How does the uncle's experience differ from his nephew's experience? (Passmore, 1987, p. 147)

The only difference Hume can find is *habit*. The uncle has different expectations than the child because the uncle has observed, in many different contexts and over a large number of cases, that rubber balls bounce when dropped. His expectations are hardly conscious, but are derived from habit. The baby is too young to have had such experience.

This explanation seems to answer the question of why the uncle has different expectations than the child. But it raises another, much more serious, problem: it implies that these habits of the mind are not trustworthy because they do not produce certain knowledge. Habits are merely unthinking products of our minds. If induction is the foundation of science (as, for example, Bacon insisted), then science (Hume implies) rests on a foundation whose veracity is impossible to demonstrate. This implication has baffled philosophers of science ever since. Indeed, throughout the nineteenth and the first half of the twentieth century, it may be fair to say that Hume's argument was the prime skeleton in the naturalist's closet.

Hume the Sceptic II: Ground Rules of Science
If induction can produce no certain knowledge, and causal explanations are nothing more than habits, justified by man's fertile imagination, how in the world can we perform science? Hume's answer was: very carefully. Scientists should lower their ambitions. They should not yield to the temptation of trying to explain too much. They should refrain from imposing causal explanations upon the world. Science should, in fact, do without causal claims altogether; it should restrict itself to identifying and observing regularities in the world. In short, scientists should focus on correlations. They should identify and map factual correlations – i.e., correlations among facts that are directly observable by the human senses.

To explain the realm of science more carefully, Hume drew a basic distinction between two types of knowledge: those based on *facts* (empirical knowledge) and those based on *values* (normative knowledge). *Empirical knowledge*, based on fact, is the foundation of science. It consists of knowledge about the observable world. It is accessible to all human beings via sensory perception. And all sensible people are in agreement about the basic properties of this observable world. This is the core element of what we have called the naturalist methodology: a Real World characterized by natural patterns that are observable to us (in other words, that we can experience). Over time, humankind has collected much common knowledge about the world from a vast number of simple sense impressions. In contrast, *normative knowledge* is based on values and beliefs: this is the realm of individual preferences. It can provide no basis for science, for we can say nothing certain about this type of knowledge. It is subjective, since different individuals tend to entertain different values and beliefs.

This distinction between facts and values – between empirical knowledge and normative knowledge – remains a key notion in naturalist science. It implies that science is based on facts, not on norms. This should not be interpreted to suggest that Hume felt that values and beliefs are unimportant or unworthy of scholarly investigations. His simple point is that they fall outside the purview of science proper. Science can help us answer questions formulated about empirical events, but it cannot settle normative disputes – these must be left to theologians and philosophers (who, after 2000 years of debate, still appear to be far from agreement).

All members of the community of naturalist science will, when push comes to shove, agree with Hume's proposition that science must be based on facts and not on values. Still, few of them would choose to formulate this claim in the draconian terms with which Hume concluded his *Inquiry Concerning Human Understanding*. If we should reassess human knowledge, if we should:

> run over libraries, persuaded by these principles, what havoc must we make? If we take in our hand any volume – of divinity or school metaphysics, for instance – let us ask, *Does it contain any abstract reasoning concerning quantity or number?* No. *Does it contain any experimental reasoning concerning matter of fact and existence?* No. Commit it then to the flames, for it can contain nothing but sophistry and illusion.   (Hume, 1983 [1748], p. 173)

The Basic Assumptions of the Naturalist Methodology

Francis Bacon, John Locke and David Hume provide us with the basic framework for a modern philosophy of scientific knowledge. In their

Figure 2.2   *Some founding fathers of the naturalist methodology and their main contributions*

Galileo Galilei	1565–1642	*The Starry Messenger* [1610]
Francis Bacon	1561–1626	*Novum Organum* [1620]
John Locke	1632–1704	*An Essay Concerning Human Understanding* [1690]
David Hume	1711–1776	*An Inquiry Concerning Human Understanding* [1748]

works, subsequent thinkers have found support for the claims that the world is real, and that it consists of independent particulars. In these works, subsequent authors have drawn sustenance for the arguments that these particular components interact in regular and patterned ways, and that human beings can experience these interactions by way of sense perception. To the basic conceptual frame built by Bacon, Locke and Hume modern naturalists have added planks and boards of their own, but their additions have hardly altered the basic design of these Founding Fathers, whose main contributions are listed in Figure 2.2.

For example, subsequent naturalists have interpreted Locke and Hume to mean that there *is* a Real World 'out there' – a Real World which exists independently of our senses. This world exists whether human beings are there to observe it or not. On the strength of this claim, naturalists have built a clear and simple definition of 'truth': a statement that accurately corresponds to a state of affairs in the Real World. This is the famous 'correspondence theory' of truth, which is today often associated with Karl Popper (1994, p. 5): a 'theory or a statement is true, if what it says corresponds to reality'.

Subsequent naturalists have also found in Hume a confirmation of the methodology of Bacon: that there are many kinds of repetitions and regularities in the world – for example, that day alternates with night, that the moon waxes and wanes, that the ocean rises and ebbs, that summer gives way to autumn and winter . . . Thus, it can be said that the main purpose of science is to identify these regularities (for example, to show the alternations between day and night, to map the patterns of the lunar phases and the ocean tides, to describe the cycles of the seasons . . .).

Also, naturalists agree that such regularities may be experienced through systematic sense perception. The naturalist trusts his senses to reveal truth. Such experience and observations can, in turn, be communicated from one naturalist to the next through the medium of language – i.e., through clear and precise observation statements, supported by clear descriptions, simple illustrations and incisive logic. Galileo's

Starry Messenger is a good case in point. It is a masterpiece of crystal-clear exposition. The argument is carried along by a lucid and crisp language (still, after 400 years); it is guided by an iron hand of strict logic, reinforced by geometric proofs; it is supported by several illustrations (sketches, figures and pictures) of what Galileo saw through his telescope.

Furthermore, subsequent naturalists found in Hume an impetus to uncover the regularities of nature and document them as accumulated *associations*. John Stuart Mill's [1891] magisterial *A System of Logic* is typical in this regard. For Mill, science involves two propositions. First, knowledge about the laws of nature is acquired through the identification of associations (or in more modern term: variable correlations). Second, human knowledge grows over time through the accumulation of observation statements, of tested and true correlations and of logical argument. New scholars rely on the disseminated texts of their predecessors, using the arguments of their elders as vantage points for their own. In this way, knowledge grows through the generations.

This empiricist epistemology gives rise to the standard definition of 'theory': a set of (verified) correlations, logically or systematically related to each other. In the naturalist tradition, 'theory' hinges on a statement which says that one phenomenon (or one class of phenomena) is connected in a certain way with another phenomenon (or class of phenomena). For the naturalist, a theory is a map of associations. Galileo's observation statement that the planets revolve around the sun would be the core of his theory of planetary orbits – i.e., the orbits of the planets are connected to the sun.

On Doubt and Reductionism: the Cartesian Revolution

The empiricist philosophy that evolved in seventeenth- and eighteenth-century England had parallels elsewhere. In France, for example, Descartes (1596–1650) shared the basic attitudes of the empiricists of his age. He was an opponent of traditional, scholastic philosophy, and shared with Galileo and Bacon a number of attitudes and new insights about the world and how we can come to know it. Indeed, Descartes pushed to its extreme the idea that the world is a material reality; that human observers can gain knowledge about the world through their senses; and that knowledge can be spread by communicating it to others in crisp and clear language. His *Meditations on the First Philosophy* [1641] is an excellent example of this. Not only does Descartes set his own observations before the reader; he tries to make the reader engage with the facts. He wants his reader to do more than just passively absorb the information he provides: he cleverly engages the reader to make him understand the importance of the question and then to follow the twists and turns of his argument.

Descartes did not question the key empiricist claim that sense experience is the basic component in knowledge acquisition. But he refused to rely on sense experience alone. He shared Bacon's concern that the human senses are not trustworthy; they must be harnessed by Reason. Actually, the famous 'Cartesian method' is not far removed from Bacon's 'way of the bee'. The difference between the two is often exaggerated (it is commonly claimed that whereas Bacon stressed the importance of induction, Descartes emphasized the importance of deduction); it is important to note that theirs is largely a difference of emphasis – both of them found a place for inductive as well as deductive procedures. Both Descartes and Bacon claimed that the business of science was to produce general statements, cultivate main features and produce simple models of the world.

Descartes, like his contemporaries Galileo and Bacon, assumed that the world ultimately *was* simple. If one could penetrate below the bloomin', buzzin' complexity of the superficial world, one would find the serene and simple mechanisms of a streamlined design. To arrive at this world, Descartes recommended two epistemological principles: systematic doubt and reductionism.

The most famous explication of systematic doubt is set out in his *Meditations*. Here, Descartes begins by asking what it is possible to know. But before he begins to build his argument about human knowledge, Descartes argues that we must first rid ourselves of all former beliefs, because many of these are bound to be false. This claim created an enormous stir in scholastic circles, and members of the Church accused Descartes of wanting to destroy truths, morals and decency. (Sound familiar?)

Descartes responded to the charges with an analogy: he who is worried about rotten apples in a barrel will be well advised to tip out all the apples and then replace each one carefully, inspecting every single apple for damage and rot. Only when he is certain that an apple is sound should he put it back in the barrel. If he makes a single mistake, the entire barrel may be spoiled. Descartes' point is that all claims should be treated as if they were false. We should only add a claim to our stock of knowledge if we are certain that it is true; if we are in the slightest doubt about a claim's veracity, we should reject it.

In 1637 Descartes published his famous book on the scientific method: *Discourse on Methods for Conducting Reason and Seeking Truth in the Sciences*. Here he expanded on the second epistemological principle of science: reductionism. This principle holds that you should always build your investigation from the bottom up, beginning with the propositions that you know to be absolutely true. Descartes' principle of reductionism is intimately connected to his principle of systematic doubt: begin your investigations into a subject by dividing every extant argument into its many component propositions. Ask of each and every proposition: how do I know that this is true? Then, reject every proposition that you cannot verify without the shadow of a doubt. By this process, in due time, you will have reduced the number of propositions about your subject to a few, true, core claims. These few, indubitably certain components will serve as the solid foundation stones upon which you can then build an argument.

How, precisely, do you build this argument? Descartes summarized his method with three pieces of advice. First, divide each problem into its smaller, constituent parts. Second, proceed in an orderly and logical way: 'always beginning with the simplest objects, those most apt to be known, and ascending little by little, in steps as it were, to the knowledge of the most complex'. And third, learn from geometry! Look at how the geometricians proceed from a few indubitable axioms and build their arguments step by step, with clear logic and discipline. Observe, writes Descartes (1973 [1637], p. 20, our translation), the 'chains of perfectly simple and easy reasonings by means of which geometricians are accustomed to carry out their most difficult demonstrations' and deduce one thing from another.

Descartes believed that his method of systematic doubt – whose procedures are so well captured by his apple barrel analogy – was the best way to clean away the cluttered growth of everyday sense perception and lay bare the simple, basic structures of the Real World underneath. He also believed that this process could be aided by the logical procedures of geometry and algebra. His principles of systematic doubt, reductionism and cool analysis are still basic rules of thumb in the empiricist tradition of science, and they underpin the naturalist methodology. Not only do they increase the certainty of an argument; they also help to make it lean and efficient in form. By eliminating all dubious assumptions, a scientist is left with a simple set of axioms upon which a rational argument can rest logically. It is, in other words, possible to cultivate simplified versions of the world. Indeed, it is not merely possible; it is the only proper way. The only way to penetrate below the complexity of the superficial world (and identify the streamlined design of the universe) is to remove superficial details and unnecessary clutter; to reduce the world to a simplified model of essential principles.

There are clear differences between the English philosophers of science and their Continental colleagues. To some, these differences are large enough to warrant different labels: whereas Britain's seventeenth- and eighteenth-century philosophers of knowledge are commonly called

Empiricists, their French contemporaries are often referred to as *Rationalists*. For us, the parallels between these schools of thought are more striking than their differences. Both schools assumed that the Real World is a material fact. Both assumed that this World is orderly and streamlined. Both argued that scientists have access to this world through sense perception. Descartes, who is often identified as a rationalist par excellence, quarrels with none of these key assumptions. The procedures of 'Cartesian doubt' and 'Cartesian reductionism' were adopted by empiricists everywhere – and developed into potent instruments of modern science. The immense analytical powers that they represented were greatly augmented by the addition of mathematical techniques – which Descartes also pioneered, and which subsequent scientists like Sir Isaac Newton applied with immense success.

Post-Cartesian Developments: from Comte to Vienna

Auguste Comte (1798–1857), Frenchman and the founder of modern sociology, was one of the first scholars who sought to carve out an academic field devoted to the scientific study of human society. Comte's *Course of Positive Philosophy* [1830–42] popularized terms like 'positive perception' to indicate the type of knowledge that was acceptable for science. For Comte, the social and natural sciences shared two important features: they shared the same epistemological form, and they both needed to be freed from metaphysical speculation. Toward that end, Comte coined the term 'sociology' to designate the science that would synthesize all positive knowledge about society and guide humanity in its search for the 'good society'.

Comte's sociological method hinged on two arguments: one epistemological, the other historical. His epistemological argument involved two simple claims. The first repeated the basic claim of earlier empiricists: that all scientific knowledge about the Real World flows from empirical observation – from sense perception or, as he called it, from 'positive perception'. Comte's second claim was a radical application of Hume's distinction between fact and value – between empirical and normative knowledge. In particular, Comte held that knowledge which does not originate in positive perception – i.e., which is not fact-based and empirical – is not knowledge about the world, and therefore falls outside the purview of science. Comte derived his two claims from observing how research was done in the natural sciences, and he saw a logical continuity between the investigation of natural and social phenomena. Knowledge about the social world, he argued, will also accumulate until it slowly arrives at general statements and fundamental insights.

The second argument that sustained Comte's sociological method elaborates on this notion of slowly accumulating knowledge and involves historical evolution. It held that human thought and science has evolved through various 'ways of knowing'. In particular, he maps three historical phases. The first phase was a mystical theological or fictitious stage – a primitive phase during which human beings tried to understand the world in religious terms. One of its key characteristics was the notion that the world was created by divine beings. The second phase was metaphysical, when humanity tried to understand the world in abstract terms. Its key notions involved abstract principles and ultimate causes. Finally, knowledge proceeded to a scientific or positive phase. Here the search for ultimate causes is abandoned, and humanity instead tries to establish laws. The only way to search for these laws was through systematic, empirical observation.

Emile Durkheim (1858–1917) fully agreed that the purpose of sociology was to search for laws in social life and to do this through systematic, empirical observation. He carried Comte's project into the twentieth century with respect to the need to develop more rigorous, empirically grounded scientific methods. In addition, Durkheim agreed that society is a part of nature, and that a science of society has to be based on the same logical principles as those that characterize the natural sciences. Durkheim – like Comte – longed to cut social science free from the metaphysical tendencies which dominated social thought in the nineteenth century. Toward that end, Durkheim went to great lengths to encourage the sociologist to move away from the study of concepts to focus on the study of things – most particularly, 'social facts'.

Durkheim did this most evidently in his *The Rules of Sociological Method* [1895]. Here he laments the lack of discussion among sociologists about the proper approach to social phenomena. To address this problem, he suggests that we must start the journey anew, and he uses the first two chapters of that book to trace these initial steps.

In particular, Durkheim argued that '[t]he first and most basic rule is: *Consider social facts as things*' (1964 [1895], p. 14, italics in original). Social scientists need to establish social facts: things that are independent of, and constrain, individuals. For Durkheim, '[a] social fact is to be recognized by the power of external coercion which it exercises or is capable of exercising over individuals' (Durkheim, 1964, p. 10). Defined in this way, social facts are not reducible to other disciplines – for example, they are not biological or psychological facts; they are socially constructed and collectively maintained constraints (for example, norms, rules, laws, economic organizations, customs . . .). On this premise Durkheim makes the case for Sociology as an autonomous social science.

For Sociology to be a science, Durkheim argues, it has to start with sense perception. To this he adds that senses are not always trustworthy.

In doing so, he begins by merely retracing the thoughts of Bacon and Hume on the problems of perception. Then, however, he adds a new concern: the epistemological problems that haunt the natural sciences are multiplied in the social sciences. Social facts, Durkheim continues, are more difficult to observe than natural facts. Social facts do not just appear to our senses; on the contrary, what appears directly to our senses is often illusory or mistaken. For this reason, the layperson is often deluded about the nature of social reality: he often substitutes the 'representations' of social facts for the real thing. To crack this problem, the sociologist needed to break away from popular perceptions and approach the social world as if for the first time. He must start anew, and build his scientific edifice on sturdier, empirical foundations. With an explicit reference to Descartes' systematic doubt, Durkheim (1964, p. 22) explains that the first step in social research is to turn away from all preconceptions and to turn attention towards the facts!

> In the present state of knowledge, we cannot be certain of the exact nature of the state, of sovereignty, political liberty, democracy, social-ism, communism, etc. Our method should, then, require our avoid-ance of all use of these concepts so long as they have not been scientifically established. And yet the words which express them recur constantly in the discussions of sociologists. They are freely employed with great assurance, as though they corresponded to things well known and precisely defined, whereas they awaken in us nothing but confused ideas, a tangle of impressions, prejudices, and emotions. (Durkheim, 1964, pp. 65–6)

Consider Durkheim's concern with the precision and clarity of language. In the above quote he sounded a loud claxon to warn against the use of ambiguous terms like 'freedom', 'democracy', socialism' and so on. Underneath this warning lies the correspondence theory of truth as a bedrock assumption: scientific discussions must be conducted in terms which correspond to phenomena in the real world – to things well known and well defined. Consider also his famous investigation on suicide. Durkheim's entire argument is built around the empiricist notion that a 'theory' involves a proposition in which one social fact (or class of phenomena; in this case 'suicide') is connected in a certain way with another social fact (or another class of phenomena; in this case 'individualism').

With his *Rules of Sociological Method*, Durkheim sought to provide a sound methodological footing for sociology in particular, and for the other new social sciences in general. His success was mixed. On the one hand, he provided sound advice – as when he insisted on relying on facts, and using concepts which corresponded to things well known and well defined. On the other hand, Durkheim introduced concerns which complicated his task. His distinction between the natural sciences and the social sciences is a case in point. When he argued that the social sciences were different from the natural sciences in terms of the objects observed, he opened up a Pandora's box in the philosophy of the young social sciences. His distinction was embraced by advocates of more constructivist approaches and used in a vast metaphysical debate that shook the social sciences at the time – and which has since been regularly resurrected by new generations of social scientists.

Durkheim provoked some scholars to wonder whether natural-science ideals were appropriate for the emerging social sciences, and to advocate more humanist and interpretive approaches. These sceptics happily embraced Durkheim's distinction between natural and social objects: they sought to prise the social and natural sciences apart and to sever the methodological links with the natural sciences altogether. As you will see, some of these sceptics return to play a larger role in subsequent chapters of this book.

In some ways this was a curious denunciation, for never before could science claim so much progress in so short a time. 'As the century drew to a close, scientists could reflect with satisfaction that they had pinned down most of the mysteries of the physical world: electricity, magnetism, gases, optics, acoustics, kinetics and statistical mechanics, to name just a few, had fallen into order before them' (Bryson, 2003, p. 153). There are reasons to argue that the humanist criticism of the naturalist approach was not exclusively driven by academic concerns. The methodological debate which exploded on the young social sciences in the final years of the nineteenth century took place in a turbulent environment. Scientists had produced great feats; but they had also produced great fears. The whole world clanged and chuffed with the machinery that modern science had produced and societies were rapidly changing as a result; there was a widespread fear that order and morality were unravelling and that the West was irretrievably descending into a deep crisis. Also, there was a growing concern that ambitious dictators might harness the insights of modern science for their own nefarious purposes. This latter worry would erupt on a grand scale with the advent of an unprecedented war between the Great Powers of Europe: a war that would engulf the West in a destructive, all-consuming struggle.

Logical Positivism

The First World War brought with it a reaction against all things Prussian – including a reaction against Prussian-based philosophy of knowledge.

One of the most significant of these reactions emerged among German academics themselves. The result was a leaner and meaner version of empiricism. In the wake of the Great War, in the Austrian capital of Vienna, a small group of German expatriates introduced a tighter and more focused philosophy of knowledge. The members of the so-called Vienna Circle were critical of the abstract and arid nature of metaphysical quarrels, and they strongly opposed what they considered to be the woolly idealism of Germany's philosophy of knowledge (as represented, for example, in the work of Hegel's idealistic followers) and the relativism that was increasingly dominating many fronts of human knowledge.

The founder of the Circle, Moritz Schlick (1882–1936), proposed to create a new approach that could provide science with more solid logical foundations. A German physicist, Schlick had moved to Vienna in the wake of Germany's defeat in the First World War. There he was joined by another German expatriate, Rudolf Carnap. These men were the Circle's driving figures. In addition, Kurt Gödel, Otto Neurath, Herbert Feigl, Philipp Frank, Hans Hahn, Victor Kraft and Friedrich Waismann were all associated with the Vienna Circle and with its philosophical journal, *Erkenntniss*.[1] Finally, it is also necessary to mention Alfred J. Ayer, a young student from Oxford's Department of Philosophy who came to Vienna in 1932 and sat in on the meetings. He synthesized the discussions in a brilliant little book, *Language, Truth and Logic* [1936], through which he became the Circle's most important ambassador in the English-speaking world.

The members of the Vienna Circle were not much interested in the history of philosophy. Their arguments tended to echo those of David Hume and Auguste Comte. In that sense, their arguments were not particularly revolutionary in content. What was most revolutionary was the form and the extreme fervour of their position.

In terms of form, the Vienna Circle insisted on using logic as the primary tool of positive (or naturalist) science. Its members developed a more far-ranging logic; a logic that provided very powerful tools of analysis that the Vienna Circle wanted to turn towards the philosophy of science. In terms of fervour, the Circle tightened and focused the positivism of Comte and Durkheim. Among other things, its members sharpened Comte's already narrow interpretation of Hume's distinction between fact and value.

The fundamental question of the Vienna Circle was this: When is an argument scientific? Deeply disturbed by the many ideologues, nationalists, mystics and faith healers who invoked science to support their arguments, members of the Circle searched for a criterion which could distinguish scientific from pseudo-scientific – or 'metaphysical' –

arguments. *Fin de siècle* Vienna was one of the most energetic and academically exciting places in Europe – if not the entire world. It was a city of extraordinary talents in the fields of literature, music, art, philosophy and science. City life was famous for its 'nervous splendour', its heady mix of gossip and intellectual brilliance. Among the many topics of Viennese conversation were new academic theories – like those of the young patent-office clerk Albert Einstein, who apparently argued that Galileo, Kepler and Newton were mistaken, and those of the smooth and charming young doctor Sigmund Freud, who claimed he could interpret dreams. The Vienna Circle wanted to know: Were these arguments scientific or not? Was Dr Freud a brilliant doctor or an influential quack? Was Albert Einstein a true physicist?

Moritz Schlick imagined that he could settle controversies like this by identifying a proper *demarcation principle* – i.e., a criterion which could distinguish scientific from pseudo-scientific arguments. With such a principle in hand, Schlick hoped that he could cut away the intellectually gangrenous tissue of the ailing body of science. Traditional philosophies of knowledge had stressed the role of empirical observations and logic as such demarcation principles. But Schlick was all too aware that pseudo-scientists could also use logic and muster empirical evidence to support their claims. Besides, scientists would inevitably err, while charlatans might stumble across occasional truths. Schlick and his colleagues wanted to hone the arguments of positivism and logic into sharper tools, still. They referred to their approach as 'logical positivism'.

The logical positivists subscribed to a single demarcation principle: the *principle of verification*. They argued that all scientific statements had one particular quality in common: that they could be tested and deemed true or false. Or, as they put it more pointedly, scientific statements are all meaningful; non-scientific statements are, by contrast, meaningless. If the Vienna Circle had a basic, founding principle, it was this principle of verification. Using it as their main stick, Circle members beat early twentieth-century philosophy of science in ways that sent shocks through the scientific communities.

'The criterion we use to test out the genuineness of apparent statements of fact is the criterion of verifiability', wrote Alfred Ayer (1952 [1936], p. 35). 'We say that a sentence is factually significant to any given person, if, and only if, he knows how to verify that proposition which it purports to express.' This was not a revolutionary thought. The basic question of the Vienna Circle was really the same as Descartes had presented in the opening of his *Meditations*: What is it possible to know? When is an argument scientific? Their project was also very similar to that of Descartes: they wanted to empty the barrel of human knowledge and examine each and every apple carefully, in order to put the good ones back for further use (while systematically discarding the bad apples). To do this, they relied on the old maxims of John Locke, David Hume, August Comte and others.

The verification principle relies on a draconian distinction between statements that are meaningful and statements that are meaningless. Science is concerned with meaningful statements. Such statements, in turn, come in two types: those that are true and those that are false. Science, then, is primarily concerned with meaningful statements that are true.

This appeared to be a straightforward conceptualization at first. But it soon gave rise to several questions. The first was: How does one know if a statement is true? The immediate answer to this question was formulated in terms of the old epistemological chestnut: the correspondence theory of truth. A statement is true if it accurately corresponds to a state of affairs in the Real World. One must, in other words, compare the statement to the Real World. Or, to put it more succinctly: one gauges the veracity of a statement by testing it!

A second question followed on the heels of the first: What does one actually do when one tests a statement? In order to respond to this question, the members of the Vienna Circle needed more time, because the answer was not as simple as it seemed at first glance. The answer depended, among other things, upon the eyes that saw and the nature of the statement to be tested.

Meaningful statements come in two main types: formal or empirical. Formal statements are self-contained or self-referential; they can be deemed true or false by investigating whether they are logically consistent (or not). 'This bachelor is an unmarried man' is a formal statement that is true, because 'a bachelor' is by accepted usage always understood as an unmarried man. Formal statements are, in other words, true or false by definition. As such, they provide no new knowledge about the world. Or, as the Circle members might have put it: the predicate merely unpacks what is already present in the subject.

Empirical statements may provide new knowledge about the world. Empirical statements refer to a state or event outside itself; they can be deemed true or false by observing the facts of the world, and then determining whether the statement corresponds to a real fact or condition in the world. 'The cheese is in the cupboard' is a meaningful sentence. To test its veracity one could simply open the cupboard door and observe its contents. If the cheese is there, the statement would be true; if there is no cheese in the cupboard, the statement would be false. Statements that were neither formal nor empirical would be deemed meaningless.

Freud and Einstein under the Microscope

We can now return to the Circle's evaluation of the scientific content of Freud's and Einstein's contributions. We begin with Sigmund Freud: was his argument scientific or not?

Freud's *Interpretation of Dreams* was ferociously discussed for several seasons when it came out in 1900 – not only in Vienna (where he lived and practised), but all over Europe. His argument had an instant influence. Authors and artists embraced the notion that our dreams are disguises for unconscious wishes; they delved into the argument that sleep relaxes the grip that the (responsible and rational) *ego* and the (partially conscious) *super-ego* have on our darker instincts and our most primitive fears. As a result, the impulses of the *id* slip past the sleeping *ego* and escape into the conscious mind. There they are picked up as dreams. Freud argued that a trained psychologist could use these dreams to gain access to the unconscious mind.

There can be no doubting that Freud had an electrifying influence, not only on novelists and artists in turn-of-the century Vienna, but upon social scientists as well – and he still does. In fact, Freud is commonly counted as one of the most influential social scientists of the twentieth century. It is astonishing, therefore, that the Vienna Circle deemed his theories to be pseudo-science at best. By its criterion of verifiability, Freud's theory does not pass muster. Freud did not know how to verify his claims in any systematic way. Indeed, Freud shied away from testing his claims. Those scientists who have tried to derive hypotheses from Freud's arguments and hold them up against competing explanations have confronted a tough task. The arguments are slippery and evasive – the basic terms (*id* and *ego*) are hard to define, and the basic mechanisms (the weakening of the ego and the escape of basic impulses into the conscious mind) are difficult to trace. Its arguments rest on anecdotes and examples that do not lend themselves to testing. As a result, Freud's theories are mostly confined to the disciplinary history of psychology, as his model of the human mind has been largely replaced by chemically and biologically based models of the brain. Outside of psychology, however, Freud can still muster a significant number of fans and followers, especially in the humanities. This is not surprising, if only because his discussions of the hidden, irrational processes of the mind made an important contribution to Western thought and exerted a formidable influence on Western culture.

How, then, do Einstein's arguments compare? Do they pass the verification threshold?

On the face of it, the 'principle of equivalence' which Einstein presented in his 1905 paper, 'On the Electrodynamics of Moving Bodies', appeared fairly meaningless to most readers – it was a short piece without footnotes, references and mathematical formulas, written by a lowly clerk in a Swiss patent office. To clarify his principle of equivalence, Einstein added a short mathematical expression a few weeks later: $E = mc^2$. Energy (E) and mass (m) are basically the same thing, he explained. Energy is liberated matter, and matter is locked-up energy waiting to be released. This may not mean much to the uninitiated; in fact, it did not mean much to the initiated either, at first. There are two reasons for this. First, its key definitions were vague: E and m were said to be equivalent and the definition of one was locked into the definition of the other. Second, the introduction of c^2 (the speed of light multiplied by itself) would yield an impossibly large number. It meant that an average human body would contain no less than 7×10^{18} joules of potential energy – an enormous amount which, if it were to be released all at once, would totally destroy several very large cities. This argument – the core of Einstein's Special Theory of Relativity – opened up an entirely new way of looking at the world and the universe. But it also opened up two related questions: Was it sensible? Was it meaningful?

Schlick and Carnap were physicists, and followed Einstein's work with great interest. Karl Popper, who rejected Freud and Marx as webs of untestable – and therefore nonsensical – statements, was thrilled by the way Einstein drew logical implications from his theory and exposed them nakedly to testing. The members of the Vienna Circle had no problem with Einstein's key concept of 'simultaneity'; indeed, they agreed that what is meant by things being simultaneous depends on how simultaneity is actually determined by observation. They were at first taken aback by the enormous amount of energy that, according to Einstein's theory, was bound up in matter. But they realized that Einstein's theory explained several questions that astronomers and geologists had wondered about for a long time. For example, how can the sun radiate heat for billions of years without running empty? How can the earth's innards remain molten without cooling off? How can a little lump of uranium emit high-level energy for thousands of years without ending up as a small heap of ash? The answer to these puzzling questions was provided by Einstein's thesis: there is an enormous amount of energy locked up in the mass of the sun, the earth and the lump of uranium, respectively. Einstein indicated this by the expression c^2 – which represented a truly enormous number.

Einstein's fame increased in the opening decades of the twentieth century – if nothing else, because his theories seemed to engender a spate of entertainingly fanciful, if not absurd, implications. Consequently, his fame skyrocketed when some of his implications were confirmed. In 1919 Arthur S. Eddington led an expedition to Principe Island off West

Africa. From there, he calculated, it would be possible to observe distant stars close to the sun's corona during a solar eclipse. If Einstein was right, and light was bent by the gravitation forces of the sun, these stars would appear nearer to the sun than they actually were. Eddington's observations corroborated the implications of Einstein's theory. Soon after, Einstein's reputation rose even higher when his theory could account for an anomalous movement of the planet Mercury that had defied explanation by Newtonian theory. In 1921 he was awarded the Nobel Prize for Physics.

Later Developments
Logical positivism flourished for just a few years before it disintegrated and died. Why did this bright star burn out? One reason is that it was too radical; another is its brusque style. The Vienna Circle applied its positivist doctrines and new logic to all kinds of ideas and arguments, in the process sorting science from pseudo-science – as their assessments of Freud and Einstein indicate. Logical positivists saw their role akin to that of H. C. Andersen's imaginary child who pointed to authoritative arguments and cried out that the emperor had no clothes. This made them unpopular, especially among dictators such as Stalin and Hitler, who banned logical positivism altogether.

The haughty little book *Language, Truth and Logic* [1936] by the young Oxford upstart Ayer, at the age of just 25, was an irritant in inter-war Britain. The logical positivists were often viewed as arrogant troublemakers; as a result they created intense and lasting enemies. In particular, they offended two important and influential academic camps: Freudians and Marxists. But there was also a less political, personal and emotional reason why logical positivism faded so quickly: it was basically flawed. Its principle of verification was problematic, and was never convincingly formulated.

Logical positivism's critics came in all shapes and sizes. The young Michael Oakeshott rejected the positivist notion of a unified science as early as 1933, and remained a fierce critic of positivism for the rest of his life. Robin G. Collingwood [1940] rejected, almost without reservation, the approach of Ayer and logical positivists – as we shall see in subsequent chapters, Collingwood was especially irritated by their short-sighted calls for the elimination of metaphysics, and hurled against them the claim that you could have no knowledge without foreknowledge. However, the most significant critic of logical positivism was probably Karl Popper. Popper's objections addressed two points: the verification principle and the attending inductivism.

Popper was critical of the role of inductivism in the positivist project. In doing so, he leaned heavily on David Hume: not on 'Hume the empiricist', but on 'Hume the sceptic'. For empiricists, science begins with sense perception and proceeds through systematic observation and the rules of induction towards the development of general laws. Sceptics, however, hold that this argument suffers from a problem of justification: on the basis of observed regularities alone, one cannot use the past to infer any certain knowledge about the future. From daily experience that the sun rises each morning, most people infer the general law that the sun always rises in the morning. However, this cannot be a logically conclusive inference, because there is no absolute guarantee that what we have seen in the past will persist in the future. The 'law' is ultimately based on an illogical leap of faith – or, using Hume's expression, on 'habit'.

Popper illustrated this with a simple example using swans. He begins by noting the universal observations (and claims) of conscientious European ornithologists: swans are always white. It would seem from the countless observations of white swans in Europe that we can infer that all swans are white. However, this inference would be sabotaged by any tourist to Australia who happens to snap a photo of a black swan. The existence of a single black swan is enough to falsify the universal claim that all swans are white.

By this argument Popper can launch a second criticism at the logical positivists: Schlick is wrong in thinking that the verification principle can provide a solid basis for knowledge. The world is simply too vast and varied for anyone to demonstrate a general claim to be accurate and true. However, Popper continues, it is easy to demonstrate that something is materially false! Rather than a verification principle, Popper argued that science could be defined with reference to a *falsification principle*.

Popper was especially critical of Marxism and used it to illustrate his larger point: for young Marxists in the wake of the Bolshevik revolution, the world was filled with verifications of Marxist theory: 'A Marxist could not open a newspaper without finding on every page confirming evidence of his interpretation of history; not only in the news, but also in its presentation – which revealed the class bias of the paper' (Popper, 1989 [1953], p. 35).

This falsification principle led Popper to criticize another aspect of the logical positivist project: most people tend to see what they want to see. Consequently, any systematic observation of the world is already affected by theory – it if were not, the observation could not be systematic. In light of this argument, the central claim by logical positivists – that a scientist could observe the world and systematically induce general statements from these observations – was impossible. Without theory, we fumble helplessly around in the dark.

At the Threshold of the Millennium

Popper has made a deep impression on twentieth-century empiricism and its naturalist methodology. His inheritance is still felt in three general areas: (1) his argument that empirical observation is theory dependent; (2) his criticism of inductivism; and (3) his refutation of logical positivism. These three contributions have left such a profound impression on late-twentieth century science that it is worth looking more closely at each of them.

On Theories

One way of illustrating Popper's argument about the theory-dependence of sense perception goes by way of the fictitious detective Sherlock Holmes, whose stated method of discovery bore an uncanny resemblance to the logical positivists' view of science. Holmes goes out in the world to collect pieces of information. He compares and contrasts facts in order to identify a pattern that constitutes the truth. His findings always astonish his faithful sidekick, John Watson, who invariably wonders how Holmes arrives at his conclusions. Holmes's answer is always the same. First, you have to acquire all the necessary facts. Then you must combine them in various ways. Finally, you systematically compare each of the various ways against the events of the Real World and eliminate, one by one, those that are not supported by the evidence. In the end, 'when you have eliminated the impossible, whatever remains, however improbable, must be the truth' (Doyle, 1930, chapter 6).

If Holmes's behaviour is observed more closely, however, there are reasons to think that he is pulling the wool over his good friend's eyes. Consider, for example, the famous case of *Silver Blaze*, which involved a missing race horse and the murder of its trainer. Sir Arthur Conan Doyle (1927, p. 343) describes how Holmes discovers a key piece of information:

> Holmes took the bag, and, descended into the hollow, he pushed the matting into a more central position. Then stretching himself upon his face and leaning his chin upon his hands, he made a careful study of the trampled mud in front of him. 'Hullo!' said he suddenly. 'What's this?' It was a wax vesta, half burned, which was so coated with mud that it looked at first like a little chip of wood.
>
> 'I cannot think how I came to overlook it,' said the inspector with an expression of annoyance.
>
> 'It was invisible, buried in the mud, I only saw it because I was looking for it!'

In this description Holmes's approach is not at all a careful, open, methodical survey of the Real World. Rather, Holmes obviously has a theory, and that theory tells him what to look for – a wax vesta – before he throws himself on the muddy ground outside the horse stable to begin his search. Holmes saw the wax vesta because he was looking for it. But how would Holmes know what to look for if he didn't already have a theory?

On Induction

Popper's notion of the theory dependent nature of observation was an outcome of his thoughts on 'Hume's problem'. In the mid-eighteenth century David Hume had begun to ask the first, awkward questions about whether observations could yield general statements, such as theories and laws. Hume had pointed out that a number of individual observations – however many – could not logically sum to a general statement that was indubitably true.

The sun may have risen every day in the past, but there is no guarantee that it will also rise tomorrow. A pragmatic physicist might brush this claim aside as idle speculation and retort that we *can*, in fact, be pretty sure that the sun will rise tomorrow. Indeed, by our understanding of the laws of physics and astronomy, it is possible to predict the precise time at which the sun will rise tomorrow! Hume would answer the pragmatic physicist twice over. First, the fact that the laws of astronomy have held good in the past does not logically entail that they will continue to hold good in the future. Second, the laws of astronomy are themselves the outcome of many individual observations of the heavens; they are, in short, general statements produced by induction. Attempts to justify induction by appealing to general statements – which are themselves produced by induction – constitutes a tautology, not a valid argument.

For Popper, then, science is not about finding the ultimate truth. Science is a process; it builds on general statements. But where these statements come from is not important. We do not evaluate a theory on the basis of where it has come from; we evaluate it on the basis of its explanatory power.

On Testing

How do we determine whether a proposition is true or false? According to the long tradition of empiricist science, we must check it against observations of the Real World to see if it can be verified. This procedure received its most pointed formulation by Moritz Schlick and the members of the Vienna Circle. Popper disagreed: he rejected empiricism's traditional demarcation principle like he rejected its inductivist ideal. He proposed an alternative principle for separating scientific knowledge from pseudo-science. As it is impossible to observe all phenomena, any inductive method will prove unsatisfactory. In their stead, Popper suggests that the

Figure 2.3   *Inductive–deductive model*

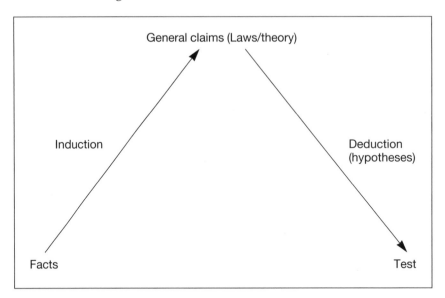

only genuine test of a theory is an attempt to *falsify* it. Popper proposed that falsifiability (rather than Schlick's verifiability) should be the demarcation criterion for evaluating the scientific status of a theory.

With Popper's critique of inductivist science, we have arrived at a place where we can sketch out some of the basic elements of the naturalist methodology. In Figure 2.3 we depict the scientific project in modified positivist terms, with both inductive (left side) and deductive (right side) components.

In distinguishing between the upside and downside of this triangular endeavour we are consciously promulgating the myth – 'sired by Kant, foaled by the Vienna School, and raced past us in our statistics textbooks' (Stinchcombe, 1978, p. 4) – that one can fruitfully separate the theoretical from the empirical parts of the research design. We do this because this myth continues to play an absolutely central role in the world view of naturalist social science. In practice, of course, even the most dyed-in-the-wool naturalists recognize that it is impossible to begin an empirical study without theoretical expectations, or a theoretical study without empirical experience – a modest combination of both ingredients is necessary before the researcher can even begin.

Popper's critique of the inductivist approach results in another model (in Figure 2.4), that provides a stronger deductive grounding for scientific study. In this model, the researcher is given freer reign to develop a deductively informed theory, which is subsequently tested (in a falsifiable

Figure 2.4　*Straight deductive model*

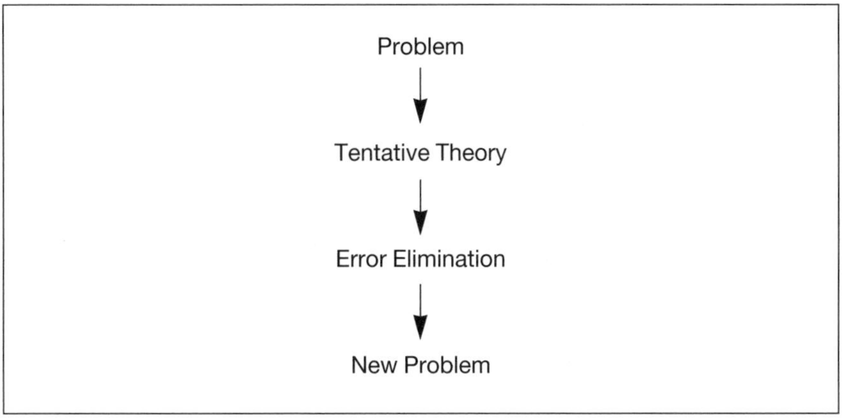

Problem

↓

Tentative Theory

↓

Error Elimination

↓

New Problem

Source: Based on Pheby (1988, p. 25).

manner) in the empirical world. Significantly, Popper's approach leads to a diversity of rival theories, which can be evaluated in hierarchical terms. Both approaches share an implicit understanding that there is a Real World filled with naturally existing patterns that can reveal themselves to the disinterested observer. It is this shared understanding that constitutes the naturalist methodology in social science.

Post-Popper

The naturalist methodology of modern social science is remarkably indebted to Popper's main arguments. This legacy is perhaps most explicit in the nature of modern hypothesis testing in statistical studies, as we shall see in Chapter 4. One reason for this is that his ideas were shored up by other thinkers who evolved arguments that ran parallel to, and were consistent with, his. One of these was Peter Oppenheim, who developed a particular technique that was tailor-made for Popper's philosophy of science: testing by way of the null-hypothesis. Another was Carl Gustav Hempel.

Hempel set out to answer the age-old (and now familiar) question of 'what is science?' His own approach, in effect, was inductive: he began by collecting several indubitable scientific explanations, and then started to compare them. In so doing, he looked for commonalities shared by these much-admired scientific explanations. What he discovered was that they all shared two common features: they all involved at least one universal law, and they all included a statement of relevant conditions. Together,

Figure 2.5   *Hempel's Definition of Science*

$$E = f[(C_1, C_2, \ldots \ldots C_n), (L_1, L_2, \ldots \ldots L_n)]$$

- C_1, C_2, etc. represents 'conditions' or partial facts – i.e., statements concerning the conditions under which the law holds true. In the text's example it is an important condition that the water is heated under an atmospheric pressure that corresponds to the usual pressure at sea level.
- L_1, L_2, etc. indicates a 'law' – i.e., some regularity in nature that can be captured, e.g. by the expression 'when X appears, then Y appears' or 'if X, then Y'. For example, when water is heated to a hundred degrees centigrade (X), it boils (Y).
- E represents the explanandum event – the thing to be explained. E, then, is a function (f) of the laws and conditions under which the laws hold true: it results 'from the particular circumstances specified in C_1, C_2, ... C_n, in accordance with the laws L_1, L_2, ... L_n' (Hempel 1969, p. 81).

Source: Based on Hempel (1969 [1962], p. 81).

these components – the law and the relevant conditions – constitute the premises (the *explanans*) from which an explanatory statement (*explanandum*) is deduced. Hempel's argument is presented as Figure 2.5.

By 'universal law', Hempel referred to an absolute regularity in nature: an association or a correlation. Such a law is usually captured by a formulation such as 'where X appears, Y also appears'. For example, when water is heated to a 100 °C (X), it boils (Y). By 'relevant conditions' Hempel referred to the conditions under which the regularity holds true. In the example above: that the water is contained in an open pot and that the water in it is heated at sea level. By 'explanation' Hempel referred to an operation that is logically the same as the operation called 'prediction'. A law implies prediction, because whenever we observe the appearance of X (and the relevant conditions are present), then we can predict the appearance of Y – if we heat water (in an open pot near the sea) we can predict its boiling at about 100 °C. An explanation, however, differs from prediction in one important respect: it follows an event (whereas a prediction precedes it). When we want to explain something, we start with that which we want to explain – we start with the dependent variable (Y). In order to explain Y, we must identify the proper universal law – plus a set of relevant conditions – that logically imply that event. In the case of a prediction, we start with the universal law – plus a set of initial conditions – from which we deduce a statement about an unknown event (Y). An explanation, in other words, is a 'prediction written backwards'.

We now have attained the tools and vocabulary of the modern naturalist scientist, who goes out into the world in search of patterns and regularities that reside in nature. The naturalist scientist engages the world with a basic hypothesis is mind – something that needs explaining. This thing in need of explanation is called the *dependent variable*, and is often denoted as *Y*. The things that explain changes in the dependent variable are called *independent variables*, and are traditionally referred to as *X*. As is common among naturalists, this relationship can be depicted in algebraic form:

$$Y = \alpha + \beta_1 X_1 + \beta_2 X_2 + \varepsilon.$$

Thus, the dependent variable (*Y*) is traditionally put on the left side of the equation, while the independent variables (X_1 and X_2) are listed to the right of the equal sign, matched to their coefficients (β_1 and β_2). In this equation there is also a constant term (α) and an error term (ε). The role that these variables play in explanation will be elaborated upon in Chapter 4. For now we need only note that this algebraic expression implies a linear relationship between the dependent and independent variables. This is a very common (if often unrealistic) assumption among naturalist social scientists, but it is not a necessary feature of the methodology itself. It is tradition and the maths-processing skills of social scientists (and their computers) that limits this approach (not the methodology itself).

Hempel's reasoning minimizes the use of induction in scientific explanations. It is therefore a good match for Popper's anti-inductivist philosophy of science. Hempel's model employs no other rules of logical inference, other than that of deduction. Its universal laws are not derived by inductive generalization from individual instances; they are merely hypotheses – inspired guesswork or conjectures – which, in turn, may be tested against empirical evidence drawn from systematic observation of events in the Real World. This reliance on hypothesis and deduction alone has earned it the label the 'covering law model'.

Hempel's deductive–nomological explanation and Popper's theory of falsification have constituted the mainstays of naturalist social science since the middle of the twentieth century. Consequently, they play a central role on the broad stage that is social science.

Recapitulation: the Naturalist Way of Knowing

The founding fathers of modern science have provided us with a powerful philosophy of knowledge. They have also provided a legitimizing philosophy; naturalists gain an argument that they can use to justify their approach. Locke and Hume, in particular, provide the philosophical foundations for the naturalist approach to social science, to which subsequent naturalists have added boards and planks. The next section will examine these component elements, or supporting joists, to the naturalist approach.

The Broad Joists of the Naturalist Methodology

Naturalist social science builds on three broad joists – all of them milled from the trunk of traditional natural science: one is ontological, another is epistemological, and the third is methodological in nature. These are presented briefly in Figure 2.6.

First, there is the ontological joist. Subsequent naturalists found in Locke and Hume an atomistic *ontology* – a clear notion that the Real World consists of independent particulars. They interpreted Locke and Hume to mean that there *is* a Real World 'out there' – a Real World which exists independently of our senses. This world exists whether human beings are there to observe it or not. On this ontological joist subsequent naturalists have built a simple definition of 'truth': a statement is true if it accurately corresponds to a state of affairs in the real world. This definition is known as the *correspondence theory of truth*.

The second supporting joist is epistemological. Subsequent naturalists entertain the same *epistemology* as their forebears about the regularities of nature and the drive to document these regularities as accumulated associations. This involves two things. First, it means that knowledge about the regularities of nature is acquired through systematic observations of associated phenomena. Knowledge about the laws of nature is, in other words, acquired through the identification of associations (or variable correlations). This suggests that the ultimate purpose of science is to uncover these regularities and to restate them as (natural) laws. Second, the empirical epistemology means that human knowledge grows over time through the accumulation of true correlations. This accumulation is reflected in the growth of more and more accurate theories.

Figure 2.6   *The three basic joists of naturalist social science*

- An *ontology* of independent particulars.
- An *epistemology* which relies on an idea of accumulated *a posteriori* knowledge of associations (or correlations).
- A *methodology* which seeks to identify regularities in the Real World.

Finally, there is the methodological joist. Subsequent naturalists have found in Hume a confirmation of the *methodology* of Galileo, Bacon and others. In particular, these authors maintain that the world is filled with many kinds of repetitions and regularities, and the main purpose of naturalist science is to identify these regularities. This means that regularities are observable by systematic use of human sense perception, and it means that such observations are communicable.

The Naturalist Hierarchy of Methods

Naturalist science sets out to discover and chart the regularities of the world. Naturalist scholars observe the world, painstakingly collect empirical evidence, then analyse and order it so that they can reveal and accumulate knowledge of the regularities of the world. From these tasks, naturalist social scientists seek to account for individual events in the past and predict events in the future. This understanding of the nature of the Real World, and the appropriate way to uncover its truths, has resulted in a firm hierarchy of methods within the naturalist approach to social science.

Francis Bacon and Galileo Galilei rank among the major thinkers in naturalist science. Although their inductive procedures and experimental designs have been probed and amended over the centuries, their basic designs still offer valid models for naturalist ventures. Neither Popper nor Hempel have strayed far from these models. Indeed, the experimental design, which was introduced by Galileo and Bacon, lies at the very core of the methods preferred by contemporary naturalists. Both Popper's and Hempel's philosophies of science are fully congruent with the experimental designs of Bacon and Galileo.

In other words, the experimental method is the ideal, which other methods strive to emulate. This method is ideal because of its ability to control and order causal and temporal relationships. Other methods are less apt in these regards. Consequently, the experiment ranks as the one, true scientific procedure; other methods are deemed less accurate or powerful and rank lower on the naturalist scale of preferred methods.

Of course, the experimental method is not always possible or convenient. In many social science projects, experiments are not practical, affordable or ethical. When experimentation is not a realistic choice, naturalist social scientists tend to fall back on the second-best approach: the statistical method. This method tries hard to emulate the basic design of experiments. However, due to lack of data, even the statistical method can prove impractical, so that the social scientist may find it necessary to use a comparative approach designed for a smaller number of observations. In the worst-case scenario, when a research question cannot even be pursued through systematic comparisons, the social scientist may be

Figure 2.7   *The hierarchy of methods in the naturalist tradition*

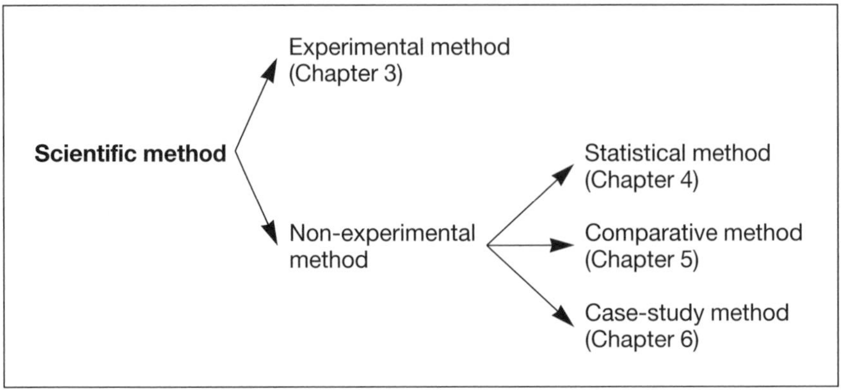

Source: Based on Lijphart (1975, p. 162).

forced to resort to the case-study or historiographic method, which lies at the bottom of the naturalist's hierarchy of methods. Naturalist social science is expected to employ this method only when faced with a yawning paucity of data.

The existence of such a hierarchy of methods is a commonly entertained notion in the naturalist social sciences. Arend Lijphart (1975) has given this notion a classic expression, which is depicted in Figure 2.7.

The first half of the book that follows is organized with this figure in mind. Thus, the next chapter – Chapter 3 – discusses the ideal, experimental, method. Subsequent chapters will then introduce other methods in descending order of usefulness to the naturalist social scientist: Chapter 4 discusses statistics, Chapter 5 comparisons, and Chapter 6 will describe case studies and historical methods.

Recommended Further Reading

Readers who want to trace the philosophical roots of the naturalist tradition should return to the original: Hume's *Inquiry Concerning Human Understanding* [1748]. For a more up-to-date introduction to larger philosophy of science issues, read Hollis's *The Philosophy of Social Science* (1994). The classic formulation of logical positivism is Ayer's *Language, Truth and Logic* (1952), whereas Wilson's *Consilience* (2003) provides a magnificent view of an expansive modern naturalist project.

Chapter 3

The Experimental Method

In closing the last chapter we introduced a hierarchy of methods associated with the naturalist approach, an approach that assumes the world is inherently characterized by regularities or patterns. These patterns are made accessible to the naturalist by the systematic use of particular methods or techniques. The most important of these are control and comparison. Control is used to isolate the cause–effect relationship from other potential explanatory variables. Comparison is used to map regularities with the aim of discovering general laws or patterns. By means of control and comparison, the scientist is able to identify, isolate and explore regularities in the world. This is done – as Hume and Mill insisted – by the systematic observation of variables.

Methods vary in their ability to deal with this type of control and comparison. In this chapter we will show why the method of experiment is the naturalist's premier means for securing knowledge about causal relationships. As you will soon discover, the experimental method is a straightforward, simple and effective approach. Consequently, we have kept this chapter short and to the point. Our intention is to provide you with a simple, but solid, introduction to a very powerful method. We see no reason to burden the chapter with additional examples or spruce it up with lots of bells and whistles. The beauty of experiment lies in its simplicity and directness.

What is the experimental method? Why is it so popular? In essence, the experimental method involves two operations rolled into one: a demonstration that when an independent variable (X) is present, then its dependent associate (Y) is present as well; *and* that when X is absent, then Y is also absent. In other words, experiments allow us to focus on particular associations, or correlations/co-variations. This focus, as we have already noted, is central to all scientific endeavours. But the prime reason for the popularity of the experimental method is that it allows us to manipulate the actual environment in which casual relationships are tested. This, in turn, reassures us that the relationships discovered are real and direct, and not the result of some accidental (contextual) influence. The simplicity and control inherent in experimentation are the very reasons why it is taken as a model for other methods in the naturalist social science tradition.

Indeed, this method is so central to the naturalist approach that it is difficult to appreciate any naturalist method without first fully understanding the logic of experimentation. This is the view of Ernest Nagel (1961, p. 425f.), according to whom 'every branch of inquiry aiming at reliable general laws concerning empirical subject matter must employ a procedure that, if it is not strictly controlled experimentation, has the essential logical functions of experiment in inquiry'.

Nagel probably had the natural or physical sciences foremost in mind, for the social sciences present a number of moral and practical hindrances for experimental research. Although we can assume that many generals long for a better understanding of the nature of war, and many ministers of finance would like to find the causes of large-scale recessions, it would be neither cheap nor appropriate to explore these topics through research projects that applied the experimental method.

But resistance to experiments is not limited to ethical concerns. Some methodological traditions in social science are leery of those very qualities of experiments that naturalists embrace: their ability to manipulate contexts with an eye to developing firm knowledge about specific causal relationships. After all, the experiment is an artificial construct: creating an experiment means creating an artificial (and controlled) context. Worse (from the constructivist perspective), the experimenter employs this context in a very mechanistic and manipulative fashion.

This is not a criticism anchored in ethics, or even generalizability (what we will refer to below as external validity). This is an ontological argument about the nature of the things we study: is the world of social science made up of atomistic, interchangeable parts (like a clock), or is it an organic whole, where the very context provides it with meaning (and where manipulating the context will change its meaning)? While social scientists in the naturalist tradition boast about the great strides that have been made in the design and application of the experimental method in recent years, constructivists tend to claim that its cavalier and ultimately destructive attitude towards context makes it an unacceptable tool. We will return to this issue in Chapter 12, when we discuss the merits of experiment from a constructivist point of view.

Despite the constructivist's scepticism, the social scientist's use of experimental methods is on the rise. Just a few decades ago, experimentation was largely confined to narrow and applied research agendas (for example, within social psychology and management studies). Furthermore, its practitioners were almost always on the defensive – a posture which may be explained in part by a general recognition of the ethical and practical problems associated with social scientific experimentation, and an intellectual context in which social scientists were more critical of the sort of damage that experimental control does to the constitutive context of social behaviour.

By contrast, experimentation today has become increasingly mainstream. Experiments in social science receive broad support – both academic and financial. The main reason for this support lies in the fact, noted above, that experiments provide a strong (perhaps the strongest) proof of causal relationships. When properly conceived, the experimental design provides us with a phenomenally strong basis for inferring causal relationships between variables. Not only are experiments designed to produce secure knowledge about causal relationships via control and comparison, but this design fits hand-in-glove with the empiricist's reliance on observational evidence. After all, experimentation is 'experience carefully planned' in advance' (Fisher, 1953, p. 8). Given this compatibility, is not surprising that experiments have been granted a leading role in the naturalist's pantheon of methods.

This chapter aims to explain this important role. In doing so, we have two main objectives. First, we examine the design of the experimental method, with an eye to explaining how it provides internal validity. Second, we aim to examine the accepted strengths and weakness of this method, in light of the design features described in the first section, and a small number of influential examples.

Historical and Definitional Preliminaries

Since experiment involves a practical, tinkering element, it is natural to return to one of history's greatest tinkerers: Francis Bacon. He conducted a classic experiment to demonstrate the effect of heat. He began by selecting two iron balls of equal size – just big enough to pass through the hole in an iron sleeve. He heated up one of the balls, and noted that it no longer passed through the hole. He observed that the other ball, which had not been heated, still glided through the sleeve. Bacon then made two observations before he drew a general conclusion. First, he observed that the two balls were equal in all respects, except that one had been exposed to heat. Second, he observed that the heated ball did not pass through the hole in the iron sleeve – although it had done so before it was heated, and that the other ball, similar but unheated, still passed through. The general conclusion? That the heated ball had expanded and that the heat was the cause of the expansion.

Bacon's procedure – his selection of objects, his systematic manipulation and observation and his comparative logic – conforms to the modern experiment in its simplest form. We shall discuss these design details below, as this is the primary objective of the chapter that follows.

But it is equally important for us that you think of Bacon's experiment in light of his larger methodological argument. Experiments can provide us with observations about the world that can then be used to make more general statements. In Bacon's experiment, the objective was not to increase the size of iron balls (for whatever purpose), but to understand the general relationship between solid objects and heat (in other words, that solid objects expand when heated).

Galileo's Design

A more famous experiment is associated with Galileo Galilei, who claimed to have dropped different-sized balls from the top of the 'leaning tower' of Pisa. Galileo was interested in testing Aristotle's claim that objects of a different weight fall with different speeds. To do this, he developed an experimental process in three neat steps. The first step involved setting up the conditions – in other words, selecting the proper objects and arranging them in ways which allowed for manipulation (that is, he selected a set of different-sized balls and carried them to the top of the tower of Pisa). The second step involved the systematic observation of the phenomenon at hand; in other words, throwing the objects off the tower and observing their fall very closely – carefully noting their gathering speed and carefully measuring the time between them when landing. Different-sized balls fell to the ground together 'with not so much as a hand's breadth between them', he observed. Galileo's third step was to *analyse*. After much careful consideration (where he twisted and turned his observation statements in ways that made them yield the information that they held), Galileo came to the conclusion that Aristotle had been wrong: all objects fall with the *same* speed.[1]

In general, experimentation is a research procedure that sets up a representation of the world: it involves the isolation of component parts in terms of *conditions* and *variables*. Experiments then manipulate these variables so as to observe (and record) the relations between them. Experimentation allows the observer to control claims made about an object; it allows the observer to check systematically – by wiggling and poking – that the claims made about an object are, in fact, correct. At the most general level, the investigations of both Bacon and Galileo square nicely with Zimeny's general definition of experimentation as an 'objective observation of phenomena which are made to occur in a strictly controlled situation in which one *or more* factors are varied and the others are kept constant' (Zimeny, 1961, p. 18, italics in original).

But this is not the only reason we have begun our discussion of experiments with Galileo and Bacon. We wanted to return to history's greatest inductivists to illustrate the important role of hypothesis testing (and hence theory) in experimental designs. As Galileo's example illustrates, an experiment does not begin by setting up a representation of a particular part of the world; it begins with a good reason for doing so! Experiments start with an initial proposition, an educated guess, or a theory; in short, they begin with hypotheses. Indeed, Bacon was known to criticize his forebears and colleagues for not using hypotheses as a guide in their experimental work. Thus, experimentation helps us answer questions that are inspired by theoretical concerns.

The Classic Design

Like Galileo and Bacon, modern scientists use experiments to better understand the world. Like our experimental forefathers, we find utility in this method because it rests critically on an ontological assumption about the existence of naturally occurring patterns in the Real World. It is, after all, these patterns that the experimenter intends to capture. Experiments allow us to construct representations of a particular part of the world, isolate its component parts in terms of conditions and variables, and manipulate these variables in order to observe (and record) any changes in the relations between them.

Since Galileo, the experiment has developed a more formal and explicitly comparative design. The researcher distinguishes between two equivalent phenomena. He then exposes one phenomenon (the *treatment group*) to a stimulus (X), but not the other (the *control group*, which remains unexposed) – as when Bacon applied two iron balls and exposed one of them to heat but not the other. The two phenomena are then compared. Since they were identical before the treatment was administered, any difference between the two must be attributed to the treatment. This method can help the scientist identify the presence of a distinct cause-and-effect relationship. When done correctly, an experiment can provide deep understanding of the causal relationship between variables.

There are two main (and related) features of the experimental design: control and random assignment. It is these two features that allow the experiment to produce such strong knowledge about the nature of hypothesized relationships. *Control* refers to the ability of the analyst to operationalize both independent and dependent variables, with the aim of measuring the impact of a given treatment or stimulus. *Random assignment* refers to the ability of the experimenter to control all extraneous factors – known and unknown, plausible and implausible – that may be linked to the phenomenon of interest. This combination of control and random assignment is critical for securing firm knowledge about causal relationships. For this reason, variations of control and random assignment are employed by all methods in the naturalist tradition. A hypothetical example may prove useful at this point to clarify what we mean by control and random assignment.

Imagine that we have developed a new way of teaching social science methods, and that we want to gauge the effectiveness of this new method, compared to more traditional approaches. To test this effectiveness, we can experiment on a group of incoming students to the course. This can be done by dividing the class in half (making sure that this 'division' is purely random). We wouldn't want to divide the group by simply drawing a line down the middle of the classroom, as friends of similar levels of intelligence may be sitting next to one another. In addition, we would want to make sure that age, gender, class, income and so on, were randomly distributed across the two sample groups. The easiest way to do this may be to flip a coin for each student, and let the coin distribute students randomly between the two groups within the class. In this way, random allocation is used to ensure that the results of our experiment are not caused by some extraneous factor in the sample (such as age, sex, friend-cohort or class).

Once the class is divided into two equal groups, each is given an examination to test their initial competence in social science methods. This is often referred to as the *pre-test*. The pre-test will give us a baseline from which we can evaluate the effect of the given treatment (in this case, our new approach to teaching methods). We then spend the semester teaching each group of students in a different way: one half is taught using the new technique (this group is the treatment group); the other half is taught the old way (this group is the control group). When teaching both groups, we make sure that the only difference separating the control and treatment groups is the method of teaching (the stimulus, X, or treatment). At the end of the semester we again test each group (a *post-test*) and compare scores. In this way, control is used to ensure that any observable difference in test results can be attributed to the treatment (the new teaching method).

This example illustrates the basic design of the experimental method, and it is captured schematically as the fourth example in Figure 3.1 below. It also illustrates the potential explanatory power of the experimental method. The ability of the experimenter to select control and treatment groups with an eye trained on random assignment provides him with a high degree of *internal validity*. Internal validity refers to the scientist's control over context, such that he can be certain of the causal relationships among them.[2] In the example above, the experiment has internal validity if students in the treatment group score significantly better (or worse) than those in the control group at the end of the semester, and there is no reason to believe that this effect is due to something other than the different teaching methods employed. For social scientists, the provision of strong internal validity is the 'crown jewel of experimentation' (McGraw, 1996, p. 772).

The reason for this lies, rather uncomfortably, in our understanding of causation, which is anchored in Hume. Because we cannot observe causation itself, we must use counterfactual analyses to confirm causal effects. In other words, to distinguish causation from correlation, the experimenter is forced to engage in a counterfactual thought experiment. If two variables are causally related to one another, the experimenter assumes that the absence of the (causal) factor would lead to the absence of an effect. In non-causal correlations, the experimenter does not expect this counterfactual to hold. Though experimenters often neglect to admit it, the internal validity of their experiments depends critically on counterfactuals.

While it is easy to admire the experiment's provision of internal validity, it is just as easy to exaggerate this feature. After all, experimental design still cannot provide us with information about the underlying processes that link treatment and outcome. As we shall discuss with respect to statistical methods (in the following chapter), confirming causal relationships requires that the social scientist considers the mechanisms, or mediators, by which treatment variables cause outcomes. Indeed, while internal validity is clearly the strongest asset of experimental designs, one of the most famous examples of experiments in social science illustrates a major difficulty associated with applying this method to thinking subjects. We are referring to the set of management experiments conducted in Hawthorne, Illinois in the late 1920s.

In the interwar period, the Western Electric Company was eager to employ new developments in social science techniques to increase the productivity of its workers. Toward that end, the company hired Elton Mayo, a psychologist at Harvard University, to examine whether minor changes in the plant's environment could enhance worker productivity. In 1927, Mayo and his associates travelled to the company's Hawthorne plant near Chicago, and proceeded to set up an experiment. The research group began by randomly segregating workers into two rooms: one containing the treatment group, one the control group. They then began to introduce a number of treatments to the first room to gauge the effect of these changes on worker productivity. For example, they might have improved the lighting, introduced paintings on the walls or music in the air, and so on.

Mayo predicted that worker productivity would increase in the treatment room as new treatments were introduced. He was therefore surprised to note that productivity increased in the control room as well, despite the absence of a treatment there. Worse (for Mayo), it seemed as though productivity at the Hawthorne plant was increasing whether Mayo's team introduced new treatments or removed them. Indeed, when Mayo dimmed the lighting in the treatment room and left the workers in semi-darkness, their productivity still increased (every plant manager should be so lucky!). After many sleepless nights, it dawned upon Mayo that the workers were not responding to the changes that he had so cleverly designed and so systematically introduced. Instead, they were responding to being observed. In other words, all the workers reacted to being observed by improving their productivity, regardless of whether they were working in the treatment or the control room.

This phenomenon has gone down in the lore of management studies as 'the Hawthorne effect'. While familiar to students of behavioural science, it is also familiar to the general lay public by way of Gary Larson's cartoon of the panicky members of an indigenous tribe trying to hide their microwaves and TVs while yelling, 'Anthropologists! Anthropologists!'

The Hawthorne effect illustrates one of the main problems with the experimental method in social science: when the researcher delves into the world, in order to isolate the features that most interest him, he also alters the nature of that world. To minimize this effect, social science experiments often try to avoid any physical separation of the treatment group and the control group. Thus, in medical experiments – for example, experiments designed to gauge the effectiveness of a new cold medicine – the participants themselves do not know the group to which they belong. All participants receive a pill – half of them receive the actual medicine, whereas the others receive a harmless placebo.

Experiments lend themselves to securing strong knowledge (based on sensory perception and observational statements) about the nature of causal relationships. For this reason, they play a vital and central role in the scientist's toolbox of methods. By manipulating the context of a relationship between variables, the experimenter can generate the conditions for studies with very strong internal validity. But this method's very ability and willingness to manipulate the environment means that the knowledge generated by experiments cannot be easily generalized beyond the controlled environment. This leads us to the issue of external validity.

Internal validity means control – it refers to a control of variables so tight that we can confidently say that correlation equals causation. *External validity* means generalizability, or the degree to which we can trust that the lessons learnt from experiments 'in the laboratory' are extendable to the real world. If internal validity is the crown jewel of experimentation, external validity is its Achilles' heel (Iyengar, 1991). Indeed, the very qualities that make an experiment produce tests with strong internal validity (that they are contextually specific), undermines their capacity to generalize: we have no way of evaluating the effects of non-controlled variables once the experiment leaves the laboratory.

Some of this tension can be resolved by employing different types of experiments. For example, it is common to distinguish between laboratory and field experiments. Laboratory experimentation is clearly the most controlled method of data collection in the social sciences. A laboratory setting allows the researcher to control certain features in the natural environment as well as manipulate independent variables in order to observe the effects produced. These types of experiments tend to have a high degree of internal validity, but a fairly low degree of external validity. Field experiments, on the other hand, occur in a natural situation. While the researcher can still manipulate the relevant independent variables, he is confined to contextual variables that can only be controlled in a loose fashion. This increases the degree of external validity of field experiments (relative to laboratory experiments), but it also makes it more difficult to control intrinsic and (especially) extrinsic factors.[3]

For an example of the problem of external validity, consider the popular resistance and scepticism to genetically modified crops. Although the consuming public is fully aware that genetically modified food crops have undergone a phenomenally large barrage of experimental tests to try to evaluate (and minimize) their negative effects on human health, they remain sceptical that the lessons learnt in the laboratory will continue to hold once these crops are set loose in a natural environment. The very complexity of the natural world makes it impossible to control for all contingencies. Theories help the natural scientist test the most likely interactions, but consumers are sceptical of the scientist's ability to consider all contingencies, or to generalize safely from the lessons learnt in the laboratory.

In the social sciences, the problems of both internal and external validity are complicated by the inability of the analyst to use random assignment at will. Not even the strongest proponents of social science experiments are willing to downplay the ethical and practical difficulties associated with conducting experiments on people, communities and nations. Because of these very real and serious difficulties, social scientists often have to develop alternatives to true experimental design, or what Cook and Campbell (1979) have referred to as *quasi-experiments*.

These alternative designs can be illustrated by returning to the hypothetical teaching example introduced above. Instead of finding a truly random way of dividing our class into two groups (one control, one treatment), we might use non-comparable groups, or groups whose composition is not strictly controlled. For example, instead of dividing one class into two, we might teach the new approach to this year's class, and compare it to the results generated from the traditional teaching approach used in a class from the previous year. Obviously, this approach is not optimal in that there may be several important differences separating the two years – differences that might affect the outcome (in addition to the 'treatment').

An alternative quasi-experimental approach could build on strong theoretical expectations about what sort of students tend to do well in a class of research methods. We might use these expectations to ensure an even (no longer random) distribution of important individual characteristics across the two groups. For example, if we know that women tend to do better than men in methods training, we would want to make sure that each group had an equal distribution of both sexes. In this way, we use theory to help us control for expected variation (for example, to make sure that the sample is equally distributed with respect to sex, age, income, class background and so on).

To illustrate the differences between real and quasi-experiments, we can draw from a colleague's graphical depiction. Kristen Ringdal (2001, p. 217) introduces four types of experimental designs, each with a single causal factor (X). The two examples in the right column are real experiments; the two in the left column are quasi-experiments. Within each group he then distinguishes between pre-test and post-test designs. His comparison is reproduced as Figure 3.1.

In the first design (I) we find a single group (there is no control), which is only tested after the treatment (X) has taken place. In this design, it is difficult to control for a number of alterative explanations, so that the level of internal validity is relatively low.

In the second design (II), the researcher has access to both a control and a treatment group, but the group members are not randomly chosen (this is what distinguishes it from a real experiment). In this design, the first group is affected by the treatment variable (X), but the second (control) group is not. The effect of the treatment is then measured by comparing the difference in outcomes between the control (C) and treatment (E) groups (in other words, $X = Y_{E2} - Y_{C2}$). This design was used in our quasi-experimental example above (where we tested the effect of our new methods teaching approach on one year's students and compared it with the results from the previous year's students).

In the third design (III) we find a random distribution of group members. This design protects against selection bias, and the researcher can be more confident that the different post-test outcomes are caused by the treatment variable (X).

Finally, the fourth design (IV) is the most common design, as it provides a strong defence against alternative explanations or bias. Not only is there random selection, but the existence of both a pre-test and

Figure 3.1 *Some examples of experimental design*

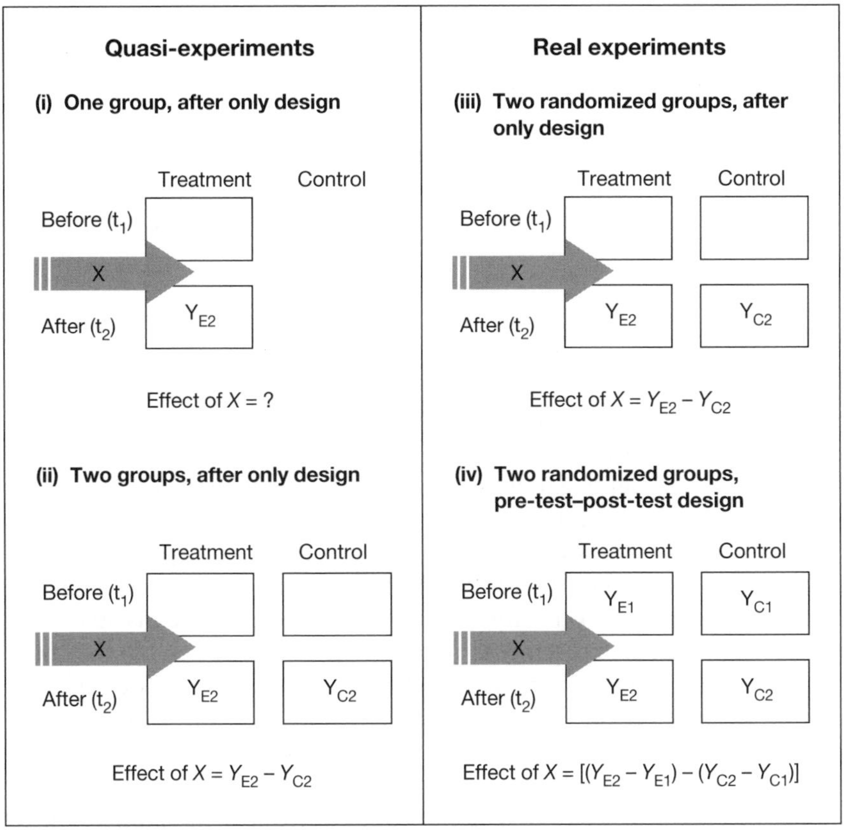

Source: Ringdal (2001, p. 217).

post-test helps to define, locate and test real causal factors. This is the design that lay behind our initial hypothetical example, where X can be understood as our new approach for teaching research methods, and the effect of X is measured by comparing the change in test scores (post-test minus pre-test) in the treatment group, with those in the control group (in other words, $X = [(Y_{E2} - Y_{E1}) - (Y_{C2} - Y_{C1})]$.

As we will see in subsequent chapters, other comparative approaches rely on the same sort of design logic as that which is found in modified or quasi-experiments. Researchers aim to control for alternative sources of variation in order to be certain that the observed variation is the only one (and hence its cause). By employing quasi-experimental designs, the experimenter accepts a lesser degree of internal validity (relative to a true experimental design). In doing so, however, the researcher can avoid some of the most difficult practical and ethical problems associated with experimentation when employed in the social sciences.

Exemplary Illustrations

The experiment is being employed with increased frequency and recognition across the spectrum of social science. Still, some academic disciplines have proven to be more comfortable than others with experimental designs.

Maier's Rats

Psychologists have a long history of relying on experiments. Most famous of these is, perhaps, Norman Maier, who used experiments to question the authority of Freudian psychoanalysis. Like any good experimenter, Maier began by setting up an experimental condition – he selected his objects and arranged them in ways that enabled him to control his variables and conditions. Given the many good reasons – material as well as moral – for not using human beings as test subjects, Maier experimented on white rats. His arrangement consisted of a jumping apparatus: a platform that faced two openings or 'doors', each marked by different, easily distinguishable symbols – a black circle on a white background on one door and a white circle on a black background on the other. One door would easily swing back at the touch of a jumping rat and reveal a landing board upon which Maier placed tasty morsels as reward. The other door would not open; the poor rat who jumped at it would meet a closed door and fall, startled, into a net below.

Maier's first question was to find out how fast rats could learn – how quickly they could identify the yielding door with the food behind it. In order to find the answer, he placed his white rats on the platform and watched them jump. He used several rats and subjected each of them to hundreds of jumps. He observed each jump and took meticulous notes on whether the animal jumped through the yielding door and landed on the feeding board, or whether it smacked into the closed door and fell into the net below. At the end he analysed his notes.

Maier found differences in learning abilities among rats – some were surprisingly quick, others were slow learners. But sooner or later, he noted, all the rats developed a preference for the yielding door with the reward behind it. This preference was the result of learning on the part of the rat. How did learning take place? Maier argued that jumps which landed the rat on the feeding platform were 'right choices' because they produced rewards that the rat would seek to repeat in the future; jumps at the closed door were 'wrong choices' that involved punishments that the rat would seek to avoid in the future.

> The selective use of reward and punishment has made one way of behaving more attractive than the other, and as long as the reward and punishment remain the same the preference continues. Since the consequence of the response determines the preference, we may speak of such responses as *goal oriented* or *goal motivated*.   (Maier, 1949, p. 26)

This argument met stiff resistance. Maier had challenged the views of established psychologists, teachers and pedagogues, who argued that learning was driven by some kind of inner motivation. In the face of criticism that his work showed behaviour to be solely goal-oriented, Maier responded with yet another rat-based study. This study began with a simple question: What would happen if the goal was removed from the rats? What kind of behaviour would the rodents develop if the food was moved around randomly? Again, Maier placed the rats on his apparatus, observed how they jumped and wrote the results down in meticulous notes. The first thing he noticed was that when food was moved willy-nilly behind the doors, the rodents sensibly refused to jump. In other words, when rewards were unpredictable and goals were uncertain, the rats saw no reason to jump at all.

But how would the rats behave if they were *forced* to jump? To answer this question, Maier wired the platform so that the rats would receive an electric shock and thus be strongly encouraged to jump. Again, he observed every rat's jump, took careful notes and analysed the results. His conclusions were striking: the rats that were forced to jump developed standard, fixed responses – some of them would consistently jump at a particular symbol (regardless of whether it was placed on the right or the left); others would always jump at a particular door (regardless of the symbol that covered it). Maier (1949, p. 27) concluded that the poor rodents faced a '*no-solution problem* and regard it as frustrating': the rats became 'frustrated', and frustrated behaviour is determined by something other than goals.

Maier thus drew a sharp distinction between *goal-directed behaviour* on the one hand, and *frustrated behaviour* on the other.[4] Goal-directed behaviour is formed by the consequences of actions and involves learning – acts that result in rewards tend to be increasingly repeated in the future, whereas those that involve punishment tend to be avoided. Frustrated behaviour, by contrast, is unrelated to the consequence of actions. Frustrated behaviour is 'stereotyped' and 'fixated' and involves no learning. Once a stereotypical behaviour pattern is formed, it persists. When food is reintroduced – even when the rats smell it and are aware of its presence – they nevertheless continue their stereotypical behaviour and jump at the same door again and again. Indeed, even when food is placed in the open door and is fully visible, rats who have become fixated on the other (closed) door will continue to jump at that door, repeatedly smack into it and fall into the net blow.

Ideological Innocence

While experiments in the disciplines of Psychology and Management Studies might be better known (as the above examples from Maier and Mayo illustrate), Political Scientists, too, rely on experiments. Some rely on them indirectly – for example, by borrowing the results of experiments conducted by others and applying their lessons to explore questions in their own fields. For example, Ted Gurr (1970) used the above-mentioned frustration–aggression hypothesis to explore the reasons behind political rebellions. Others conduct their own experiments.

One of the best-known experiments in Political Science is the influential 'question wording experiment' conducted by Sullivan, Piereson and Marcus (1978). Their experiment was a direct response to Philip Converse's (1964, 1970) thesis about 'ideological innocence'. As was common in much of the early (1950s) research on public attitudes and opinion in the USA, Converse held that Americans were innocent, even ignorant, of ideological concepts, and that they lacked true opinions on most policy questions. In the mid-1960s, this concept of ideological innocence was under increasing criticism, with several authors suggesting that American public opinion had become more sophisticated and ideological in its assessments of issues, parties and candidates. These new arguments were largely based on evidence from changing responses to questions in the National Election Study. In particular, after 1964, it would appear as though respondents were becoming more ideologically sophisticated. As the 1964 election was a hotly contested ideological campaign, it made good intuitive sense that voters had become more ideologically aware.

Because of their familiarity with National Election Study questions, Sullivan, Piereson and Marcus devised an alternative explanation for the (apparent) change in public attitudes. They thought that the changes did not reflect underlying attitudes, but (rather) a change in the way that the questions were framed to gauge ideological competence (after 1964). To check the validity of their hunch, and to challenge the growing evidence of a more ideologically sophisticated American voter, they developed a classic experimental design, where respondents were divided into two groups. Half of the respondents were given pre-1964 questions concerning ideological competence; the other half were posed questions in the new, post-1964, format. The results of their experiment showed convincingly that the observed change in attitude was not due to any real change in the electorate, but rather to changes in the survey questions themselves! This example is one of the most elegant (and most referenced) demonstrations of a cause-and-effect relationship in the social sciences, and it is one that would have been difficult to demonstrate in a non-experimental form.

A second example is provided by the work of Shanto Iyengar and Donald Kinder on the role of the media in influencing public opinion. Iyengar and Kinder (1987) used a series of well-designed experiments to show how the presentation of news affects public opinion in a number of subtle ways. In contrast to much of the (then) conventional wisdom about the minimal effects of the media, Shanto and Kinder conclude that television news shapes the American public's conception of political life in pervasive ways. Their book, *News that Matters*, offered 'more persuasive evidence than parallel work in the critical, rhetorical, content-analytic, or even correlational schools' (Chaffee, 1989, p. 277).

Iyengar has also used experiments in subsequent studies on the effects of mass media. In his 1991 book *Is Anyone Responsible?*, Iyengar divided respondents into two groups: one was shown a videotape that included an *episodic* news report on a particular issue problem; a second group was shown a *thematic* report on the same problem. The issues of crime, terrorism, poverty, unemployment, racial inequality and the Iran–Contra affair were included in the experiments. After their exposure to the videotape, which contained seven news stories including the story that was subject to experimental manipulation, participants completed a post-test questionnaire that included open-ended questions about the causes and treatment of the problem at issue. A comparison of the episodic and thematic treatment groups revealed that the episodic group's response usually contained more individualistic and punitive attributions and fewer societal attributes.

Media-related issues lend themselves to experimental design, if only because they are fairly easy to replicate under controlled conditions. Many social scientists have easy access to a deep (and cheap) reservoir of experimental subjects (read students). Better still, it is fairly easy to entice these subjects to sit and watch a short patch of television, after which they exchange their impressions (answer a questionnaire) for money. Experiments of this kind are helping us realize the important role of the modern media in shaping political, economic and social attitudes.

Conclusion

The power of experiment in the naturalist methodology can be traced to its relationship to observation. Observation and observation statements are the premier epistemological devices used by naturalists; experiments place these observations on centre stage. More importantly, observations are seen to be most useful when done in a systematic way, and experiments provide this systematization. Experiments allow the scientist to control and compare relevant variables (and contexts) in order to secure knowledge about posited relationships. In those experimental designs where researchers have the most control (for example, in laboratory experiments), the researcher is able to produce remarkably strong and dependable knowledge about specific causal relationships.

This is what attracts many naturalists to the experimental method. But this very characteristic is what makes it such a problem for constructivists. Traditional experimental designs harvest information at the expense of the context from which the information was originally derived. Because the experimental method is the most invasive and destructive with respect to original context, it is often shunned by scholars in the constructivist tradition. For them, these types of experiment are an extreme choice of method.

Of course, the researcher can develop experimental designs that are more realistic, but this gain in external validity tends to come at the expense of internal validity. To be honest, many social scientists are willing to make this trade-off, and sophisticated field experiments are becoming increasingly common. This should not surprise us, as field experiments still allow us to develop remarkably firm knowledge about specific causal relationships. This is because field experiments, like their laboratory brethren, allow the scientist to control and manipulate variations in the most relevant variables.

Still, there are many areas of social life that do not lend themselves to experimental design – whether in the laboratory or out in the field. In some cases, experiments would violate norms of ethical conduct. For example, one doesn't distribute cigarettes to children to see if they develop cancer later on in life. For that matter, even Maier's treatment of his rats makes many of us uncomfortable. In other cases, experiments would involve such complex, large and expensive preparations as to be practically impossible. For example, an experiment designed to establish the causes of economic development in poor countries would prove to be terribly difficult to conduct. In still other cases, experiments would be both practically unfeasible and morally reprehensible. Clearly, for example, we would not want to identify the causes of war through experimentation.

To avoid awkward situations such as these, social scientists have found it necessary to develop other, alternative, tools, which try to mimic the experiment in design. In these situations, statistical analysis appears as the next best choice of methods, as its access to large numbers of independent observations allows the scientist another (yet similar) means of controlling and monitoring variation. It is to this method we now turn our attention.

Recommended Further Reading

There are several good introductions to experimental designs in the social sciences. A good place to begin is with Fisher's classic *The Design of Experiments* (1953). Donald Campbell's work – with Julian Stanley, *Experimental and Quasi-Experimental Designs for Research* (1966), and with T. D. Cook, *Quasi-Experimentation* (1979) – may be particularly useful. Finally, Christensen's *Experimental Methodology* (2001) provides an up-to-date overview of experimental methodology.

Chapter 4

The Statistical Method

Naturalist social scientists agree that their task is to identify patterns and regularities in nature. Applied methods of comparison, or what J. S. Mill [1891] referred to as 'experimental methods', are used to flush out these patterns. While Mill's methods of experiment refer mostly to what we call the comparative method today, they have been elaborated on by statisticians in ways that have secured statistics a very high status in the pantheon of naturalist methods.

Although naturalists can agree on the importance of identifying regularities in the world, there is a tension among them as to how much we can infer about the nature of these observed relationships. As we saw in Chapter 2, David Hume distrusted causal explanations and cautioned scientists against their use. For Hume, scientists should limit their activities to identifying, observing and charting the regularities of the world.

By contrast, J. S. Mill's faith in the uniformity of nature allowed him to see the Real World as held together by intricate webs of causal relationships. Although he acknowledged that causality cannot be observed by the naked eye, Mill suspected that some kind of cause will be lurking nearby whenever a co-variation is identified. For Mill, then, co-variation and cause are different things; yet the two always appear together. The presence of co-variation can indicate the presence of a cause – in the same way that the eager fly-fisherman who observes rings in a lake can be alerted to a trout. The task of the scholar begins by observing the co-variation; he proceeds below the surface of mere appearances; and he concludes by capturing the causal mechanism at work, deeper down.

In short, there is an important ontological difference separating Mill from Hume, and we intend to exploit this difference to distinguish between the two main ways in which statistical methods are used by scholars in the naturalist tradition: descriptive and inferential. Descriptive statistics are most frequently used to supplement narratives; as such they are a conventional tool in the naturalist's toolbox of methods. But, as we shall see later, descriptive statistics are also welcomed by the constructivist scholar. Inferential statistics, however, is a much more ambitious project: it extends the inductive enterprise to infer about characteristics of a population, in order to generate predictions, explanations and hypothesis tests. This type of statistical approach is most at home among naturalists, as it replicates many of the design features of the experimental method (examined in the previous chapter).

Descriptive Statistics

Statistics involves the systematic collection of quantitative information along lines specified by the rules of inductive logic. Its etymology is revealing: the term 'statistics' literally referred to information about the 'state' – it was quantitative information for statesmen, about the inhabitants of the country (for example, their number, gender, age and so on), and those of their enemies. From time immemorial, rulers have tried to assess the number of people over whom they exercise authority. Recall, for example, that Christ was allegedly born in a Bethlehem stable because King Herod ordered a gigantic census (which required that all his subjects had to return to their place of birth). Throughout the millennia, the Christian Church has kept baptismal registers, cemetery registers and confirmation books. When these numbers are collected in order to infer some other information – for example by a ruler to calculate the tax returns of his lands, or to assess the military strength of his nation – this sort of bookkeeping can qualify as statistics.

Pioneers: Graunt, Petty and Conring

While the collection of statistics has been around for a very long time, its modern application can be traced to the seventeenth century. John Graunt (1620–74) was one of the first people to apply numbers in the systematically inductive way that we now recognize as 'statistics'. Although Graunt was, by occupation, a haberdasher, he seems to have had a morbid preoccupation with death, and a brief account of this preoccupation may help convey the essence of the method he helped to develop.

Graunt processed death records that had been kept by the London parishes. It was in grouping and regrouping these records, according to the various causes of death, that he discovered how large numbers displayed patterns and regularities that were not evident in smaller numbers. He noted, for example, that the proportion of suicides remained remarkably constant over time, and that fatal diseases and accidents (events that seemed to be triggered by pure chance) possessed a surprising regularity. He discovered that the death rates in towns exceeded those in the countryside, and he noted that the population was divided equally between the sexes (despite the fact that the birth rate of boys was greater than that of girls – suggesting that the greater birth rate of boys was offset by a greater mortality rate for males, later in life).

In essence, Graunt applied various bookkeeping techniques to group facts and statistical records. He collected facts, invented categories and taxonomies for them, counted up the entries (or 'scores') of their different categories, and applied simple arithmetic techniques. These bookkeeping techniques allowed him to describe the general characteristics of a set of data and to derive 'some truths and not commonly believed opinions' (Graunt, 1996 [1662], preface, §3).

Thus, from his infamous 'Table of Casualties' in the 1662 edition of his *Natural and Political Observations . . . upon the Bills of Mortality*, we learn that the least common causes of death during the period surveyed were 'Shingles', 'Stitch' and (our favourite) 'Fainted in Bed'. Deaths of this nature occurred only once over a 20-year period. By contrast, the most common cause of death in the Table of Causalities is 'Ague and Fever'. The *Observations* showed readers how many of the varied causes of death (accident, suicide and various diseases) remained remarkably stable over time, but it also illustrated how the incidence of certain diseases varies greatly over time. Graunt recognized that these diseases were likely to have very particular causes, and he argued that lives could be saved if such causes could be found and removed. On the strength of this argument Graunt set about creating a system to warn of the onset and spread of bubonic plague in the city.

Graunt died in London – reportedly of jaundice and liver disease – in 1674, but his statistical legacy was propelled by a friend and supporter, Sir William Petty (1623–87). An army physician and professor of anatomy and music, Petty had neither the morbid inclination of his bookkeeping friend, nor his patience for note taking and systematization. However, Petty did have a scientifically-trained mind and a capacity to marvel at Graunt's discoveries. Thus endowed, he began to speculate about the practical and scientific implications of them. Indeed, with time, Petty came to the conclusion that Graunt's method was the *only* viable method for investigating medical, economic and political subjects. He eagerly demonstrated the application of this new method to his friends and colleagues at the newly established Royal Society (of which he was a founder). Naming this method 'Political Arithmetic', Petty defined it as 'the art of reasoning by figures upon things relating to government' (Pearson, 1978, p. 2).

Petty and Graunt compiled information, sifted through it, classified it, and grouped it in various ways in an attempt to uncover the world's uniformity and hidden patterns. In this they were not alone. Around 1650, Herman Conring (1606–81), at the University of Helmstädt, had introduced a system which allowed him to collect quantitative information about countries and compare them according to size and structure. In addition, he elaborated on the kind of inferences that could be drawn from descriptive facts concerning the rules of conduct for responsible statesmen – a skill which earned him a profitable reputation among German princes, many of whom hired him as an adviser.

These men instigated a remarkable revolution – but its effect was slow and muted. The eighteenth century saw comparatively few efforts to pursue the scientific promise contained in the works of Petty, Graunt and Conring. Still, there was some activity on the ground, and it was not insignificant. In particular, the early eighteenth century saw new Dutch and English insurance companies beginning to use statistics to gauge the probabilities of accidents at sea (in order to establish premiums for ships and cargoes). In France, academic gamblers began to develop more formal theories of probability – first, by systematically observing games of chance; later, by extending their observations to problems of economics, insurance, warfare, politics and medicine.

One of the main reasons for this hiatus in interest may have been resistance to the use of statistics within the scientific community itself. This resistance can be seen in an early attempt to bring statistical methods under the umbrella of British science. In 1830, when it was first proposed that a statistics section of the British Association for the Advancement of Science be formed, the Association found it necessary to appoint a committee to evaluate whether statistics was a proper branch of science. Chaired by Thomas Malthus, this committee soon became divided (as was the entire scientific community at the time). While they could agree that the collection and orderly tabulation of data was consistent with scientific objectives, they were sceptical about whether the statistical interpretation of results was scientifically respectable. This sceptical view was clearly evident in the motto of the Statistical Society of London (later the Royal Statistical Society), which was subsequently formed in 1834. Indeed, their motto – *Aliis exterendum* – can be translated literally as: 'let others thrash it out' (Cochran, 1976, p. 8)! This motto appeared on a binding ribbon around a fat, neatly bound, sheaf of wheat. This, presumably, was meant to represent a collection of abundant, well-tabulated data. In short, the scientific community's embrace of statistics was limited to its descriptive capacity. The data collected would be 'objective'; its interpretation would be 'thrashed out' by others.[1]

Galton: Basic Concepts and Examples

To get a feel for the power of the statistical approach we need to begin by describing some of its component parts. We can do this by way of examples and by tracing the roots of this approach back to one remarkable man: Francis Galton (1822–1911).

Galton was multi-talented: geographer, tropical explorer, anthropologist, meteorologist, criminologist, contrarian, mathematician and bestselling author. In short, Galton was a polymath and a fascinating one at that. His intellectual legacy lives on by way of a long autobiography, *Memories of My Life* (1908) (in which he boasts about it all), and an impressive website dedicated to spreading his work (www.galton.org).

Galton's legacy is perhaps most evident in two subsequent innovations that transformed modern statistics: the explicit phrasing of social-science questions in variable terms; and the construction of arithmetical and mathematical formulae designed to capture such variable relationships. These innovations function as a bridge to the use of statistical inference (the theme of the second part of this chapter).

Variable Analysis

As we noted in this chapter's introduction, John Stuart Mill believed it was possible to use inductive approaches to capture causal relations. To do this, the scientist needed to break down the chaos that appears on the world's surface, and distil it into single, well-defined, facts. When this is done, each fact can be related to other facts – one, or two, or a few at a time. Through systematic observation of relationships, and meticulous mapping of co-relations of facts, the uniformity of the world can be slowly uncovered. This is possible, averred Mill (2002 [1891], p. 248), because every observed fact has a cause and this cause will be found in another fact which immediately precedes it. Once a scholar identifies a clear co-variation between two facts – X and Y – he knows that there are only two simple ways in which this co-variation can be logically understood: either X causes Y, or Y causes X.

As an example, let us return to our proposed new approach for methods teaching. In the previous chapter we showed how an experimental design could prove the effectiveness of our new teaching approach by separating students into control and treatment groups. A statistician might approach the same question from a slightly different angle (as he does not have the ability to actually create control and treatment groups, for whatever reason). The promising statistician, recognizing the utility of our new teaching method, might begin by noting that this method can only be effective if students actually attend lectures. He then might consider the escapades of two students: Aurora and Bruce. Both students attend lectures regularly, and both tend to get very good grades. On the basis of this observation our statistician may wonder if there is a more general co-relation at work here.[2] To explore this hunch further, he begins to observe other students to find out how often they attend lectures. Later, he finds out what grades these students get, and searches for the hypothesized co-relation between 'lectures attended' and 'getting good grades'.

The statistician proceeds by ranking the students according to how often they attend lectures. In so doing, he notes that the course drew from ten lectures in total, and that the best possible student score was seven good grades (where 'good' grades are defined as an 'A' or 'B'). He then compares the attendance and grade scores to see if there is any systematic co-relation across cases. He then notes his observations in a data matrix, presented as Table 4.1.

A data matrix is a composite of three different things: units, variables and values. In this example, the *units* of analysis are the people who are observed – in other words, the 20 students (Aurora, Bruce, Carol and so on). There are two *variables* in this example, 'Number of Lectures Attended' and 'Number of Good Grades' – denoted as variables X and Y, respectively. As we observe each of the units in turn, we allocate observation *values* to each unit on each of the variables. For example, as we

Table 4.1   *Good grades and lectures attended*

Observation	Students	Number of lectures attended (X)	Number of good grades (Y)
1	Aurora	8	6
2	Bruce	7	5
3	Carol	6	3
4	Dina	5	3
5	Elisabeth	3	3
6	Freddy	3	1
7	George	2	0
8	Harry	1	0
9	Irene	2	1
10	Jon	4	2
11	Kim	4	3
12	Lorraine	6	4
13	Mike	8	6
14	Nelly	9	6
15	Oprah	9	7
16	Peter	10	6
17	Quincy	10	7
18	Robert	10	7
19	Shelly	10	7
20	Thandeka	10	0

observe that Aurora attended eight lectures, we give her a value of eight (8) on variable X; since Harry doesn't have a single good grade, he is given a value of zero (0) on variable Y. 'Units', 'variables' and 'values' are some of the most common terms in the modern naturalist trade. Consequently, it is important to know these terms in order to follow discussions in the naturalist approach to social science.

The relation between the two variables in Table 4.1 – number of lectures attended (X) and good grades (Y) – is clearly visible in this matrix, since high attendance values in column X are associated with high grades in column Y. There is, in other words, a positive relationship between variables X and Y. (Regarding the anomalous values for observation 20, Thandeka, see the discussion on Figure 4.3 further on in this chapter.)

Note that the central actor in this familiar story is the 'variable'. A variable is something that varies: it is a phenomenon that assumes different (varying) values according to different cases (for example, grades for each student). In the experimental method we can make values vary by manipulating reality. In the social sciences, this is often not possible: we cannot artificially change the sex of a person, increase his age, and so on. We therefore need to create variation by taking many different cases with different values, according to a number of properties (variables).

Capturing Variable Analysis: On Peas and People

The initial establishment of the Statistical Society of London reflected a renewed growth of interest in statistical approaches. Few individuals played a more important role in that resurgence than Sir Francis Galton. Taking a page from the books of Graunt and Petty, Galton began to investigate the distribution of attributes among human beings.

Graunt had measured the world, but he had measured it one variable at a time. His contributions – such as the measures of central tendency and dispersion – were designed to capture the shape or form of a data set collected along a single variable; they pertained to univariate statistics. Francis Galton elaborated on and systematized Graunt's univariate devices – he captured the logic of central tendency and dispersion in statistical formulae; he elaborated on Graunt's notion of 'the average' and refined it by distinguishing between three measurements of central tendency: the 'arithmetic mean', the 'median' and the 'mode'. These contributions are spelled out in Figure 4.1.

Subsequent calculation of the standard deviation built on a concept Galton had pioneered: that of the 'normal distribution', which he defined as a curve in which the mean, the median and the mode coincide. He conceived of it as an ideal pattern for the distribution of attributes in a population. In addition, he elaborated on univariate techniques by

Figure 4.1 *Important concepts in early statistics*

- **Arithmetic mean** is a simple calculation for an average measure – the sum of the values of all observations, divided by the number of observations. The mean is commonly denoted as $\bar{x}$, and can be summarized by the formula: $\bar{x} = \sum x/N$. If Bob earns £100, Doug earns £150, Sam earns £150, Ed earns £250 and Lucky Eddie wins £650 in the lottery, their total income equals £1300 and the arithmetic mean equals £260.
- The **mode** is the most common value in a distribution – or, more formally: the value with the greatest frequency (in the example above: £150, because it is the only value to appear twice).
- The **median** is that value which divides a distribution exactly in half – or, more formally: that value above and below which one half of the observations lie (i.e., £150).
- The **standard deviation** is denoted by the Greek letter σ (or *sigma*), and is defined as follows: $\sigma = \sqrt{1/N \sum (x_i - \bar{x}_i)^2}$. The standard deviation is a measure of dispersion, used to capture the spread of scores in a distribution of scores. In the example above, because of Eddie's incredible luck, the standard deviation is a whopping £201, or $\sqrt{1/5 \sum [(100 - 260)^2 + (150 - 260)^2 + (150 - 260)^2 + (250 - 260)^2 + (650 - 260)^2]}$.
- The **correlation coefficient** is designed so that it will vary between the values of +1 to –1. A correlation of 1 indicates a perfect positive correlation (so that when one variable is large, the other is large); when one variable rises (or falls) the other does the same. A correlation of –1 indicates a perfect negative correlation (so that when one variable is large, the other is low); when one variable rises, the other falls. A correlation of 0 means that there is no association (that the variation of one variable has nothing to do with the variation of the other).

expressing his data in terms of figures and he made important contributions to bivariate analysis. In fact, it was in the field of bivariate statistics that Francis Galton made his most significant contributions.

To put a little meat on this skeleton, we can take a closer look at one of Galton's interests. Galton was the original pea counter. His contribution to modern social science techniques had its humble beginning in 1875, when he put sweet peas in seven envelopes, marked them K, L, M, N, O, P and Q, and distributed them among his friends. Each envelope contained ten peas of exactly the same size. His friends then planted their peas and dutifully tended the plants. In the autumn they harvested the new generation of peas, returned them to the marked envelopes and gave them back to Galton. He, in turn, carefully measured the diameter of each pea down to a hundredth of an inch and noted the results, which are reproduced in Table 4.2. Finally, he compared the notes of these new measurements with the notes he had already made about the sizes of the peas he had distributed earlier among his friends.

Table 4.2   *Parent seeds and their produce*

Packet name	Diameter of parent seed (in/100)	Mean diameter of filial seed (in/100)	Diameter of filial seeds (in per cent)							
			Under 15	15	16	17	18	19	20	Above 21
K	21	17.5	22	8	10	18	21	13	6	2
L	20	17.3	23	10	12	17	20	13	3	2
M	19	16.0	35	16	12	13	11	10	2	1
N	18	16.3	34	12	13	17	16	6	2	0
O	17	15.6	37	16	13	16	13	4	1	0
P	16	16.0	34	15	18	16	13	3	1	0
Q	15	15.3	46	14	9	11	14	4	2	0

Source: Galton (1889, p. 226).

Galton summarized his results in a matrix, several pages of drawings and deliberations, and a two-dimensional graph which he used to conclude that the mean diameter of filial seeds from a particular diameter of parent seeds approximately described a straight line with positive slope less than 1 (see Pearson, 1930, vol. III, p. 3). What he meant to say was that big peas tend to produce other big peas. Galton had, by all appearances, taken a fairly uninteresting topic and made it difficult too! Charles Darwin seemed to agree. In a letter to Galton (dated 7 November 1875), Darwin admits: 'I have read your essay with much curiosity and interest, but you probably have no idea how excessively difficult it is to understand. I cannot fully grasp, only here and there conjecture, what are the points on which we differ – I daresay this is chiefly due to muddle-headiness on my part, but I do not think wholly so' (cited in Pearson, 1930, vol. II, p. 187).

Galton got more attention when he began to count and measure people. In 1886 he published a paper which was based on measurements of the height of 1000 people: 500 men and their grown-up sons. This study was designed using the same logic as his pea study. The conclusion was that big men (like big peas) tend to produce big offspring. Not the most surprising of conclusions. Yet, Galton's argument reverberated through the scientific community and occasioned no less than a revolution in the social sciences.

This reaction might be explained by the fact that a study of people is more interesting than a study of peas. But the reaction was also, in part, because of the *technique* that Galton developed for his second study. Indeed, Galton introduced a new way of thinking about social-science phenomena – a way which allowed him to visualize his two observations in spatial terms. Furthermore, he expressed his new vision in an algebraic formula, termed the 'correlation coefficient' (see Figure 4.1). Galton's correlation coefficient provided the social sciences with a standard measure, according to which its practitioners could assess the strength and direction of a co-relation (or co-variation or correlation) between two variables. This technique, and the way of thinking that undergirded it, allowed social scientists to demonstrate the patterned variations of their units of analysis in new and convincing ways.

Galton's new visualization technique is easy to follow if we apply it to his earlier data on seven packets of sweet peas rather than on the more complicated set of 1000 fathers and sons. The observations he made of his peas was summarized in Table 4.2 above, which is reproduced from Galton's 1889 book *Natural Inheritance*. This table offers hours of excitement for any devoted pea counter. He will, upon the sight of it, rub his hands in joy and immediately begin to draw the distribution curves of these packets of seeds – individually and in various combinations – calculate their spread, their central tendency, their standard deviation, and so on.

For our present purpose we will limit our focus to the first two columns in Galton's table: the columns labelled 'Diameter of Parent Seed' and 'Mean Diameter of Filial Seed'. If we study the numbers, it seems pretty obvious that big parent peas tend to produce big filial peas. We see that the largest parent seeds (in packet K, whose peas measured 21/100 inches in diameter) produced the largest filial seeds (17.5/100 inches as an average); and that the smaller the parent seed – from packets L, M, N and so on, in descending order) produced filial seeds of a steadily declining average size. At the smallest end we find parent seeds (in packet Q with a diameter of 15/100 inches each), which produced the smallest filial seeds (with an average diameter of 15.3/100 inches).

Exciting as this is, we can do more. In addition to describing one variable or comparing single variables, we can co-relate them. Such a co-relation is depicted in Figure 4.2, where the column 'Diameter of Parent Seed' is measured along the horizontal axis, and the column 'Mean Diameter of Filial Seed' is delegated to the vertical axis. The figure shows very clearly how big parent peas produce big filial peas. This graph is, in effect, Galton's invention. He developed it by making two clever moves. The first was to transform the values from a data matrix into a set of coordinate points. The second move was to plot these points into a Cartesian graph. Presto! He had produced a 'scatter plot'.

To appreciate more fully the brilliance that lay behind Galton's two

Figure 4.2   *Parent seeds and their produce*

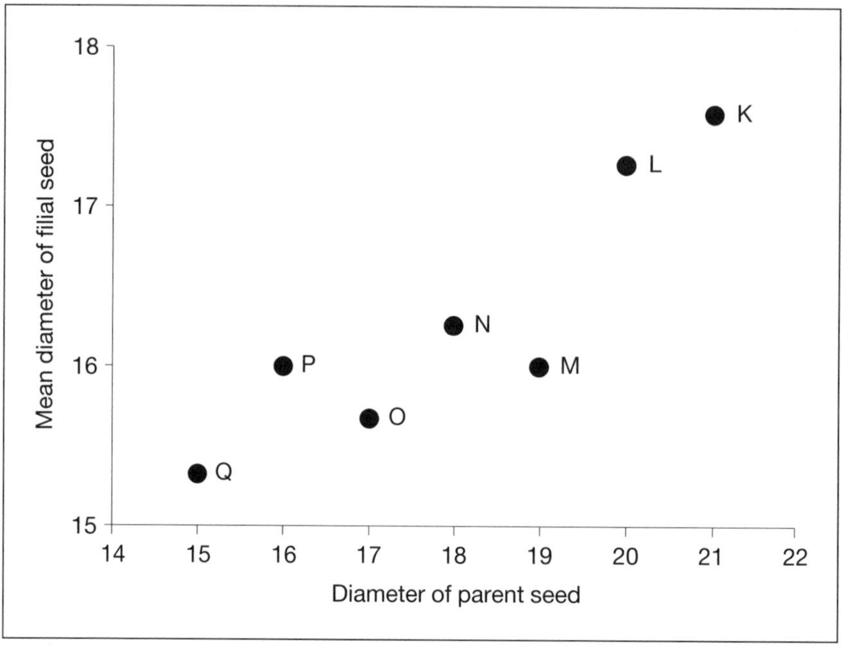

Source: Based on Galton (1889, p. 226).

moves, it is necessary to return briefly to René Descartes. Descartes'
Discourse on Method had suggested to Galton the true importance of
converting his data matrix into a spatial graph. When Galton read
Descartes, he was amused by the author's story of how he once lay ill in
bed and watched a fly walk on the ceiling above him, a ceiling that
consisted of square tiles. As Descartes watched the fly's movements, he
was struck by the thought that he could describe the position of the fly by
considering each ceiling tile as a coordinate point – in other words, as a
point where a horizontal line (or row) of tiles crossed a vertical line (or
column) of tiles. On the strength of this idea, Descartes developed the
concept of reference lines and coordinate points. Galton pursued
Descartes' logic and applied the notion to pairs of variables.

Galton's original presentation of this material was made before the
Royal Institute and published in *Nature* (1877). Actually, this publica-
tion does not include a scatter plot or regression line of the pea data.
However, from Karl Pearson (1930, vol. III, pp. 3–4) we know that
Galton had used the pea data to produce the world's first regression line.
At any rate, ten years later – in 1886 – we find its graphical presentation
in a paper on people (instead of peas). Galton had collected data on the

heights of fathers and their eldest sons and plotted all the individual values onto a Cartesian graph. Galton ended up with a scatter plot, which showed him that big fathers (like big peas) produce big offspring. But because his later study included a Cartesian graph, Galton had acquired a more powerful tool of analysis and he could perform a more penetrating analysis.

In this history lie the roots to modern regression, so it is worthwhile to recap. In his early work with peas, Galton used measurement techniques like arithmetic mean and standard deviation to show that big parent peas tend to produce big filial peas. Ten years later, he used the correlation coefficient and a scatter plot to demonstrate that tall men tend to have tall sons. In addition, he showed that very tall men tend to have sons who are smaller than themselves, whereas very small men tend to have sons who are bigger then themselves. With his new Cartesian tool in hand, Galton could formulate this insight in a new, simple and revolutionary way: filial size regresses towards the mean of the race. Galton had discovered *regression analysis*, the workhorse of modern social-science statistics.[3]

Galton would later apply his regression techniques to other subjects and studies. When he applied it to a study of the distribution of intelligence in society, he concluded that intelligence, too, is distributed unevenly in society; and that intelligent parents tend to have intelligent children (but that filial intelligence tends to regress towards the mean). On the base of several such studies, Galton claimed that he had discovered a social law: although various properties are unevenly distributed among men, such differences tend to even out over the longer haul, because with each new generation these properties will tend to regress towards the mean of the race.

Galton's statistical techniques are today universally applied; they are included in the analytical armoury of every serious social science student. Galton's subsequent influence rests on a number of factors, but we might focus briefly on three on these. First, he managed to popularize statistical measurements like the correlation coefficient, on which his fame deservedly rests.

Second, Galton made scholars critically aware of the dangers of comparing fundamentally similar units: the so-called *Galton's problem*. In 1888, when Galton was President of the Royal Anthropological Institute, he heard a talk by Edward Taylor that aimed to explain the development of a cluster of institutions (related to marriage and kinship) by organizing data from a worldwide sample of 350 societies. After hearing the presentation, Galton asked Taylor about the independence of each unit – to which Taylor apparently could not respond. Hence: 'Galton's problem'.

Finally, Galton taught other men who contributed further to the development of modern statistics. Foremost among them was Karl Pearson (1857–1936), who pioneered the study of frequency curves, elaborated techniques for measuring correlations – such as the 'chi-squared "goodness-of-fit" test' – and coined important terms in the statistician's working vocabulary (for example, 'standard deviation'). Pearson continued the statistical work of his mentor, recruited talented students and gave them projects to work on. Many of Pearsons' students, in turn, pioneered new methods and techniques. One of these was W. S. Gossett (1876–1937). Better known by his pseudonym, 'Student' (as in '*Student's t*'), Gossett worked as a chemist for the Guinness brewery in Dublin in 1899, and developed methods for measuring (ingredients') quality on the basis of small samples. This *t* distribution is especially important for interpreting data gathered on small samples when the population variance is unknown.

At this point it is important to emphasize that the early application of statistical methods were still mostly aimed at describing relationships. Pearson's developments, in particular, began to push statistical studies in a more inferential direction. While these developments have had an enormous impact on the way statistics are used as part of a larger, inferential, project, Pearson himself was quite clear about the limitations to his 'scientific' approach:

> Science of the past is a description, for the future a belief; it is not, and has never been, an explanation, if by this word is meant that science shows the necessity of any sequence of perceptions.   (Pearson, 1892, cited in Sayer 1992, p. 193)

Émile Durkheim

This new mode of describing the world was quickly seized upon by social scientists. Among these was the French sociologist, Émile Durkheim. Although Durkheim didn't develop any new statistical techniques, he placed descriptive statistics at the centre of social scientific activity.

Durkheim's *Suicide* serves as a useful example. The study begins by demonstrating how different countries in Europe have different rates of suicide. For example, Durkheim establishes that the suicide rate in England was twice as high as that in Italy, and that the rate in Denmark was four times the English rate. From these observations Durkheim inferred that suicide is unevenly distributed across countries. In addition, he found that the suicide rate remains fairly stable in any given society from year to year. Thus, it 'is not simply a sum of independent units, a collective total, but is itself a new fact *sui generis*, with its own unity, individuality, and consequently its own nature' (Durkheim, 1952, p. 46). Suicide is, in effect, a 'social fact'.

If we acknowledge that suicide is a patterned phenomenon, how can we account for its pattern? Durkheim argued that if we systematically investigate the various European societies with an eye to *other* patterned phenomena, we should, sooner or later, be able to identify co-variations between suicide rates and other patterned phenomena. Thus, Durkheim was struck by the evident fact that suicide co-varies with religion – and he demonstrated (through the use of statistical tables) how the suicide rate was systematically low in Catholic countries, while it was systematically high in Protestant countries (and that countries with mixed populations of Catholics and Protestants tend to have rates in between these extremes). Religion, then, must have something to do with the patterned distribution of suicide.

Since Catholicism and Protestantism condemn suicide with equal severity, it is unlikely that the character of doctrine or beliefs affect a country's rate of suicide. However, Durkheim noted that the two religions differ systematically in social structure, and argued that this may provide a clue. In Protestantism, the individual is alone with God; in Catholicism, on the other hand, the individual has a priestly hierarchy between himself and the deity. Thus, whereas Protestantism is severely individualistic, the Catholic Church represents a 'more strongly integrated' social hierarchy.

The degree of social integration of the Church, then, can account for differences in suicide rates across European societies. With this proposition Durkheim established a causal generalization which links suicide to social solidarity in churches. In particular, the suicide rate of a religious community is inversely related to the level of social integration in that community – the more strongly integrated the religious society, the lower its rate of suicide.

This claim led Durkheim to suspect that the connection between social integration and suicide can be extended further – that the principle of social solidarity applies not only to religious communities, but to communities more generally. For example, Durkheim noted that the suicide rates of unmarried people were generally higher than those of married people of comparable age. Marriage may involve burdens and responsibilities which single persons do not have; yet, marriage is also a small community with integrative mechanisms of its own that have a protecting influence against suicide.

Inferential Statistics

By the end of the nineteenth century, developments in statistical techniques were propelling the method into new, more explanatory, realms of science. No longer was statistics confined to simple Political Arithmetic, or numerical descriptions of the world. Statistics became gradually more connected with characterizing (and implicitly, explaining) the relationship between two (or more) variables. Consequently, the role of modern statistics is increasingly associated with attempts to infer beyond the data to something (laws, theories, hypotheses) that is not directly observed.

Indeed, one of the most influential new texts in social science methods, King, Keohane and Verba's *Designing Social Inquiry* (1994, p. 8), argues that 'the key distinguishing mark of scientific research is the goal of making inferences that go beyond the particular observations collected'. For them, there is a single logic of explanation common to all empirical social science research, and that logic is statistical. Their intent is to proselytize few-N social science researchers to the logic of statistical inference.[4]

The workhorse of modern statistical inference is the regression analysis. Regressions allow us to predict the value of a dependent variable (in other words, the variable to be explained), given the value of an independent variable (an explanatory variable). Generally speaking, regression analyses are of two types: bivariate and multivariate. Bivariate regressions, like correlational analysis, provide a depiction of how changes in the level of a single independent variable are related to changes in a dependent variable. Multivariate regressions allow us to expand on the number of independent variables. In the name of simplicity and clarity, we will begin with a simple bivariate example to describe the general logic of the method. We can then add additional explanatory (independent) variables to illustrate how mathematical manipulation of data allows the analyst to control for the effects of a variable which cannot be controlled in practice.

Let us return to the class attendance example from earlier in the chapter, as it can help us illustrate simple statistical relationships. After all, most of us have fairly strong priors of, and experience with, the factors that influence grades. Off the top of our head, we can conceive of several possible factors that influence grades: time spent in the library, time spent doing homework, class attendance, level of education, social status, sex, and so on. As a first cut at the problem, we begin by examining how an individual's grades are related to class attendance. Of course, in framing the question in this way, we are ignoring other important causal influences (that is, the model is mis-specified, or it suffers from omitted-variables bias), but our primary purpose here is pedagogic, not scientific.

To test the relationship between attendance and grades, we first need to consider how to measure each variable, collect data on both, and then map them in a two-dimensional space. The first two steps have already been taken (in Table 4.1). For convenience, we can provide these variables with shortened names, such that the number of good grades is shortened

Figure 4.3 *The spatial relation between class attendance and good grades*

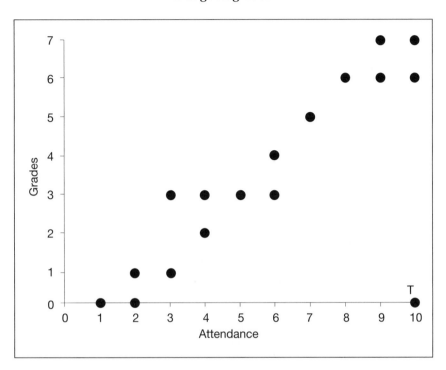

to the variable name *GRADES*; and the number of lectures attended is abbreviated by the variable name *ATTENDANCE*. The third step is produced as the scatter plot in Figure 4.3, where each point in the diagram represents an individual in the sample.

From this simple scatter plot, a trained statistician will see a clear relationship between attendance and grades. This relationship is captured by the apparent pattern in the scatter plot of individual observations: individuals who attend classes more often tend to do better in the class (get more good grades). This is evidenced by the fact that the data are clustered in a line-like cloud that appears to stretch upward and to the right.

Before the statistician proceeds to quantify this relationship, however, he will need to deal with a particular observation in the scatter plot – one that doesn't seem to fit the general pattern. This observation, labelled 'T' (in the bottom right-hand corner of the graph) corresponds to the 20th observation in Table 4.1. For some inexplicable reason, Thandeka seemed to have attended all of the lectures, but didn't secure any good grades. Before the statistician can proceed, he must decide what to do with this *outlier* observation.

After contacting both of us, the statistician discovers that Thandeka is the daughter of one of the teachers, and that she was forced to attend lectures every week (as the class was offered very early in the morning, and the teacher in question was not able to secure a babysitter). For this reason, Thandeka's attendance had been perfect, but she never delivered any work to be graded (hence her 'lack' of good grades). Because Thandeka's experiences are not directly relevant for understanding the relationship between attendance and good grades, the statistician can discard this observation from the subsequent analysis.

To generate an estimate of how many better grades might be secured by attending an extra lecture, we can develop a mathematical expression that captures this relationship. To do so, we need to think about the relationship in terms of interpreting Figure 4.3. For the sake of simplicity, we'll assume that the relationship is linear (in other words, that each additional lecture attended delivers the same payoff in terms of good grades). This assumption is not problematic by looking at these data (which 'line up'), but it might be very problematic if the data should reveal another pattern (or given alternative theoretical expectations). Unfortunately, this rather common assumption is a legacy of the limits to regression analysis in the pre-computer era. Contemporary statistical programs allow us to think of these relationships in much more sophisticated terms (for example, quadratic or cubic), but the weight of history bears heavily on the shoulders of statisticians – at least in this particular case.

In the language of statistics, we can summarize the hypothesized relationship depicted in Figure 4.3 as:

$$GRADES = \alpha + \beta ATTENDANCE + \varepsilon$$

where α is a constant term (the grade a person can expect to earn without attending any lectures); β is the effect on grades (in number of 'good grades') of attending an additional lecture; and ε is an 'error' term which is used to capture the effect of other factors on grades. We use the Greek letters (α, β and ε) to remind us that these are estimates generated by the analysis – they are *not* directly observable. We only have observations of *GRADES* and *ATTENDANCE*. Because it does not make sense to speak about a negative number of good grades, or attending lectures a negative number of times, we can use this knowledge to set the lower limit, or baseline, to the relationship. In particular, we will constrain the constant term (α) to zero.

In this relationship, the dependent variable (that which we aim to explain) is *GRADES*, the independent (explanatory) variable is *ATTENDANCE*, and the β term is referred to as the coefficient (in this case, for our independent variable, *ATTENDANCE*). As the β coefficient is positive, we are assuming that the relationship between grades and attendance is positive (in other words, more attendance leads to better grades). If we expected a negative relationship (more attendance leads to poorer grades) we could capture this with a negative coefficient (for example, $GRADES = \alpha - \beta ATTENDANCE + \varepsilon$).

To generate the estimates for α and β, we begin by ignoring ε (actually, we simply assume that it is, on average, equal to zero). We then try to fit a line that comes closest to all of the points in Figure 4.3. There are a number of ways to do this, but we will focus on the most common (minimum sum of squared errors) approach. This line will intersect the Y axis at a given point (this is represented by α, the constant), and the line itself will have a slope of β .

To generate this line, we simply ask a computer to find a line which minimizes the estimated vertical distance between each observation and the hypothesized line. We refer to this distance as the estimated error term associated with each observation. In practice, the computer starts with a hypothesized line, calculates the error estimates, then tries to minimize these by moving the line around. When it is satisfied that these errors have been minimized, the computer generates numerical estimates for α and β. This hypothesized relationship is depicted in Figure 4.4.

With this statistical summary we can predict how attendance, generally, affects grades. Traditionally, the relationship is depicted with an algebraic equation and statistic; in other words:

$$GRADES = 0 + .6804\ ATTENDANCE$$
$$R^2 = .9224$$

The first figure to the right of the equals sign, (0), was imposed on the equation so we would not have to deal with odd interpretations of the data.[5] The second coefficient (.6804) represents the slope of the line in Figure 4.4 (a positive number means the line slopes upward, from left to right; a negative number means that the line slopes downward). We can interpret this to mean that for each additional class attended, a given student can expect .6804 more 'good grades'. Not at all a bad return on one's investment in time! The R^2 statistic (.9224) captures the model's degree of fit: that is, 92 per cent of the variance in grades is captured by this very simple model!

Among other things, the accuracy of this prediction depends on the sample's degree of representativeness. For example, we need to know if the sample is a good indicator of the population at large. If we were to find out that the sample included only men, and we know that that the relationship between attendance and grades varies between men and

Figure 4.4   *Regression line on attendance/grades data*

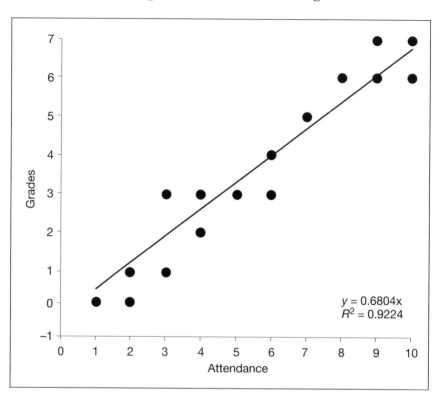

women, then we would not be able to generalize to the whole population from a study based solely on male subjects. There are other assumptions that could prove problematic as well. For example: Why should we assume that the relationship is linear? Is it reasonable to assume that attendance is the most significant influence on grades?

In this case, there is little justification to develop any generalizations from the observations in Figures 4.3 and 4.4. After all, the generalization is based on very few observations (19!). We have purposely chosen a small number of observations in order to illustrate how these relationships can be captured empirically. Worse, the data themselves are fictitious: we have constructed them to suit our purpose. Because of this, the estimates for α and β will necessarily be nonsense. However, if there was some empirical basis to the observations for *GRADES* and *ATTENDANCE*, and if we had more observations upon which to draw, we could use these estimates to predict, exactly, what attending an additional lecture would yield in terms of better grades.

Multivariate Analysis

As we mentioned at the outset, however, there are good reasons to expect that other factors may influence a student's grade. To the extent that these factors are important, they can undermine the interpretive validity of the coefficients produced in the *bivariate* regression. Under these conditions, the analyst turns to a *multivariate* regression technique. As the name implies, multivariate refers to an explanatory relationship with more than one explanatory variable. The procedure for incorporating additional independent (explanatory) variables is very straightforward, but it is difficult for us to depict these developments in two-dimensional space. Conceptually, we begin to estimate planes, instead of simple lines – but the logic is exactly the same: we allow the computer to select a plane so as to minimize the sum of squared errors.

When we add more explanatory variables we can see why these explanatory variables are referred to as 'independent variables' by statisticians. Statistical inference proceeds on the basis of a number of simplifying assumptions about the nature of relationships in the real world. One of the most important of these is the assumption that the independent variables are independent of one another (in other words, that they are not capturing the same thing). In short, when employing multivariate analyses we choose explanatory variables that are assumed to be unrelated to one another. If this assumption is violated, then the estimated coefficients can be misleading.

This is not a minor issue for social scientists, as many of the things we are interested in have common (and complex) causal backgrounds. This is the matter of Galton's problem, as noted above. Nor is this problem of interdependence limited to the right-hand side of the explanatory equation. A serious difficulty in much social science enquiry is the problem of endogeneity, where the relation under study can also be understood in a more complicated and indirect way: both X and Y might be caused by a third and hitherto unknown variable, called a lurking variable.

Thus, it is conceivable that in the example above, both attendance and grades can be explained by social situation. What we mean by this is that a student's social status might be the underlying explanation for both attendance and grades. For example, it is not unreasonable to expect an underprivileged student to find employment while studying, and work obligations can easily conflict with class attendance. It is also possible that an underprivileged student can grow up in an environment where academic performance is not encouraged or prioritized. In this situation, the relationship between attendance and grades is *spurious*,[6] as both can be explained by another, endogenous, factor. While there are several empirical means for limiting the endogeneity problem (see, for example, King et al., 1994, section 5.4), a sound theory is the most reliable defence.

Let us now consider the effect of sex *and* attendance on grades. As we mentioned earlier, there may be some reason to expect that women students tend to get better grades than male students. To test whether this is the case, we simply add gender observations (*SEX*) to our model, so that the computer will produce coefficients (in this case β_2) for that variable as well. Because sex is a dichotomous variable (there are usually only two sexes), its coefficient will behave in a somewhat different way, but we hope that the choice of a dichotomous variable will clarify the conceptual procedure below. Thus, our new model can be depicted as:

$$GRADES = \alpha + \beta_1 ATTENDANCE + \beta_2 SEX + \varepsilon$$

When we run this equation, we are now asking the computer to estimate the nature of the relationship between attendance and grades, for women and for men. In short, the computer divides up the data into two groups: women and men. It then estimates the nature of the relationship between attendance and grades for each group. By comparing these differences, the computer can estimate the effect of sex. At the same time, the computer can divide the sample up into, say, three groups: high, medium and low levels of attendance. It then estimates the effect of sex on grades within each of these three sub-groups. Here too, the computer compares estimates for men and women across each attendance sub-group. Given sufficient data, this process of adding additional (independent) variables can be extended to produce very complex models of the world.

At this point we might reflect on how control and comparison are being used here, in contrast to their use in experimental method. After all, as we already suggested in the previous chapter, it is possible to conceive of an experimental approach to studying this relationship, but this requires that we physically manipulate our data and their contexts (for example, randomly dividing subjects into control and treatment groups). The statistical method allows us to bypass these difficulties. Instead of physically altering the context of our subjects to control for the influence of a particular variable, we can use the computer to divide the sample into sub-groups, and run partial correlations for each group. In doing so, we can estimate the effect of a given 'treatment' on an outcome. It should be clear that the analyst's demand for data increases significantly with the number of partial correlations.

Regression analysis provides a remarkably strong foundation for making predictions. This predictive capacity relies heavily on an underlying naturalist ontology. The statistician (implicitly) assumes that it makes sense to divide up the social world into variables and search for patterns among them. In addition, he assumes that the Real World patterns are so stable that we can expect them to hold beyond our narrow sample of observations. The statistical method allows us to manipulate data in ways that can uncover hidden patterns in the data. The predictive capacity of the regression analysis (for example, our ability to predict that a student who attends an additional lecture can expect to get 0.6804 better grades) is based on this ability.

Perhaps these ontological assumptions are even more evident when we think about how statistical techniques are so conveniently used in counterfactual analyses. This is done schematically in Figure 4.5, where we ask you to consider the impact of a new policy (X), in a given policy space (the effect of which is measured on the Y axis). Using the language of experiments, we can understand the effect of the introduced policy as a treatment variable introduced at time T_1. In order to measure the impact of this policy, we need to compare a real policy outcome (Y) with a counterfactual outcome (Z), at some time in the future (T_2). In this case, the counterfactual (Z) represents the way we expect the world to look in the absence of the posited treatment or policy change (X). To gauge the effectiveness of the policy in question, we can't simply compare the pre-treatment score (at T_1, prior to X) against the post-treatment outcome (Y), as we can't assume that time stopped in the absence of the new policy. In

Figure 4.5   *Counterfactual depiction*

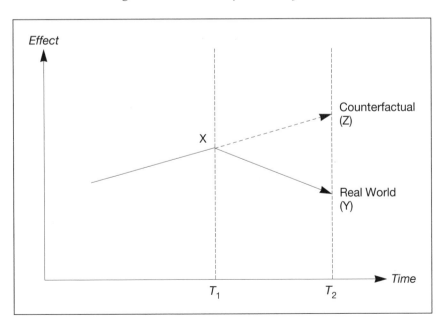

short, we have to compare the real (post-policy) and counterfactual outcomes. The counterfactual point of comparison is generated by using regression analysis to project a trend (based on pre-treatment data) into the future. This trend is depicted by the dotted line, XZ: it provides us with an empirically informed image of what the world would have looked like in the absence of the imposed policy change.

This is, in effect, what Robert Fogel – the 1993 Nobel Prize Co-Laureate in Economics – does. Fogel pioneered a research tradition, called cliometrics, which combines economic theory, quantitative methods, hypothesis testing, counterfactual analyses, and more traditional techniques of economic history to explain economic growth or decline. He uses these techniques to ask difficult questions about fundamental tenets of American economic historiography; for example, that the railroad was an indispensable and driving force behind American growth in the nineteenth century (Fogel, 1964); or that American slavery was not as unprofitable as traditionally assumed (Fogel and Engerman, 1974). In doing so, Fogel's analyses build on naturalist assumptions about the nature of the Real World and exploit the patterns they offer to generate counterfactual histories that can probe and challenge deeply held assumptions (even truths) about economic history.

The basic regression model has become the workhorse of modern scientific analysis and its influence is spread broadly across the social scientific landscape. Most developments in statistics over the past 30 years have been aimed at extending this basic regression model to an ever broader set of problems (and to overcome an increasingly wide set of violations to the basic model). In particular, many developments in the specialized field of econometrics have spread to other social science disciplines. Among these are refinements of so-called 'structural equation models', that allow researchers to incorporate systematic hypotheses about measurement error and missing variables into a wide variety of models; innovative time-series approaches that have allowed statisticians to deal with data shortages in cross-national studies; and models with very complex (non-linear) parameter functions.[7] In addition, specialized statistical applications (and software) have developed within each of the social science disciplines – making it nearly impossible to try to provide any sort of comprehensive overview of the developments.

Conclusion

On concluding this chapter it is easy to understand this desire to use statistical inference as the logical point of departure in social science study. For most social scientists, statistics is the closest alternative method we have to the experiment. Because statistics does not involve the physical manipulation of data, it is a method that lends itself to the study of social phenomena – where we tend to study events that have already occurred. Instead of manipulating the physical data itself, statistical approaches allow us to manipulate already existing data in a conceptual (or logical/mathematical) manner. For that very reason, statistical approaches cannot possibly control for all other variables – merely the other key variables that are known to exert influence.

This chapter has outlined the important role that the statistical method plays in contemporary social science from a naturalist perspective. We have divided the chapter in a way that emphasizes the role of descriptive as well as inferential statistics in this methodological tradition. While social scientists have come to prioritize the sort of knowledge generated by statistical approaches, its very logic depends heavily on that of the experiment. The utility of statistical analysis depends critically on the availability of data – in sufficient numbers. Unfortunately, not all that interests social scientists lends itself to statistical study – either because the objects of study are too few in number (for example, outbreaks of nuclear conflict) or because there is insufficient data already collected. For these unlucky scholars, the only option is to descend one step further down the hierarchy of naturalist methods: to the few-N comparative study.

Recommended Further Reading

We think that the best way to learn statistics is through history. For that reason, the curious student might begin by reading Stigler (1986) or by browsing through the *Journal of Statistics Education*. Good and influential statistics texts include Hanushek and Jackson's (1977) *Statistical Methods for Social Scientists* and Lewis-Beck's (1980) *Applied Regression*. For more fun and playful applications, see Best's (2001) *Damned Lies and Statistics* and Knapp's (1996) *Learning Statistics through Playing Cards*. Finally, King, Keohane and Verba's (1994) *Designing Social Inquiry* offers a broader methodological approach anchored in statistical inference.

Chapter 5

The Comparative Method

Let us return to the basic philosophical components of the naturalist approach: that there is a Real World out there, independent of the observer; that the World is uniform and orderly; that observations and observation statements allow us to access that World; and that a careful process of induction and deduction can be used to identify the ordering principles of the World, so as to determine its component parts and their causal relations. This chapter describes how the comparative method is employed within this methodological perspective.

In one sense, of course, all scientific endeavours are comparative in nature. Francis Bacon used the comparative method in his laboratory to identify the optimal condition for the sprouting of seeds. He steeped wheat seeds for 12 hours in nine different liquids: cow dung, urine, three different wines and four different water solutions. He then carefully observed the speed of germination and the heartiness of growth in each dish and compared each sample of seeds carefully with all the others – as well as with a sample of unsteeped seeds. After doing this several times over, he drew two general conclusions: first, seeds steeped in urine is a sure winner, every time; second, seeds steeped in claret is a waste of good drink (Bacon, 1627, p. 109f).

Sometimes Bacon referred to this exercise as a systematic comparison, sometimes he referred to it as an experiment. The label hardly matters. For an experiment always involves systematic comparison; and a comparative investigation is usually modelled after the experiment. Indeed, Talcott Parsons (1949, p. 743) made the same point when he noted that: 'Experiment is . . . nothing but the comparative method where the cases to be compared are produced to order and under controlled conditions.' When John Stuart Mill explained the main variations of the comparative method – and he is, as we will soon see, the major authority on the subject – he did this in a chapter entitled 'The Four Experimental Methods'.

For Arend Lijphart, the comparative method is modelled after the statistical design. It is the 'method of testing hypothesized empirical relationships among variables on the basis of the same logic that guides the statistical method, but in which the cases are selected in such a way as to maximize the variance of the independent variables and to minimize the variance of the control variables' (Lijphart, 1975, p. 164). This does not matter much in the end, since statistics is, in turn, modelled on the experiment. The point here is that the comparative method mirrors experimental (and statistical) methods: they all involve variable analysis, and they all try to establish general empirical relationships between (at least) two variables, by means of control.

Yet, there are differences, and they are important. First of all, the comparative method does not select its cases in random ways (as do experimental and statistical studies). Rather, comparative studies unabashedly select their cases on the dependent variable. For example, a student of revolutions would select France as an interesting case precisely because of the revolution that took place there; or a study of America's best-run companies would surely want to sample from among these (for example, Peters and Waterman, 2004). Alternatively, comparativists often search for 'negative' cases (for example, the absence of a war) in analyses that seek to explain positive outcomes of something that interests them (for example, war) (Mahoney and Goertz, 2004). As we shall discover, case selection is one of the great strengths of the comparative method – but it also introduces some problems. Primary among these is the problem of selection bias, which continually haunts comparative projects. This problem is compounded by another characteristic feature: the comparative method distinguishes itself from statistics in its number of cases. Whereas statistical studies regularly rely on hundreds – sometimes thousands – of cases, the comparative method rarely relies on more than three or four. Indeed, only exceptional cases – such as the much-admired work of Barrington Moore (1966) – tend to brave more than this.

The reason is quite simple. The number of possible comparisons increases rather substantially by the following formula:

$$([n(n-1)]/2).$$

Thus, a comparativist wishing to compare nine cases must consider ($[9(9-1)]/2) = 36$ different combinations. This is quite a lot to consider and juggle. For this reason, comparative studies are often referred to as 'small-N' or 'few-N' studies. We prefer to use the term 'few-N', as some students seem to harbour the curious illusion that 'small-N' methods apply best to diminutive phenomena (rather than to a small *number* of cases, regardless of their size). Because the number of cases is so few, problems of over-determination are a constant threat to comparative analyses.

In recent years, this numerical gap has been closed by an important methodological approach associated with Charles Ragin (1987). To fill the gap that separates few-N studies (working with three or four cases) and statistical studies (that begin with – say – 60 observations), Ragin introduced a Qualitative Comparative Analysis (QCA) approach for conducting comparative analyses based on Boolean logic. More recently, new tools have been developed to apply QCA to an even broader area: Multi-Value QCA (or MVQCA) allows analysts to pursue QCA logic while using richer (in other words, non-dichotomous) data (see Moses et al., 2005, pp. 61ff.).[1] These developments have made it more difficult to refer to a quantitative/qualitative divide in social studies.

Still, there is a significant amount of work done at the lower end of the observation count, and this work tends to suffer from problems related to over-determination and selection bias. These shortcomings reduce the comparative method's ability to generalize about the nature of the Real World. It is for this reason that comparative analyses are often surrounded by methodological controversy and that comparativists are often considered poor cousins to statisticians and experimenters. But what can a poor cousin do? 'The answer is that the comparative method is not the equivalent of the experimental method but only a very imperfect substitute. A clear awareness of the limitations of the comparative method is necessary, but need not be disabling, because, as we shall see, these weaknesses can be minimized' (Lijphart, 1971, p. 685). The lessons used to correct for these shortcomings will be discussed in the final pages of this chapter.

The Methods of John Stuart Mill

One of the most confusing aspects of the comparative method is the many names given to it. For example, in the literature we can find references to different systems/similar systems (Przeworski and Teune, 1970), comparable case strategies (Lijphart, 1975), focused comparison (Hague et al., 1998), case-oriented comparisons (Ragin 1987), method of systematic comparative illustration (Smelser, 1973), and others. Because comparisons are used in all social scientific methods, it is easy to confuse their various sub-types. For this reason, we have decided to return to the beginning: to the early classic work of John Stuart Mill. Not only was his description the first systematic formulation of the modern comparative method; he remains the conceptual instigator for much work since.

John Stuart Mill (1806–73) had a remarkable education, not least because he was raised by a very determined father, James Mill, with the advice and assistance of the utilitarian philosopher, Jeremy Bentham. The result was an extraordinary boy. Little John Stuart began to learn Greek at the age of three; by the age of eight, he had read famous Greek classics in their original language. He was introduced to Latin, Algebra and elementary Geometry at a very early age. By the time he had reached twelve, he had studied differential calculus and written a history of Roman government. (In case there are any attentive or inspired parents among our readers, we hasten to point out that Mill suffered a severe nervous breakdown at the age of 21.) Although J. S. Mill's influence is rightfully recognized in several fields (among them, philosophy, economics, as a publicist, as an exponent of Utilitarianism, logician and ethical theorist), we will focus our attention on his *A System of Logic* (2002 [1891]).

As we saw in the previous chapter, Mill begins by assuming that there is order and uniformity in nature. This assumption clearly reflects the ontological foundation of the naturalist's methodology. As we know, the very complexity of nature means that its uniformity is not always understood: it is not easy to see the complex ways in which the things in nature are related to one another. Empirical regularities may overlap and give the appearance of irregularity. However, because of the order and uniformity of nature, naturalists can be certain that there are stable connections and causal regularities lying beneath the apparently complex and confusing surface of things. These causal regularities may not be immediately obvious, but it is possible to discover them by using scientific methods – by experiment or by systematic comparison.

Mill finds no need to distinguish sharply between the experimental and the comparative method, because they both conform to the same logical design. Or, more precisely: to the same logical designs. Mill identifies four of them: The Method of Difference, the Method of Agreement, the Indirect Method of Difference and the Method of Concomitant Variation.[2] Before they are more properly introduced, it is worth noting that Mill was quite sceptical of applying these methods outside the natural sciences; to apply them to the political sciences was 'out of the question' (Mill, 2002, p. 297). Needless to say, this caveat is seldom heeded by students of social phenomena, who continue to use them undeterred.

The Method of Difference

The two simplest methods are the Method of Difference and the Method of Agreement. The Method of Difference relies on the logical design of the experiment and is the more reliable method of the two. Mill describes it thus:

> If an instance in which the phenomenon under investigation occurs, and an instance in which it does not occur, have every circumstance in

common save one, that one occurring only in the former; the circumstance in which alone the two instances differ is the effect, or the cause, or an indispensable part of the cause, of the phenomenon.   (Mill, 2002, p. 256)[3]

The Method of Difference compares political/social systems that share a number of common features as a way of neutralizing some differences while highlighting others. In other words, case selection is used in a way to control for causal effect. By choosing cases that are mostly similar at the outset, any observed difference between the cases cannot be explained by those similarities. In short, all cases share basic characteristics (effective control), but vary with respect to some key explanatory factor. The presence or absence of this factor can then be used to explain any variation in outcomes (as the other relevant explanatory variables are controlled for by case selection).

When the appropriate conditions are met, this method is closest to that of artificial experiment, but Mill himself was quite sceptical about whether these conditions were met in the social sciences:

> If two nations can be found which are alike in all natural advantages and disadvantages; whose people resemble each other in every quality, physical and moral, spontaneous and acquired; whose habits, usages, opinions, laws and institutions are the same in all respects, except that one of them has a more protective tariff, or in other respects interferes more with the freedom of industry; if one of these nations is found to be rich and the other poor, or one richer than the other, this will be an *experimentum crucis* – a real proof by experience which of the two systems is most favorable to national riches. *But the supposition that two such instances can be met is manifestly absurd.* Nor is such a concurrence even abstractly possible. Two nations which agreed in everything except their commercial policy would agree also in that. (Mill, 2002, p. 575, second emphasis added)

This scepticism has not stopped social scientists from employing the Method of Difference. Indeed, they tend to do so in four different ways: comparisons over time, within nations, over areas and in counterfactuals. As we descend down this list of applications, we begin to stray further and further from Mill's original intent. By the time we reach the fourth application we have distanced ourselves from Mill's inductivism, and find investigators engaging the method in more deductive frameworks.

The first applications of the method of difference are so-called *longitudinal* or *diachronic* comparisons. Mill's example is of a man shot through the heart. He argues that we can be certain that the gunshot killed the man 'for he was in the fullness of life immediately before, all circumstance being the same, except the wound' (2002, p. 256). Most circumstances were the same before and after the shot, except for two: (1) after the shot the man was stone dead; and (2) he had a gaping wound in his chest. As these circumstances were the two most obvious, it is tempting to infer that the second was causally related to the first.

By a similar logic we can compare the social conditions of a single country at two different points in time – before and after a major event – in order to establish the cause of the event. A useful example is Theda Skocpol's comparison of the abortive Russian revolution in 1905 with the revolutionary success in 1917. Russia was in all major respects the same country in 1917 that it was in 1905, save two major differences: (1) by the end of 1917 Russia went through a social revolution; and (2) Russia was weakened to the point of collapse by a major war. It is thus tempting to infer that the second is causally related to the first. In other words, the application of the Method of Difference can 'validate arguments about the crucial contribution to social-revolutionary success in Russia of war-related processes that lead to the breakdown of state repressive capacities' (Skocpol, 1979, p. 37).

The second application of this method compares intra-state differences. Examples include comparisons of policy variations within the United States' 50 states, or the different provinces, counties or municipalities in a single state. Thus, it is meaningful to assess the efficiency of hospital management by comparing how hospitals are financed and run in two or more Norwegian counties. Similarly, it can be meaningful to assess an educational reform by comparing its effects in two or more adjacent Swedish counties. These are all pairs of cases that are so similar that they will – to a major degree – fulfil the criterion of having, in Mill's terms, 'every circumstance in common save one . . .' These types of comparisons exploit the fact that a common national context provides enough similarity across sub-national units to control (in effect) for the causal effect of shared influences.

In a third type of application, investigators control for a number of contextual variables by choosing states or polities that are relatively similar (for example, with respect to wealth, regime type, religion, culture and other key variables). Thus, it would be meaningful to assess the efficiency of hospital management by comparing how hospitals are financed and run in Sweden and Norway; or it would be meaningful to assess the quality of education in Chile and Argentina; or the workings of democracy in Poland and Slovakia. These are all pairs of states that are similar enough to approach Mill's condition for using the Method of Difference. Indeed, the establishment of Area Studies in traditional Political Science – a field with a long and proud record – is predicated on this argument.

It is assumed that countries in the same region (for example, Latin America, the Middle East, East Africa) have so many significant variables in common that it is meaningful to compare them with respect to selected variables. Area Studies use geographic proximity as a means for controlling for many potential contextual explanations.

The fourth and final application is counterfactual. This approach takes Mill's caveat above seriously, and recognizes that it is not possible to find cases similar in all respects but one (the explanatory factor). However, even if this is not the case in practice, it is possible to *imagine* a case that is exactly similar – a theoretically pure instance of the phenomenon of interest (Fearon 1991). In this application of the Method of Difference we can use counterfactual cases as a way to increase the number of observations (even if one of them is fictitious). In addition, a counterfactual application allows the analyst to consider causal relationships in a way that is very similar to the role played by counterfactuals under experimental conditions (see Chapter 3). By this point, however, we've strayed some distance from Mill's inductive method. Still, the application of the Method of Difference follows exactly the same procedural design.

In theory, the Method of Difference is a powerful method, for when its (rather demanding) conditions are met, the Method of Difference is closest to that of the artificial experiment. In practice, however, analysts should realize that it is highly unlikely that these conditions will ever be met in the real world. The examples above tend to rely on rather heroic assumptions about similarities across time, and within states and regions.

The Method of Agreement

Because the Method of Agreement is not encumbered with the same sort of strict conditions as we saw in the Method of Difference, it more easily lends itself to the social scientist. Also, its logical design is simple. Mill explains:

> If two or more instances of the phenomenon under investigation have only one circumstance in common, the circumstance in which alone all the instances agree is the cause (or effect) of the given phenomenon. (Mill, 2002, p. 255)

Mill's variable analysis is clearly present in this quote. It is worth noting that Mill thinks in terms of co-variation between 'instances' of phenomena. As in the Method of Difference, he reasons in terms of dichotomies, in which phenomena are either absent or present. The Method of Agreement is simple in that the investigator merely collects cases of a particular phenomenon in an attempt to find common factors in these cases that are otherwise quite different.

Indeed, the Method of Agreement is by far the simplest and the most straightforward of Mill's methods, but it is generally regarded as inferior. This is because it has a tendency to lead to faulty empirical generalizations. As with the Method of Difference, there is much resistance to applying the Method of Agreement to social science studies. In particular, Émile Durkheim was critical of applications of either the Method of Difference or the Method of Agreement, on the grounds that the social world was simply too complex. By relying slavishly on these methods, Durkheim felt that comparativists were jeopardizing the good reputation of sociologists:

> [T]he conclusions of sociologists have often been discredited because they have chosen the method of agreement or of difference – especially the former – and have occupied themselves more with accumulating documents than with selecting and criticizing them. (Durkheim, 1964, p. 133)

As with the Method of Difference, the Method of Agreement controls for variation on the basis of case selection: the investigator merely begins to collect cases of a particular phenomenon in an attempt to find common explanatory factors in cases that are otherwise quite different. Each case is acknowledged to be inherently different, with the exception of a key explanatory factor. The phenomenon is then explained by the common presence of that factor.

For example, Eric Wolf (1968) compared revolutionary movements that had significant peasant participation in Mexico, Russia, China, North Vietnam, Algeria and Cuba. Because these countries shared few common features, Wolf argued that the penetration of capitalist agriculture was the key explanatory factor (common to each account) for the appearance of revolutionary movements with broad peasant support. In short, the penetration of capitalist agricultural regimes appears as the only relevant factor common to all these disparate cases.

We can depict this process in the form of a simple (and fictitious) example. Imagine four friends driving home from Pop's Food Barn. These friends are of different age, size and weight – the only thing they seem to share in common is the fact that they were driving home from an extraordinary meeting of the Sons of Norway meeting (called to take advantage of a special on Pop's famous seafood platter). Thus, they are all men, and all of Norwegian descent, but they don't seem to share any other relevant qualities. Suddenly and without warning, Eddy begins to complain about queasiness. Soon his other companions – Doug, Sam and

Bill – are also noticing growing unease. Eddy, who is driving, pulls on to the hard shoulder so that the four can jump out of the car before becoming seriously ill.

To understand what is going on, we apply Mill's Method of Agreement. If we assume that sex (male) and ethnicity (Norwegian-ness) are not generally associated with nausea and stomach cramps, then we can begin by recognizing that the only circumstance that these four unlucky fellows share is dinner at Pop's. All four victims had ordered the same $6.99 seafood platter with hushpuppies, catfish, shrimp and oysters. (This was, after all, the point of the gathering.) But we can investigate even closer, to see if there was something that these unlucky chaps ate at the Food Barn that caused this common illness. Table 5.1 lays out the relevant variables for us.

In the language of the naturalist, we begin by defining the dependent variable – the phenomenon to be explained – and labelling it 'Fallen Ill' or Y. We then define the four potential explanatory factors: Shrimp (X_1); Oysters (X_2); Hushpuppies (X_3); and Catfish fillets (X_4). The Method of Agreement allows us to examine cases of the phenomenon with an eye towards eliminating any of the four explanatory variables. We begin by creating a Table (5.1) where we examine one case after the other. Thus, in the first case (Eddy) we find all four explanatory variables present, so that we cannot be certain about which is the causal factor (any one of the platter items could have caused the illness). We then proceed to the next case (2). Here we see that Doug consumed neither shrimp (X_1) nor hushpuppies (X_3), so these two dishes can safely be dropped as explanatory factors. In the third case we find that catfish fillets (X_4) cease to be a potential explanation. For this reason, we have not filled in the remaining scores in the matrix. At this point we can conclude that the falling ill (Y) was caused by the oysters (X_2).

Table 5.1   *The method of agreement and Pop's $6.99 seafood platter*

Case	Name	Outcome	Food eaten			
		Fallen ill (Y)	Shrimp (X_1)	Oysters (X_2)	Hushpuppies (X_3)	Catfish fillet (X_4)
1	Eddy	Yes	Yes	Yes	Yes	Yes
2	Doug	Yes	No	Yes	No	Yes
3	Sam	Yes	.	Yes	.	No
4	Bill	Yes	.	Yes	.	.

Or can we? Mill believed that the main problem with this method is its inability to establish any necessary link between cause and effect. For example, the fact that all instances of illness occurred after eating oysters is no guarantee that oysters caused the illness. Both oysters and the illness might be affected by some unidentified (underlying or lurking) third factor (in other words, *Galton's Problem*). For example, perhaps Pop's Food Barn was not a particularly hygienic eating establishment; it could be that bacteria near the oysters at the Food Barn caused the illness. Another serious shortcoming of this method is that it is completely incapacitated by the problem of multiple causations (what Mill called plural causation, see also Lieberson (1991) and Ragin (1987)). If illness results from *either* hushpuppies *or* catfish fillets, then there may be instances where hushpuppies have caused people to fall ill and other instances when catfish fillets have caused people to fall ill. The Method of Agreement would lead to the incorrect conclusion that neither of these factors caused the illness.

These examples show that the Method of Agreement (like the Method of Difference) is really a method of *elimination*. The investigator begins by collecting examples of the event he is interested in: say, revolution, economic development, or illness after Pop's Food Barn. He then begins to gather evidence of possible causes (for example, oysters, shrimp, hushpuppies and catfish). He compares all cases carefully for each of the proposed causes, eliminating one potential explanatory factor after the other, until he is left with one factor that all cases have in common.

Finally, it is important to point out that Table 5.1 reveals an *over-determined* relationship. The analysis depends on too few cases relative to the number of explanatory variables. This is a very common and serious problem in few-N comparative studies, one to which we return below.

The Indirect Method of Difference

The most reliable comparative method is the Indirect Method of Difference or the Joint Method of Agreement (as Mill also called it). This application is closer to the statistical in that it involves cross-tabulations of causes and effects.[4] By combining two (mirror) applications of the Method of Agreement, it allows the investigator to come closest to approximating experimental design with non-experimental data. In other words, the Indirect Method of Difference is also modelled on the procedural design of the experiment. It allows the investigator to draw on non-experimental data yet approximate the logic of the experiment. This is evident in Mill's description of its procedural design:

If two or more instances in which the phenomenon occurs have only one circumstance in common, while two or more instances in which it does not occur have nothing in common save the absence of that circumstance, the circumstance in which alone the two sets of instances differ is the effect, or the cause, or an indispensable part of the cause, of the phenomenon.   (Mill, 2002, p. 259)

The Method of Indirect Difference is not as complicated at it sounds. In effect, it relies on a double application of the Method of Agreement. This can be shown by extending the example of the four unfortunate friends to include 'negative' cases, and by comparing all cases systematically for agreement as well as for difference.

Imagine, now, a second car driving home from Pop's Food Barn filled with three other members of the Sons of Norway's local chapter: Robert, Jens and Tom. Noticing their friends curled up in a state of nausea, they pull over to offer some assistance. Robert, who was driving, interviewed each of the four prostrate victims to uncover what was amiss. From that information he was able to assemble a mental matrix of his own – not unlike the one found in Table 5.1. But he could now extend that table to include 'negative cases'. Grabbing a stick, he quickly traced Table 5.2 in the sand at the side of the road. Note how the (shaded) top part of Table 5.2 reproduces his mental matrix (and copies Table 5.1 above)

Having established, by means of the Method of Agreement, that oysters were the likely cause of the illness, Robert sets to work employing the Indirect Method of Difference. He begins to collect cases where no illness occurred (remember, Robert was one of the few students who had attended all ten methods lectures in Chapter 3). If it is true that

Table 5.2   *The indirect method of difference*

Case	Name	Outcome	Food eaten			
		Fallen ill (Y)	Shrimp (X_1)	Oysters (X_2)	Hushpuppies (X_3)	Catfish fillet (X_4)
1	Eddy	Yes	Yes	Yes	Yes	Yes
2	Doug	Yes	No	Yes	No	Yes
3	Sam	Yes	.	Yes	.	No
4	Bill	Yes	.	Yes	.	.
5	Robert	No	No	No	No	Yes
6	Jens	No	Yes	No	No	No
7	Tom	No	No	No	Yes	Yes

oysters caused his friends to fall ill, Robert expects to find that those who had *not* fallen ill had *not* eaten oysters. To search for this evidence Robert didn't need to look any further than his own passengers, as neither himself, Jens nor Tom had eaten oysters that evening.

By juxtaposing the positive and negative cases in Table 5.2 we can be more certain of the causal relationship at work. Not only did illness occur after every instance of oyster consumption, but the lack of illness was also associated with the lack of oyster consumption. Thus, the major difference between the Indirect Method of Difference and the Method of Agreement is that the indirect method uses negative cases to reinforce conclusions drawn from positive cases.

Two elegant applications of the Method of Indirect Difference are mentioned in most introductions to the comparative method – and deservedly so. The first is Barrington Moore's *Social Origins of Dictatorship and Democracy* (1966). The other is Theda Skocpol's *States and Social Revolutions* (1979). Moore seeks to explain how different countries have developed from agrarian to industrial societies. He selects five important countries that have all gone through this modernization process – England, France, USA, Japan and China. To explain the routes they took, he focuses on historical relationships among the main (economic) classes in these countries. In particular, he shows how different classes have cooperated and competed in different ways, and how different class alignments produce very different political results. In cases where the rising bourgeoisie allied with the aristocracy and the rural masses (and allowed agriculture to be commercialized), the result was liberal democracy – as in England and the USA. In cases where the rural masses allied with the traditional aristocracy against the bourgeoisie, the result was fascism (for example, Japan). In cases where the rural masses took power, the result was communism (as in China). Thus Barrington Moore demonstrates that countries can travel three different routes towards modernization; only one of them, however, leads to democracy. Towards the end of the book he introduces a final case, India, to examine more closely the complicated relationship between democracy and modernization (as India managed to secure the former before the latter).

Social Origins of Dictatorship and Democracy provides a unique understanding of 400 years of economic development and political history. It is a story rife with insights and commentaries and an argument that dispels traditional theories of development as it unfolds. It has fascinated two generations of social scientists, and is a monument to the power and fertility of the comparative method. From the naturalist's perspective, the problem with Moore's argument is that its comparative design is implicit; it takes a skilled methodologist to disentangle all the threads that the author weaves into his argument. We return to this important observation in Chapter 10. Theda Skocpol, by contrast, has explicitly advertised her application of the Method of Indirect Difference.

Her book, *States and Social Revolutions*, begins by discussing three social revolutions – the French (1789), the Russian (1917) and the Chinese (1947) – in order to identify a few probable causes of revolution (using the Method of Agreement). Skocpol then proceeds to study instances of social unrest which did *not* produce social revolution – the Reform Movement in Hohenzollern Prussia (1807–14), the German upheavals (1848–50) and Meiji Restoration in Tokugawa Japan (1868–73) foremost among them. She then integrates these cases of non-revolution into her discussion as 'negative cases', 'contrasts' or 'counterpoints'. This integration of 'contrasts' or 'counterpoints' lifts Skocpol's method up from the Method of Agreement to the Method of Indirect Difference – and produces 'the best book that has ever been written on revolutions' (Collins, 1980, p. 647).

Perhaps the reason for such acclaim can be found in the fact that the basic logic of her argument is very simple: the main cause of social revolution is a factor that is systematically present when revolution is present, but systematically absent in cases of turmoil when social revolution is absent. As she discusses her various revolutions in light of one variable after the other, Skocpol can home in on 'state collapse' as the most probable cause of revolution. On the one hand, all of her positive cases of revolution – France, Russia and China – were preceded by the unravelling of state institutions. On the other, all of her negative cases involved rebellions that were struck down by the force of the state. The state apparatus, in other words, did not unravel in these negative cases. Rather, when the revolutionary movement gathers force, governments rely on state forces to block and stop the revolutionary process.

One of the qualities that makes Skocpol's book so worthwhile is that she doesn't rest after she has identified her independent variable. Instead of proudly displaying state collapse as a cause of revolution, she pursues it even further: she asks what might have produced the collapse. By beginning to unravel the chain of causality in this way, Skocpol ends up with Great Power wars. State collapse is a key causal variable for social revolution; however, when she revisits her positive cases (all the weakened states that experienced revolution), she finds that each of them was weakened by a great war. Through a virtuoso application of the Indirect Method of Difference, Skocpol concludes that social revolutions are produced by the confluence of three developments: (1) an initial collapse or incapacitation of the central administrative and military apparatus of the state – occasioned, for example, by loss in a major war; (2) widespread peasant rebellions; and (3) shifts of political allegiance among elite groups.

The Method of Concomitant Variation

We have arrived at the fourth, and final, of Mill's methods. The Method of Concomitant Variation is more sophisticated than the others because it is not limited to binary cases (as are the other applications): it observes and measures the quantitative variations of the operative variables and relates these to each. Consequently, the Method of Concomitant Variation can track variation in strength rather than in the simple presence or absence of a variable. As such, this method comes closest to the statistical method described in Chapter 4. Here, more than anywhere else, we see how closely related these (experimental, statistical and comparative) methods are to one another. Mill described this fourth method of comparison thus:

> Whatever phenomenon varies in any manner whenever another phenomenon varies in some particular manner, is either a cause or an effect of that phenomenon, or is connected with it through some fact of causation.   (Mill, 2002, p. 263)

While Durkheim was sceptical about applications of the Method of Agreement and the Method of Difference to social phenomena, his scepticism did not extend to Mill's Method of Concomitant Variation. Durkheim saw this method as the instrument par excellence of sociological research. For this reason, we might quote Durkheim at length on this subject:

> for [the method of concomitant variation] to be reliable, it is not necessary that all the variables differing from those which we are comparing shall have been strictly excluded. The mere parallelism of the series of values presented by the two phenomena, provided that it has been established in a sufficient number and variety of cases, is proof that a relationship exists between them. Its validity is due to the fact that the concomitant variations display the causal relationships not by coincidence, as the preceding ones do, but intrinsically. It does not simply show us two facts which accompany or exclude one another externally, so that there is no direct proof that they are united by an internal bond; on the contrary, it shows them as mutually influencing each other in a continuous manner, at least so far as their quality is concerned.   (Durkheim, 1964, pp. 130–1)

Because this method not only examines the existence of correlations, but also gauges their relative strength, it is remarkably similar to the statistical approach described in the previous chapter. To underscore the difference that non-dichotomization can make, we can replace the

Table 5.3   *The method of concomitant variation*

Case	Name	Outcome in °F (°C)	Food eaten (Number of helpings)			
		Body temp. (Y)	Shrimp (X_1)	Oysters (X_2)	Hushpuppies (X_3)	Catfish fillet (X_4)
1	Eddy	102 (38.8)	1	4	1	1
2	Doug	99 (37.2)	0	1	0	4
3	Sam	100 (37.7)	.	2	.	0
4	Bill	101 (38.3)	.	3	.	.
5	Robert	98.6 (37)	0	0	0	5
6	Jens	98.6 (37)	5	0	0	0
7	Tom	98.6 (37)	0	0	3	1

dichotomous scores in Table 5.2 with non-dichotomous scores. In particular, we can use body temperature as a measure of illness, instead of falling ill (Yes/No). Similarly, we can note the number of helpings each Son of Norway took at the Food Barn, rather than using dichotomous scores for consumption (Yes/No). This is done in Table 5.3.

If, for the sake of convenience, we focus our attention on the two relevant variables (number of oyster helpings and body temperature), we can note that the two variables not only co-vary, but they do so in a very structured way. With closer observation we can note that a single increase in the number of oyster helpings corresponds to an increase in body temperature of one degree Fahrenheit (F). For example, Doug only had one oyster helping, and his temperature was only a little above average (99°). Sam was not satisfied before he had two helpings of oysters, and his temperature was a degree higher (100°). This pattern continues all the way up to Big Eddy, who seems to have had an enormous appetite. His toll for consuming four helpings of oysters was a feverous temperature of 102 °F (38.8 °C).

While the Method of Concomitant Variations has significant analytical potential, it can easily be employed in a less ambitious, more inductive fashion, where testing causal relationships is downplayed in favour of understanding underlying commonalities. Indeed, this is the approach that underlies a classic work in comparative politics: Gabriel Almond and Sidney Verba's (1965 [1963]) *Civic Culture*. In their contribution to a 'scientific theory of democracy' (1965, p. 10), Almond and Verba conducted 5000 interviews, scattered across five different countries (Britain, Germany, Italy, Mexico and the United States), with an eye to identifying the political culture that is associated with democracy.

In particular, Almond and Verba compared levels of political participation and diverse citizens' attitudes towards government and politics in the five countries. Following J. S. Mill's lead, they begin by providing clear definitions and measurements for the variables of interest. In this case, Almond and Verba had to operationalize a number of very slippery and amorphous concepts, such as 'pride'. To do this, they surveyed broad swaths of the population in each country and asked them similar questions with the aim of providing compatible, cross-national data. On the basis of these responses, Almond and Verba could map systematic patterns across nations:

> Thus the Americans and the British with greatest frequency take pride in their political systems, social legislation, and international prestige. Italians in the overwhelming majority take no pride in their political system . . . To the extent that they have national pride at all, it is in their history, the physical beauty of their country, or in the fact of being Italian.   (Almond and Verba, 1965, p. 65)

On the basis of several such investigations and comparisons, Almond and Verba concluded that democracy relies on a participant culture – what they call a 'civic culture'. But they added that democracy is most stable in societies where participation is tempered by elements of subject and parochial attitudes. For example, they found that their measure of pride correlated with civic culture – noting that the citizens of the more democratic nations tended to be more proud of their polities.

Shortcomings

In the presentation above we have used influential and real, as well as fictitious, examples to illustrate the breadth and appeal of the comparative method for social scientists. We wish to conclude this chapter by returning to the caveats with which we began: the comparative method often suffers from two significant shortcomings when viewed from the demands of the naturalist's methodology: over-determination and sampling bias. We close this chapter with a short discussion of each. It is important to point out that these problems are not restricted to few-N comparative projects – they only tend to be more common here.

Over-determination

Over-determination concerns our ability to generalize from the observations we have. To generalize we use inference, which is itself restricted by the amount of information we already have. As a general rule, we tend to assume that one piece of information cannot give independent information for more than one other fact. This rule translates into the concept of *degrees of freedom*, which you may recall from your introductory statistics course: degrees of freedom are the number of cases minus the number of explanatory variables, minus one.

Thus, when the analyst has only one case, and at least one explanatory variable, he/she is working with negative degrees of freedom: under these conditions, any claims about causation are worthless (see, for example, Campbell 1975). The reason for this is clear: without more observations we can say nothing about the spread of the phenomenon. Without a grasp of the spread (or variation) of a given phenomenon, it is impossible to generalize with any degree of accuracy.

Consider a simple example: we begin with an observation of a poor state, whose GDP/capita (PPP) is $1308. From this observation we have a rough estimate of the average wealth of poor states, but no information about the spread of national incomes. Consequently, it would be difficult to know if this state finds itself at the high or the low end of the 'poor state' scale: we can say nothing about the representativeness of this observation with respect to poor states generally. However, if we were to gather more observations (for example, find that another poor country in the same year had a per capita income of $429, while a third had $2484), then we could begin to develop a better understanding of what the universe of 'poor states' looks like. Thus, from a single observation, we can say nothing about other poor states. It is only when we have more than one observation that we can get information about the spread of the population. These problems can be particularly troublesome in few-N comparative studies. Indeed, we noted it in relation to Table 5.1.

Following Lijphart (1971), we can divide the over-determination problem into its two main components: (1) too few observations and (2) too many variables. To solve these problems, Lijphart suggests four solutions: two for each of the component parts.

The first lesson corresponds to the mantra of naturalist science: 'increase N'. Researchers are encouraged to expand their analysis both spatially and temporally to allow for more possibilities of control. By increasing the number of observations we improve our ability to control variations. Eventually, we may even be able to graduate to statistical analysis, climbing another rung up the methods ladder. Increasing the number of observations also helps us to generalize, as we can assume that the sample becomes more representative as the N increases and we get a better mapping of potential spread.

The second lesson aims to reduce the property space of the analysis by combining variables and/or categories. Researchers are encouraged to combine similar variables that encompass underlying characteristics. In this way, the number of explanatory variables will decrease relative to the number of observations – increasing the analyst's degrees of freedom. Although this entails discarding costly information, the costs are generally seen to be affordable. In doing so, the analyst increases his analytical purchase and degrees of freedom.

Lijphart's third lesson requires that we use theories more vigorously to aid in choosing only the most likely (important) variables. In other words, we can initially scan all the potential explanatory variables, but in the end analysis we need to economize in order to maximize the degrees of freedom. The fourth lesson returns us to the choice of method, discussed by Mill. If we can choose our cases carefully (in other words, in light of theory), we can effectively control for many of the potential operative variables in an analysis.

It is worthwhile noting that the last three solutions encourage the comparativist to engage theoretical issues, providing a larger role for theory. To improve on the potential shortcomings of the comparative approach, as developed for inductive studies, we need to introduce theories that will help us define key variables, reduce the property space of variables, and focus on appropriate cases. Good comparative research exploits both deductive and inductive approaches to testing causal relationships.

Sampling Bias

Whereas experiments and statistical designs are based on the principle of random selection, the essence of the comparative method is case selection. We choose our cases with an eye towards control. While this is one of the strengths of the few-N comparative method, it is also its bane: sampling bias can threaten the generalizability of any results we might generate. In its most blatant form, social scientists select only cases that support the theory in question, or draw only from certain types of sources. But it is not uncommon to find comparative studies where the cases are chosen by their score on the dependent variable. This can (but needn't always) raise some serious problems. As this last example is the least understood, we shall examine it more closely.

Most students learn in their introductory statistics courses that selecting on the dependent variable is forbidden. But few students remember why, or what the implications are of violating this taboo. The problem stems from the logic of explanation and we might understand it better by returning to our sick friends on the side of the road. In the example depicted in Table 5.1 above (Method of Agreement), four cases were introduced on the basis of their score on the dependent variable (all four men were sick). To elaborate on the problem of selection bias, we can consider what we might infer about the world on the basis of these four cases.

To do this we need to return to the scene of the four sick men – before their friends joined them in the second car. Imagine now that a state patrol car pulls up instead: seeing a car pulled off to the side of the road, two state troopers arrive to investigate and provide support. Imagine also that inside the patrol car we find Officer Delaney and Officer Kaitlin; the first had just finished her graduate training in statistical criminology; the second had majored in historical sociology at the University of Minnesota. When the two troopers arrive, their (very different) mental processes shifted into high gear.

Delaney, the statistician, was least worried of the two. She saw these four instances and realized immediately that there was no need to generalize on the basis of four individual cases. To illustrate the point, Delaney drew Figure 5.1 in the sand beside the four prostrate Sons of Norway. In Figure 5.1 we see the four observations from Table 5.1 nested in the upper right-hand corner of the graph (and labelled by their case number: **1, 2, 3, 4**). By only studying these four cases, Delaney realizes that we can say nothing about the location of the other cases. Without that knowledge, Delaney simply assumes that the remaining cases (*a, b, c, d, e, f, g, h, i, j, k, l*) line up in a vertical fashion as depicted in Figure 5.1, below the

Figure 5.1   *The statistician's assumed relationship*

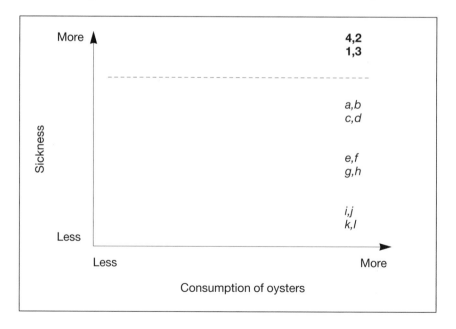

dotted line (in other words, that the illness was not related to consumption of oysters). In this (as we have already discovered) she would have been wrong. But it is not an unreasonable interpretation, especially for someone trained in statistics. Delaney is rightfully leery of sampling on the dependent variable and generalizing on the basis of a very small number of observations. Delaney can assume that this is an isolated incident and that there is no need for alarm.

Given an opportunity, however, Officer Kaitlin would jump in to erase Delaney's drawing in the sand and replace it with her own. Given her training as a historical sociologist, she realizes that causal relationships can reveal themselves – even in areas characterized by a small number of observations, and where there is little variation in the dependent variable. From her methods training, Kaitlin would expect to find a different pattern in the remaining (unobserved) data – a pattern similar to the one depicted in Figure 5.2. If Kaitlin is correct, it is important to investigate further. Somebody needs to tell Pop that his oysters are foul, and other Sons of Norway should be contacted in order to map out the extent of the phenomenon.

This time Kaitlin was lucky, but it is important to note that Delaney's inferences were just as capable of being right (or wrong). Our point is not to show how the biases that drive statistical or comparative studies are

Figure 5.2   *The comparativist's assumed relationship*

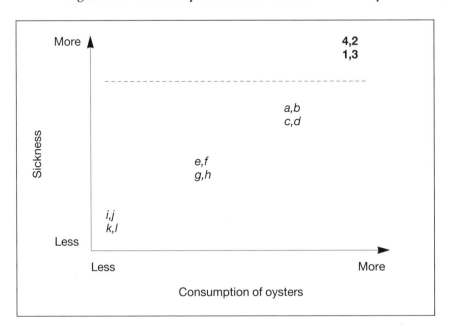

better or worse than the other. Rather, our intention is to illustrate the problems associated with research projects that select a subject of study on the basis of the dependent variable, and where there is no variation in that variable (in other words, that the analyst only chooses from one outcome on the dependent variable). The example above is inspired by Barbara Geddes (1990), in a piece that documents the seriousness of this problem in Area Studies that were used to generalize about factors that can explain economic development. Because certain factors can be used to explain economic development in a given region of the world, it does not mean that we can generalize from these findings to the universe of developing states.

By selecting cases on the basis of single scores on the dependent variable, we may mistakenly jump to the wrong conclusion about the nature and location of the remainder of the (untested) population. In short, if we had selected a different set of cases, we might have derived a completely different conclusion about the nature of the relationship between these two variables.

Conclusion

We conclude this chapter by looking back on the path we have just travelled. We began by showing how comparative methods attempt to mimic the scientific logic of experimentation and statistical methods by employing their own means of control. In comparative studies, control is conducted by way of case selection, and this introduces a number of problems that comparativists are always trying to correct.

We then described the main methods of comparison, as first introduced by J. S. Mill. These methods were originally designed as inductive tools for mapping the complex empirical patterns that exist in the Real World. To the extent that these methods are used in a purely inductive fashion, their shortcomings were clearly evident to Mill, Durkheim and many others. As a consequence, their application to the social sciences was strongly discouraged.

To correct for the main shortcomings of this method, social scientists are encouraged to increase their number of observations, in hopes of being able to apply (eventually) a statistical approach. Alternatively (and most commonly), social scientists can use theory as a way to overcome both of the major problems of this method: over-determination and sampling bias. In the end, good comparative studies combine deductive and inductive approaches to test hypotheses concerning causal arguments, even when the number of observations is relatively small.

Recommended Further Reading

As always, we recommend that you turn to the original source. In the study of comparative methods, this means J. S. Mill's *A System of Logic* [1891]. Still, there are a number of good and influential introductions to the comparative method, including Przeworski and Teune's *The Logic of Comparative Social Inquiry* (1970) and Landman's *Issues and Methods in Comparative Politics* (2000). Of these, our favourite is Ragin's *The Comparative Method* (1987).

Chapter 6

History and Case Studies

In this chapter we discuss the role of history in the naturalist's toolbox of methods. Perhaps the easiest way to do this would be to return to the study of cliometrics, introduced in the closing pages of Chapter 4, where we find quantitative methods and behavioural models from the social sciences applied to the study of history. After all, this relatively new 'scientific' approach to history has proven to be both popular and fruitful. Yet cliometrics itself does not provide us with a method that is distinct from those already covered in previous chapters; cliometricians such as Robert Fogel are simply borrowing statistical methods and theories from naturalist social science and employing them to historical queries.

There is another way to think about historical methods: as case studies. Here, the social scientist uses historical methods (or relies on the work of historians) to collect data on an individual case of a larger phenomenon. In this context, historical studies are seen as intricate parts of larger comparative projects – they become the building blocks of subsequent scientific comparison and analysis.

To say that the historical approach is used as part of a case study strategy in naturalist social science is to say very little about what the method actually entails. To answer this important question, the first part of this chapter describes what might be called the technical aspects of traditional historiography. This description builds on two particular aspects of the historical approach: the criteria used to establish reputable sources, and the way in which these data are utilized (in other words, the overall objectives of historical analysis). Both aspects have a long and established lineage in contemporary historiography.

These two features do not make historical studies scientific – but they do provide a strong empirical foundation for subsequent social science. It is for this reason that we focus so long on the historical approach: it provides the groundwork for so much subsequent social scientific analysis. The utility of the historical method for naturalists is derived from its application in case studies – where the case under study is understood as one observation in a larger comparative study, or as a useful illustration in the development of theory. As such, historically informed case studies tend to occupy an important, if relatively low, rung in the naturalist methods hierarchy. As Lundberg (1926, p. 61) disparagingly noted, they too often become 'a helpless tail to the statistical kite'.

The Historical Method

Before we can understand the utility of historical methods in case study strategies, we need to grapple with the tenuous relationship between history and science. To do this we can try to anchor the historian's method in the naturalist's methodology, by distinguishing and delineating the historian's approach or method.

This, as it turns out, is no easy task. At one level, the historical approach is as straight as an arrow: historians build cases around evidence. The core of the historical method is to probe the evidence in order to ascertain if it is solid. Beyond that, however, it is hard to identity any particular properties of the historical method. After all, there is no clear demarcation principle separating history from fiction. Indeed, the community of historians does not even possess a technical vocabulary that is distinctive to its members. This is one of the most refreshing qualities of historical research: a historian presents his case in everyday language. Another endearing quality is history's variety of approaches and ideological perspectives. Historians do not limit themselves to specific hypothetico–deductive techniques or experimental controls in order to determine the veracity of their claims. Among historians, Isaiah Berlin (1954, p. 5) once observed, 'there plainly exists a far greater variety of methods and procedures than is usually provided for in textbooks on logic or scientific methods'.

While the historian's approach is remarkably varied, there is a certain simplicity and practicality to it that might be summarized as the practical application of common sense. It was no less an authority than Lord Acton (1834–1902), who noted how 'common sense' lay at the core of the historical method. In his [1895] inaugural lecture at Cambridge on the study of history, Acton noted that common sense was meant to complement the more 'technical' aspects of the historical method. The main thing to learn, he insisted,

> is not the art of accumulating material, but the sublimer art of investigating it, of discerning truth from falsehood and certainty from doubt. It is by solidity of criticism more than by the plentitude of erudition, that the study of history strengthens, and straightens, and extends the mind. And the accession of the critic in the place of the indefatigable compiler, of the artist in coloured narrative, the skilled limner of character, the persuasive advocate of good, or other, causes, amounts to a

transfer of government, to a change of dynasty, in the historic realm. For the critic is one who, when he lights on an interesting statement, begins by suspecting it. He remains in suspense until he has subjected his authority to three operations. First, he asks whether he has read the passage as the author wrote it. . . . Next is the question where the writer got his information . . . third . . . is their dogma of impartiality. (Acton, 1906a, pp. 15–16)

These technical and commonsensical aspects of historical methods are aimed at generating dependable, verifiable knowledge of past events as they actually happened. For this reason, perhaps, Evans (1997, pp. 65–6) suggests that the best way of training young historians is to be very pragmatic, and to view history less as an exact science and more as a craft.

Most historians, in practice, would agree that at least some degree of training and supervision is necessary to equip young scholars for a career in the profession, and that the PhD is probably the best way of doing this. The historian's training through the PhD is necessarily mostly training on the job, learning through practice. But historians also have to learn theories and techniques before they are let loose on their materials; they must absorb not only the Rankean principles of source-criticism and citation but also relevant skills such as languages, paleography, statistics and so on. Moreover they also have to read and digest a large amount of contextual material and master the secondary literature relating to their subject. This kind of training, it has been argued, is more characteristic of a craft than a science.

At the core of the historical method lies a kind of systematic doubt that is trained on the historians' sources. If we are to believe Lord Acton, historians do not have much more than this by way of scientific procedures – for the historian's work is distinguished neither by the use of particular equipment nor by special processes. However, historians know what they have and they make the most of it. Indeed, historians are so adept at what they do, social scientists might do well to observe their procedures and learn from them. For the historical method of systematic doubt – often referred to as 'source criticism' – is, really, the core component in all social science methods.

Leopold von Ranke

The purpose of historiography is to generate dependable knowledge about the past, as it really happened – *wie es eigentlich gewesen war*. This, at least, was the maxim of Leopold von Ranke (1790–1886), the name most closely associated with the modern historical method. With him we can begin to trace the unique traits of the modern, scholarly approach to historical study. Ranke's impact on that approach is enormous, as it builds on his three important legacies: (1) he helped to establish history as a separate discipline, based on describing history as it actually happened; (2) he established that discipline with a reputation for impartiality; and (3) he developed an explicit outline of historical methods based on source criticism. Although the third point alone focuses on the technical aspect of good history writing, all these contributions helped to secure a foundational role for historical work in the naturalist hierarchy of methods. For this reason it behooves us to spend a little time examining von Ranke's contribution.

Ranke's quest for objective historiography was prompted by his concern about the nature of contemporary public education in Europe (and especially Germany). In the wake of the French and industrial revolutions, public education was gradually introduced to Europe – and history played a central role in this education. But Ranke feared that the history being taught was little more than the inculcation of patriotic myths by the old in the young.

History, along with language and religion, was part of the basic curriculum of early nineteenth-century state schools. Although history was included because it helped children learn the basic skills of critical reasoning and communication, history could also have a socializing effect: it included patriotic myths and edifying inventions and imparted to every new generation the knowledge and values of the old. In the hands of the eager nation builders of early nineteenth-century Europe, the past became the servant of identity politics and the teaching of history repeated the myths of national glory. This socializing effect did not go unnoticed by political leaders aware of the growing need for an educated and coordinated infantry in modern warfare.

This was how the role of history was conceived at the time of Ranke's youth. The early nineteenth century was an age of nation building and basic education aimed at teaching children nationalism – if not patriotism. In this context, languages, religion and history were all subjects intended to have a socializing effect on new generations of citizens. While *language* education could provide children with elementary skills of communication (such as reading and writing), it could also connect each young pupil to the spirit of a distinct human community and a common sense of belonging to a larger society (à la German idealists such as Herder and Fichte). Teaching *religion* (or Christianity) communicated the norms of ethically responsible values and socially responsible behaviour; while signalling a sense of belonging to a larger, particularly fortunate, civilization.

Similarly, the teaching of *history* was used to inculcate a sense of social belongingness, but in a more explicit fashion. History introduced children to a common heritage with a common set of heroes and myths, but it also had an edifying, moralizing function. During the age of nationalism, these functions were becoming increasingly self-conscious – and in many school curricula the same functions are still encouraged.[1]

Quellenkritik

Von Ranke was mostly concerned with the effect of this approach to the study of history as a scholarly discipline. Ranke's original training was in philology, where he learned of methods recently developed in the study of ancient and medieval literature. These methods were used to determine whether a given text was true (or corrupted by later interpolations), whether it was written by the author to whom it was usually attributed, and to determine which of the available versions was the most reliable.

After turning to the study of history in the 1820s, Ranke established a seminar at the University of Berlin where he instructed advanced students in the approach to historical research. His instruction focused on the critical study of sources – *Quellenkritik*, which he had largely imported from his training in philology. In particular, Ranke established a hierarchy of sources, ranked according to their reliability. History, he taught, should be written from sources that were located as close as possible to the events in question. Most preferably, history should be based on eyewitness reports and what Ranke called the 'purest, most immediate documents' (Ranke, 1956, p. 54).

Soon Ranke became Europe's premier teacher of historiography: students came from across the continent to study his new, scientific, approach to history. On leaving Berlin these students came to learn that history should avoid edifying and moral-raising projects: the task of the historian was to recreate the past, truthfully and objectively. By carefully unfolding events, the historian could show how they produced a specific condition, event, or event sequence. To do this properly, the historian would have to find the proper sources and use them in a self-conscious and critical way. In short, behind all serious historical research lies a systematic quest for original source material. At the core of any good historical narrative lies a systematic assessment of the nature and the quality of every identified document.

Ranke distinguished between two kinds of sources: primary and secondary. Historical research, he argued, should rely on *primary sources* to the greatest degree possible. Primary sources are the direct outcomes of historical events or experiences. They include eyewitness accounts (for example, interviews and oral histories), original documents (for example, diaries and school records), and diplomatic reports (for example, the original assessment and papers given to decision makers, papers and minutes from committee meetings, and so on).

But the historical researcher also has access to *secondary sources*: those that are once removed from original events. For example, the historian might find information in the form of a narrative that is (itself) based on primary sources; a newspaper report that is based on eyewitness accounts; or even a summary of important statistics. Secondary sources can help the historian establish a theme for his work; they can aid in mapping out the field of research, to find out what is written and what is not; they can be useful for finding out which issues are raised and which are not – to identify which questions are raised and how they are answered. However, the very distance of secondary sources from the actual historical event makes them less trustworthy.

For Ranke, the job of the historian was to root out forgeries and falsifications from the historical record. To do so, the historian was to stick to primary sources, and to establish internal and external consistencies. This should not appear as surprising to the modern reader, and it is surely an exaggeration to claim that Ranke was the first to employ these techniques. After all, Islamic tradition holds that the early Caliphs (from the first half of the seventh century) authorized Zaid bin Thabit to supervise a team that would collect and transcribe the Qur'anic revelation. As the Qur'an is held to record the voice of Allah himself, it was absolutely essential that Thabit's team made no mistakes in its task. To ensure an authentic version of the voice of Allah, each verse of the Qur'an is said to have been verified by at least two witnesses who had heard them spoken by the Prophet Muhammad himself.

Even if Ranke wasn't the first to employ careful source criticism, his mark is firmly planted on modern European historiography:

> Whatever the means they use, historians still have to engage in the basic Rankean spadework of investigating the provenance of documents, of enquiring about the motives of those who wrote them, the circumstances in which they were written, and the ways in which they relate to other documents on the same subject. The perils which await them should they fail to do this are only too obvious.   (Evans, 1997, p. 19)

The Aim of History
The uncovering of indubitable facts through basic spadework among primary sources is the first, fundamental component of historical research. The second fundamental component is loftier: it concerns the goal of history. Ranke saw history as a corpus of ascertained facts. These

facts constitute a series of witness statements, available to the historian in document form. The historian reads these documents, systematizes their content and creates a narrative of 'what really happened'.

It may be useful to compare Ranke's maxim with that of Sherlock Holmes. As we have already seen in Chapter 2, Holmes explained the investigative part of his method to Dr Watson in terms of a two-step procedure: first, collect all relevant evidence; then sort through it: for 'when you have eliminated the impossible, whatever remains, however improbable, must be the truth' (Doyle, 1930, Chapter 6). The comparison is useful, for both Ranke and Holmes were products of the same historical epoch and the empiricist spirit that marked it. They were birds of a feather in an age characterized by progress and scientific innocence where 'the new historians walked in a Garden of Eden, without a scrap of philosophy to cover them, naked and unashamed before the god of history' (Carr, 1987, p. 20).

Ranke was affected by nineteenth-century philosophy of science. Yet, it is too simple to depict him as a naïve empiricist. Ranke's famous phrase, *'wie es eigentlich gewesen war'*, is most literally translated as 'what actually happened', but it may be better to interpret the phrase to mean 'how it essentially was' (Evans, 1997, p. 17). This is because Ranke's goal was not just to collect facts but also to understand the inner being, or the essence, of the past. A deeply religious and conservative man, Ranke did not believe that God would prioritize different historical epochs: each had to be similar in His eyes. For this reason, the past could not (should not) be judged by the standard of the present. It had to be understood on its own terms. Thus, the objective of history was to come to understand these universal truths of each historical epoch. It was this view that separated Ranke from the Prussian school of (deeply nationalistic) German historians: all states (not just Prussia) were examples of God's will; no state's history could be prioritized. It is this position that underlies Ranke's reputation for impartiality.

This approach to impartial history is not itself an artefact of history; it is clearly evident in several subsequent generations of historians. Most famously, Lord Acton encouraged the ideal of objectivity in his letter of instruction to the authors of the first book in the multi-volume work *The Cambridge Modern History*: a historian's account of the battle of Waterloo must be painstakingly impartial; it must be Waterloo 'that satisfies French and English, German and Dutch alike; that nobody can tell, without examining the list of authors, where the Bishop of Oxford laid down the pen, and whether Fairbarn or Gasquet, Libermann or Harrison took it up' (Acton, 1906b, p. 318).

The Cambridge Modern History, then, was to offer the modern reader:

a unique opportunity of recording, in the way most useful to the greatest number, the fullness of the knowledge which the nineteenth century is about to bequeath . . . By the judicious division of labour we should be able to do it, and to bring home to every man the last document, and the ripest conclusions of international research.

Ultimate history we cannot have in this generation; but we can dispose of conventional history, and show the point we have reached on the road from one to the other, now that all information is within reach, and every problem has become capable of solution.   (Acton, 1907, pp. 10–12)

Thus, it would appear that history could not only be impartial, it could also be definitive. By combining the technical expertise and common-sensical aspects of historical research, the modern scholar could contribute to human progress and understanding.

It is here that we can clearly see a naturalist's affinity in this approach. 'Out there, in the documents, lay the facts, waiting to be discovered by historians, just as the stars shone out there in the heavens, waiting to be discovered by astronomers; all the historian had to do was apply the proper scientific method, eliminate his own personality from the investigation, and the facts would come to light' (Evans, 1997, pp. 20–1).

Barbara Tuchman

In modern form, the Rankean tradition is reflected in the works of a number of contemporary historians. The most readable of them is surely Barbara Tuchman, the price winning author of *The Guns of August, The Zimmermann Telegram* and several other very popular books. Tuchman explains that historiography is first and foremost narrative history. She sees herself as a storyteller – 'a narrator who deals in true stories not fiction' (Tuchman, 1981, p. 18). She agrees explicitly with Leopold von Ranke who saw it as his purpose to reveal 'how it essentially was'.

The Phase of Research
In the spring of 1963 Barbara Tuchman was invited to Radcliffe College to present a lecture on her research method. This lecture was eventually published as a chapter in her 1981 book *Practicing History*. As soon as she spoke, it became evident that she subscribed to Holmes's maxim of dividing the research process into two distinct phases: the phase of research and the phase of processing.

In the phase of research, Tuchman explained, she would collect all relevant evidence. In practice, she would begin by reading books by other historians. However, she warned against doing too much of this introductory reading; it may be a hazardous thing to read such secondary sources too carefully. It is best to use them as guides at the outset of a project 'to find out the general scheme of what happened', and then to jump quickly into the primary sources (Tuchman, 1981, p. 19). The primary sources would include memoirs, letters, diaries, minutes, generals' campaign reports, and so on. Such sources are systematized in national archives. Serious research into international events must include visits to such archives, and will therefore involve much travel. A research project on the outbreak of the First World War would most certainly include visits to archives in London, Paris and Berlin – often also to national libraries and special collections. In addition, it is useful to visit the places where the action occurred in order to get a sense of the geography, the landscape and the climate in which the events occurred.

Tuchman knew perfectly well that historians seek to explain. But explanations need not take the same form as those we find in the sciences. Adhering to Ranke's dictum, Tuchman argued that the historian should not even think about causality in the natural science sense of the term. For the historian who worked carefully with his sources, the causal chain of events would somehow emerge all by itself. 'As to the mechanics of research', she explained,

> I take notes on four-by-six index cards, reminding myself about once an hour of a rule I read long ago in a research manual, 'Never write on the back of anything.' Since copying is a chore and a bore, use of the cards, the smaller the better, forces one to extract the strictly relevant, to distill [sic] from the very beginning, to pass the material through the grinder of one's own mind, so to speak. Eventually, as the cards fall into groups according to subject or person or chronological sequences, the pattern of my story will emerge.   (Ibid., p. 20)

The main problem with this phase of research has nothing to do with knowing how to explain; rather, it is knowing when to stop. Her advice to young historians is this: 'One must stop *before* one has finished; otherwise, one will never stop and never finish' (ibid.).

The Phase of Processing

Knowing when to stop is difficult in the research phase as this is heady, fun and 'endlessly seductive' (Tuchman, 1981, p. 21). By contrast, the processing phase is hard and difficult work. It involves much thinking. Most of all, it involves writing. 'One has to sit down on that chair and think and transform thought into readable, conservative, interesting sentences that both make sense and make the reader turn the page' (ibid.). It is laborious work that involves writing, revising, rearranging, adding, cutting, rewriting . . .

This work can be gruelling. First of all, the writing process is itself slow, often painfully so. Sometimes the writing is agonizing; for example, when last week's text is found to stray from its object and has to be rejected *in toto*. If that wasn't hard enough, the historian must keep tabs on the many references and sources that trail along with any serious history text. For the historian must back every claim with sources through a painstaking process of reference and bibliography. Different scholars use different rules and conventions here. Social science authors tend to refer to their sources simply, by putting the name of the author and the publication year of his text in parentheses and injecting this into the text – like this (Ranke, 1956). They follow this up by supplying full details in a bibliography at the end of the book. Historians do this as well. However, some historians prefer more elaborate systems.

The most common alternative is to use notes – either footnotes (which are printed at the bottom of the text page) or endnotes (which are collected in a special section at the end of the chapter or the end of the book), which refer not only to sources, but to specific documents in carefully ordered archives as well. In other words, historians may use a wider diversity of sources than social scientists, and put different demands on their reference system. Some authors do not want to interrupt the narrative flow by any visible reference. They may prefer to publish a list of sources as a special section of the book; here the book's narrative is substantiated page by page, and the sources used are accounted for in the order they are used. These different referencing and source systems are outlined in Figure 6.1.

The point, of course, is a dual one. First of all, any scholarly text must display its sources blatantly and clearly. Second, the display must help the reader find his way through the sources that have been relied upon in making the analysis! It is worth repeating this second point, because an astonishingly large number of students suffer through years of education without paying attention to references – although they encounter them every day in their readings – and without noticing the strict logic to which they are subjected. In short, students can study, study and study, and still waste much of their time if they overlook some of the most basic of scholarly points: (1) scientific research is a public act; (2) science depends on testing; and (3) scholarly references provide the key to both of them!

A highly influential methods book established these basic points in its introductory pages: 'Scientific research uses explicit, codified, and public methods to generate and analyze data whose reliability can therefore be assessed' (King et al., 1994, p. 8). That's it! That's the core of science and scholarship – historical or otherwise. Any author who wants to write a

Figure 6.1   *Denotation of sources – references and bibliographies*

References

There are two common systems of reference: author–date and footnote.

1. The *author–date system* has been the standard among social scientists for many years. Here, the source (the vast majority of the cases) is the name of a *person* – an author whose work has been relied upon in crafting an argument. The author's name is set in parentheses, together with the publication year of the work (and the relevant page number), thus: (Rampolla, 2002, p. 67). This author–date system is particularly convenient when relying on secondary sources. It needs to be complemented by a bibliography, which is usually printed after the main text.

2. The *footnote (or endnote) system* is still used by many historians. One reason that historians still use it, rather than the author–date system, is that footnotes are more convenient when using primary sources. It does not have to be complemented by a bibliography – but a bibliography is always a very helpful addition, especially if the work is long and the sources are many.

    Typical footnotes will include references to a book,[1] an article[2] or an archival document.[3] This method tends to rely on Latin abbreviations to help the reader locate the first (and full) bibliographic reference. The most common of these are:

    - *ibid.*: short for *ibidem*, which means 'in the same place';
    - *idem* (or *id.*): means 'the same';
    - *op. cit.*: short for *opera citato*; means 'in the work cited';
    - f. (pl. *ff.*): means 'and following'.

Bibliography

A bibliography is a listing of books on a particular topic, usually arranged alphabetically according to the authors' last names. It is bound by very strict rules. Two of these will be mentioned here:

- Titles of books are referred to in italics; publication information – year and publisher – clearly denoted, thus:
  Tuchman, Barbara (1962) *The Guns of August* (New York: Macmillan).

- Journal articles are referred to in quotes; the journal's name is written in italics; the volume and issue in which the journal appeared must be clearly denoted, together with the page numbers it spans. For example:
  Holland, Paul (1986) 'Statistics and Causal Inference', *Journal of the American Statistical Association*, 81(4): 945–60.

Notes

1   For example: Mary Lynn Rampolla (2002) *A Pocket Guide to Writing History* (New York: St. Martin's).
2   For example: Paul Holland (1986) 'Statistics and Causal Inference', *Journal of the American Statistical Association*, vol. 81, no. 4, pp. 945–60.
3   For example: Carnegie Endowment for International Peace (1916) *Diplomatic Documents Relating to the Outbreak of the European War*. 2 vols. Ed. James Brown Scott (New York: Oxford).

scholarly text must *publish* his work somehow. In the doing, he must bare his sources, thus laying his argument open for any reader to test! A scholarly author must afford *everyone* the opportunity to check and double-check his scholarly claims. If he does not do this, his text is not scholarly!

As if writing well was not difficult enough, good historiography also involves writing objectively. Tuchman (1981, p. 22) explains that this is best ensured if she tries to write '*as of the time*, without using the benefit of hindsight'. The critical reader may question whether this type of objectivity is even possible. After all, the historian *does* know the outcome of the story.[2] Worse, it is this very knowledge that establishes an event as interesting or important. There can be little doubt that this knowledge will affect the historian's approach to the material: it will necessarily influence the way he reads the documents, selects material for his database, and converts his data into a coherent, flowing narrative. Such knowledge must influence the way the historian selects, emphasizes and adds causal connections to make the narrative flow.

But Tuchman insists that it *is* possible to be objective. Indeed, to do this she warns that the historian must not be concerned with causation. She writes:

> To find out what happens in history is enough at the outset without trying too soon to make sure of the 'why'. I believe it is safer to leave the 'why' alone until after one has not only gathered the facts but arranged them in sequence; to be exact, in sentences, paragraphs, and chapters. The very process of transforming a collection of personalities, dates, gun calibers, letters and speeches into a narrative eventually forces the 'why' to the surface. It will emerge of itself one fine day from the story of what happened. It will suddenly appear and tap one on the shoulder, but not if one chases after it first, before one knows what happened. Then it will elude one forever.   (Ibid., p. 23)

Like good historians, we do not wish to exaggerate. Tuchman is an artist as much as a scientist, and she reveals this in a short note on references that closes her *Guns of August*. Here, Tuchman is willing to relax the Rankean constraint:

> Through this forest of special pleading the historian gropes his way, trying to recapture the truth of past events and find out 'what really happened.' He discovers that truth is subjective and separate, made up of little bits seen, experienced, and recorded by different people. It is like a design seen through a kaleidoscope; when the cylinder is shaken the countless colored fragments form a new picture. Yet they are the

same fragments that make a different picture a moment earlier. This is the problem inherent in the records left by actors in past events. That famous goal, '*wie es wirklich war*,' is never wholly within our grasp. (1962, pp. 441–2)

If Tuchman pulls back from definitive objective history, there are still others who are willing to carry on. In particular, there remains an influential strand of neo-Rankean history represented, for example, by the works of Elton (1967) and Goldstein (1976). This is a tradition that Ian Lustick (1996, p. 12) despairingly refers to as the Forrest Gump theory of history, where 'History is as historians do'. In Elton's *The Practice of History*, history is the search for an objective truth about the past. Like Lord Acton's preface to the *Cambridge Modern History*, Elton is suggesting that it is possible to write a definitive history of something, so definitive that it would never need to be written again.

Criticism

Critics of Ranke have noted that his approach produces a very slanted view of history. His demand for primary sources – for official documents, letters and diaries – tends to favour those historical agents who leave traces behind in the form of such documents; this, in turn, marginalizes those actors who do not. As G. R. Elton notes (1967, pp. 20–1): 'Lively minds of little knowledge like to charge historians with asking the wrong questions or with treating uninteresting problems. The history of princes and politics, of war and diplomacy, is often called dull and insufficient; why do we not hear more about "ordinary people", the lives of the poor, the whole of "society"?' The problem, Elton notes, is that we do not have direct evidence of this history: 'The past is over and done with: it cannot be relived' (ibid.). For this reason, traditional history was largely political history, as official state papers were the most carefully preserved and easily accessible.

While this is a popular criticism of Ranke's method, it is hardly a devastating one. The individual historian begins a research project by formulating a research question. He then casts about to determine which sources are available and which are most appropriate. It is the responsibility of the historian to choose appropriate sources; these, in turn, are a reflection of the questions asked – not the other way around. A historian who allows the content of a well-known archive to determine his topic is akin to the drunk who arrives home late one night and loses his house key. Although he has dropped the key in the dark grass by his front door, the drunk chooses to begin his search under the lamp post further down the road (where the light is better).

There is another kind of criticism that is more to the point: Ranke, and the tradition that shadows him, seems to have an unadulterated faith in objectivity. In a multicultural age of many perspectives, this faith may appear anachronistic, if not naïve. However, to those scholars fatigued by postmodern study, this quest for objective courses of events makes the historical method all the more appealing.

> It is right and proper that postmodernist theorists and critics should force historians to rethink the categories and assumptions with which they work, and to justify the manner in which they practice their discipline. But postmodernism is itself one group of theories among many, and as contestable as all the rest. For my own part, I remain optimistic that objective historical knowledge is both desirable and attainable. So when Patrick Joyce tells us that social history is dead, and Elizabeth Deeds Ermarth declares that time is a fictional construct, and Roland Barthes announces that all the world's a text, and Hans Kellner wants historians to stop behaving as if we were researching into things that actually happened, and Diane Purkiss says that we should just tell stories without bothering whether or not they are true, and Frank Ankersmit swears that we can never know anything at all about the past so we might as well confine ourselves to studying other historians, and Keith Jenkins proclaims that all history is just naked ideology designed to get historians power and money in big university institutions run by the bourgeoisie, I will look humbly at the past and say despite them all: it really happened, and we really can, if we are very scrupulous and careful and self-critical, find out how it happened and reach some tenable though always less than final conclusions about what it all meant. (Evans, 1997, pp. 252–3)

Evans has a good point: historians cannot just write anything. A meticulous anchoring in sources is not enough in itself. This becomes apparent when we consider one of the dark blots on the record of recent historiography: how the historical profession seriously debated and found scholarly virtues in the histories of the right-wing author, and self-taught historian, David Irving. Many historians, focusing more on his method than his message, found Irving to be a meticulous tracer of sources, and a powerful writer of scholarly works. His biographies on Hitler, Göring and Rommel were reviewed among other, similar books, their noxious message all but obscured.

It was a shameful moment for professional historians when an English courtroom did what scholarly historians ought to have done years ago: debate Mr Irving's books and make them an object of scholarly scrutiny. On the basis of convincing evidence, after a highly publicized trial that lasted for several weeks during the spring of 2001, the judge – Mr Justice Grey – concluded as follows:

> Irving has for his own ideological reasons persistently and deliberately misrepresented and manipulated historical evidence; that for the same reasons he has portrayed Hitler in an unwarrantedly favourable light, principally in relation to his attitude towards and responsibility for the treatment of the Jews; that he is an active Holocaust denier; that he is anti-semitic and racist and that he associates with right wing extremists who promote neo-Nazism.[3]

What lessons can we draw from this awkward episode? First and foremost, it is important to recognize that even though an account of the past is meticulously anchored in sources, it may still be bad history. Second, historians cannot write as if time is just a fictional construct, or as if historiography is just an ideology. Historians must answer to common standards of truth and decency. While some may argue that objectivity is an unattainable goal, Irving's example should show us why we cannot jettison it as an ideal. To deny the Holocaust is clearly beyond the pale. This denial cannot be tolerated because it runs counter to historical facts and it offends common sense. It is also politically repugnant (although that is not the decisive issue here).

The Case Study Method

This chapter began with a long introduction to the historian's approach: perhaps too long for a book aimed at introducing social science methods and methodologies. We risked such a long introduction because basic Rankean spadework lies at the bottom of all social scientific work, whatever its methodological point of departure. Also, social scientists can only benefit by paying close attention to the historian's high standards of referencing. For reasons such as these, we need to know how historians approach their subject. In particular, we have used the above review to show how the historian provides naturalists with the very nuts and bolts of everyday social science. Aided by the historical method, the naturalist can accumulate solid facts (like Descartes examining each apple for potential rot before returning it to the barrel), with which subsequent scientific arguments can be constructed.

We can now proceed to an introduction of how these historical 'techniques' are used by social scientists of the naturalist persuasion. To do this, we need to return to the basic ontological and epistemological precepts of naturalism. In Chapter 2 we outlined this methodology in terms of several basic components: for example, a willingness to distinguish between normative and objective statements about the world; an understanding that there exist regularities or patterns in nature that can be observed and described; that statements based on these regularities can be tested empirically; that human knowledge is cumulative; and that knowledge is singular.

It must be said at the outset that many of these claims make the traditional historian blush. After all, much of modern history can be contrasted against the social science project; we doubt that the debates about 'methodological naturalism' or 'methodological unity' have made much headway into the historian's den. Indeed, it is remarkable how little explicit reference there is to history in Edward O. Wilson's book, *Consilience*: his table of contents explicitly aims to integrate the social sciences, the arts, ethics and religion into a natural science framework, but the study of history is conspicuously missing.

To put it bluntly, what distinguishes the social scientist from the historian is his willingness (or perhaps audacity or honesty) to employ deductive frameworks to 'tease' out lessons from the historical record. For social scientists, it is almost axiomatic that comparison is both possible and fruitful (although they may disagree on the appropriate unit of comparison); many historians do not easily accept a comparative framework that extends beyond a single historical period, nation or culture.

The reader might think of these differences in terms of responses to the building which houses the Pompidou Centre in Paris; a building where the functional skeleton is itself on display. Historians, we argue, prefer the form of an argument to conceal its function; social scientists, in contrast, prefer the opposite. If this is the case, then historians should recoil from any suggestion that writers and builders alike should proudly place elevators, plumbing, wiring and ductwork on the outside of their edifice. Social scientists, on the other hand, may celebrate this as honest progress. In short, historians do not differ from social scientists in questioning the need for such structures; the two groups only differ in their need, or desire, to exhibit them. Social scientists love to display their ductwork. Historians find this inelegant; their taste runs to more traditional architecture.

This is, of course, another exaggeration (let's call it a rule of thumb): some of the best historians have relied on explicit comparative and analytical frameworks with great effect. The work of Marc Bloch (1953, 1967) is exemplary in this regard. On the other end of the spectrum, many naturalist-minded social scientists rely on the methods of historiography. Still, we do not think it is an exaggeration to argue that the social scientist aims for broader theoretical statements and relies on a more formal, explicitly conceptual, apparatus that is more self-consciously selective of the facts.

It is in this context that the case study enters at the lowest, foundational, step in the naturalist's hierarchy of methods. Case studies are histories with a point. They are 'cases' of something – and the thing under study is interesting, relevant, or 'in focus' because of a larger theoretical concern or a specific research design. Although case studies often draw on the techniques of historical scholarship, history itself is usually employed as a database for the construction and testing of theories. The naturalist tradition is leery of case studies, as it believes that studying a single case can only yield one reasonable theoretical outcome. King et al. (1994, p. 211) don't mince words on this account: 'the single observation is not a useful technique for testing hypotheses or theories'.

Types of Case Studies

In spite of the case study's relatively low stature among naturalist social scientists, it remains one of the most frequently employed research designs. Case studies are used in all the social sciences and are employed in a remarkably large number of different ways. Indeed, an entire book (Ragin and Becker, 1992) has been dedicated to debating the definitions of, selections of, and criteria for evaluating cases in social scientific enquiry.

This cross-disciplinary variety of definitions and applications of case studies has resulted in an equally large literature aimed at providing case study typologies. From this literature we choose one influential typology (Lijphart, 1971) to show the variety of different roles that case studies can play when lined up along an imaginary continuum stretching from descriptive to theoretical designs.

Lijphart (1971, p. 691) distinguishes between six types of case study:

1   atheoretical case studies;
2   interpretive case studies;
3   hypothesis-generating case studies;
4   theory-confirming case studies;
5   theory-infirming case studies;
6   deviant case studies.

The first two types of case studies are uninteresting for the naturalist, as cases are examined because of an interest in the case per se. In *atheoretical* or *interpretive* case studies there need not be a generalizing dimension to the cases. Consequently, they fit uncomfortably with the analytical ambitions of the naturalists (though they would be gleefully embraced by historians). The last three types (*theory-confirming*, *theory-infirming*, and *deviant* case studies) are case studies that aim to test an existing hypothesis or theory. It is this type of case study that fits most easily under the naturalist's rubric. To economize somewhat, we combine the theory-infirming and the deviant cases into a single category, called 'mis-fitting' in the discussion below.

The third type (*hypothesis-generating*) is a little bit different. Its aim is to use a case to help formulate definite hypotheses or theories (for further subsequent testing). Although naturalists loathe to generate theories (or to generalize broadly) on the basis of a single case, they can recognize the heuristic value of case studies. Indeed, as we shall see, the utility of this type of case can be seen an example that Hempel himself embraced.

Thus, we find it convenient to distinguish between three types of case studies: fitting, mis-fitting and generalizing. The typical features of each type come from the way in which it connects up to general propositions or theory.

Fitting or Theory-confirming Case Studies

'Fitting' or 'theory-confirming' case studies investigate the degree to which a given case fits a general proposition. These types of case studies tend to provide descriptive frameworks based on existing conceptual schemes. In other words, this design serves to demonstrate the explanatory power of a particular theory. In a 'fitting' exercise, a case is chosen as an empirical venue for applying a particular theory. As such, this type of case study tends to be less ambitious than its more critical brethren (the mis-fitting case). In short, it is illustrative. It resembles an attempt to verify a given theory, in a way not unlike the 'verification' principle introduced by the Vienna Circle (see Chapter 2).

As Karl Popper pointed out (whenever he could), early Marxist historiography is rife with examples of this type of 'fitting'. Committed socialists would regularly study historical events and then demonstrate how they conformed to – and confirmed – the Marxist theory of historical materialism. Some of the more obvious examples were written by party intellectuals and published by party presses. Others are far more subtle and possess high scholarly qualities. One case in point is the work by the famous French historian Albert Soboul. He occupied the prestigious chair of the French Revolution at the Sorbonne for many years, and studied the French Revolution from a Marxist perspective. His doctoral dissertation from 1958 on the Parisian sans-culottes, is a study of the 'revolution from below' – over a thousand pages of deep and detailed analysis of popular revolutionary movements in Paris during one year of the phase of Terror. Conservative critics have insisted that his work strayed far and wide from the Rankean ideal; that Soboul's (1958, 1962) influential books were not objective history at all but, rather, an application of Marxist social theory to the causes and courses of the French Revolution. A similar criticism has been levied against the immensely popular books of Eric Hobsbawm (most notably his famous trilogy: *The Age of Revolution, The Age of Capital* and *The Age of Empire*).

One of the most common applications of a fitting case strategy is what Harry Eckstein referred to as a *plausibility probe*. In a world with limited resources, Eckstein suggests that researchers might choose to run a sort of trial test of a given theory on a particular case (before investing too much time and money into a full-blown test): 'In essence, plausibility probes involve attempts to determine whether potential validity may reasonably be considered great enough to warrant the pains and costs of testing, which are almost always considerable, but especially so if broad, painstaking, comparative studies are undertaken' (Eckstein, 1975, p. 108).

Eckstein's reasoning was clear. If it is possible to find a case that 'fits' or illustrates a particular general proposition or claim, it may have some scholarly promise. Consequently, it might be worthwhile to pursue the claim and perhaps develop it into a full-fledged theory. This is what plausibility probes aim to accomplish.

Mis-fitting, Theory-infirming or Deviant Case Studies

Whereas 'fitting' case studies seek to demonstrate how a case fits a general proposition, the 'mis-fitting' case study seeks to show how a case does *not* easily fit a general or a universal claim. In Lijphart's (1971, p. 691) typology, mis-fitting cases correspond to his theory-infirming (case studies that weaken a theory marginally) and deviant cases (case studies where cases are known to deviate from established generalizations). In this way, the mis-fitting case employs a logic that mimics that of the falsification principle associated with Popper. A well-chosen case can provide strong support for, or falsify, a given theory. The point is to choose a case which is, in theory, falsifiable and which tests a central theoretical claim.

A good example is Mark Peceny's (1997) study of the Spanish–American War. Peceny's theoretical vantage point is the popular 'democratic peace' theory – a voluminous literature that links democratic governance with peace. This posited relationship between the two variables, 'democracy' and 'peace', is so strong that it encouraged Levy (1989, p. 270) to refer to it as the nearest 'we have to an empirical law in international relations'. In the context of such strong theoretical expectations, Peceny chose to study a case where the co-relation does *not* hold; a case which seems to challenge the democratic peace contention. Democratic peace theory claims that democracies do not go to war against other democracies. By the standards of the late nineteenth century, both the

USA and Spain are considered to be democracies – yet war broke out between them in 1898. Peceny examined this case with an eye to testing the validity of different strands of the democratic peace literature.

Peceny finds that only one particular version of the democratic peace literature can explain the outbreak of the Spanish–American War – a version he calls the 'constructivist' theory. This theory invokes the power of global norms and shared international identities to account for the peaceful relationship between democracies. Peceny shows how Spain in 1898 did not share these global norms nor any form of common identity with the United States; indeed, the USA did not really consider Spain to be a liberal democracy. Hence none of the solidarity-building mechanisms that tend to maintain openness, dialogue and a will to compromise among democratic governments existed in the Spanish–American case. Thus, when conflict increased and the threat of war presented itself, there were no mechanisms to prevent war from breaking out. The outcome of Peceny's argument is twofold. First, he can explain the outbreak of the Spanish–American War – and do so in light of a general theory. Second, Peceny singles out one particular version of the democratic peace theory and shows how its explanatory power outperforms other versions of the same theory. As a consequence, Peceny can use the Spanish–American case to refine and deepen the general proposition of democratic peace theory.

By employing either fitting or mis-fitting types of case studies, it is possible to anchor the case study approach firmly in the naturalist tradition. Indeed, one of that tradition's central philosophical contributors, Carl Gustav Hempel, explicitly embraced historical explanations, as long as they followed his simple definition of science. As the attentive reader will recall, Hempel held that scientific explanations invoke a universal law and a description of relevant conditions. This kind of explanation has become known as 'Hempel's covering law'. All meaningful questions can be given scientific answers in accordance with this covering law, Hempel averred.

This covering law is broad enough that even historians can find shelter there. All historians need to do is to heed the advice of John Stuart Mill (2002, pp. 549ff.): they must relate their events-specific arguments to regularities and laws. After all, argues Hempel:

> Historical explanation, too, aims at showing that the event in question was not a 'matter of chance', but was to be expected in view of certain antecedents or simultaneous conditions. The explanations referred to is not prophesy or divination, but rational scientific anticipation which rests on the assumptions of general laws. (Hempel, 1942, p. 39)

Generalizing Case Studies

While the first two types of case studies lean heavily on the deductive side of the inductive–deductive model introduced in Chapter 2 (more precisely in Figure 2.3), it is possible to use case studies in ways that lend themselves to the inductive side of the same figure. In short, case studies can be used to generate hypotheses. They can even – on more ambitious occasions – give room for theory building. These are what Lijphart (1971) referred to as 'hypothesis-generating case studies', or what Eckstein (1975, pp. 104ff.) called 'heuristic case studies'. These studies exploit the author's familiarity with a given case to help generate new hypotheses or theories, which can be subsequently tested in a more rigorous design.

Given the complex nature of the relationship between an analyst's familiarity with the empirical terrain and his capacity for theory building, Eckstein (1975, p. 104) – following Becker (1968) – suggests we should think about these types of cases in terms of 'building blocks'. The analyst studies a given case to generate a preliminary theoretical construct. Because this construct is based on a single case, it can do little more than hint at a more valid general model. This model, then, is confronted with another case – which, in turn, might suggest ways of amending and improving the construct. These cases can then be assembled, like building blocks, into a stronger theoretical edifice. While this sort of inductive procedure may appear to be antithetical to the sort of covering law approach advocated by Hempel, a closer look at his own examples might suggest that there is room for generalizing case studies in the naturalist tradition.

One of the scientific explanations that Hempel included in his comparison of several indubitable scientific explanations (cf. Chapter 2) was clearly inductive. The example begins with some thoughts that the American philosopher, John Dewey, made one day in 1908, as he was washing dishes. Dewey noticed that when he had washed the glasses and placed them on a tray, small bubbles emerged from under the edge of each glass. These bubbles grew in size for a few seconds, before they became smaller again and finally disappeared altogether. Dewey observed how this pattern repeated itself with each new glass that he placed on the tray. From these observations he developed an explanation.

The glasses were washed in hot water, to which dishwashing soap was added. When a dirty glass was immersed in the sink, it was both covered in soapy water and heated up. When washed, and lifted out of the water, the glasses trapped cold air as they were moved to the tray and placed upside down to drain. This would cause dishwater to collect on the tray. After a few glasses had been placed on the tray, newly arriving glasses – wet, warm, and filled with cold air – were placed in the accumulated water on the tray. The air inside would be heated by the warm glass that surrounded it. Since heated air expands, it would be pressed under the edge of the glass. And since the glasses were placed upside down on a watery tray, the escaping air would pass through a thin layer of water – where it was trapped by a thin film of soap. As a result, the escaping air created soap bubbles around the rim of the newly washed glasses. After a short while, however, the glasses on the tray would cool. As they did, the air inside them would also cool; consequently, the air inside them would no longer expand and the bubbles would no longer grow. Indeed, as the glasses cooled the air trapped inside would contract, creating an under-pressure inside the glass and causing the bubble-trapped air to return to inside the class.

Dewey wrote down this explanation – and he did so in great detail. The reason for this detailed description was not that his causal reasoning was a great philosophical insight. Rather, he realized that he had constructed a good scientific explanation. The musings that began with soap suds in 1908 grew to a book-length manuscript published in 1910 under the title *How We Think*. Here Dewey explains that he wrote down his soap-bubble theory because it represented a typical *case* of a scientific explanation. He also realized that if he analysed this explanation, and managed to isolate its distinctly scientific qualities, then he could understand what it was that characterized scientific explanations in general! In other words, Dewey sought to induce general claims on the basis of one case.

Hempel, in turn, found Dewey's argument so enlightening that he included it among his own cases of scientific explanation. By elaborating on Dewey's argument, Hempel formulated his influential definition of a 'scientific explanation' as an explanation that invokes a universal law and includes a description of relevant conditions under which the law(s) is (are) valid. Together, these components – the law and the relevant conditions – constitute the premises (the *explanans*) from which an explanatory statement (*explanandum*) could be deduced (see Figure 2.5 above). In effect, Hempel would have to acknowledge that it is legitimate to induce a hypothesis from a single case, as this is precisely what Dewey did, with great effect! And it affected Hempel's very definition of science.

At this point, however, we are coming close to the edge of what naturalists can embrace in case studies. Before we cross over that border, we can summarize the different ways in which naturalists employ case studies. This is done in Table 6.1. Here you will find a description of the main functions associated with each type of case study, as well as examples from two prominent comparativists (Arendt Lijphart and Harry Eckstein).

Table 6.1   *Three types of case studies*

Type	Function	Logic	Corresponds to Lijphart (1971)	Corresponds to Eckstein (1975)
Fitting	Illustrate a general proposition	Verification	Atheoretical Interpretive	Configurative–idiographic Plausibility probes
Mis-fitting	Explore the limits of a general proposition; theory-testing	Falsification	Theory-confirming Theory-infirming Deviant	Crucial case
Generalizing	Generate hypotheses and theory building	Cumulation	Hypothesis-generating	Heuristic

As we have already seen in Chapter 2, naturalist social science is strongly indebted to Popper and Hempel, both of whom leaned heavily on the principle of deduction. For this tradition, induction cannot produce reliable knowledge; attempts to generalize on the basis of a single case are seen to be risky endeavours indeed. Having said this, it is useful to note a simple truth. While the likes of Hempel and Popper do not trust induction to produce general truths in any case, they do not really care where hypotheses come from, as long they can be tested for veracity. For this reason, induction should not be rejected out of hand; we just need to lower our analytical sights. There is nothing to prevent a scholar from inducing a general proposition on the basis of deep familiarity with a single case, and run the risk of his statement being proven false. Indeed, in practice, general social science statements are often induced from single cases. In so doing, however, scholars do not – of course – present these inductions as true statements; they present them as hypotheses. And hypotheses, as we know from previous chapters, are tentative statements. They are created for the explicit purpose of being tested.

Conclusion

Case studies, in their sundry forms, are frequently used to test and apply various types of theories. Indeed, case study tests are most appreciated when the theories being tested involve complex relationships. At the same time, case studies provide the analyst with a familiarity of detail and context that lends itself to developing new theories.

In principle, there is a great difference separating historical studies from case studies; so great, in fact, that case studies can be counted as science (because they have a generalizing purpose), while history cannot (for the very same reason: it lacks a generalizing purpose). In practice, however, the difference between them is slight. After all, good histories and good case studies both rely on the same method: Ranke's method of *Quellenkritik*.

As we have endeavoured to show, a case study relies on the historical method. Yet, it is something more. A case study is a case of something. It points beyond the object immediately at hand. It seeks to move from a purely empirical level of exposition to a level of general statements. A history of the French revolution seeks to set the revolutionary events straight. A case study of the French revolution aims higher. If it covers the entire revolution, its ambition is to say something about revolutions in general. If it only discusses an aspect of the revolution, its ambition is to assess that aspect in general.

In practice, case studies force the analyst to jump right in the middle of the methodological muddle. The analyst's nearness to the empirical detail and his heavy reliance on theory mean that he is constantly forced to address the sundry ways in which theoretical claims and empirical evidence often collide. As a result, case study researchers need to be extremely careful about their research design, objectives and case selection.

This concern and focus is – itself – evident in our desire to emphasize the various ways that case studies use different theories, and are used in different research designs. Because of their nearness to the empirical detail, practitioners of case studies are often forced to be much more conscious and explicit about the way in which they engage their theories, design their research programmes, and choose their cases. Case study researchers tend to be more aware of the practical limitations of dividing scientific work into deductive and inductive projects. As a result, case studies tend to involve, in complex ways, a combination of scientific objectives: including both theory development and theory testing.

While case studies provide the researcher with a more direct experience of the interplay between theory and data, and a credibility that is itself derived from the researcher's familiarity with context, these qualities are the very handicap that limits the case study's appeal to the broader community of naturalist social scientists. In particular, the focus on single cases makes it difficult to test hypotheses in systematic and complex ways against empirical evidence beyond the specific case in question. It is for this reason that the case study method remains at the bottom of the naturalists' hierarchy of methods.

To close this chapter we draw on two insightful quotes. The first is from Arend Lijphart. It eloquently summarizes the awkward, but important, role of case studies in the naturalist's social scientific project:

> The great advantage of the case study is that by focusing on a single case, that case can be intensively examined even when the research resources at the investigator's disposal are relatively limited. The scientific status of the case study method is somewhat ambiguous, however, because science is a generalizing activity. A single case can constitute neither the basis of a valid generalization nor the ground for disproving an established generalization.   (Lijphart, 1971, p. 691)

The second closing quote can be traced to Hempel, as he – more than anybody else in this chapter – provides us with a strong anchoring tether to the solid ground of naturalist social science. But Hempel can, as attested to in the quote that follows, also function as a bridge to the constructivist approach in the second half of this book:

[In] history no less than in any other branch of empirical inquiry, scientific explanation can be achieved only by means of suitable general hypotheses, or by theories, which are bodies of systematically related hypotheses. This thesis is clearly in contrast with the familiar view that genuine explanation in history is obtained by a method which characteristically distinguishes the social from the natural sciences, namely *the method of empathetic understanding.* The historian, we are told, imagines himself in the place of the persons involved in the events which he wants to explain; he tries to realize as completely as possible the circumstances under which they acted, and the motives which influenced their actions; and by this imaginary self-identification with his heroes, he arrives at an understanding and thus at an adequate explanation of the events with which he is concerned. (Hempel, 1942, p. 44)

Recommended Further Reading

As Hempel's 'The Function of General Laws in History' (1942) ties history to the naturalist science project, it is a good place to start. There are a number of good and well-written introductions to historiography – we recommend Elton's *The Practice of History* (1967) and Evans's *In Defence of History* (1997). Finally, there are several very good introductions to case studies in social science. Among them, the inquisitive reader might look at Eckstein's 'Case Study and Theory in Political Science' (1975); Lijphart's 'Comparative Politics and the Comparative Method' (1971); Ragin and Becker's *What is a Case?* (1992); Burton's 'The Use of Case Studies in Social Science Research' (2000); and Yin's *Case Study Research: Designs and Methods* (1994).

Chapter 7

Sowing Doubts about the Naturalist Methodology

So far, the discussion has been rather straightforward and mainstream. Our intention has been to provide a firm and common starting point – familiar to social scientists in a wide range of subject areas – from which to proceed. We hope that our depiction of this mainstream tradition is reasonable, as both of us – to varying degrees – locate our own research programmes within it. In short, we are trying hard to avoid creating a straw man for what is easily the hegemonic methodological tradition in social science.

Still – and despite its hegemonic status – it is possible to raise doubts about important elements in this methodological tradition, and reasonable people voice these doubts in different ways. As students of social phenomena, it behooves us to understand the nature and bases of these doubts before we decide on an appropriate strategy for dealing with them. Some of us find these doubts to be serious enough that they encourage us to explore alternative methodological vantage points: these scholars refuse to be caught in what is seen as the methodological straitjacket of the naturalist approach. Beginning with the next chapter, Chapter 8, the remainder of the book outlines one such methodological alternative: a constructivist approach to study the social world.

Others among us caution against throwing the baby out with the bathwater. Recognizing important shortcomings to the naturalists' approach does not mean that we must jettison the whole naturalist project *in toto*. From this view, raising doubts about particular shortcomings might make it possible to modify the naturalist approach in ways that will strengthen its analytical powers or more accurately delineate the areas in which it works best.

This chapter is written with both audiences in mind. In a sense, this chapter functions as the book's fulcrum, upon which the naturalist and constructivist approaches teeter. In particular, we aim to show how sensible people can hold different opinions about the nature of social reality, and that these different ontological positions lend themselves to new epistemologies that are less beholden to the naturalist tradition. We conclude the chapter with a call for methodological pluralism, the motto for which might be summed up in a quote from Albert Einstein (1953, p. 38): 'Whoever undertakes to set himself up as a judge in the field of Truth and Knowledge is shipwrecked by the laughter of the gods.'

The chapter itself is divided into three sections, each of which sows seeds of doubt in a particular aspect of the naturalist approach. We hope to bring these seeds to fruition in the chapters that follow. The first section looks at some of the most troubling ontological assumptions that underlie the naturalist approach. The second section questions the strong empiricist basis to naturalist epistemology (in light of the ontological doubts raised in the first section). As ontological, epistemological and methodological issues are intricately related to one another, the final section ties these ontological and epistemological doubts together in a way that allows us to open up the methodological foundations of the naturalist approach.

It is important for us to reiterate why we sow these doubts. It is *not* our ambition to undermine the naturalist approach; nor do we proselytize for any methodological alternative. Our intent is much broader than promoting one particular approach over another: we wish to present different methodological approaches (in ways that expose both potential and faults) so that students can best decide which approach is most appropriate. Personally, we find the world is big enough, complicated enough and curious enough to accommodate several competing views of social reality.

Ontological Doubts

Since Chapter 2 we have granted several important naturalist assumptions. Most important of these are: (1) that there exists a Real World out there; (2) that this World exists independent of our interrogation of it; and (3) that it is patterned or orderly. We have trusted the arguments of John Stuart Mill and others, and accepted the claim that the world is characterized by patterns and regularities. This trust has not been blind or frivolous. After all, there can be no doubting that these ontological assumptions have yielded great rewards. Elaborate theories, grounded in these assumptions, have taught us much about our world and allowed us to master many aspects of our universe. It is difficult to imagine sending a rocket to the moon, building an artificial heart, or connecting the world together in a dense network of computers, without theories that rest on these important ontological assumptions.

Nevertheless, doubts about these assumptions have a long and influential pedigree. Most famously, perhaps, Plato argued forcefully for the ephemeral and unreliable nature of the material world (and knowledge that is derived from it). Indeed, it is worth recalling that many of the naturalist approach's founding fathers did not take the material world for granted: most notably, René Descartes and David Hume both struggled with the nature of reality, and its relationship to a benevolent God.

In order to consider the meaning of such doubts with respect to social science research, we can organize them under two headings: doubts about the realness of the natural world, and doubts about the realness of the social world. For obvious reasons, we want to spend most of our time addressing the latter type of doubts.

The Natural World

Assumptions about patterns in the world are most common (and more reasonable) in the natural sciences. It is not controversial to suggest that hydrogen's relationship to oxygen is relatively fixed in a given context; it is more difficult to say the same about, say, Islam and democracy. After all, it is in the natural world that the naturalist ontology was born, and it is in this context that it clearly thrives. Still, even here, it is possible to raise doubts about whether the basic ontological assumptions of naturalism hold at all levels of the physical world. These doubts can be raised at two levels: one metaphysical, the other physical.

At a metaphysical and religious level, it is easy to question assumptions about the existence of an ordered nature – in other words, that the Real World consists of regularities, patterns and recurrences. As we have already noted on several occasions, this assumption is absolutely crucial to the naturalist's endeavour: it allows scientists to formulate universal laws, and to employ inductive methods in their search to uncover them. This assumption was easier to accept at a time when the scientific community believed in the existence of an all-powerful God, who – himself – could be held responsible for the order that scientists sought to uncover. In the era after which Nietzsche (among others) proclaimed that God is dead, it may be less convenient to assume that the world is characterized by an underlying order. For Nietzsche (1967, p. 113, emphasis his), anyway, 'our attitude toward God as some alleged spider of purpose and morality behind the great captious web of causality, is *hubris*'. Without the convenience of a Great Designer or Conductor, does it make sense to assume that the world is still characterized by an underlying order?

But ontological doubts needn't always sprout from metaphysical terrain. There are also empirical grounds for doubting the existence of universal laws and patterns in nature. Because we are not physical or natural scientists, we turn to another, more authoritative, voice to tell us about how physicists have come to raise their own ontological doubts over the last century. Fritjof Capra (1982, p. 76), the distinguished physicist from the University of California, Berkeley, tells us:

> This exploration of the atomic and subatomic world brought scientists in contact with a strange and unexpected reality that shattered the foundations of their world view and forced them to think in entirely new ways. Nothing like that had ever happened before in science. Revolutions like those of Copernicus and Darwin had introduced profound changes in the general conception of the universe, changes that were shocking to many people, but the new concepts themselves were not difficult to grasp. In the twentieth century, however, physicists faced, for the first time, a serious challenge to their ability to understand the universe. Every time they asked nature a question in an atomic experiment, nature answered with a paradox, and the more they tried to clarify this new reality, scientists became painfully aware that their basic concepts, their language, and their whole way of thinking were inadequate to describe atomic phenomena. Their problem was not only intellectual but involved an intense emotional and existential experience, as vividly described by Werner Heisenberg: 'I remember discussion with Bohr which went through many hours till very late at night and ended almost in despair; and when at the end of the discussion I went alone for a walk in the neighboring park I repeated to myself again and again the question: Can nature possibly be so absurd as it seemed to us in these atomic experiments.'

This is not the place to introduce Heisenberg's uncertainty principle.[1] We simply wish to show how an important swath of the physical sciences has called into question some of the ontological assumptions associated with naturalism. Nor is this sort of doubt confined to quantum physics. In the realm of Chaos Theory, for example, certain physical processes (for example, turbulent gaseous and liquid flow, population dynamics in predatory prey species, multiple mechanical collisions, and so on) have shown themselves hesitant to abide by universal laws, even when their behaviour is wholly deterministic.

In short, natural scientists increasingly acknowledge that their world of study may not be characterized by the universal laws and patterns that have traditionally anchored their ontological point of departure – at least not at all levels of inquiry. Over time, the religious context of science has changed in ways that make it less compelling to assume a patterned logic to nature. Finally, there is an increased realization that the world is a very complicated and complex place.

The Social World

Since the very beginning of social science, concerns have been voiced about whether approaches to studying the natural world were applicable to studies of the social world – concerns which have only grown with the realization that some of the basic ontological assumptions don't seem to hold, even in the natural world. Still, for many observers, the natural and social worlds are inherently different, and this difference is obvious: people, unlike particles, think. The subjects of social studies are self-aware, reflexive, creative and intentional: they rationalize their actions; they are motivated by purpose; and they enjoy a certain freedom of action. All of these inherently human capacities make it possible to doubt whether mechanistic assumptions about natural patterns in the real world make sense when studying the social world.

Once we open a fissure between the social and natural worlds, we can begin to see how patterns in the social world might appear as fleeting, subjective and even unreal to the careful observer. Sceptics among us begin to wonder if the patterns we observe are not of our own doing.

This possibility is evident in the way in which the world seems to have changed following Samuel Huntington's extremely influential 'Clash of Civilizations' argument (1993, 1996). Writing after the end of the Cold War, when it was still entirely unclear as to what post-Cold War international politics would look like, Huntington proposed that a new international cleavage was developing across civilizations. At the time when Huntington's argument was first introduced, few observers would have been willing to recognize the existence (or importance) of such civilizational cleavages. In contrast, many of our students find in Huntington an accurate depiction of the nature of today's international community (as witnessed by the terrorist attack of 11 September 2001, and America's subsequent wars in Afghanistan and Iraq).

Herein lie several important ontological points of inquiry. The first has already been mentioned: is the international community characterized by a division along civilizational lines? (Framed in other words: What is the nature of the subject we study?) If the answer to this question is yes, we are led to another series of related questions: Is this pattern constant? Has it always been there? If not, why has it become so obvious now? In addressing these questions, we might begin to wonder whether Huntington's very observation was an important factor in bringing this pattern to life (or relevance). Given Huntington's stature and influence in the field of political science (and among policy makers), it is conceivable that his argument became a self-fulfilling prophesy (rather than a remarkable prediction, based on solid evidence and theory). Perhaps the world *is* as we see it, because a respected authority has told us to see the world in this way.

At this point, we should note that we are not talking about a problem with faulty definitions and/or operationalizations[2] (as was first brought to our attention by J. S. Mill and Émile Durkheim, both of whom were concerned with the confusion that results from faulty and overlapping definitions). Indeed, attempts to apply very precise definitions to a social phenomenon often help us reveal the remarkable way that our understanding and perception of social concepts tends to change over time and across space.

Consider democracy. Until the end of the eighteenth century, democracy was generally assumed to be an unattractive form of government: it was mob rule. Then, in the wake of the American and French revolutions, the promise of democracy became more obvious, and its institutions spread at a remarkable pace – so much so that Freedom House (2000) labelled the twentieth century 'The Democratic Century'. Yet early critics of democracy would hardly recognize today's states as democratic: they were, in fact, looking at different beasts. After all, modern democratic states have nothing that looks like the 'rule of the people' (in Greek, δημος, *demos*, means the people; κρατειν, *kratein*, means rule; hence 'democracy' = 'rule of the people'). Indeed, when we look closely at the way social scientists measure (for example, Polity IV, 2005; Freedom House, 2005) or conceptualize (for example, Schumpeter, 1950; Dahl, 1971; Downs, 1957) democracy today, there is remarkably little focus on the degree to which the people participate in governing themselves. It is for this reason that John Dunn (2005, p. 18) claims: 'When any modern state claims to be a democracy it necessarily misdescribes itself.'

Our point is not to belittle empirical research on democracy, but to note how the things we study can change in appearance when viewed from different contexts and perspectives. Indeed, recognizing the constructed nature of social reality is the starting point for many postmodern approaches, which aim to rid social inquiry of rigid assumptions about fixed identities. In most cases, this ontological pluralism (or nihilism) can be traced back to Friedrich Nietzsche (1844–1900). From Nietzsche's view of consciousness, the world is fundamentally disordered: there is no intelligible world to be known. To the extent that we find the world intelligible, it is a result of the observer imposing her intelligibility platelet on the subject.

Michel Foucault (1984, p. 127) has popularized this position among contemporary social scientists by arguing:

> We must not imagine that the world turns toward us a legible face which we would have only to decipher; the world is not the accomplice of our knowledge; there is no prediscursive providence which

disposes the world in our favor. We must conceive discourse as a violence which we do to things, or in any case as a practice which we impose on them.

Each of us has these 'illegible' faces. You and we, our football club, our political party and our nation (to name just a few examples) have multiple identities. You might consider yourself a student, a sailor, a drinker, a denizen of the world, a mother, and any number of other (perhaps more private) things. You can be all of these things, at different times, in different places, to different audiences.

Larry Preston (1995) has made this point in one of the most readable pieces ever published in the *American Political Science Review*. Preston is mostly concerned with how the voices of the marginalized are appropriated and perverted by scholars who allegedly represent them. His personal anecdote of a return to the hospital in which he worked as a younger man shows how identity can be triggered by representations (here by clothing). As a young man, working as a janitor in the local hospital, Preston was consciously aware of how 'invisible' he was to the hospital staff. As a janitor he was unimportant. Later, as a professor, he happened to return to the hospital – this time armed in the professional's body armour of suit and tie. The staff's reaction to him was now one of respect and acknowledgement. He was a different person now, an important person.

These sorts of flexible identities exist at all levels. Norway, as a nation, can be many things to many observers: a just social democratic state; a homogenous and xenophobic fortress of white-dom; a voice for environmentalism and human rights in the world community; the slaughterer of whales; home of the reluctant Europeans . . . These competing (even conflicting) identities make Norway difficult to study with a methodological approach that assumes the existence of a single and fixed object of study.

If we accept that signals and interpretations can vary from time to time, or from context to context, then it becomes increasingly difficult to be certain about the realness, the concreteness, the singularity of the objects/actions that we are surveying as social scientists. Recognizing this, however, does not leave the analyst helplessly stranded on the sidelines. These very 'weaknesses' (in the eyes of the naturalists) can be turned, judo-like, to the analyst's advantage. Meaning, understanding, empathy and purpose become keys to understanding when simple observation escapes us.

To conclude this section, it is possible to raise doubts about three central ontological assumptions associated with the naturalist approach. First, it is clear that some law-like patterns exist in nature, and that these can be exploited to great advantage. But it is not at all clear whether it is reasonable to assume that the social world can (or should be) characterized in this way. Second, there are sufficient reasons to doubt that the social world exists as a single entity – equally accessible to any observer with the proper instruments and attitude. The social world seems less certain, more contingent, and capable of presenting itself in many different forms. Finally, given the role of agency and meaning in human activity, there may be good reasons to doubt whether the social world exists independent of its interrogator. Indeed, one might even see this as a major justification for doing what we do. In the words of Thomas Schelling (1978, p. 19):

> Social scientists are more like forest rangers than like naturalists. The naturalist can be interested in what causes a species to be extinct, without caring whether or not it does become extinct. (If it has been extinct for a million years his curiosity is truly without concern.) The ranger will be concerned with whether or not the buffalo do disappear, and how to keep them in a healthy balance with their environment.

Social scientists study the social world with the aim of improving it. We hope to exploit the patterns we discover. It is for this reason that we seek to understand the true nature of these patterns, and employ the appropriate epistemological techniques for comprehending those patterns. It is to these techniques we now turn.

Epistemological Doubts

Once we relax some of these (naturalist) assumptions, and consider the possibility that some of the social world's apparent patterns might not be universal, natural and independent of our observations, we immediately become aware of the limitations associated with the naturalists' reliance on an empiricist epistemology. In a world that reveals itself in so many complex ways, can observation alone be sufficient for understanding it? The limits of the naturalist epistemological approach can be grouped under three headings, concerning the role of: presuppositions; meaning; and scientific authority. These limitations, in turn, provide support for alternative epistemological traditions – less anchored in the empiricist tradition. To illustrate the power of alternative epistemological traditions, we close the section with an example.

Presuppositions

The first epistemological doubt arises from the role of presuppositions in framing our empirical investigations. Today, this position is associated with Robin W. Collingwood (although earlier authors, in particular Immanuel Kant [1787], play an important role in getting the ball rolling). In his *Essay on Metaphysics*, Collingwood (1962 [1940], pp. 144ff.) argues against the (naïve scientific) view that it is possible to ascertain facts objectively by way of the senses, and to classify them by means of logical thought.

Facts themselves, he argues, are historical phenomena: they are man-made, a function of a concept or vision of the world. Actually, Collingwood's argument is evident in the very etymology of the word itself: 'fact' is derived from the Latin *facere*, which means 'to make'. This logic is also evident in other languages whose word for 'fact' is not so directly derived from the Latin root. In French, for example, a fact is *un fait*, from the verb *faire* ('to make'). In Spanish, a fact is *un hecho*, from the verb *hacer* (again, 'to make'). In Italian: *un fatto* (from the verb *fare*, 'to make'). In German a fact is *das Faktum* or *die Tatsache* (*Sache* = 'matter', 'fact'); *Tat* = deed, from the verb *zu tun* ('to make' – literally: a thing that is made).

As facts are historical phenomena, observations of them (and the classifications that follow) depend critically on what Collingwood called *presuppositions*. The notion of presuppositions is really very simple – and this simplicity is the main reason we use Collingwood (rather than, for example, Kant) to illustrate this important epistemological point. Collingwood discovers this point on the open sea; on a voyage made to improve his failing health. The first chapter of his *Essay on Metaphysics* was written aboard the motor vessel *Alcinous* and refers to a seemingly trivial event:

> I write these words sitting on the deck of a ship. I lift my eyes and see a piece of string – a line, I must call it at sea – stretched more or less horizontally above me. I find myself thinking 'that is a clothes-line', meaning that it was put there to hang washing on. When I decide that it was put there for that purpose I am presupposing that it was put there for some purpose. Only if that presupposition is made does the question arise, what purpose? If that presupposition were not made, if for example I had thought the line came there by accident, that question would not have arisen, and the situation in which I think 'that is a clothes-line' would not have occurred.   (Collingwood, 1962, p. 21)

In order to observe anything, Collingwood argues that we must observe it in relation to something – to some pre-existing criterion or condition. In other words, we must first have some idea of what we are supposed to see. Otherwise, the 'facts' under our noses make no sense to us.

In order to make the same important point to a group of his students, Karl Popper (1989) recalled that he once began a lecture with the following instructions:

'Take pencil and paper; carefully observe, and write down what you have observed!' They asked, of course, what I wanted them to observe. Clearly the instruction, 'Observe!' is absurd. (It is not even idiomatic, unless the object of the transitive verb can be taken as understood.) Observation is always selective. It needs a chosen object, a definite task, an interest, a point of view, a problem. And its description presupposes a descriptive language, with property words; it presupposes similarity and classification, which in their turn presuppose interests, points of view, and problems.

Popper, then, continued with another example:

'A hungry animal', writes Katz, 'divides the environment into edible and inedible things. An animal in flight sees roads to escape and hiding places . . . Generally speaking, objects change . . . according to the needs of the animal.' We may add that objects can be classified, and can become similar or dissimilar, only in this way – by being related to needs and interests. This rule applies not only to animals but also to scientists. For the animal a point of view is provided by its needs, the task of the moment, and its expectations; for the scientist by his theoretical interests, the special problem under investigation, his conjunctures and anticipations, and the theories which he accepts as a kind of background: his frame of reference, his 'horizon of expectations'. (Popper, 1989, pp. 61–2)

These presuppositions can give rise to different frames of reference for understanding the world. They raise doubts about the ability of sensory perception to guarantee objectivity – perceptions can be framed by presuppositions to help us see one of many potential faces of reality. It is in this light that Dick Sklar once noted, 'theories are conceived in ideological sin rather than scientific virtue' (cited in Geddes, 2003, p. 21).

There are numerous graphic examples that challenge this depiction of singular sensory interpretations. Hanson's (1961) book *Patterns of Discovery* is filled with amusing examples of how a picture can be interpreted in a variety of ways. Sometime in our life, each of us has probably seen one of a series of fun illusions that depict a pretty young maiden and an old hag (concomitantly). In Figure 7.1, we have reproduced the famous wife/mother-in-law illusion. As often appears to be the case (although neither one of us speaks from personal experience!), the wife

Figure 7.1   *Wife and mother-in-law*

Source: The original source of this picture (*left*) is said to be an anonymous German postcard from 1888. The picture was also used as part of an advertising campaign for the Anchor Buggy Company from 1890 (*right*).

of one's dreams can turn instantly into the mother-in-law from hell. Both creatures, it seems, coexist in the fragile frame at the alter.

As love would have it, we are – at first – drawn to the lovely wife. The unsightly mother-in-law (from within) escapes our detection. It is only after we are told that the mother-in-law actually exists (perhaps by our best mate), that we begin to see a different picture. Under this new investigatory light the other identity emerges.

Being told to look for a mother-in-law is akin to having a theory that tells you to search for something in the empirical data before you (as Sherlock Holmes knew what to look for in the mud outside Silver Blaze's stable). Indeed, as Martin Hollis (1994, p. 79) has it: 'Observation has become so bound up with interpretation and hence with theory that, in deciding what the facts of observation are, we may be deciding between rival theories.'

A wonderful example of this dilemma is found in the way that natural scientists have attempted to capture psychic 'talents'. Consider the highly publicized feats of Uri Geller in the 1970s. Geller was investigated and endorsed by several prominent scientists – although none of them actually witnessed his spoon-bending powers under controlled conditions. Remarkably, Geller convinced the investigating scientists that many of the control arrangements being suggested were 'aesthetically unappealing' and the scientific observers succumbed to this argument:

> To comprehend how such prominent scientists can paint themselves into such a corner we must view the situation from their perspective. When they wrote their article, they had already become convinced of Geller's paranormal powers. They realized that no such powers had ever yet survived scrutiny by scientific methods. From their perspective, then, the major task was to find a way to keep the powers they credited from fading under investigation. If they could find conditions that enabled the 'psychic' to produce his phenomena reliably in the laboratory, then they could later bring in the skeptics and use more traditional scientific methods.   (Hyman, 1989, p. 148)

This is a remarkable illustration of how the scientist's presuppositions affect the independence of her sensory perception.

Meaning

You may recall that we closed the last chapter with a quote from Hempel; a quote that deplored the fashion of using empathetic understanding (as opposed to empirical, scientific, inquiry) to explain historical events. The reason for the popularity of empathetic approaches is a recognition that the social world is saturated with meaning – meaning that can help the analyst understand actor motivation.

It is generally assumed that this extensive web of meaning is one of the most important differences that separate the natural and the social world. Richard Rorty, however, thinks this is a mistake: the natural world, too, is caught up in its own webs of significance and meaning:

> when it is said that 'interpretation begins from the postulate that the web of meaning constitutes human existence,' this suggests that fossils (for example) might get constituted *without* a web of meanings . . . To say that human beings wouldn't be human, would be animal, unless they talked a lot is true enough. If you can't figure out the relation between a person, the noises he makes, and other persons, then you won't know much about him. But one could equally well say that fossils wouldn't be fossils, would be merely rocks, if we couldn't grasp their relations to lots of other fossils. Fossils are constituted *as* fossils by a web of relationships to other fossils and to the speech of the paleontologists who describe such relationships.   (Rorty 1982, p. 199, emphasis his)

While it is relatively novel to argue for the existence of webs of meaning in the natural world, it should not be controversial to suggest that social and political agents have their own sets of ideas, self-understandings, wills and motivations . . . and that these factors influence the 'realness' of their actions. This understanding of the social world is often associated with Wilhelm Dilthey (1833–1911), who focused on the role of meaning in distinguishing between the natural and the social worlds. In particular, Dilthey held that the human world – unlike the natural world – can be understood with reference to different aspects of meaning (for example, purpose, value, ideal, and so on). The epistemological consequence of this is that social facts are not things which can be simply observed.

Recognizing this difference requires that we employ different epistemological approaches. Following William Outhwaite (1975, pp. 16–17), we might allow that:

> social phenomena and, in particular, human actions are not 'given' to the investigator in the same way as natural phenomena. The social scientist must begin with data which are already partially interpreted in the ordinary language of everyday life. Moreover, social scientists cannot coherently aim to provide a natural science of human life, but rather to deepen, systematize and often qualify, by means of empirical and conceptual investigations, an 'understanding' which is already present.

Most of us are familiar with the important role that meaning plays in interpreting everyday events. A classic example of this was made famous by Clifford Geertz in his introduction to *The Interpretation of Cultures*. Geertz refers to Ryle's discussion of 'thick description', where we are asked to consider:

> two boys rapidly contracting the eyelids of their right eyes. In one, this is an involuntary twitch; in the other, a conspiratorial signal to a friend. The two movements are, as movements, identical; from an I-am-a-camera, 'phenomenalistic' observation of them alone, one could not tell which was twitch and which was wink, or indeed whether both or either was twitch or wink. Yet the difference, however unphotographable, between a twitch and a wink is vast; as anyone unfortunate enough to have had the first taken for the second knows. (Geertz, 1993 [1973], p. 6)

To distinguish one meaning from the other, the observer has to interpret the phenomenon in its context. To the extent that naturalists embrace an 'I-am-a-camera' perspective (and we think this is a pretty good description of their empiricist epistemology), they will have trouble distinguishing between similar phenomena of this type. To distinguish one meaning from the other, the observer has to interpret the phenomenon in the constitutive context to which it is anchored. As a consequence, preserving and enhancing constitutive contexts must be a central objective for those who hope to employ meaning to explain social phenomena.

Scientific Authority

This brings us to our final epistemological challenge: the naturalist's reliance on scientific authority. As we noted in Chapter 2, the naturalist approach leans heavily on an empiricist epistemology, mixed with a healthy dose of rationalism. Thus far we have mostly questioned the empiricist basis of scientific authority. In this section we want to suggest that naturalism's reliance on reason is not without problems. In fact, much of the power of science comes not from its reliance on reason or sense perception, but on rhetoric and on science's own image as an important source of authority in the modern world.

We begin with the power of reason. Although academics often loathe acknowledging it, privileging reason introduces and sustains a number of biases into the nature of our study. Reason can make us ignore and devalue important parts of the human experience. This approach leads us to:

> favor the head over the heart; the mechanical over the spiritual or the natural . . ., the inertly impersonal over the richly personal . . ., the banal collective over the uniquely individual, the dissociated anomic individual over the organic collective; the dead tradition over the living experiment; the positivist experiment over the living tradition; the static product over the dynamic process; the monotony of linear time over the timeless recurrence of myth; dull, sterile order over dynamic disorder; chaotic, entropic disorder over primordial order; the forces of death over the forces of life.   (Graff, 1979, p. 25)

Worse, once we recognize the fleeting and subjective nature of social activity, we might begin to doubt the utility of prioritizing 'scientific' insights, derived from sterile and structured empirical proofs, mixed with reason. In this new ontological setting we might wonder whether the Harvard-trained sociologist is really a better student of contemporary human behaviour than the popular rap or country music artist (whose exposure to the real world may be more authentic).

Post-structuralists, such as Michael Shapiro, are quite adamant in their critique of the social scientists' over-reliance on scientific authority:

Part of what must be rejected is that aspect of the terrain predicated on a radical distinction between what is thought of as fictional and scientific genres of writing. In the history of thought the distinction has been supported by the notion that the fictional text, e.g., the story, play or novel, manufactures its own objects and events in acts of imagination, while the epistemologically respectable genres, such as the scientific text, have 'real' objects and events, which provide a warrant for the knowledge-value of the text's statements purporting to be about the objects and events.   (Shapiro, 1988, p. 7)

Shapiro's book *Reading the Postmodern Polity* (1992) is a masterful example of how the voices of novels and myths have a legitimate and convincing voice in social scientific discourse. His comparison of DeLillo's *Libra* (1988) and Bellah et al.'s *Habits of the Heart* (1986) shows how a fictional biography might outperform a large scientific project in capturing America's cultural diversity. If novels are legitimate authorities for social understanding, why not graffiti? Beavis and Butthead? Prisons? The body itself? Indeed, analysts have explored all of these venues (and more!) in search of insights to the social condition.

The economist Donald McCloskey makes a similar – if more explicit – point in his *The Rhetoric of Economics* (1986). While mainstream economists tend to market themselves as top-shelf methodologists, adorned in sophisticated formal and econometrical labels, the bite of their argument (if, and when, it holds) usually rests on masterful rhetoric: reference to a popular truth, a myth, an established authority, and so on.

The power of myth among contemporary economists was clearly evident in recent debates about exchange rate regimes. Today's consensus in Europe for fixed exchange rates was frequently argued and defended in terms borrowed explicitly from Homer's *Odyssey* (for example, Giavazzi and Pagano, 1988). Like the Sirens, whose crying beauty bewitches sailors far from home, inflation and devaluation are said to coax the vote-lonely politician. It is best, this argument holds, that the hands of public officials be tied to a rigid (fixed) mast:

Therefore pass these Sirens by, and stop your men's ears with wax that none of them may hear; but if you like you can listen yourself, for you may get the men to bind you as you stand upright on a cross piece half way up the mast, and they must lash the rope's end to the mast itself, that you may have the pleasure of listening. If you beg and pray the men to unloose you, then they must bind you faster.   (Homer, 1999, p. 105)

The Homeric myth was a very effective rhetorical device in debates among economists over the utility of fixed rates of (currency) exchange.

Presumably, the modern economist is familiar enough with *The Odyssey* to understand the relevance of the 'binding to the mast' parable. (But, perhaps, not familiar enough to remember Lady Kirkê's second caveat: to impair the hearing of the crew – presumably the *demos* – by filling their ears with beeswax.)

We are not suggesting that economists cannot wield good empirical and rational arguments for why (and when) a country should adopt a fixed exchange rate regime. Our point is simply that we need to be more aware of the role that rhetoric (and in this case, the role of myth) play in convincing us of this option.

Przeworski and Teune

To consider how some of this chapter's ontological and epistemological doubts apply to social scientific study, we propose to take a closer look at an influential textbook in comparative methods for social scientists.

Przeworski and Teune's *Logic of Comparative Social Inquiry* is a classic example of the naturalist approach to social science, where the authors introduce students to the explanatory and predictive goals of science with reference to the voting behaviour of an imaginary Monsieur Jacques Rouget. In particular, readers are asked to explain why it is that Monsieur Rouget votes Communist. To do this, Przeworski and Teune sketch a two-staged research activity, not unlike the one depicted in Figure 2.3 above. First, the social scientist is encouraged to collect a number of relevant observations about M. Rouget: he is a male, aged 24, with blond hair, brown eyes, and he works in a large factory. (As we shall see, not all of these observations are relevant; but too much information is always better than too little.)

The social scientist is then encouraged to draw upon generally probabilistic statements that are relevant for explaining voting behaviour. (In other words, the second step of this research design finds us at the apex of the research triangle depicted in Figure 2.3.) These statements have already been induced from previous empirical studies, so that we can be confident of their applicability. In particular, we know that:

> One out of every two workers votes Communist; and employees of large organizations vote Communist more often than employees of small organizations; and young people vote Communist more often than older people.   (Przeworski and Teune, 1970, p. 19)

From the empirical observations about M. Rouget, and the probabilistic statements listed above, the social scientist can generate a hypothesis about M. Rouget's voter behaviour: it is likely that he will vote

Communist.[3] This hypothesis can then be tested empirically by observing his future vote.

The example of Monsieur Rouget is a wonderfully concise illustration of the power of modern naturalist explanations. The power of this explanation rests on its strong inductive foundation and the implicit recognition that there are law-like patterns in social behaviour. The patterns allow us to predict the probability of a young male worker in a larger factory voting Communist. On this foundation, empirical observations are combined with generalized statements (themselves based on previous induction) to formulate hypotheses that can be verified empirically. This careful procedure provides the social scientist with secure knowledge that can better help us interpret future voter behaviour. Although Przeworski and Teune explicitly recognize that this explanation is incomplete – several other factors may be relevant for predicting M. Rouget's behavior – this particular explanation enjoys a relatively high level of probability. It is, after all, for these reasons that the naturalist's approach to social phenomena is today hegemonic.

But this approach is not the only way to predict Monsieur Rouget's voting behaviour. Just as M. Rouget was a hypothetical construction of Przeworski and Teune to illustrate the power of naturalist social science methods, it is possible to construct a hypothetical context around M. Rouget, imbued with patterns and meaning. For example, we can consider an entirely different epistemological vantage point, one provided by M. Rouget's wife, Kikki.

Kikki has lived with Jacques Rouget for the past six years in a small flat in a middle-class suburb just north of Paris. Jacques drives a BMW that he cannot afford and appreciates the finer things in life. As a result, Kikki and Jacques are always short of money – which Jacques unfailingly blames on the French state's passion for taxing his small factory salary. From Kikki we learn that her husband's main passion in life is football. This is, we learn, the main reason he joined the factory union: it was a prerequisite for playing on the team. When he is not following market developments on his computer at home, he is watching, playing or dreaming about football. Jacques manages the factory's football team, having held (unchallenged) the position of centre forward for the last five years. As team manager, he travels a great deal, and increasingly socializes with the factory's management (who also follow the team with great interest). In addition, we learn that Jacques has become increasingly conservative in his view of the world, especially his political view, since his father died three years ago. When we ask Kikki, she could tell us with complete certainty that Jacques will vote Gaullist (RPR) in the next election.

We have now presented two very different means of explaining M. Rouget's future voting behaviour: Kikki's understanding of M. Rouget's behaviour is quite different from that of Przeworski and Teune's. Both provide important insights that allow us to predict and understand Jacques's voting behaviour.

At first glance, the most significant difference between the two examples may concern questions of efficiency. Can we really expect to have detailed, familiar knowledge about every voter in France? While recognizing that this is an important consideration for the investigator in the field, it is not one that we feel is significant in itself, for two reasons. First, money will flow to legitimate projects: the initial struggle is about legitimization. Second, there are several political issues where resources are not an important part of the analysis: interpretive studies of nations, parties or government decisions, for example, needn't be more expensive or time-consuming than 'naturalist' ones.

Rather, we would like to focus on the more significant differences distinguishing these two approaches. In particular, Kikki's explanation is different in that it:

- recognizes Jacques Rouget as a conscious political being, one that can formulate his political perspective independent of the structural determinants that are said to inform political behaviour;
- understands that Jacques's voting behaviour depends critically on a thorough or complete interpretation of Jacques as a complex creature in a given context saturated with meaning; and
- relies on a broader scope of authority. Our confidence in Kikki's interpretation depends on her authority (as Jacques's wife), and her ability to describe how his political vision is a product of several larger developments in his life over the last decade or so.

In short, the ontological doubts that we considered in the first section of this chapter have made alternative epistemological approaches more attractive. No longer does the scholar need to confine herself to empirical or rational proofs, or authorities who rely on these 'ways of knowing'. Myths, revelation and other authorities (such as novelists, film characters, wives and so on.) become potentially relevant interpretive authorities.

It is on the basis of these ontological and epistemological doubts that we can understand why it is that Kikki Rouget's explanation of her husband's voting behaviour might be more convincing. Her familiarity with Jacques's life and experiences provides her with an interpretive perspective that is more legitimate than that provided by inductively derived generalizations of voter behaviour. At the same time, these ontological and epistemological doubts provide us with a critical vantage point from which we might question the way in which mainstream (naturalist) approaches use reason and sensory perception as part of their rhetorical tool kit.

Look again at Przeworski and Teune's explanation of M. Rouget's voting behaviour; but pay particular attention to its *style*. For Przeworski and Teune (1970, p. 19), the explanation took the following form:

```
One out of every two workers votes Communist; and
employees of large organizations vote Communist more
often than employees of small organizations; and young
people vote Communist more often than older people.
Therefore, it is likely that
    M. Rouget votes Communist.
```

There are three particularly relevant observations about the form of their explanation (we can assume that the 'content' is correct). First, the explanation is framed in the form of a covering law (indeed, Hempel is referred to higher up on the same page). Second, the language is authoritative/scientific. Consider the following (immediately preceding) passage, which oozes scientific authority:

The second premise consists of a conjunction of general statements describing with a high likelihood the behavior of skilled workers, employees of large factories and young persons (No interaction is assumed.).   (Ibid., p. 19)

Finally, the very style, or form, of exposition is meant to mimic a mathematical theorem: note the nature of the indentations and the structured format! The last sentence is broken in two, with 'M. Rouget votes Communist' whisked off to a new line, as if placed on a pedestal for all to see. QED. What other role can this style of presentation play if it is not to parrot scientific authority?

This is McCloskey's (1986) 'rhetoric' of social science, as introduced above. To the extent that the reader is convinced by Przeworski and Teune's argument, it could be that the conviction is grounded in the authors' use of authoritative reference, voice and form (as much as rational and empirical support). The empirical content of the covering law is not at all supported (of course, this is a fictitious example), nor is there any explicit attempt to explain why these factors (and not, say, the man's hair or eye colour) are relevant.

Methodological Doubts

By introducing a number of ontological doubts we can free the social scientist to consider other epistemological outlets. No longer are we limited to the sort of reason, facts and authority that has permeated scientific discourse for so long. The methodological consequences of this revolution are wide-ranging – they stretch across a continuum that includes subscribers to a weak methodological hierarchy, to those who might be called methodological anarchists. Straddling these two ideal types, offering a radical solution, is Paul Feyerabend.

Beyond this continuum lies the ideal of methodological holism, or the idea that one single methodology should suffice for the study of both social and natural phenomena. Indeed, there is a long, and fairly varied, tradition – one that includes such disparate authors as Comte, Mill and even Marx – that strives for methodological unity. But this consensus is itself divided. On the one hand, we find a hard core of this tradition, exemplified by the logical positivists of the Vienna Circle, who argue that all sciences should be modelled as closely as possible on physics. Today, this tradition is represented by Edward O. Wilson's (2003) campaign for *Conscilience*. On the other hand, we can find a softer school, exemplified by Marx, which argues for a sort of methodological rapprochement between the natural and social scientific approaches: 'Natural science will in time incorporate into itself the science of man, just as the science of man will incorporate into itself natural science: there will be *one* science' (Marx, 1844, III, §4). In this camp we might also place today's scientific realists.

But this chapter has provided a number of illustrations that should encourage people to question the utility of striving for methodological unity. This position is best exemplified by Michel Foucault. In the English preface to his *Order of Things* – which is, itself, one of the great epistemological projects of our generation – Foucault describes the dilemma:

> Discourse in general, and scientific discourse in particular, is so complex a reality that we not only can, but should, approach it at different levels, and with different methods. If there is one approach that I do reject, however, it is that (one might call it, broadly speaking, the phenomenological approach) which gives absolute priority to the observing subject, which attributes a constituent role to an act, which places its own point of view at the origin of all historicity – which, in short, leads to a transcendental consciousness. It seems to me that the historical analysis of scientific discourse should, in the last resort, be subject, not to a theory of the knowing subject, but rather to a theory of discursive practice.   (1970, p. xiv)

Those who criticize methodological holism tend to subscribe to two different positions. On the one hand, we find those who want to argue for methodological pluralism. These analysts are willing to accept that some methodologies are more appropriate than others for studying certain types of phenomena. The problem, however, is agreeing on the measure of 'appropriateness'. Some remnant of a demarcation principle(s), no matter how diluted, remains.

At the other end of the spectrum, many postmodernists find methodological assumptions to be both alien and violent. These authors tend to speak about strategies, not methodologies, and they are especially doubtful of any attempt to impose a demarcation barrier. For McCloskey, the imposition of any strict methodological criterion as a demarcation barrier constitutes a conversation stopper: 'In practice, methodology serves chiefly to demarcate Us from Them, demarcating science from nonscience' (1986, p. 26). For many who are unfamiliar with (or unsympathetic to, or both) this approach, this sort of methodological agnosticism seems like cheating: if there is no methodological standard by which to evaluate scientific contributions, then arguments about authenticity appear little more than shouting matches about who has better access to the authentic.

To illustrate this problem we can refer to a real-life classroom example. Several years ago, one of us invited a guest lecturer on postmodernism to his introductory political theory class. This guest ended his entertaining discussion about the postmodern subject with a short (and equally entertaining) analysis of why young, middle-class, white kids buy rap music. His argument was that these kids bought rap music because it reinforced their stereotypes of violent, sex-driven, black youth. As the lecture was presented to a bunch of young, middle-class, primarily white kids, its objective was surely to provoke argument – which it did. When this interpretation was challenged by a young African male student in the front row (who wanted to explain the inherent qualities of the music, and its deep roots in African tradition and culture), the two ended up in a shouting match. Without any methodological criteria for reference, each needed to convince the audience of his authenticity and experience. The student claimed authority with reference to his ethnic background; the lecturer with reference to the academe. In a situation like this, how can we decide which argument is better? On the other hand, we might ask: is it important to know who wins?

This problem of authority is difficult to shake. Even those of us trained in the naturalist tradition can be (and often are) influenced by alternative (non-scientific) authorities of social events (such as songwriters or storytellers). For example, a convincing argument could be made that two critical turning points in modern American history (the American decision to join the Second World War and the assassination of J. F. Kennedy) are best explained by novels, not academic treatises. Gore Vidal's (2000) *The Golden Age* and Don DeLillo's (1988) *Libra* are not academic histories, with proper references and detailed footnotes. But each author is an authority in his own right, and each is able to convey very authentic and plausible depictions of historical events in an allegedly fictional form. It is *because* these authors do not pretend to be authentic or universal that their fictional accounts carry so much explanatory punch.

There may be other reasons for shunning methodological standards as well. Stanley Fish (1987), the well-known American lawyer and literature scholar, argues that a preoccupation with methods belongs only to those logocentric systems that claim to be externally valid, seeking transcendental truths. Worse, as McCloskey was hinting at in an earlier passage, methodological criteria often serve as a means for narrowing discussion – keeping out the voices from the margins; narrowing the rhetorical discourse.

Across these two methodological positions straddles a monster of contemporary philosophy of science: Paul Feyerabend (1924–94). While his methodological position is probably closer to the first ideal type (methodological pluralism) than it is to the latter (methodological anarchy), the solution he proposes is suitable for both camps.

Feyerabend's work is grounded in actual examples of scientific change. This sort of grounding encourages a proliferation of new and incompatible theories, competition, and notions of scientific progress. For Feyerabend, scientific progress is derived from theoretical and methodological pluralism.

Indeed, in his most famous work, *Against Method*, Feyerabend (1975) argues that science has no special features that render it intrinsically superior to other kinds of knowledge such as ancient myths or voodoo:

[S]cience is much closer to myth than a scientific philosophy is prepared to admit. It is one of the many forms of thought that have been developed by man, and not necessarily the best. It is conspicuous, noisy and impudent, but it is inherently superior only for those who have already decided in favour of a certain ideology, or who have accepted it without ever having examined its advantages and its limits. (Feyerabend, 1975, p. 295)

In short, Feyerabend wished to downgrade the importance of empirical arguments by suggesting that aesthetic criteria, personal whims and social factors have a more decisive role in the history of science than rationalist or empiricist epistemologies would indicate. We might note that this description of science seems to mesh pretty well with our depiction of the Lomborg affair in the introductory chapter. Feyerabend's argument about methodological pluralism (like that of many postmoderns) is an argument about emancipation: individuals should be free to choose between science and other forms of knowledge. Feyerabend sees our dependence on scientific authority today as a parallel to the dominance of the Catholic Church at the time of Galileo: our high regard for science is a dangerous dogma, and a direct threat to democracy. To solve this problem, Feyerabend argued that free, democratic societies needed to ensure that 'all traditions have equal rights and equal access to the centers of power' (Feyerabend, 1978, p. 9). He argues that to defend society from scientific experts, science should be placed under democratic control: experts should be consulted, and controlled democratically by juries of laypeople.

Recommended Further Reading

For a description of how Galileo's telescope changed the nature of truth and altered our understanding of the world, see Burke's *The Day the Universe Changed* (1985). Capra's *The Turning Point* (1982) also provides a very accessible introduction to a new way of understanding the world. For a very broad introduction to philosophy of social science issues, see Hollis's *The Philosophy of Social Science* (1994). Collingwood's *Essay on Metaphysics* (1962) and his *The Idea of History* (1956) provide central contributions to an alternative to the naturalist methodology, while Feyerabend's *Against Method* (1975) provides additional philosophical support.

Chapter 8

A Constructivist Philosophy of Science

Behind us, in Chapters 1–6, we have left the empirical quest for certain knowledge; ahead of us lies doubt, difference and dissent. Chapter 7 planted the seeds of these doubts. The present chapter seeks to identify some of the wild methodological vines that have grown from those seeds. Our intention is to harvest a constructivist alternative to the naturalist philosophy of science, as described in Chapter 2.

We begin by retracing our steps back to David Hume, and then explore a road previously not taken by examining the effect that Hume's argument had on Immanuel Kant. It is in Kant that we find the ontological tap root for what we term the constructivist approach to social science – a recognition that the patterns we study are of our own making. While the naturalist and the constructivist traditions both recognize the need to map and explain patterns in the world, they differ over what they see to be the source of these patterns. As reflected in their respective titles, constructivists trace these patterns back to the scholarly mind that observes them, whereas naturalists understand the patterns to be an essential part of nature. Consequently, constructivists and naturalists tend to have different attitudes towards, and approaches for, uncovering the truth – indeed, some constructivists wonder if there is a truth out there to be attained at all.

To gain access to Kant, we reintroduce a forgotten Kantian scholar from the nineteenth century: William Whewell. Whewell helps us consider the different ways in which we are responsible for the patterns we observe in the social world. With Whewell it is easier to see how knowledge is contextualized: history, society, ideas and language influence the patterns we use to explain and understand social phenomena. Consequently, Whewell's approach is less beholden to empiricism and encourages us to embrace a much larger range of epistemological outlets.

From the vantage point provided by Whewell, we can survey the broad field of contemporary constructivist approaches and elaborate on the core components of constructivist social science. By focusing on common methodological components we can help students to compare a constructivist philosophy of science with its naturalist counterpart, as depicted in Chapter 2. In addition, these common methodological elements can help us better understand how constructivism is applied in the particular methods chapters that follow.

On Natural and Other Worlds

Constructivists begin by recognizing that there is a world of difference separating the natural from the social world. As we saw in the preceding chapter, constructivists share this position with a much larger group of social analysts. As a result, we can come to expect different types of explanations for events that occur in either the natural or the social worlds.

To understand these difference we can return to J. S. Mill, who held: 'A bird or a stone, a man or a wise man, means simply an object having such and such attributes' (Mill, 2002 [1891], p. 59). Mill is referring to the simple fact that birds and stones (for example) share many similarities: most important of these may be that they are both material objects (for example, they have mass and extension). As material objects, both birds and stones obey physical laws. At this level, of course, there is little room (or need) for difference: as material objects, birds, stones and wise men find themselves subject to the same natural laws.

If Galileo should have wondered whether this actually was the case, we can imagine him climbing the stairs of Pisa's leaning tower bearing a stone, a bird in its cage, and a smart Italian. After dropping each one from the top, and taking careful notes, we might expect him to conclude that all three objects in principle drop with equal speed. After all, each of these three objects acts as material objects. *When dead.*

Alive, of course, the objects might behave quite differently. Should Galileo drop a live bird from the top of the tower, its behaviour would deviate radically from the stone: the bird would most likely fly away (assuming it was a type of bird that could fly – i.e., not a penguin or some such fowl). The smart Italian, on the other hand, would probably behave in a way very similar to the stone: when dropped, we can expect even a live Italian to drop like a stone (albeit in a somewhat more animated fashion).

If we twist this example one more turn, we might think about how a puzzled observer on the ground would respond after witnessing the entire procedure. We can imagine her, when interviewed by a local journalist about these odd circumstances, revealing answers to a string of questions:

Journalist:	Why do you think he dropped the stone?
Witness:	I guess it was to see how quickly it dropped. Galileo is known in the neighbourhood for doing these sorts of things.
Journalist:	Why did he drop the bird?
Witness:	I suppose he wanted to see if it could fly. Why else would you drop a bird from the top of a tower?
Journalist:	Why, then, do you think he dropped the man off the top of the tower?
Witness:	How the hell would I know? I didn't see any sort of struggle. Perhaps the guy was a rival scientist? This is all very unsettling. . . .

In short, when we begin to look beyond an object's material capacities, and come to recognize the real differences that distinguish stones, birds and men, then we begin to discover that different principles of explanation may apply to each of them. There is nothing particularly odd about a dropping stone, so the observer focuses on the natural factors pulling the stone: we want to know how it works. A bird's actions are more varied, so we begin to look for explanations in the bird (it can fly) or in forces external to the bird (Galileo). With the most complex object, man, we begin to search for more complex and complicated reasons; we search for meaning. The sundry attributes of diverse objects encourage us to think in terms of different explanations for their behaviour.

This is the sort of puzzle that David Hume worked on when speculating about the nature of causation. But Hume's laboratory of choice was not a leaning tower, but a billiards hall. Hume wanted to know why a particular billiard ball moved. He reasoned that we must search for a *cause* that is external to the ball – for example, that it was hit by another billiard ball. Likewise, if we want to know the *reason* why that second ball moved, we may find that it was set in motion by a pool player – again, an instance of an external cause. But if we want to *explain* why the pool player set his ball in motion, the search for an external cause becomes more complicated. In one sense, we can find an external cause in the rules of the game of billiards. But game rules are hardly an external cause in the material sense of the term. The rules of the game are a social construct: they are something that pool players have invented; they are a convention. Herein lies a dilemma, then, as the cause can also be seen to be internal, for the rules of the game *are* the game of billiards – they constitute the game! As such, they also give meaning to the pool player's action (i.e., setting the ball in motion).

To summarize from Hume's example, we can distinguish at least four distinct reasons (or causes) for why a man sets a billiard ball in motion:

Table 8.1   *Objects, sciences and their principles of explanation*

Object	Properties	Science	Principle of explanation
Inanimate	Mass and extension	Physics	Causality
Animate	Mass and extension		
Plants	+ vital force	Botany	Adaptation
Animals	+ vital force	Zoology	Function
Humans	+ vital force + will and reason	Social sciences	Volition, interest, meaning, rules, institutions, praxis

(1) a physical cause; (2) an intentional cause (the man wanted to play snooker); (3) an institutional cause (the rules of billiards told the man what he could do); and (4) a functional cause (the man knew what would happen if he used the pool cue in the usual way).

While it is rather common to elaborate between two main types of causes (physical and intentional), the example above illustrates that there is no reason to limit ourselves to these. In Table 8.1 we present a typology of different types of explanations. We hasten to point out that this is a very simple typology for thinking about the different principles of explanation and their relationship to their objects of study (and their requisite scientific discipline). We do not mean to suggest that we are limited to these types of explanations; that some types of explanation are better than others; or that students of human behaviour should not use causal or functional arguments (for example).

In the left-hand column of the table we distinguish between inanimate and animate objects (the latter of which are further divided into plants, animals and humans). The middle two columns describe the properties and scientific disciplines usually associated with these types of objects. While the scientific disciplines are fairly straightforward, we might explain the contents of the second column in a little more detail. Here we see that inanimate and animate objects share material qualities (mass and extension), but animate objects are different from inanimate objects in that they are alive (they are characterized by what Whewell calls a 'vital force'). Among animate objects, humans distinguish themselves further by having recourse to will and reason (in addition to having both mass and extension, and the vital force).

In the column entitled 'Principle of Explanation' we indicate several ways in which the various objects may be explained. Inanimate objects lend themselves to *causal* explanations – this is the traditional explanatory principle in Physics. Animate objects, however, may be accounted for in many different ways. The behaviour of plants and animals can also be explained in terms of causality; but more often they are accounted for in terms of *adaptation* or *function*. Human behaviour can also be explained in these terms. However, because human beings are endowed with reason, language and free will, human actions can also be explained by other principles as well (for example, *volition*, *interest* or *meaning*).

There are two points worth emphasizing in this table. First of all, it is possible to detect a pattern: the simplest objects are associated with the simplest explanations, while the more complex objects come with more complex explanations. Second, we note that the typology is inclusive: all objects (both inanimate and animate) have mass and extension. For this reason, all of these objects can be measured, weighed and counted – and their behaviour can be explained in terms of external causality. But when we begin to note the more unique attributes of an object, we see that other principles of explanation can also apply: because of the 'vital force' inherent to them, the behaviour of plants and animals (including humans) can be explained in terms of adaptation and function (in addition to causality). Finally, humans can be further distinguished by their use of reason, will and meaningful speech. These capacities give rise to an even wider variety of potential explanations.

These examples are used to describe the complicated nature of the relationship between the natural and social worlds. In many important respects, the two worlds are quite alike, and these similarities mean that explanatory principles developed for studying the natural world can often be employed (and with great effect) to social phenomena. On the other hand, the examples also suggest that the nature of human interaction is quite different from the way in which inanimate objects interact. Consequently, it is possible to explain this interaction with recourse to a much larger set of explanatory principles.

Beneath all this complexity lies a view of the world that recognizes the subjectivity and illusiveness of social patterns. The next section will introduce the ontological foundations of just such a view.

The Awakening

In the beginning there was Hume. In Chapter 2 we learned that Hume was an empiricist and that, like other empiricists before him, he believed that we have access to the Real World through our senses: we look out of the window and see trees and bushes, rocks on the ground, buses on the roads, and birds in the air. From these observations we gather systematic knowledge about the world; if we are scientists, we seek to induce general statements from our observations.

But Hume was also a sceptic. In spite of his empiricist sympathies, Hume warned us of induction's potential pitfalls. After all, we cannot trust inductive reasoning to produce general statements that are true; for induction is based on observed events, and observed events can never embrace *all* possible objects/events of the world. Our experience with past regularities is no guarantee that the future will bring similar regularities. This simple point can be illustrated by considering the 'inductive turkey' example often attributed to Bertrand Russell. From the first morning after a turkey arrives at a farm he notices that feeding time is five o'clock. Each day the turkey experiences the same thing: food comes at five. With the passing of time, and with the turkey having noted the regularity of his feeding time, the turkey eventually infers that he is always fed at 5 a.m. Unfortunately for the turkey, this inference proved to be faulty. At 5 a.m. on 25 December, the unlucky turkey was not fed, but slaughtered for Christmas dinner.

In a similar way, Hume argued that we cannot infer beyond our own limited experience. This is a big step for any empiricist. To make this step easier, Hume retreated from the most radical destination to which it led and took refuge in a pragmatic argument that rested on the principle of human habit. In short, Hume came to accept that there are natural limitations to what we can know about causality.

On Pure Concepts and Natural Ideas

Hume's argument was earth-rattling stuff for scientists of his day. Causation was (and is!) a central object of scientific discovery, and to suggest that it rested on such flimsy ground had the effect of shaking the very foundations of science and metaphysics. The effect was strong enough to wake Immanuel Kant from what he later described as his 'dogmatic slumber' (1969 [1783], p. 302). Kant understood the serious implications of Hume's argument, and he was not willing to leave causality resting on such shaky foundations.

If Hume was correct, all of science was in danger. Worse (for Kant, who was a philosopher by profession), if causality proved to be beyond the grasp of our knowledge, it is possible that other metaphysical concepts might prove to be just as elusive. Kant immediately began to construct a sturdier basis for understanding causation. As he sought to improve on Hume – who understood causation as a habitual expression (mechanically produced by the association of ideas) – the scope of Kant's enquiry expanded. Causation is not habit, Kant averred; it is part of a bigger and more general property of the nature of the human condition.

On the surface of things, it appears as though Kant ended up in the philosophical vicinity of Hume; both developed a philosophy of knowledge that directed attention away from the Real World and turned it on the nature of the human mind. But surface appearances are often misleading – as is the case with Hume and Kant. The two philosophers developed very different understandings of human knowledge, and ended up informing very different philosophies of science.

To understand the differences that separate these two great thinkers, we need to remember how Hume's understanding of causation rested on his theory of sense perception: i.e., that the human mind absorbs impressions through the senses. Kant was willing to accept this theory of sense perception, in part. He agreed that the senses presented perceptions to the mind. However, he could not agree with the notion that the human mind is an empty vessel, into which sense impressions fall passively. For Kant, the senses merely brought perceptions to the doorstep of the mind. It was then up to the mind to organize these perceptions, categorize them, and store them for later use. To perform this task, the human mind comes from the dealer already equipped with basic preconditioning concepts – which it uses to harness the flux of sense perceptions that are delivered at its doorstep. Thus, Kant concluded that the mind is an agent in its own right; it is an interpreter of the impressions that come to it from the external world!

But if each human mind is an active interpreter of sense impressions, how is it possible for different people to agree on what the world looks like? How is it possible to agree on anything at all? The answers to these important questions are not as daunting as they first appear. Kant argued that we all share certain basic, preconditioning or organizing, ideas. Indeed, possessing these basic ideas is part of what it means to be human. In other words, all human beings share a set of basic categories and concepts that organize the perceptions that our senses deliver to the mind from the outside world.

In the end, Kant identified 12 such pure concepts (or forms of understanding), through which all human perceptions must pass on their way to objective knowledge. These are listed in Table 8.2, where we can see that Kant organized these basic ideas into four sets: (1) quantity of objects; (2) quality of objects; (3) their relation to each other; and (4) their mode of existence (or modality). After these 12 pure concepts had done their work – after their sorting work was done – the processed sensations were conveyed to the conscious mind.

Everything we perceive is channelled through these categories of our mind. Without them we could not perceive or know anything. In arguing thus, Kant was able to save modern science from Hume's excessive scepticism. Newtonian physics and the universal laws of nature (for

Table 8.2   *Kant's pure concepts of understanding*

Quantity	*Quality*	*Relation*	*Modality*
Unity	Affirmation	Substance–accidents	Possibility
Plurality	Negation	Cause–effect	Actuality
Totality	Limitation	Causal reciprocity	Necessity

Source: based on Kant (1929 [1787], p. 113).

example) were saved from the horrible uncertainty to which Hume had exposed them. With Kant, scientists could continue to assume that the laws of nature would apply indefinitely. But Kant's rescue came at a very high cost. In providing the necessary groundwork for assuming the universality of nature's laws, Kant shifted the ontological terrain from nature to the human mind. In other words, Kant shows us how Newton's ordered universe (for example) is not anchored in nature; it is anchored, instead, in universal and necessary concepts of the human mind.

This is an important argument. We should point out that Kant is *not* making a distinction between the social and natural world, as we did in the introduction to this chapter. Instead, Kant is distinguishing between a Real World and the way it is perceived by us. In other words, Kant is telling us that the laws of nature do not belong to the Real World! Worse (for naturalists, at least) Kant is claiming that those real world patterns (that we observe so clearly) belong to the human mind; that the human mind imposes its own patterns on nature and the world. The implication, of course, is that we can never observe or know the Real World – 'objectively' as it were. We can never say anything about how the Real World is 'in itself'. The only thing we can observe are the perceptions of the world: how the world appears to us.

The World of Our Making

This discussion is leading us down a very difficult and winding path. At its end is the unanswerable question about whether there actually exists a Real World, independent of our existence. For Kant it was important to emphasize that he was not denying the existence of a Real World.[1] He was simply saying that we have no way of knowing anything about that Real World (the *noumena*). All we know is that our perceptions (*phenoumena*) of the Real World are somehow related to it. But the nature of that relationship remains complex and ambiguous: they seem to coexist simultaneously. (As Kant's pure concepts include causation, it is problematic to say that the *noumena* cause us to have perceptions of *phenoumena*.) Nor was Kant advocating more metaphysical speculation; he was committed to pursuing philosophy within the narrow 'limits of pure reason', and to recognizing that most positive knowledge could only come about through sense perception.

Kant introduces a rather serious problem for social scientists interested in understanding the world. He forces us to recognize that our human faculties are limited: our sense perceptions and our reason pertain only to the world of *phenoumena*, not to the *noumena*. In effect, Kant makes us realize the limits of both reason and sensory perception as tools that can help us to understand the Real World.

The Unwieldy World of William Whewell

In Immanuel Kant we have found a philosophical sponsor for the constructivist approach.[2] Kant introduced an important ontological twist: the realization that the world we live in is a world as it appears to us – a world of *phenoumena*. Again, this is not to say that the Real World doesn't exist; only that it is beyond our capacity to observe and understand it. Under these very different ontological conditions, we need to rethink the role of our senses and reason in providing neutral or objective knowledge. Before we can do this, however, we need to think about how these pure concepts might generate patterns of relevance for social scientists. For this, we turn to William Whewell.

From today's vantage point, William Whewell (1794–1866) appears as a rather obscure British philosopher of science. In his own context, however, Whewell was well known. He was also controversial, because he explicitly challenged the naturalist ontology and engaged in debate with John Stuart Mill – the very embodiment of the naturalist tradition in mid-nineteenth-century Britain.

Whewell seems to have been joined at the hip to Trinity College, Cambridge: he studied there, became a fellow, then a tutor, and finally served as its Master from 1841 until his death. His academic output was exceptional, in both abundance and diversity. He taught and published on subjects as diverse as astronomy, tides, technology and moral philosophy. However, his principal work – in length and by the central position it occupies in his thought – was in the field of scientific methodology, as collected in two major studies: his *History of the Inductive Sciences* [1837] and his *Philosophy of the Inductive Sciences* [1840]. The former is a general history of the natural sciences with a strong critique of empiricism; the latter provides a systematic summary of the lessons Whewell drew from his historical investigations.

Whewell's critique of naturalism took aim at one of its originators: John Locke. Although Locke had argued that induction lies at the heart of modern science, his own approach was remarkably theory driven. As Whewell showed, all indications suggest that Locke subscribed to his theory of sense perception long before he had found the facts needed to support its presuppositions. Whewell, by contrast, did what Locke and other empiricists should have done: he looked carefully at how science had actually evolved, and how its method was revealed in history. The result was his impressive three-volume *History of the Inductive Sciences*.

The cumulative result of Whewell's work was three strong broadsides on the naturalist tradition. First, Whewell argued that the naturalist's *methodology* is just plain wrong. Naturalists (such as Locke and his followers) had misunderstood Bacon and his concept of induction. Scientists do not begin with particular observations and infer general theories from them. Scientists begin with a question. They then imagine many possible answers. Finally, they test various answers against the available facts in a process of active tinkering and systematic experiment.

Whewell singles out the breakthrough case of Johannes Kepler to illustrate the actual praxis of science. Kepler had many observations of the night sky at his disposal – he knew where lots of heavenly bodies had been on thousands of different dates. He struggled to find a pattern into which all of them could fit; he worked for years to make these heavenly bodies fit into a simple, general conception. Writes Whewell:

> [We] know from his own narrative how hard he [Kepler] struggled and laboured to find the right conception; how many conceptions he tried and rejected; what corrections and adjustments of his first guesses he afterwards introduced. In his case we see in the most conspicuous manner the philosopher impressing his own ideal conception upon the facts; the facts being exactly fitted to this conception, although no one before had detected such a fitness. And in like manner, in all other cases, the discovery of a truth by induction consists in finding a conception or combination of conceptions which agrees with, connects, and arranges the facts.
>
> Such ideal conceptions or combinations of conceptions, superinduced upon the facts, and reducing them to rule and order, are *theories*. [. . . A theory, then,] is a truth collected from facts by induction; that is, by superinducing upon the facts ideal conceptions such as they truly agree with.   (Whewell, 1996 [1840], p. 42f.)

Whewell's approach seems to be very close to what the nineteenth-century American philosopher Charles S. Peirce referred to as 'retroduction'. The essence of retroduction involves the forming and accepting (on probation) of a hypothesis to explain surprising facts. Peirce argued that retroductive reasoning was similar to induction in that it involves a movement from individual observations to a connective proposition; but it was different from induction in that it created new knowledge.

Whewell's second broadside was aimed at the naturalist's reliance on empiricist *epistemology*, which he held was sadly incomplete and half right at best. The naturalists correctly assume that sense perception is vitally important to the acquisition of scientific knowledge; but Whewell argued that sense perception is only half the story. Science also depends on the appropriate processing of perceptions and on this count the naturalists fall woefully short. In this argument, Whewell draws heavily on Kant. Indeed, he freely admits that he 'adopted Kant's reasoning respecting the nature of Space and Time', although he distanced himself from the metaphysical system of Kant and his followers (Whewell, 1996, p. x). Whewell was not the person to push this argument and probe its deeper implications; he did not direct his scholarly attention on speculations on the inner workings on the human mind. Instead, Whewell focused his attention on the empirical world (which scientists investigate), and on society (in which scientists live).

Finally, Whewell charged the naturalists with being *ontologically* arrogant. Here, too, he borrowed arguments from Kant, but sharpened them to a polemical point. Naturalists, he claimed, are full of themselves: they are cocksure that there is a Real World out there, but they have few if any metaphysical arguments to show that this is the case.

In short, Whewell argued that naturalists are methodologically wrong, epistemologically incomplete and ontologically shallow. We can now understand better why he drew so much critical attention. Whewell showed how naturalists claim to have accumulated a good deal of knowledge about the world. But they cannot show that it is *true* knowledge. Indeed, they cannot even show that their knowledge (even if it was true) is knowledge about the *real* world.

Disparate Pieces to a New Philosophy of Science

It is not enough to recognize that the mind uses pure concepts (or 'fundamental ideas' as Whewell calls them). We need to know how these concepts can create patterns – patterns that attract the interest of the social scientist. Whewell recognized that we acquire knowledge through our senses, but not through our senses alone. Clearly, more factors are involved, but what can they be?

Whewell's work on the history and nature of science is encyclopaedic. Consequently, the modern reader can easily follow its rich seams and mine from them arguments about how we create and grasp the patterns central to our understanding about the world. Here we want to focus on four such seams: the role of history, society, ideas and of communication (or language). Although Whewell himself did not produce this particular quartet of factors, it is not difficult to trace them in his writings. In doing so, we hope to show the breadth and power of constructivist approaches, as represented in the work of a number of more recent authors. In other words, we follow up Whewell's initial insights with a number of influential and more contemporary examples. By dividing the literature in this way, it is important to emphasize that our list is not meant to be exhaustive. We provide one possible path through a vast and varied terrain.

The Role of History

On the basis of his vast study of the history of ideas and of scientific discoveries, Whewell concluded that history displays no steady pattern of accumulation of singular insights. There is no clear and obvious pattern of cumulative growth in the history of human knowledge. Instead, human knowledge displays periods of rapid progress, interspersed with periods of stagnation. If the history of science had a pattern, argued Whewell, it was not steady progress, but a dialectical movement in which inductive periods alternate with periods of generalizations.

Instead of entertaining a simple, historical teleology of human knowledge, Whewell cast human knowledge in sociological terms. He argued that societies share a pool of common knowledge, and he envisioned these pools as dynamic and ever-changing. Knowledge changes over time – often in fits and starts. For example, half a millennium ago, people did not commonly recognize that the planets orbited the sun; even learned Renaissance astronomers claimed that the planets travelled in perfect circles around the earth. When Copernicus, Kepler and Galileo argued that this was an erroneous view, they ignited a scientific revolution, in which the old idea of a geocentric universe was replaced by a new and heliocentric one.

With examples such as this, Whewell argued that science – indeed, human knowledge in general – is historical in nature. More recently, this basic notion has been popularized by one of the most influential philosophers of science in the twentieth century, the American physicist and historian Thomas Kuhn (1922–96).

Brother, Can You Paradigm?

Kuhn's first book, *The Copernican Revolution* (1957), was a case study of the episode that Whewell used to illustrate his view of scientific change: the story of how the old Aristotelian approach to the physical sciences broke down when confronted with the observation-based arguments of Copernicus and Galileo. Kuhn concluded that this change involved something more than a simple victory of 'reason' over prejudice; it involved a more basic change in perspective and world view.

In his second book, *The Structure of Scientific Revolutions* (1970 [1962]), Kuhn cultivated this conclusion and argued that scientists are not as open-minded as commonly assumed. Rather, scientists are committed to established truths – 'conceptual, theoretical, instrumental and methodological' (Kuhn, 1970, p. 42). Indeed, the Church scholars who defended Aristotle against Galileo and the New Sciences were representative of the way in which scientists generally behave: they seek to defend established theories and reject the arguments of their critics.

Most scientists conduct problem-solving tasks within an orthodox, commonly accepted, theoretical framework. Kuhn calls this framework a 'disciplinary matrix' or a *paradigm*, which he defines as 'the entire constellation of beliefs, values, techniques and so on shared by the members of a given community' (Kuhn, 1970, p. 173). He then calls the puzzle-solving routine activities that take place within these paradigms *normal science*.

The practitioners of normal science form a collegial group: they are tied together by a common solidarity and a commitment to the kinds of questions asked; they follow similar procedures to answer those questions; and they agree about the form that those answers should take. These questions asked, procedures followed and answers inferred are then assessed by colleagues. This peer-review process draws on the most relevant experts to evaluate the research produced. In the doing, the process reproduces normal science as a self-sustaining, puzzle-solving process within the framework of a dominant paradigm.

A revolution occurs when one of these dominant paradigms breaks down. This might result from some observant scientist discovering an inconvenient fact that does not easily fit within the established theories – as when Copernicus observed that the planets did not travel in perfect circles around the earth, or when Galileo noted that there were mountains on the moon. Efforts to explain new and anomalous observations complicate existing theories and introduce inconsistencies. Normal science no longer performs in the expected manner; it cannot provide satisfactory answers. It fails or goes astray:

And when it does – when, that is, the profession can no longer evade anomalies that subvert the existing tradition of scientific practice – then begin the extraordinary investigations that lead the profession at last to a new set of commitments, a new basis for the practice of science. The extraordinary episodes in which that shift of professional commitments occurs are the ones known in this essay as scientific revolutions. They are the tradition-shattering complements to the tradition-bound activity of normal science.   (Kuhn, 1970, p. 6)

The basic point of Kuhn's argument is that scientists typically go around for years believing one thing – despite mounting evidence to the contrary – and happily practising the established routines of normal science. All of a sudden they notice a mass of conflicting evidence, change their minds, and wonder how they could ever have believed otherwise. Naturalists may accept this basic idea, admitting that scientific knowledge is not merely a product of slow and steady accumulation; however, they do it reluctantly. Some naturalist social scientists embrace Kuhn's description of the structure of scientific revolutions by arguing that the social sciences are pre-paradigmatic; that the social sciences are younger than the natural sciences, and that they have not been able to draw on the same amount of resources as the natural sciences (despite the extra levels of complexity associated with human activity). This argument holds that when social science matures and is properly funded, we can expect to see it reach the same paradigmatic stage as the natural sciences: becoming cumulative, stable and predictive.

Constructivists, by contrast, embrace enthusiastically the idea that human knowledge has evolved, not through accumulation but through sudden shifts and bounds. Actually, most constructivists would probably embrace Whewell's hazy original more readily than Kuhn's souped-up argument that science goes through revolutionary periods driven by the discovery of new sensual evidence. This is because constructivists like to point out that old paradigms in the social sciences may be replaced, but they seldom fade entirely away. Constructivists like to situate such changes in a larger, social context and point to the way in which social scientific fashion swings in tandem with various constellations of power.

The Impact of Society

This discussion of the fashionable swings of social scientific knowledge brings us to the second framing device we find in Whewell. This is a recognition that knowledge is affected both by individuals (as 'carriers' of knowledge) and by the societies they compose (as 'pools' of knowledge). Before we cover the concepts of 'carriers' and 'pools', it is necessary to add a word or two about Whewell's understanding of 'science' and 'knowledge'.

Science, Whewell avers, tends to be specialized knowledge, produced by specialized scholars. Scientists – a word that Whewell seems to have invented[3] – are knowledgeable people. Yet, knowledge alone does not make scholarship; and knowledgeable people do not always become scholars and scientists. A scientist is not a scientist simply by virtue of the many facts that she knows.

Individuals as Carriers of Knowledge

How, then, is an economist different from other people who talk about money? How is a political scientist different from other people who talk about politics? One important difference concerns the *nature* (not the amount) of their knowledge. Scholars are self-conscious about the methods and theories that they have at their disposal; 'other people' may be interested in money and politics, but they do not master the methods and theories of professional economists or political scientists (and may not even desire to do so!).

Another difference concerns the *context* of the knowledge. Scholars command facts, methods and theories; but these are always subjects of controversy and objects of discussion. Facts and arguments presented by one scholar are immediately seized upon by others and subjected to scrutiny, checking and criticism. Scholars are both aware of and familiar with these sorts of professional debates. As professionals they know the history of their discipline – including its history of controversies.

Finally, there is the *social* or the *communal* aspect of scientific knowledge. Scholars are tied together in distinct scholarly communities by a common knowledge of debates and arguments – in the past, as well as in the present. These communities have always institutionalized themselves as professional societies and associations. In the earliest times, this was done on an informal basis, in terms of acquaintance networks. More recently, scholars have organized themselves in scientific societies, with formal memberships, annual conferences and membership journals.

These societies of scholars facilitate the circulation of arguments and encourage scientific discussions. In particular, they help to ensure that new arguments are subjected to scrutiny, control and criticism by fellow scientists. The result is the development of distinct disciplinary heritages, myths and academic traditions, and a web of interrelationships and acquaintanceships among scholarly colleagues, strengthening professional solidarity. These professional societies are, in other, words community- and identity-building mechanisms that tie distinct communities of scholars together by a common knowledge of debates and arguments.

Society as Pools of Knowledge

William Whewell considered Locke's philosophy of science to rest on a simplistic and dubious claim: that sense perception is the basis for all knowledge. If this were true, knowledge would depend on the individual and on the perceptions of the individual. As a consequence, all knowledge would be contingent. But knowledge is *not* contingent. Furthermore, it is clearly more than the sum of individual perceptions. Whewell argued that facts, ideas and arguments do not always originate with individuals; they are sustained and maintained by social relationships and thus have an impersonal quality to them.

In theory, knowledge is based on sense perception. In practice, however, people do not obtain knowledge by observing the world. Rather, they obtain knowledge by interacting with other people. Two consequences flow from this view of science as a social activity. First, people get most of their knowledge by learning from others – by watching others, by listening to others and by reading texts written by others. People, in short, obtain knowledge by consulting a pool of available and common knowledge produced and maintained – or carried by – members of the society that exist around them. Second, knowledge is social and impersonal – or better, transpersonal or interpersonal. Knowledge is part and parcel of the social community in which people live. This community, then, shapes people's knowledge and affects the way they perceive the world.

Whewell inferred this argument from the philosophy of Immanuel Kant. In this, he was not alone. The claim that neither perception nor reason alone can provide us with understanding about the Real World has encouraged many subsequent scholars to ponder the nature of perception, the limits of reason and the vulnerability of the Enlightenment project. Such ponderings – and the attendant search for the limits of reason – were taken to new and sophisticated levels by inter-war sociologists.

The label 'sociology of knowledge' (*Wissenssoziologie*) was coined by Max Scheler in Germany in the 1920s. He drew on Marx, Nietzsche and others to show how human ideas, knowledge and consciousness in general are conditioned by social conditions, albeit not determined by them. His writings triggered a debate in Germany, which was quickly carried to the English-speaking world – to a large extent by Jewish refugees from Hitler's Nazi regime. It was introduced to Great Britain by Karl Mannheim (1936), who held a more radical view than Scheler – arguing that the social context determined not only the appearance but also the content of human knowledge. It was brought to the United States by authors like Alfred Schütz and members of the Marx-inspired *Institut für Sozialforschung* in Frankfurt am Main.

This so-called 'Frankfurt School' had a political agenda.[4] They reflected on the limits of claims made for certain kinds of knowledge. They used their analyses to question the foundations of knowledge and science, as practised in modern society. In particular, they pointed out that contemporary society was filled with repressive and inhuman mechanisms that distorted or alienated people. For these critical theorists, political liberalism could be decadent, and science could be the instrument of political oppression. In short, critical theorists believed it was important to use their knowledge to criticize the status quo and promote radical change.

Members of the Frankfurt School were engaged in a project that sought to specify the ways in which the community we belong to influences the way we perceive and understand the world. Individual members of the School disagreed about *how*, and through which mechanisms, society influences its members in practice. They also quarrelled about whether individuals, in turn, affect the nature of society. Some held that individuals constantly (re)create society through their patterned behaviour; others held that changes occur from the self-conscious and wilful acts of reform, rebellion or revolution. But they all entertained the basic notion of individuals as carriers, and societies as pools.

The Role of Ideas

Social scientists are also people. They are members of society and, like everybody else, are influenced by it. Whewell did not systematically explore the nature of this influence and the mechanisms at work. Although he discussed the nature and importance of ideas, he let others tackle the relations of ideas to society, social institutions and to social identities (class, gender, age group, ethnic and religious background, and so on). This section will first present Whewell's basic notions of the nature and role of ideas, and then trace the way in which subsequent social scientists like Dilthey, Gadamer and Giddens have produced influential modern variations on Whewell's theme.

Whewell summarized his main argument as an aphorism on one of the very first pages in the first volume of *The Philosophy of the Inductive Sciences*:

> *Fact* and *Theory* correspond to Sense on the one hand and to Ideas on the other, so far as we are *conscious* of our ideas: but all Facts involve Ideas *unconsciously*; and thus the distinction of Facts and Theories, is not tenable, as that of Sense and Ideas is.   (Whewell, 1996, pp. xvii)

A few pages later, he reiterates the point: 'Facts are the materials of science, but all Facts involve Ideas' (1996, p. xxxvii). In other words, human knowledge comes from sense perception, yet scientific knowledge hinges on more than perception alone. Perception is conditioned by ideas. Without ideas we cannot make sense of the things our senses bring to us. Ideas perform a crucially important role in guiding the flux of sensory impressions as they enter the mind. Consequently, our knowledge of the world depends on the way in which ideas affect our perceptions – how they are evaluated, discussed and strung together. Or, as modern philosophers of science put it: observation is theory dependent!

Science is more than the collection of reams of facts. Science also involves the creative organization, interpretation and assessment of those facts. Whewell claimed that the naturalist tradition undervalues these other aspects of science: it routinely overlooks the role played by individual inspiration and scholarly imagination, and it ignores the important role that ideas play in creating scientific knowledge.

For Whewell, the decisive act of scientific discovery involves the 'colligation' of facts. Good science relies on both facts and ideas. But Whewell draws this argument out even further by arguing that a good idea eventually becomes incorporated into experience. When an idea is convincing enough, it becomes so tightly integrated into experience that we come to think of it as a fact. By Whewell's account, yesterday's theories become the facts of today! The facts of today (for example, that the earth revolves around the sun), began as yesterday's ideas. Our susceptibility to facts is framed by ideas, readily available in the pool of common knowledge.

This claim is intimately related to the concept of foreknowledge – a concept that flies in the face of the inductivist position of the naturalist methodology, described in Chapter 2. Foreknowledge, it must be noted, is not bias. For the constructivist, foreknowledge is both necessary and integral to any research project. Thus, right from the start, the hermeneutic approach assumes that we form an expectation about the unknown from what we already know. Diesing (1992) suggests that foreknowledge must be made explicit and formulated as an initial hypothesis:

> The initial hypothesis guides the search for and interpretation of details, which in turn revise the hypothesis, which leads to reinterpretation and further search, and so on. In case of conflict, the circle tends to widen farther and farther into the contexts on the one side and our foreknowledge on the other side.   (Diesing, 1992, p. 109)

This circular or dialectical aspect of constructivist science is one of its characteristic features. It is also its main point of criticism. In effect, this dialectical approach tries to explain something (x) in terms of something else (y), before turning around and explaining y in terms of x. In short, there is no clear verification principle upon which we can fall back: we can only continue to offer competing interpretations. Aware of this problem, proponents of this approach argue that it is the most honest. Our understanding of the world is not based on a secure ontological starting point: it is circular in nature. Indeed, Otto Neurath (1959, p. 201) once likened the problem to repairing a faulty boat at sea: 'We are like sailors who must rebuild their ship on the open sea, never able to dismantle it in dry-dock and to reconstruct it there out of the best materials.'

Teutonic treatments: Verstehen *and* Hermeneutik
It is easy to see how Whewell's argument lends itself to the concept of *verstehen* – a concept associated with an important branch of modern social research. The concept of *verstehen* is a shoot from the Kantian root, tended and groomed by German gardeners such as Wilhelm Dilthey, Heinrich Rikert, Georg Simmel and Max Weber.

At the very outset, Wilhelm Dilthey (1833–1911) maintained that understanding was an outcome of *empathy* – that in order to understand an action or an argument, it is necessary to put oneself in the agent's (or author's) shoes, relive her historical experiences and image oneself in her social location, as it were. Our attempt to tap into Kikki Rouget's empathetic understanding of her husband (in the previous chapter) is an example of this sort of understanding.

Eventually, Dilthey distanced himself from this approach because he saw that it might easily lead down the garden path to subjectivism, at the end of which loomed the threatening ghost of relativism. For if all our perceptions are phenomenal, and all knowledge is personal, then there is no guarantee that different observers have common knowledge of the world. It becomes hard to assess whether you and I (and the woman next door) understand the same thing when we refer to trust, marriage, power, deceit and so on.

Clearly, Dilthey needed to find a way to show that some understandings are truer than others; that some propositions are good and others are bad. To do this, he invoked the ancient technique of *hermeneutic understanding* – an old and recognized procedure of interpretation of texts, particularly biblical texts, whereby any understanding must be shown to fit a distinct context. The first hermeneuticians were theologians, and for them the privileged position was granted an omniscient God: Hermes carried God's messages, and the art of reading those messages was thus labelled 'hermeneutics'. God has since retreated from the sciences; however, the notion of a privileged position remains.

Hermeneutic understanding offered Dilthey a way to do two things. First, it could separate the natural from the human sciences – the *Naturwissenschaften* from the *Geisteswissenschaften*. Natural science hinges on the principle of *Erklären*; it seeks to explain natural phenomena in terms of cause and effect. The human sciences (and the budding social sciences) involve the principle of *Verstehen*; they seek to understand social phenomena in terms of relationships.

Second, hermeneutics offered Dilthey an independent perspective from which the human and social sciences could privilege knowledge – in other words, sort good understanding from bad. This independent perspective can be obtained by interpreting particular passages by reference to the larger whole. As we learn from Outhwaite (1975, p. 34), Dilthey argued: 'The totality of a work must be understood through its individual propositions and their relations, and yet the full understanding of an individual component presupposes an understanding of the whole.' This is the famous 'hermeneutic circle', which Dilthey calls 'the central difficulty of the art of interpretation'.

Dilthey's arguments were pushed further by others. His distinction between explanation and understanding was elaborated on by sociologists such as Max Weber. His hermeneutic approach was pursued by sociologists and social philosophers – most famously by the controversial Martin Heidegger. In the late twentieth century, the hermeneutic approach is often associated with Paul Ricoeur and with Heidegger's student Hans-Georg Gadamer. For Gadamer, knowledge is not about providing universal truths, but about expanding our own horizons and understandings. We do this by examining life as a product embedded in culture, and reflecting practical activity. For Gadamer, understanding is based on a feeling for the individuality and uniqueness of persons; it is a way to understand the inwardness of the other (Gadamer, 1984, p. 57). Thus, understanding a text does not involve recovering the author's original intention; rather, it is a matter of encountering a text from one's current position:

> [E]very age has to understand a transmitted text in its own way, for the text is part of the whole tradition in which the age takes an objective interest and in which it seeks to understand itself. The real meaning of a text, as it speaks to an interpreter, does not depend on the contingency of the author and whom he originally wrote for.   (Quoted in Gunnell, 1982, p. 317)

In short, the meaning of each particular item comes from its place in the whole. For example, if we want to know the meaning of a particular word or phrase in a sentence, we often use the context of the sentence (or paragraph, or section, or piece) to understand what is meant. The same sort of interactive method can be used to interpret social phenomena. The researcher starts with an initial hypothesis, uses this hypothesis to search for and interpret details, then returns to revise the hypothesis (which leads to another reinterpretation and further search, and so on). The common hermeneutic strategy of 'tacking' back and forth between the particular and the general allows the interpreter a more flexible relationship to his/her subject.

For the British sociologist Anthony Giddens (1982), however, this is not enough. Like many constructivists, Giddens calls for yet another level of hermeneutic understanding, one which he referred to as the 'double hermeneutic'. At the first hermeneutic level, we come to understand the world by tacking back and forth between it and our perceptions of it. However, this direct and simple understanding of the hermeneutic circle will not suffice for scientists who study the social world. For they (unlike scientists who study the natural world) are members of the society which they study; they have to interpret a social world which is already interpreted by the actors that inhabit it! As social actors have the capacity to understand and respond to our analyses, our knowledge of the social world can actually change that world. This is where the second hermeneutic level comes in: as a description of the two-tiered, interpretive and dialectical relationship between social scientific knowledge and human practices, where social analysts are part of the social world that they analyse.

Even the Nobel Prize-winning economist Douglass C. North has pursued a similar argument. Why has no one managed to explain properly why some countries are rich and others poor, he asked? One reason, he suggested, is that social science explanations are difficult – far more difficult than natural science explanations. Natural scientists, he explains:

> can build from the fundamental unit of their science to explore the dimension of the problem they seek to comprehend. Social scientists do not have anything comparable to genes, protons, neutrons, elements to build upon. The whole structure that makes up the foundation of human interaction is a construct of the human mind and has evolved over time in an incremental process; the culture of a society is the cumulative aggregate of the surviving beliefs and institutions.
>
> It is important to understand that while the constructs humans create are a subjective function of the human mind, humans are continually testing the constructs (read theories) against evidence to see if they have explanatory value. But note that both evidence and theories are constructs and both at best are very imperfect mirrors of what we are trying to comprehend and therefore control. (North, 2005, p. 83)

Gallic contributions: structures quotidien and habitus humaine

Until recently, it has been controversial to claim that evidence, against which social theories are tested, is itself a construct of the human mind. It has been more commonplace to recognize that theories are human constructs. So too is the argument that human (inter)actions depose social sediments or 'institutions', which – in turn – determine further human interaction. The latter view is most commonly associated with the French scholarly journal *Annales d'histoire économique et sociale*. Its imaginative editors and authors – foremost among these are Marc Bloch and Lucien Febvre – enriched their understanding of past events by combining history with geography, sociology, collective psychology and other social sciences. In the process they produced a distinctive approach often referred to as 'the *Annales* school'.

One of the most influential expressions of this basic idea comes from the *annaliste* historian Fernand Braudel, in the first volume of his magisterial study on the evolution of early capitalism – a volume fortuitously entitled *Les structures du quotidien* [The Structures of Everyday Life]. In early modern history the lives of most people consisted of routine behaviour. Over time, this routinized behaviour came to have diverse effects on people: imprisoning some, while giving meaning to the lives of others. Braudel (1977, p. 7) argues that this still applies:

> I think mankind is more than waist-deep in daily routine. Countless inherited acts, accumulated pell-mell and repeated time after time to this very day become habits that help us live, imprison us, and make decisions for us throughout our lives. These acts are incentives, compulsions, ways of acting and reacting that sometimes – more frequently than we might suspect – go back to the beginnings of mankind's history. Ancient, yet still alive, this multicenturied past flows into the present like the Amazon River pouring its water into the Atlantic Ocean of the vast flood of its cloudy waters.

The basic idea behind Braudel's 'structures of everyday life' has been developed by other authors as well – some of them emphasizing (like Braudel) the material routines of daily work, others (like Michel Foucault) exploring more abstract exchange acts or patterns of thought and speech. French sociologist Pierre Bourdieu seems to have tried to capture most of them in his concept of *habitus* – a term that denotes socialized subjectivity or 'the internalization of externality and the externalization of internality' (Bourdieu, 1977, p. 72). In short, habitus can be understood as those socially constructed tendencies or dispositions that come to influence both social structures and practical activity in a dialectical fashion.

Constructivists – be they French, German or whatever – emphasize the role that the surrounding community plays on the way we perceive and understand the world around us. However, they disagree markedly about the nature of this influence. Some (such as Giddens, and like Braudel) seek to capture it through the concept of structure. Others (for example, Gadamer and Bourdieu) doubt the notion of lasting but latent structures and prefer to see this influence in terms of strategic or (re)constitutive acts. These authors are often influenced by theories of communication and language.

On Communication and Language

As we have already noted, scientists live in society and must relate to all kinds of people; among them, their fellow scientists. In doing so, scientists read and review each other's writings; they discuss procedures and results; and they exchange facts and ideas. In short, they communicate, and their communication is mediated by language. Whewell was aware of the importance of language in science, and he began his *Philosophy of Induction* with a discussion 'concerning the language of science'.

Later, Thomas Kuhn elaborated on Whewell's claims about language and weaved them into a more systematic discussion. In doing this, Kuhn took Whewell's arguments a long step further. For example, Kuhn did not just recognize that the distinction between fact and theory was unclear; he argued that facts are theory dependent – facts are only meaningful in relation to some theory. In addition, Kuhn introduced a new and troublesome twist to this argument: he argued that facts are language dependent. This threw an enormous wrench into the naturalist machinery. If facts are language dependent, then so too is the world (as the world is composed of facts). Following Kuhn, we find ourselves in a reality that can not exist independently of language.

Of course, Kuhn was not the first to make this connection. Members of the Vienna Circle had touched on similar arguments a quarter of a century earlier. Recall that Ayer's [1936] influential introduction to Logical Positivism was entitled *Language, Truth and Logic* (emphasis ours). The Vienna Circle had not, however, probed these questions directly, as this would have drawn the logical positivists too far away from their focus on truth and logic. After all, the question of language does not only concern the relationship between the observer and the thing being observed; language is a social phenomenon that also concerns the relationship between the observer and the society (within which the observations are being communicated).

What kind of relationship is this? What does communication entail?

How does it happen? The major contributors to the naturalist tradition – Locke, Hume, Mill and the Vienna Circle – are uncharacteristically silent in response to these important questions. Naturalism simply assumes that observations are written down and disseminated to others in a neutral, or instrumental, fashion. For the naturalist, language is partly a tool through which observations and knowledge are expressed, and partly a transparent medium that preserves the vast body of human knowledge.

The Linguistic Turn

Over the years there have been many rebel forces that have launched linguistic offensives on the naturalist camp. There has been no single, unified philosophical movement or a particular linguistic impulse behind these offensives; what we find instead is a plethora of guerrilla snipers. Thus, it is hard to get a proper handle on the nature of this linguistic turn. To simplify, we can distinguish between two kinds of influences: a formalist approach to linguistics that originated in Eastern Europe towards the end of the nineteenth century; and a structuralist social philosophy that emerged in France.

The formalist approach to linguistics can be traced to the Swiss philologist Ferdinand de Saussure (1857–1913). Saussure ignited a revolution in the 1890s when he drew a sharp distinction between words (*paroles*) and language (*langue*). The word, he claimed, is the elemental unit of language. But a language is much more than words hobbled together; it is more than the sum of its individual components (words). For Saussure, there is an underlying principle that determines the interrelationships among words and affects the form which individual words assume (for example, whether it is conjugated or declined according to tense, case, number or gender). Language, then, contains two different things: words and the principles that direct their use. Saussure called the latter the 'structure' of a given language. What's more, Saussure added a claim that fired imaginations far beyond his own discipline: he added that the meaning of a word is not determined by its content, but by its context or structure.

In the wake of the First World War, this claim revolutionized the study of language everywhere. In America, linguists like Leonard Bloomfield embraced Saussure's notion of 'structure' to develop a new science of 'structural linguistics'. In Europe, similar developments were nursed by Louis Hjelmsklev in Denmark and Antoine Meillet in France. Most significantly, Saussure made an enormous impression on Eastern European linguists. In Russia, Saussure stimulated a distinct school of linguistic formalism which influenced thinkers such as Mikhail Bakhtin. In Prague, Roman Jakobson and Nikolai Trubetzkoy pursued Saussure's notion that the meaning of a word is determined not by its content but by its placement – 'not by what it contains but by what exists outside of it' (Saussure, 1986 [1916], p. 114). This so-called Prague School developed a now standard theory in linguistics, where the inventory of sounds in a particular language could be analysed in terms of a series of contrasts or opposites. The Prague School also contributed to the electrifying effect that Saussure's imagery had on scholars in other fields.

Around the Second World War, the notion of structure came to animate the social sciences. In France, the anthropologist Claude Lévi-Strauss applied Saussure's discussion about *langue* and *parole* in his ambitious, Kant-like search for the basic structures of the human mind. A Jew, Lévi-Strauss fled France during the war, spending most of the war amongst a community of intellectual émigrés in New York City. Here he met Roman Jakobson, whose work inspired him to search for the formal codes and universal mental structures that he believed lay beneath all myth and kinship structures. In particular, Lévi-Strauss's work examined the structures associated with parenthood (*The Elementary Structures of Kinship*, 1949); the notion of pre-logical primitive/totem mentalities (in *La Pensée sauvage*,[5] 1962); and myths – first in *Mythologiques* (1964–71), later in the particular myths associated with different eating habits (for example, *The Raw and the Cooked*, 1964, and *From Honey to Ashes*, 1967). In these studies Lévi-Strauss examined social relationships with an eye to uncovering the underlying structure of societies.

The title of this section, 'The Linguistic Turn', is a reference to an influential book from 1967 with the same title, edited by Richard Rorty. In the decades that followed, work in the humanities and social sciences increasingly recognized the importance of language in framing the way we see and interpret patterns in the world. This linguistic turn parallelled other developments in a broader structuralist movement, which searched for underlying structural relationships upon which meanings rested. Although individual members were reticent about being associated with it, the structuralist movement in France is usually associated with people such as the psychoanalyst Jacques Lacan, the philosopher Michel Foucault, and Marxists such as Louis Althusser and Nicos Poulantzas.

While structuralism allowed its followers to distance themselves from the normative framing that accompanied Western academia, it did so at the cost of local knowledge. This is a tremendous liability for most constructivists. Indeed, the structuralist's willingness to distance herself from historical and contextual reference points produced a backlash in the form of post-structuralism (as associated with people such as Julia Kristeva and Jacques Derrida). Post-structuralists reintroduced the importance of culture and context in understanding a text or social situation.

Typically, post-structuralists hold that the meaning of any work is itself a cultural phenomenon.

Summing Up: Context Matters

The examples above, taking Whewell and Kant as their points of departure, provide evidence of the important role of context in the constructivist approach. History, ideas, community and language are all important contextual factors that provide order and patterns to the world as we know it. This recognition is the central feature that distinguishes constructivist from naturalist social science. As a consequence, and as we shall see in the chapters that follow, constructivists tend to draw on methods that can preserve and employ these contexts as an aid to our understanding.

Recapitulation: the Constructivist Way of Knowing

In this chapter we have tried to paint a portrait of an alternative approach to social study. Although this portrait is rather sketchy, and made with broad strokes, we hope to have captured some of constructivism's most distinctive features. In doing so, we have granted Immanuel Kant a central role in the constructivist tradition. As a consequence of the ambiguous and contentious nature of Kant's arguments, they continue to influence the nature of contemporary debates about what constitutes science.

Thus far we have swept quickly through a wide swath of the Western world's academic history – from historical authorities like Kant and Whewell, to the many interwar intellectuals who fled the rise of fascism in Europe, to even more recent authorities on context and meaning. At first glance, it appears difficult and daunting to unify this disparate and varied group of thinkers under any single methodological claim. We realize that the diversity of these thinkers makes it difficult to find among them any single ontological claim, any uniform epistemological vision, or any particular methodological stance. Indeed, we worry that many constructivists will balk at the idea of trying to unify such diverse thinkers as Kant, Kristeva and Kuhn. But we take some comfort in realizing that the very same thing could be said of scholars from the naturalist camp. After all, both traditions are diverse; the difference between them is more a matter of degree than of nature.

In a pinch, we are prepared to argue that the naturalist camp is the less diverse of the two. The vast majority of naturalist scientists are willing to share a small handful of philosophical assumptions – for example, they agree that there is a Real World out there, and that scientists have access to it through their senses. In contrast, it is more difficult to find consensus among constructivists on any given ontological or epistemological position. While many constructivists would accept that social scientists do have access to a Real World by way of their senses, many others question the very existence of that World. Still others would argue that there is a Real World, but that neither perceptions nor human reason allow us guaranteed access to it, as it is buried under so many layers of conceptual and contextual meaning. In short, the constructivist camp covers much territory; as a consequence it may house a more heterogeneous lot of fellow travellers than the naturalist camp.

If we are to discuss the constructivist camp at all, however, it is necessary to provide it with some unifying properties – if only to help us juxtapose it with the naturalist tradition described in the first part of the book. Such unifying properties do exist; the problem is that they are distributed unevenly among members of the constructivist camp. To understand and depict these unifying characteristics we might think of them in terms of Wittgenstein's (1999, §66–71) reference to 'family resemblances': a set of features that are recognized as similar, but which have no one thing in common.

The Constructivist Other

Family photographs depict a group of individuals who share noticeable traits. That is not to say that every member of the family shares one or two dominant features; rather, they resemble each other in that they together, on closer scrutiny, share a set of features, distributed unequally among them. A few of the men may have the same big ears, some of the women may have the same thick neck, some (both men and women) may have the same kind of blunt nose, others may share the same jet of black, straight hair, and so on. But compared to the physical characteristics shared by other families, it is possible to distinguish a family resemblance. It is in these ways that we can think of the family of constructivist social scientists: we recognize that no methodological feature is shared by every member of the constructivist troop, but some features are shared by some of the members in a way that distinguishes them from other methodological families.

One of the most commonly held family features in the constructivist camp is a deep scepticism of the naturalist approach to social science. This scepticism takes aim at the core ontological, epistemological and methodological claims of the naturalist tradition. As this scepticism is broadly shared, residents of the constructivist camp might be construed as a collective Self by virtue of their common opposition to a naturalist Other.

Figure 8.1   *The three basic joists of constructivist social science*

- An **ontology** based on the precepts that women and men are malleable, and that each of us participates in the construction of our own world.
- An **epistemology** which, in addition to sense perceptions and human reason, relies on a much broader repertoire of epistemological devices (such as empathetic and dialectical approaches).
- A **methodology** which seeks to identify the (socially constructed) patterns and regularities of the world.

At the end of Chapter 2, we identified three broad joists that sustained the naturalist tradition: the notion that the Real World exists; that this world is a realm of independent particulars that relate to each other in regular and patterned ways; and that humans have access to this world through systematic observation. In Figure 8.1 we identify three basic joists in the constructivist tradition. It is important to note that none of these joists were milled from the trunk of the natural sciences. In fact, all three were developed in self-conscious opposition to naturalism. It is this opposition to the naturalist tradition that is, perhaps, the most important single feature that can unify the disparate constructivist camp.

The first joist is *ontological*. Constructivists convey a basic uncertainty about the nature of the world. For them, the world does not exist independent of our senses; it is a world of appearances. More to the point: the world we study is one that appears to people who find themselves situated in different contexts. Consequently, the world appears differently to different observers; its appearance varies with the contextual setting (temporal, geographical, gendered, ideological, cultural etc.) of the observers.

This constructivist ontology is at odds with the one shared by empiricist philosophers like John Locke and David Hume in at least two important ways. First, constructivists do not eagerly embrace the naturalist notion of a Real World. Rather, they tend to argue that the world is man-made. Second, constructivists harbour a deep suspicion towards Locke and people like him, who endow humans with fixed and permanent attributes. Constructivists are not fond of invoking human nature; they tend to portray human beings as adaptable and malleable.

In short, the common point of departure for most constructivists is an agreement that the naturalist tradition provides an unsatisfactory basis for social science. On this point, constructivists tend to distance themselves from scientific realists, as we explained in the introductory chapter.

Constructivists also agree that it is important to discuss and consider the nature of the relationship that links the mind and its world. For as long as this relationship remains unsettled, constructivists and naturalists cannot agree about the source of the patterns that both traditions agree exist (and which cry out for explanation). Naturalists are familiar with Kantian arguments – they tend to sample them, feign polite interest in their basic tenets, and then move on quickly to more practical tasks. Constructivists, by contrast, tend to linger on these Kantian arguments. While many constructivists would agree that the physical world is material, concrete and given by nature, they are loathe to accept the same description of the social world. For them, there is no clearly delineated social world: there are many. None of these worlds is naturally given; each and every one is socially constructed. Each world is created by human beings – not in the sense that humans consciously set about building their world from some original blueprint, but in the sense that this world has evolved as a result of human interaction in society, through history, with ideas, using language. Having said this, we should point out that constructivists disagree about how much of the naturalist philosophy we can and should keep. Also, they differ markedly on the distance they want to travel to find a more credible alternative.

This has significant consequences for the constructivist attitude towards truth. Given the ontological certainty of the naturalist approach, it is common to find naturalists who are firmly committed to uncovering real and unyielding truths about the world. It is this very commitment to truth that can be said to lie beneath the spirited reactions by the natural science community to Bjørn Lomborg's book, as described in the introductory chapter. In this way, naturalism appears to many of its critics as religion does to the atheist. Although this commitment to singular truths can be found among some constructivist scholars, constructivists generally tend to be more agnostic on issues of truth. To paraphrase Rorty (1979, p. 377), the point for many constructivists is to keep the conversation going rather than to find objective truth.

This brings us to the *epistemological* joist of constructivist science. Given the more open-ended ontological position shared by constructivists, we should not be surprised to find their epistemological joist to be of sizeable dimensions. Constructivists refuse to be limited to just sensual perception and reason as the only means to access knowledge. Instead, they tend to embrace a much broader selection of epistemological devices, prioritizing those which protect, enhance and exploit contextual meanings.

In short, constructivists tend to be epistemological pluralists. They are willing to employ different tools for understanding the unique nature of the social world. This willingness flows from two related claims. The first is ontological: that there is a distinction between the natural world and the social world. The second is epistemological: that in order to obtain knowledge about the social world, it is necessary to break away from the individualist notion than the whole is the sum of the parts. For the social sciences, knowledge is carried by individuals but anchored in collectives.

For the constructivist tradition, then, knowledge is not a subjective thing rent through and through with relativism (as some of its critics charge). Knowledge is intersubjective. The world is real. It is an object – a *phenoumenon*, a thing-for-us – and we can obtain knowledge about it. But how do we do that? The short constructivist answer to this important question is: very carefully!

The reason for being so careful is related to the constructed nature of the social world. Truth isn't just 'out there'. Knowledge about the social world is always knowledge-in-context; it is socially situated and has social consequences. As a result, knowledge is always somebody's knowledge. Knowledge is, in Robert Cox's famous formulation, '*for* someone'; it serves somebody's purpose. To 'know' is to be in a position to dominate or enslave.

Because knowledge and power are so closely associated, constructivists hold it is necessary to approach knowledge with scepticism and great self-awareness. We need to be attuned to the context in which knowledge is engendered, by whom and for what purpose. We also have to approach knowledge with the proper attitude. For example, we need to consider knowledge in political solidarity with the more marginalized members of society or with the proper respect for (and empathy) with the object at hand. In short, constructivists approach the world and its knowledge *critically*.

But, besides being careful and critical, how do constructivists approach the social world when they search for knowledge about it? On this point constructivists differ. Some are pragmatic and argue that the question, the purpose and the sources at hand must determine the method: for example, sometimes statistical analyses and hypothesis testing is the way to go; sometimes an interpretive case study method is the more natural choice. Others shun any procedural design that smacks of naturalism. Some constructivists have found in hermeneutics a basic method that dovetails nicely with the ontological and the epistemological tendencies of constructivism. Our point is that constructivists rely on the same basic methods as do naturalists, but they do so in different ways and towards different ends. This important lesson is elaborated upon in the chapters that follow.

From these ontological and epistemological commitments we find a confirmation of the constructivists' *methodology*. Constructivists realize that the world is filled with repetitions and regularities, but they insist that these patterns are socially constructed even as the world appears to us as objective fact. For this reason, constructivists approach their area of study with tools and approaches that can identify these socially constructed patterns in the world, and understand them in light of the contexts that give them meaning.

Conclusion

The modern constructivist tradition can be traced back to the time when Hume shook Kant from his dogmatic slumber. The result of this rude awakening was a contentious, important and ambiguous argument that has managed to keep entire philosophy departments busy and lively for well over two centuries. Kant's argument about our (in)ability to understand (directly) the Real World still lies at the heart of constructivist approaches today.

Given Kant's well-deserved reputation for opaqueness and obscurity, we have employed William Whewell to shine light on some of the key precepts of constructivist thought. Among these precepts is a healthy scepticism of: (1) the division of the examining subject from the object being examined; and (2) the separation of facts from ideas. Whewell, for example, argued that science is a social practice and that science, as well as practising scientists, are embedded in society (as well as its history).

Whewell's ideas took on a new urgency in the closing decades of the twentieth century. The result has been a varied and multifaceted approach to social science which shares certain ontological beliefs, but little else (save, perhaps, a common antagonism to the naturalist approach). This new, constructivist, approach to social science is sceptical of the naturalist quest for truth and order; it is willing to embrace new epistemological outlets; and it is leery of rigid demarcation principles. As a consequence – and as we shall see in the chapters that remain – constructivists use social scientific methods in ways (and towards ends) that differ radically from the naturalists.

Among constructivists it is possible to find scholars who do believe that there are better, and more accurate, means of interpreting human actions. For the vast majority of authors in this tradition, however, we find resistance to specifying a clear and explicit hierarchy of methods or a demarcation principle. Unlike the naturalist approach, there are few attempts in this tradition to try and push all scholars towards adopting one particular method (for example, the experimental). Nor are other methods used in an attempt to mimic the experimental (or any other) method.

This is not to say that constructivist scholars do not favour some methods over others. As we shall see in the chapters that follow, most constructivists have a soft spot for narrative approaches: these provide scholars with a nearness to the data and context that is necessary to gain insight. Comparisons are also made by constructivists, but they are used in ways that differ radically from those of naturalist scholars – in ways that protect and nurture the contexts and meanings that constructivists cherish. Having said this, it is important to emphasize that constructivists favour narrative approaches and few-N comparisons that allow the analyst to keep close to the particulars at hand.

We seldom find constructivists who are willing to employ statistical and experimental methods. Yet there is nothing inherent to either statistics or experiments that need alienate the constructivist scholar. Properly designed and executed, statistical and experimental techniques may be fruitful additions to the constructivist repertoire of methods, as we seek to show in Chapters 11 and 12.

Recommended Further Reading

To begin at the beginning, read Whewell's *History of the Inductive Sciences* [1837] and his *Philosophy of the Inductive Sciences* [1840]. Kuhn's *The Structure of Scientific Revolutions* [1962], Winch's *The Idea of a Social Science* (1958) and Wittgenstein's *Philosophical Investigations* [1953] are classic references. For more accessible introductions to the philosophy of constructivist science, see Berger and Luckmann's *The Social Construction of Reality* (1966) and Searle's *The Construction of Social Reality* (1995).

Chapter 9

From Story Telling to Telling Histories

The social scientific project, regardless of its methodological point of departure, seeks to find and explain patterns. For naturalists, the project is a fairly straightforward process of observing (or experiencing) and noting the patterns found naturally in the world. For constructivists, however, the patterns of interest are illusive and complex – and are themselves in need of explanation. In short, while naturalists believe that facts speak for themselves, and that knowledge will grow by their relentless accumulation, constructivists tend to doubt the innocence of facts and question whether facts come to the social analyst 'like fish on the fishmonger's slab' (Carr, 1987, p. 9).

The main reason for this difference lies in the naturalist's assumption that the subject can be separated from its object of study; that the student of social phenomena can be separated from her facts. When facts are understood to be (wo)man-made, the relationship between the analyst and her facts becomes more complicated. This difficulty can be divided into two parts: the nature of social data; and the analyst's relationship to that data.

The nature of social data is a two-edged problem for students of social phenomena: facts are both too plentiful and too sparse. On the one hand, we can find ourselves overwhelmed by the sheer mass of facts. As E. H. Carr (1987, p. 14) notes with some envy, few facts survive from the very distant past, and scholars of ancient history appear competent 'mainly because they are so ignorant of their subject. The modern historian [or social analyst] enjoys none of the advantages of this built-in ignorance. He must cultivate the necessary ignorance for himself.' In other words, students of social phenomena often find themselves suffocating under the massive weight of potentially relevant information. Method, for both naturalist and constructivist approaches, is the traditional means for lightening this load.

On the other hand, students of social phenomena often find themselves at the mercy of too little data. This problem is especially acute for those interested in historical phenomena. As we have already noted (in Chapter 6), one problem is the historian's reliance on primary sources. As

Figure 9.1   *Representing the past*

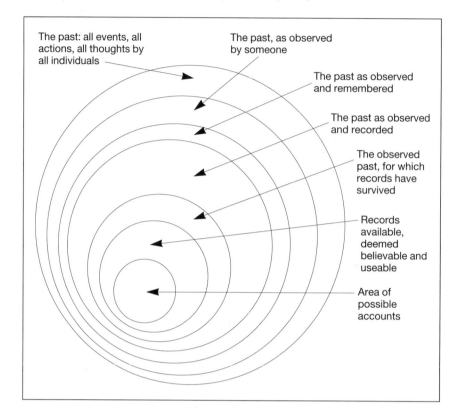

The past: all events, all actions, all thoughts by all individuals

The past, as observed by someone

The past as observed and remembered

The past as observed and recorded

The observed past, for which records have survived

Records available, deemed believable and useable

Area of possible accounts

a result of this, the historical analyst is often confined to a narrow field of research: kings, generals and MPs are more likely to leave primary accounts than are housewives, gravediggers, fishermen, bakers and mimes. The problem is exacerbated by the fact that sources (even primary sources) tend to shrivel up with time. By the time a phenomenon finds an interested sponsor and/or interpreter, its remnants may be vastly incomplete. Worse, there are no guarantees that the surviving historical record is – in any way – representative. The nature of this problem is illustrated in Figure 9.1, where the past – and our access to it – can be understood in terms of concentric circles.

If we let the outermost circle in this diagram represent the entire past, we see how a number of mostly random factors can severely restrict our access to it. For this past to enter into the analyst's account (represented here by the innermost circle), it has to be observed, remembered and recorded – and the records must have survived. Each of these steps is represented by smaller circles within the largest circle (representing the entire past). These more or less random factors (observation, remembrance, recording, survival) determine the representativeness of the account that remains. For example, if we assume that the outermost circle in Figure 9.1 captures the entire past in some sort of Cartesian space, and we note that the final account ended up in the lower left 'corner' of that space, then we have ended up with an account that is not 'centred' or representative. Without additional information to explain or interpret this bias, the analyst would probably assume (in error) that history is centred on the analyst's account.

It is because of these difficulties that constructivists tend to be critical of the three basic assumptions of naturalist historians: (1) that there is 'a past' that can be captured by the scholar; (2) that data are available to her that are somehow objective or representative of that past; and (3) that these data are simply there for the taking. Thus, Edward Carr speaks disparagingly of the naturalist who considers his facts as fish on the fish-monger's slab. In practice, of course, the social analyst interacts with her data:

> The facts are really not at all like fish on the fishmonger's slab. They are like fish swimming about in a vast and sometimes inaccessible ocean, and what the historian [or social analyst] catches will depend, partly on chance, but mainly on what part of the ocean [s]he chooses to fish in and what tackle [s]he chooses to use – these two facts being, of course, determined by what kind of fish he wants to catch. By and large, the historian [or social analyst] will get the kinds of facts [s]he wants.   (Carr, 1987, p. 23)

While traditional historians are aware of this problem, it would seem that they prefer to ignore it (or disarm it with humour), rather than tackle it head-on. Thus, in 1867, the English Rankean James Anthony Froude (1963, p. 21), noted: 'It often seems to me as if history is like a child's box of letters, with which we can spell any word we please. We have only to pick out such letters as we want, arrange them as we like, and say nothing about those which do not suit our purpose.' Or, following Catherine Morland on History (from the dedication to Carr's book): 'I often think it odd that it should be so dull, for a great deal of it must be invention.' In contrast, constructivists have come to a sober realization about the importance of their relationship to their data.

Constructivists also appreciate a good story, but they differ on the role such stories can (or should) play in the social scientific project. This means, first and foremost, that constructivists favour thick descriptions, where the analyst can climb into an intricate (hi)story and learn to know it from the inside out. But it also means that the constructivist is attracted to many unique histories and the storytellers behind them. For this reason, much of this chapter focuses on the storytellers themselves (rather than the way that histories can be placed in a larger social scientific context, as we saw in Chapter 6).

To illustrate the sundry roles that historical depictions can play in constructivist accounts, this chapter lays out a broad continuum of different motivations, styles and considerations. At the most relativistic end of this continuum, we describe a serendipitous approach, where patterns and connections are pulled from thin air (yet still provide meaning and understanding). At the other end of the continuum we find authors that recognize the contextuality and relativity of different historical accounts, but still wish to establish explicit rules for choosing 'better' accounts. This end of the continuum can flow seamlessly into naturalist accounts, as described in Chapter 6. In between these two end points, we describe how historical accounts can be framed by literary forms, ideas and social contexts.

By employing historical accounts in these different ways, constructivists problematize the way in which naturalists employ historical accounts as unbiased 'facts' in larger social scientific analyses. Given the constructivist's ontological starting point, they do not feel a need to commit themselves to a single historical account (and tend to see attempts at depicting history in this way as misleading and dishonest). But constructivists do not employ historical approaches only to criticize naturalist accounts. Constructivists celebrate the diversity of perspectives, while producing better interpretations of the phenomena under study. For them,

> '[b]etter' interpretations do not aim at arriving at the final, objective (in the [naturalist] sense) truth of the matter but rather are those that are at one and the same time aware of their own conditionality and are open to the distortions occasioned by conditions of radical inequality . . . 'Better' interpretations are readings in which the subject might recognize himself or herself, his or her meanings, his or her actions, and might even agree. And 'better' interpretations are those that are simultaneously attentive to participants' self-understanding and the way power functions in language . . . (Euben, 1999, p. 45)

The Mysterious Ways of Miss Marple

Naturalist scholars rely on disciplined and repeatable procedures, transparent designs, logical arguments and publicly verifiable sources to reveal and understand the patterns they seek. As we have seen, their method of choice is the experiment and their mascot is the professional London detective, Sherlock Holmes. Holmes exemplifies the naturalist historian with his unflinching faith in empiricism and his insistence that there is, in fact, a truth to be found.

Given the constructivist's scepticism towards a singular truth, and the role of empiricism in uncovering it, analysts in this tradition seek another detective mascot – one more sympathetic to their own methodological priors. One likely candidate is Agatha Christie's marvellous Miss Jane Marple, from the small English village of St Mary's Mead. Spinster, busybody and a shrewd observer of human nature, Miss Marple also exposes thieves and murderers. However, she relies on a radically different approach than her male counterpart.

Sherlock Holmes subscribed to the traditional correspondence theory of truth. For him, a statement was true if it corresponded to the facts in the case. Miss Marple is more circumspect. On the one hand, it would be unfair to suggest that Miss Marple denies a claim to be true when it corresponds to the facts. On the other hand, however, she seems to have a very different notion of what constitutes a fact. Also, she seems more reluctant to confirm the existence of one, unchangeable world; she may see many worlds – and consequently, she may also see many truths. Finally, Miss Marple is not bound to induction as the only way of gaining knowledge. She trusts her imagination to provide explanatory principles and associations.

This novel approach is demonstrated in one of her most famous cases, *A Pocket Full of Rye* (Christie, 2000 [1953]). When a wealthy financier, Rex Fortescue, is found murdered at his desk, his discontented wife is at first suspected of the crime. But then his wife, too, is murdered – poisoned with cyanide at teatime. Soon after, their maid is murdered while hanging up newly washed clothes to dry – strangled with a stocking in the garden, and found with a clothes-peg on her nose. Not surprisingly, the police are at a loss to explain the string of murders. When it turns out that all three victims were found with grains of rye in their pockets, their confusion is complete. Miss Marple, however, is able to discover a pattern and prods Inspector Neele to investigate the involvement of blackbirds.

The inspector brushes aside the batty old spinster, who – for good measure – begins to recite a traditional nursery rhyme from the *Mother Goose* collection:

The king was in the counting-house, counting out his money.
The queen was in the parlour eating bread and honey.
The maid was in the garden, hanging out the clothes.
There came a little blackbird and snipped off her nose . . .

Suddenly insight shines on the inspector as well: Rex is the king, of course; he was murdered while working at his desk, counting out his money (as it were). His wife represents the queen: she was murdered in the parlour while having tea. The maid was murdered in the garden, hanging out the clothes. In short, Miss Marple had seen that the murders all seemed to be connected to the old nursery rhyme 'Sing a song of sixpence'. It dawns on the inspector that the old bat may be on to something. But what? And where do the blackbirds enter in?

Miss Marple is well positioned to answer these questions. First and foremost, she is as well-informed about the wealthy Fortescue family as she is about every other family in the village. Her approach to solving crimes depends on her intimate knowledge of the people and context in which the crimes are situated. For example, she knows that the murdered financier had two sons from a previous marriage, both of whom had spent some time abroad, exploring possible investments in mines and minerals. Further investigations would reveal that father and sons quarrelled over the ownership of an apparently worthless venture in the USA: the Blackbird Mine.

This brief example illustrates why Miss Marple constitutes a reasonable representative of the constructivist approach. Like the naturalist, Miss Marple begins her investigation by looking for patterns or regularities. To do this, however, she does not rely on induction – at least, not on induction alone. Miss Marple suggests that there are many different ways of making sense of events – and one of them goes by way of Mother Goose's rhymes. As the perpetrators of the crimes are familiar with Mother Goose, their actions were influenced by the nursery rhyme – either consciously or subconsciously. The point is that once the pattern is recognized, Miss Marple can use it to piece together the missing pieces of the puzzle and come to a better understanding of what had happened. Like Sherlock Holmes, Miss Marple can use her approach to solve baffling mysteries.

The Serendipitous Approach

Miss Marple's method, though clearly unorthodox, delivers the criminals. Like many constructivists, she does not seem to be too concerned about formal or explicit rules or methods. It is for this reason, perhaps, that naturalists might refer disparagingly to the constructivist method as 'serendipitous' or an approach of 'accidental discovery'. This method, the naturalist will argue, does not involve systematic reasoning. Rather, it relies on dumb luck; and dumb luck does not deserve a place among the methods of scientists.

Despite its poor reputation among naturalists, this serendipitous method enjoys a wide entourage. Journalists use it all the time, with an expectation of observing some event first-hand and producing newsworthy eyewitness accounts. Anthropologists use it as well; their fieldwork method exploits the virtues of 'thick description' based on insight, which only participant observation can yield. Historians often work in the same way: they delve fully into some past society with the hope of gaining deep insight about its people and culture. While the method is often belittled by naturalists for its simplicity, there can be no denying that it remains an important and influential way for analysts to explain and understand social behaviour. The insight and meaning generated by this serendipitous method can have an enormous impact on the way we come to see the world.

Where does this serendipitous method come from? It should not surprise us that such an unruly method draws on non-academic roots. The word that lends its history to this method (serendipity) is actually an ancient name for Sri Lanka – or Ceylon or Serendip. One of the kings of ancient Serendip, King Jafer, had three sons who were all well versed in history and logic. All three possessed keen powers of observation and they travelled in search of adventure and further enlightenment.

One day, having made camp for the evening, the three boys were approached by a camel driver. He had lost one of his animals, and asked if they had seen it. Was the camel blind in one eye, they asked? Was it missing a tooth? If so, they knew where it had gone. They pointed out the direction, and the driver immediately set off in search of his camel.

A few hours later, the camel driver returned empty-handed. He was hungry, frustrated, and in a foul mood because he was convinced that the three young men had amused themselves at his expense. No, no, they assured him. Had not the beast been laden with butter on one side and honey on the other, asked one of the princes? And was it not being ridden by a woman, asked the other? And wasn't this woman heavily pregnant, asked the third? The camel driver answered each question in the affirmative. His mounting frustrations exploded in an indignant rage, however, when the three young men added: No, they had seen neither his camel nor the pregnant woman!

The camel driver was now convinced that the three brothers had sent him on a wild goose chase. Worse, he now suspected that they had stolen his camel to boot! Determined to get his animal back, he had the three princes arrested and brought before the Emperor Behram. There they explained that they had never seen the animal (which had subsequently been found and returned to its owner). They told the Emperor that their rich descriptions had been the simple result of clues observed and inferences drawn. The camel must have been blind in one eye, for it had eaten grass on only one side of the road – and the side with inferior feed at that. Its missing tooth had caused it to leave bits of chewed grass on the road. Ants love butter and flies love honey, and each kind of insect was found on its respective side of the road. They had seen the footprints of a woman who had often stopped to sit down and rest, and her heavy pregnancy had forced her to use both hands to get back on to her feet.

The story is related in *The Travels and Adventures of Three Princes of Serendip*, an anonymous book, translated from Arabic in 1722. The book itself reflected a strong, emerging interest in Oriental history and literature, an interest that characterized polite society in eighteenth-century England and France. It also spurred the envy of philosophers and historians: for what wisdom and insight could be gained if they might possess the princes' powers of observation, contextual imagination and playful ability to reason backwards!

Many constructivists aim to mimic the method of Serendip's three princes. They realize that this method depends on a good deal of careful empirical work. Sorting through this empirical detail may appear as guesswork, but it is – at least – well-informed guesswork. More than that, the constructivist uses her familiarity with the subject to follow a causal chain backwards: from a given event she seeks to unravel the chain of causation until she arrives at the most probable cause. This is like the process employed by the three Oriental princes; it is a method that is interpretive, imaginative, retroductive and playful. Like the camel trader's reaction, however, the serendipitous method often generates irritation and anger in those who do not appreciate the mixing of play and scholarship. But we mustn't let this playfulness distract us into thinking that the serendipitous approach somehow lacks logic or technique.

Ethnomethodology

Ethnomethodology is an approach that shares many qualities of the approach employed by the three princes of Serendip. Associated with the American sociologist Harold Garfinkel [1967] – but with roots that can be traced back to Weber's concept of *Verstehen* and Alfred Schütz's notion of phenomenological reconstruction – ethnomethodology refers to the study of ways in which people make sense of their social world. What distances this approach from the other framing devices described in the remainder of this chapter (and explains why we have positioned it at the serendipity end of our continuum) is the fact that ethnomethodologists begin by assuming that social order is illusory. Ethnomethodologists hold that the order we see in social life is constructed in the minds of social actors. In particular, society confronts us as a series of sense impressions and experiences which we must somehow organize into a coherent pattern. For Garfinkel, this organization process (what he called 'the documentary method') was individual and psychological in nature. When faced with a given context, we tend to select certain facts; we use these to establish a pattern which is subsequently used to make sense of the remaining facts (in terms of that pattern).

To illustrate how this documentary method works, Garfinkel invited a number of students to take part in an experiment. The students were told that they could talk to an 'adviser' about their personal problems, but they could only pose yes/no questions. The students could not see the adviser, and were forced to communicate with him/her through an intercom. What they *weren't* told was that the adviser was not actually listening to the questions being asked, but responded instead with a list of predetermined and random sequences of yes/no answers.

As we might expect, the advisers were not able to give consistent or (apparently) meaningful answers. Despite this, the students managed to make sense of these answers by placing them in a patterned context which allowed them to balance and weigh contradictory evidence. For example, one student asked whether he should drop out of school and was surprised to hear the adviser respond in the affirmative. Confused, he asked again: 'You really think I should drop out of school?' This time, the adviser responded in the negative. Rather than doubt the sincerity of the adviser, or dismiss the advice as nonsensical, the student struggled to find its meaning. Indeed, most students seem to have found the advice given was both reasonable and helpful!

This documentary method is used by ethnomethodologists to show how we use cultural competence and contextual (indexical) knowledge to make sense of commonplace events. This reflexive characteristic is what makes our actions (and interpretations) mutually intelligible. With this knowledge in hand, ethnomethodologists employ research strategies which force subjects to 'break' with commonplace routines in order to reveal the way in which cultural competence is always framing our understandings (for example, by examining how family members react when we pretend to be a stranger, or when we blatantly cheat at a game.) In studying these sorts of examples, ethnomethodologists can demonstrate the creativity with which we (as members of society) are able to interpret and maintain social order. In short, ethnomethodologists show us how we construct a social reality to make sense of our often senseless interactions. By using the documentary method we bring order to what is, in fact, a chaotic situation.

Presentational Approaches

Not all constructivists will rejoice in their approach being described as serendipitous. Often a great deal of reflection and polish goes into the presentation of the historical material. What's more, many constructivists are quite aware of how their historical narratives can be affected by the very form that they impose upon their material. Our stories, they argue, are shaped by the way we choose to *present* them.

After all, once we accept that the social analyst is telling a story, the next step must be to investigate the narrative form taken by these stories. Indeed, to the extent that constructivists are willing to focus on the story, at the expense of explicit methodological criteria, then the role of narrative structure in framing the story becomes all the more important. This section will show how even the most inductivist and dispassionate social analyst often organizes her narratives in standard forms that are similar to those used by writers of fiction.

From Facts to Narrative

Barbara Tuchman's explanation of the historian's writing process is a very good one. When Tuchman examines her sources, the key information in each source is, ideally, distilled into a few sentences and written on a small four-inch by six-inch card. When the research is completed, the cards can be arranged chronologically and, as Tuchman (1981, p. 20) explains, 'as the cards fall into groups according to subject or person or chronological sequence, the pattern of my story will emerge'.

This works. It is a good method; perhaps the best. It is tested, true, and drawn from the experience of a professional historian with a string of successful books to her record. Yet, even this technique ignores the key element in writing history; it is silent about the very act of historiographical creation. For if the scholar simply arranges (notes on) her sources in chronological order and writes it up, she has written nothing more than a catalogue of events!

Events, on their own, do not produce a story. The (notes on) sources are absolute central elements in the story, but the scholar needs to assemble them in particular ways in order to produce a legible and convincing story. Hayden White (1987, p. 92) formalizes the process in the following way. He begins by assuming that the social scientist has collected a box full of event-notes, and that she has arranged them in chronological order. In the depiction below, each letter represents a social fact; and chronology is depicted by alphabetical order:

$$a, b, c, d, e, \ldots \ldots \ldots, n$$

For these ordered facts to result in a story, they have to be combined in a narrative. In providing this narrative, the social analyst takes many (mostly hidden) steps. First, the analyst has to add descriptive elements that tie together various facts into a coherent whole. In addition, she needs to add an active or binding component that provides meaning. Finally, the analyst needs to interpret the different sources – emphasizing or de-emphasizing particular facts according to the role or function that these will play in the larger story.

Of course, a list of facts can be assembled in an almost infinite number of ways. Four of these potential assemblies are suggested below, where we have maintained chronological order for the sake of simplicity. In this matrix of facts, the capital (large) letters represent events or facts that are somehow privileged over the others. For example, in the second assembly of facts, event (b) is emphasized by the analyst as a determining event (B), and given a key role in the analyst's story.

$$A, b, c, d, e, \ldots \ldots, n \qquad (1)$$
$$a, B, c, d, e, \ldots \ldots, n \qquad (2)$$
$$a, b, C, d, e, \ldots \ldots, n \qquad (3)$$
$$a, b, c, D, e, \ldots \ldots, n \qquad (4)$$
$$etc. \ldots$$

White's argument is not particularly novel. It is possible to find traces of it in the work of a number of different historians, ranging from the Hegelian-inspired R. G. Collingwood to the proto-Rankean, Barbara Tuchman. But White's discussion is richer than the others in that he is searching to explain how the historian (or social analyst) moves from data to argument; how she transforms a collection of facts to a plausible story; how she structures her facts through the operation of 'emplotment' (White, 1973, p. 7).

Narrative Structures

White argues that to create a story out of a collection of facts the social analyst needs to utilize literary techniques. Drawing on Northrop Frye (1957), White distinguishes among four main types of emplotment:

- *Romance* celebrates the triumph of the good after a series of trials and tribulations. Romantic stories are filled with progress and happy endings. The evolution (or progress) is propelled by deep, conflicting forces that ultimately produce a state of harmony or bliss.
- *Tragedies* are stories of potential progress, failed; they stress the irreconcilable element of human affairs, and lament the loss of good

that is inevitable when values collide. The tragic struggle is seen as heroic (as it is in romantic stories), but it is a struggle that ends in failure (and this failure is usually rooted in some notion of human flaw).

- *Satire* is a reaction to romance, but a critical and mordant reaction: a reaction with a normative agenda of its own. In satires, human affairs are not depicted in terms of success or failure; satirical stories see only meaningless change in human life. Indeed, a satire doesn't just seek to present an alternative story, it wants to show that the romantic story is naïve and simple-minded.
- Finally, a *comedy* celebrates the conservation of human values against the threat of disruption. Like the other plot structures, comedies are also a reaction to romance (but comedy breaks less with it than do the others). In short, the basic structure of a comedy is ultimately a story of progress toward a happy ending, but where the progress is neither clear nor linear.

To give the reader a taste of how these plot structures can be read into different types of social analyses, we turn to four influential attempts to summarize the twentieth century at its close: Eric Hobsbawm's immensely popular *Age of Extremes* (1994); François Furet's *Passing of an Illusion* (1999 [1995]); Mark Mazower's *Dark Continent* (1998); and Bruce Russett and John Oneal's *Triangulating Peace* (2001).[1] These historians saw the transition to a new millennium as a convenient occasion to summarize our age, systematize its key themes, and identify its most conspicuous patterns.

The books by Hobsbawm, Furet and Mazower share many features. They agree that the twentieth century was the bloodiest in history: more people were killed in conflict and war than in any other century. They also tend to agree about what constitute the key events of the century. With respect to the first half of the century, they all emphasize the First World War, the postwar recession, the revolution in Russia, the Nazi take-over in Germany and the impact of the Second World War. In the second half of the century, all of them emphasize the nuclear rivalry between East and West and the dangerous decades of the Cold War.

Despite these important similarities, each of these authors tells a radically different story about the twentieth century. Each book can be discussed in terms of the narrative tissue that connects the (largely known and largely common) historical facts – with concepts drawn from Frye (1957) and along lines developed by White (1973). For example, Hobsbawm and Furet have both written stories in which Marxism and Marxist movements play leading roles. However, whereas Hobsbawm has cast Marxism in the role of the hero, Furet has given it the role of the villain. Both authors have concluded that Marxism dies in the last act. But for Hobsbawm this death is a tragic event; it means that the forces of light and promise have lost out to the forces of darkness. For Furet, by contrast, the death of Marxism means the ultimate retreat of the story's seductive scoundrel, and the restoration of a natural order. In terms of literary form, Hobsbawm has written a tragedy, whereas Furet has written a comedy.

Mazower, by contrast, has written a satire. *The Dark Continent* paints a deeply disturbing portrait of the twentieth century. Although he recognizes that the twentieth century is marked by democratic progress, he warns that democracy is far more fragile than most people assume. Instead of rejoicing in democracy's victory after the Cold War, Mazower questions the very notion of victory. Instead of seeing communism and fascism as horrible aberrations from Europe's past, he sees them (along with democracy) as natural products of the twentieth century.

When actively searching for plot structures in these summaries of the twentieth century, we are struck by the distinct absence of a romantic story line. To find a romantic depiction of the twentieth century we must leave the historian's den and search among social scientists. Indeed, a good number of the romantic histories of the recent past have been written by social scientists: by economists who challenge Hobsbawm's tragic tale with up-beat stories about the steady evolution of wealth and liberty; by political scientists and sociologists who see a global development of democracy and political stability. One case in point is the Hegelian-inspired argument that history has come to an end (Fukuyama, 1992). Another is the Whiggish claim that democracies do not to go to war against each other (Russett, 1993).

It is in this, romantic, way that our fourth book, by Russett and Oneal, can be read. The main claim of *Triangulating Peace* is that the twentieth century has been marked by the hopeful evolution of a zone of peace among the world's democracies. This has been orthodoxy among peace researchers for many years, but Russett and Oneal provide new and more convincing explanations for the phenomenon. In particular, they invoke Immanuel Kant's 'Perpetual Peace' [1795] essay and see Kant as a visionary advocate for a 'triangular peace' – that is, for peaceful relations among states, conducted within the civilizing frameworks of three interacting sets of institutions: republican constitutions, 'cosmopolitan law' (which guarantees free commercial transactions) and multilateral treaties and international organizations.

These four accounts of the twentieth century tell the same (basic) story, but in different ways. They share many common concerns, and draw on many of the same social data and events. In other words, they look at the real world, and see different things. This is the essence of the constructivist approach. Each interpretation encourages us to see that world through the eyes of the respective author. Indeed, it is significant and useful to recognize and stress the differences that separate these interpretations – there is no need or desire to prioritize one over the other. What utility can there be in claiming that Hobsbawm's history is better than Furet's (for example)? Rather, constructivists embrace the remarkable differences that separate these authors' individual interpretations.

Ideational Approaches

We have already noted the importance of ideas in the work of earlier philosophers of science: Whewell foreshadowed it with his discussion on the nature and impact of natural ideas, as did Collingwood in his discussion of presuppositions. More recent authors have continued this tradition, while tackling the issue head on. Among these is the early French sociologist, Émile Durkheim, who set out to investigate the basic principles that maintained order in society. Durkheim introduced the concept of solidarity, and conceived of it as a set of generally accepted norms or rules embraced by all of society's members. This way of thinking exerted a great influence on French social sciences in the twentieth century, most noticeably on the *Annales* school. This section uses examples such as these to elaborate on the importance of an author's ideational context in framing how she comes to see and understand the patterns that she studies.

From Mentalities to Discourse

The *Annales* school, as represented by two of its better-known member – Lucien Febvre and Marc Bloch – studied the history of human knowledge. From this study they came to the conclusion that most of the history of human knowledge could be described in terms of calm pools of collective knowledge (*longue durées*). Sometimes, however, this history could be characterized by sudden rushes of foaming, revolutionary change (*ruptures*). These early *Annalistes* conceived of their object of scrutiny in terms of mentalities or 'epistemologies'. Epistemologies are understood as mindsets or common assumptions that characterize the inhabitants of entire regions in certain epochs: different epistemologies evolve in different historical eras, cultures and socio-political contexts.

For example, Bloch's (1973 [1924]) book *The Royal Touch* was a serious historical investigation into the early kings' ability to cure certain diseases by touching the ailing persons. Other historians had brushed aside this purported royal ability as superstitious nonsense. But clearly, Bloch argued, people had faith in their monarch and his magical properties. This faith cannot just be discarded – indeed, it is a bad historian who appoints himself judge over the people he investigates. According to Bloch, this kind of faith in royal properties was intimately connected to the business of government and it is interesting for at least two reasons. First, such faith in royal powers was part and parcel of royal authority. It was an element of the political mentality of medieval and early modern society that legitimized the authority of the regime. As such, it should be of great interest to any historian who investigates political issues. Second, it was interesting because it alerts us to the difference between our own, late modern notions of power and the notions held by earlier societies.

The notion of collective mentality is equally evident in Lucien Febvre's (1983 [1942]) study of irreligion in sixteenth-century France, *Le problème de incroyance au XVIe siècle: la Religion de Rabelais*. As the title suggests, this is not merely a study of religious faith and free thought; it is a study on the limits of thought. Febvre argued that it was practically impossible not to believe in God in early modern France. Consequently, it is possible to delineate clearly between what was possible to think and what was impossible to think (and say) in sixteenth-century French society.

Similar studies were subsequently made by other *Annaliste* historians – among them Emmanuel Le Roy Ladurie (1966) and Carlo Ginzburg (1980). Each of them studied peasant societies against a common backdrop: the importance of 'mentalities'. Le Roy Ladurie and Ginzburg sought to understand the behaviour and arguments of the villagers; they discuss past mentalities and seek to identify the characteristic properties of past thought – to define their major mental preoccupations, the structures of their thought and the limits to what they could think.

This is another way of claiming that truth varies. Bloch, Febvre, Le Roy Ladurie and Ginzburg all demonstrate that social truths vary from one era to the next. Similarly, constructivists concede that truths vary from one society to the next – that Germans, Americans, the French and the Dutch are likely to describe events (such as wars) very differently. By the same logic we must concede that social truth varies from one social group to the next – that workers have different histories than capitalists – or that male and female historians, given exactly the same sources, can be expected to write very different histories (or herstories). This is, in part, because social analysts draw from different social experiences and perspectives. This is the guiding insight behind the historical works of the French philosopher Michel Foucault.

Foucault was deeply influenced by the *Annaliste* approach to the past. His doctoral thesis – which he wrote under the direction of Georges Canguilhem – examined the ways in which the French medical profession in the past had treated the mad and the insane. One of his guiding arguments was that the definition of madness has varied over time (in other words, what was considered mad in the seventeenth century was not the same thing as what was considered mad in the eighteenth or nineteenth centuries). Another of Foucault's arguments is that such definitions are part and parcel of the collective mentalities of the medical experts of a distinct epoch. A third argument is that such mentalities help form and reform society. They lay down the criteria for what kind of behaviour can be considered an innocent deviation, and what kind of behaviour requires public intervention or incarceration in a mental institution. Mental (pre)suppositions, in other words, affect people's freedom. They order society. They affect the exercise of political power.

In the early 1960s, Foucault published his thesis as a book, *Folie et déraison* (ironically published in English as *Madness and Civilization*, 1965). It was well received: several prominent French critics – Fernand Braudel, Roland Barthes and Gaston Bachelard among them – gave it good reviews for the boldness of its thesis, the quality of its research and (since this was in France) the beauty of its language. During the 1970s Foucault used the same basic argument on other kinds of social deviation: first on crime (1977), and later on sexual behaviour (1978).

Five years later Foucault published his second book, *Les Mots et les Choses* (literally: 'The Words and the Things', but often translated as *The Order of Things*). Here, he broadened his focus: not only did he discuss the disciplinary exercise of bio-political power; he turned his attention towards more subtle mechanisms of power: to the power of discourse. To do so, he drew on Bachelard, Canguilhem and on the *annaliste* notion of a social mentality – on the notion that certain claims are more likely than others and that there are discursive limits to what can be said (and generally understood) in a given society. It is an ambitious book, which seeks to write the history of Western mentalities over the last 300 to 400 years. It is also an idealist project in that Foucault explains how investigating mentalities of a society make it possible to understand why people in that society have thought and acted in the way that they have.

Foucault's argument is a variation on a basic theme introduced by Kant and explored by Whewell: ideas matter and the way people think and talk about society is systematically related to the way that they act. More precisely, human beings are equipped with a distinct set of natural ideas, and these deeply condition the way humans perceive the world.

Archaeology
What *are* these collective preconditions? And by which mechanisms are they maintained? In order to identify and investigate these collective

preconceptions, Foucault developed a method he called 'archaeology of knowledge'.

Foucault borrowed this term from Immanuel Kant – who had coined it to designate 'the history of that which makes a certain form of thought necessary' (Kant, 1942, p. 341). According to this view, the past can be treated as akin to an archaeological site; it can be 'excavated' by a special set of analytical tools, layer by layer as it were (see Foucault, 1972). This archaeological method enabled Foucault to rope off sections of the past in order to excavate them.

Through his excavations, Foucault hoped to uncover various layers of collective presuppositions. He conceived of these as historical systems of thought, and called them *epistemes*. The word '*episteme*' is borrowed from Aristotle and used to denote those structures of thought that make argument and reasoning possible. For Aristotle, the term refers to human knowledge. For Foucault, however, an episteme does not refer to knowledge itself so much as to the *preconditions* for knowledge – it refers to those structures of thought which make thought possible. Epistemes form the preconditions for thought and define the limits of that which can be thought or said.[2]

Here too: the basic idea was not new. Critical theorists, relying on the arguments of Marx, had argued for decades that the basic categories of human understanding were socially constructed. However, Foucault made the point very differently. Most critical theorists argued (with Marx) that the economic base of society determines the nature of its superstructure; they were, ultimately, materialists. Foucault was not. He agreed that the categories of human knowledge were socially constructed, but he argued that the formative mechanism in the construction process is language itself. To explain what he meant he introduced the concept of 'representations'.

Representations are socially (re)produced facts. They are things as they appear to us (not to be confused with the things themselves). Thus, a representation is an understanding or a description of the world: it is repeatedly presented – it is literally *re*-presented – to us as fact. This repeated presentation instils in us a sense of permanence. When a series of such representations appear together in a lasting way, they produce a discourse. A discourse, then, is a lasting system of representations. It is also a system of meaning, in light of which meaningful claims can be presented (and *re*-presented).

Foucault demonstrated the nature and role of representations and discourses in several books. Of these, *The Order of Things* may be his most famous example, as he analyzes Western scholarship – from about the Renaissance to the mid-twentieth century – to demonstrate how Western science has conducted its investigations within the discursive framework of three epistemes: the 'renaissance' system; the 'classic' system; and the 'modern' system of thought.

The object that Foucault seeks to capture and analyse in *The Order of Things* is nothing less than the basic framework of scientific knowledge for the last few centuries. He argues – like Kant, Whewell and many others – that this discursive framework affects the scientific process. It affects the questions raised, the ways in which the questions are pursued, and it affects the way that research results are formulated. In addition – and this is one of Foucault's major points – the system of thought also rules out certain questions, methods and concluding formulations. Discourses, in other words, not only determine what can be meaningfully said; they also define the limits for what can be said.

In his later works, Foucault pursued this limiting or disciplining role of discourse. He studied the history of French asylums in order to demonstrate how the definitions of insanity had changed over the centuries. He studied the history of prisons in order to demonstrate how the definitions of crime and criminals had changed over time. Finally, in his book on the history of sexuality, Foucault wanted to:

> account for the fact that [human sexuality] is spoken about, to discover who does the speaking, the positions and viewpoints from which they speak, the institutions which prompt people to speak about it and which store and distribute the things that are said. What is at issue, briefly, is the over-all 'discursive fact', the way in which sex is 'put into discourse.' Hence, too, my main concern will be to locate the forms of power . . .   (Foucault, 1978, p. 11)

Contextualizing Approaches

We have now wandered a great distance along our imaginary continuum. Starting with serendipitous approaches, we have considered the role that narrative framing and ideology or epistemes can play in determining the sort of swings in fashion we see in what constitutes knowledge and truth. This section will examine more material contextual effects, by looking at how an author's context can affect the way in which she understands and explains a given historical phenomenon.

Scholars and their Contexts

E. H. Carr's (1987 [1961]) little book *What is History?* is a classic among the many volumes that have aimed to criticize traditional historiography. There are many reasons for this. First, the book is extremely well written:

it is peppered with seductively formulated eruditions and pithy claims. Second, Carr did a marvellous job of capturing the mood of his day – the book was written in the early 1960s, and found many adherents among rebellious students of the time. Finally, *What is History?* is a learned book, written by an extremely well-read man who himself was a practising historian as well as an analyst. Indeed, Carr was one of his age's most important and influential analysts of current international events.[3] Although there is much depth to this little, readable book, we will focus on just one of its more influential currents: its discussion of context.

Carr argues that history constitutes a dialectic between general statements and facts. We wish to extend this argument to social analysis, generally.[4] He places the historian, as a social creature, centre stage. While this has always been acceptable for historians with respect to the objects of their study (for example, that a historian of Thomas Hobbes should recognize that Hobbes's thought is a product of his time), Carr insists that we must do the same for the subject – that is, for the historian – as well. After all, historians are also individuals, born of a specific time and context.

Although naturalist social scientists may be aware of how context affects the actions of those they aim to study, they are less eager to apply the same principle to themselves. Instead, they tend to hide behind the naturalist ideal of scientific objectivity. Constructivists, in contrast, emphasize the fact that the social analyst always acts from within a context, and under the influence of a distinct society (although they may disagree about the significance we should attribute to this context). The analyst is a product of, and spokesman for, the society to which she belongs.

Of course, this argument is not new. Aristotle adumbrated it. Marx expressed it most forcefully when he divided society into base and superstructure. For Marx, the 'base' could be understood as the material, economic foundation of society, while 'superstructure' was the world of ideas – the collective consciousness of society, including its philosophy, its literature, its political and social norms and values, its codes of morality and law. For Marx and the early Marxists, the base determined the nature of the superstructure.

The old Marxist argument echoes strongly in critical theory as well as in the contextual historical method. Its influence is easy to spot in Carr's discussion of social context in the case of Grote's famous *History of Greece*. George Grote was a British banker – and hence a member of the upper bourgeoisie – in the 1840s; he invested the aspirations of the rising and politically progressive British middle class in an idealized picture of Athenian democracy. The same logic is apparent in Carr's discussion of Mommsen's celebrated *History of Rome*. Theodore Mommsen, a

German liberal, was disillusioned by the German revolution of 1848–9 and was imbued with a sense that Germany needed to be saved by a strong leader. This sentiment was clearly reflected in Mommsen's admiration for decisive Roman emperors. Grote's book tells us much about Greece, of course; but it also provides a good deal of (indirect) information about the English society of Grote's day. Likewise, Mommsen's history provides us with a great deal of indirect information about the Germany of his time. Carr's basic point is that, 'you cannot fully appreciate the work of a historian unless you have first grasped the standpoint from which he himself approached it; secondly, that that standpoint is itself rooted in a social and historical background' (1987, p. 38f.).

From the Lessons of History to the History of Lessons

This point is easily illustrated if we follow the evolution of a particular historical project over time – preferably a project where sources are scarce, so that there is some room for the historian to compensate for missing facts with flights of fiction-like fancies. This may give us a chance to monitor the waves of fashion that wash across history and the social sciences with depressing regularity.

Consider the historiography on the lost city of Troy. Homer's *Iliad* is the only source of the decline and fall of this fabled city. Consequently, Troy's fate has tickled the curiosity of scholars for nearly 3000 years. Indeed, Troy's fall is one of the great conundrums of Western historiography: several generations of learned scholars have sought to determine the causes of its decline and fall. Despite this, Troy eluded scholars for centuries. Its very location remained a mystery until the final quarter of the nineteenth century, when a German expedition, led by the controversial archaeologist Heinrich Schliemann, claimed to have found its ruins in Hisarlik at Mycenae in northwestern Turkey. Schliemann's findings triggered a ferocious debate that preoccupied the world of ancient historians for several decades.

Given the paucity of data, historians and archaeologists had a tendency to read their own social conditions in the remnants of Troy. These interpretations suggest that the patterns that develop in the data are not just the outcome of chance (or deposited by History). Archaeologists, historians and social analysts are not isolated individuals, acting in a vacuum. They analyse and interpret their data in – and under the impulse of – specific social contexts. Different archaeologists did not just devise different explanations; they devised explanations that reflected the major preoccupations of their own time.

In the first round, before the First World War, the German archaeologists Heinrich Schliemann and Wilhelm Dörpfeld devised explanations that reflected the preoccupations of a young, insecure, German nation. A victorious war against France in 1871 had helped unify the German state, but the state always existed nervously in the shadow of war, constantly fearing France's revenge. Schliemann's and Dörpfeld's interpretations of the fall of Troy focused on a savage war that swept through the area between 1193 and 1184 BC (Wood 1986, p. 68).

Subsequent interpretations by the American archaeologist Carl Blegen, and others, during the interwar period focused on the role of economic crises in the fall of Troy – reflecting the economic uncertainties of their own age. Blegen's account of the crisis which took place in Troy before its fall employs an imagery which Blegen himself must have witnessed in the USA during the years of the Great Depression – indeed, there are instances where Blegen actually interprets his finding at Troy with reference to 'soup kitchens'. Later, when Blegen revisits some of his findings in the 1950s, American politics is preoccupied with the implications of the 'fall of China', the Korean War, and a tense and uncertain phase in the Cold War. This context was marked by a powerful fear by Americans of a surprise Soviet (nuclear) attack, and these contextual preoccupations are reflected in Blegen's new interpretation, where Troy was seen to have been sacked in a vicious attack that engulfed the city in flames.

More recent archaeologists and historians have rejected Blegen's account of the fall of Troy. During the 1980s and 1990s, Schliemann's and Blegen's war-based theories fell from fashion and new explanations became more popular (and were supported by new evidence, collected by new expeditions). These more recent arguments have stressed hitherto neglected factors pertaining to the social texture and the environmental context of ancient Troy. We might expect that our own generation of explanations will tend to reflect our own, post-Cold War, context: mass migrations, multiethnic problems, biological deterioration, over-population, over-development, popular epidemics and ecological imbalance.

Multiple Stories

The principle of contextualization can be extended in a number of directions. The section above maintained that social analysts are influenced by the fads and fashions that mark the societies in which analysts live. John Maynard Keynes once noted that the easiest thing in the world was to guess the opinions of educated people. When challenged (by educated interlocutors, who else?) to explain what he meant, Keynes argued that educated people tend to be products of the same academic culture; a culture which instilled in them the same kinds of knowledge and encouraged them to think in very similar terms. Keynes then expanded on his argument, relying on a 'theory of the framework' to make a more general proposition: all people in a given culture – English academics, Welsh fishermen or Chinese peasants – are likely to hold certain views and arguments in common. Consequently, according to Keynes, members of a given culture can agree on a general level of probability that holds for a given statement.

Keynes's argument must be supplemented by another, similar claim: that the material position of social scientists in the real world – including (but not limited to) class, gender and ethnicity – will shape their perspective of that world. The academic's social position will affect the way she formulates her theories and selects her facts. For example, an analyst whose background or sympathies reside with the working class may allow her values and norms to influence the selection of sources and her analytical narrative to highlight the role of, or the effect on, that class.

It is also important to recognize that the influence of social context need not be seen as a handicap – as the above illustration of Troy seems to suggest. 'Great history', writes Carr, 'is written precisely when the historian's vision of the past is illuminated by insights into the problems of the present' (1987, p. 37). It was to prove this point that Carr had introduced the historical works of Grote and Mommsen. They help Carr illustrate 'two important truths': (1) 'you cannot fully understand or appreciate the work of the historian unless you have first grasped the standpoint from which he himself approached it'; and (2) 'that the standpoint is itself rooted in a social and historical background' (Carr, 1987, p. 39).

An insightful example that recognizes the role of contextualization is provided by Norman F. Cantor (1991) in his *Inventing the Middle Ages*. Cantor shows that there is no single historical record for the medieval period – but many historical records, each of which is a function of a given expert's personal context, the more general political/ideological context and/or the expert's choice of method. These individual biases are not the result of poor scholarship – indeed, Cantor traces these autobiographical tendencies in the 'Great Medievalists' of the twentieth century (a less than motley crew that includes some of the biggest names in historiography, such as Bloch, Curtius, Gilson, Halphen, Haskins, Huizinga, Kantorowicz, Knowles, C. S. Lewis, Mommsen, Maitland, Panofsky, Postan, Power, Schram, Strayer, Southern and Tolkien). Cantor hammers Carr's point home: to understand history we must first understand the historian who writes it.

Approaching Naturalism

At the far end of this imagined continuum we find ourselves looking at historians and social scientists who recognize that there can be many competing histories, and that these histories can be influenced by (amongst others) the context, method and disposition of the author. Some naturalists think it is possible to recognize this relative nature of historical work, and still try to use history as an objective database for the testing of social scientific theories.

In an influential article in the *American Political Science Review*, Iain Lustick (1996) recognized this significant problem and proposed a number of solutions for trying to control for the 'bias' associated with different (and competing) historical accounts. Lustick is writing in the naturalist tradition, but he is critical of the way that naturalists employ historical data in social scientific projects. He shows the folly of, and difficulty facing, those naturalists who believe that some historical accounts are true, while others are false – or even how some accounts are more accurate than others (Lustick, 1996, p. 605). While naturalist social scientists are increasingly aware of the possibility of several, even competing, historical accounts, they have yet to develop a strategy for dealing with them.

The naturalist response to the problem is articulated by Theda Skocpol (1984, p. 382): 'Comparative historical sociologists have not so far worked out clear, consensual rules and procedures for the valid use of secondary sources as evidence.' With such a demarcation principle, Skocpol appears to think it would be possible to distinguish between true and faulty histories, and be more certain that our historical accounts do not suffer from selection bias.

But Lustick is sceptical of attempts to establish firm rules of this sort. Instead, he offers a bridge to link naturalist and constructivist historical accounts. This bridge consists of different strategies 'for coping with or exploiting the multiplicity of partially inconsistent historical monographs' (Lustick, 1996, pp. 615ff.). These strategies are meant to encourage the social scientist to recognize the distinctiveness and uniqueness of historical descriptions, and to consider explicitly the sort of contextual commitments that can explain this very uniqueness.

> [S]ocial scientists explicitly cognizant of the dangers of selection bias, of the absence of an unproblematic 'Historical Record,' and of both the limits and opportunities of diversity in the historiographical arrays available to them can choose where in their narratives they need to justify choices, how best to do so, and when to use patterns in the historiography itself as the target of analysis. (Lustick, 1996, p. 616)

Conclusions

With this chapter we have aimed to show how an historical method is employed by scholars who subscribe to a constructivist methodology. By realizing that the patterns they aim to explain are creations of their own making – rather than some permanent artefact of the social world – constructivists refuse to recognize a single form for history. This provides for a remarkable diversity of approaches, some of which appear serendipitous or casual to the untrained eye. In the hands of a well-trained constructivist, however, this serendipitous approach can generate great understanding and insight.

That is not to say that everyone who uses this approach does so equally well. As in the naturalist tradition, there are those on the margins of constructivist scholarship who employ these techniques poorly. We have aimed to limit our focus to some of the best examples, as we recognize that each methodological tradition includes examples that can undermine the legitimacy of their respective approaches. This is, perhaps, most evident in the constructivist camp, as much ink has been spilled over the threat to social science scholarship represented by 'postmodern' approaches. This chapter aims to show how many of the approaches associated with postmodernism can make (and have made) important contributions to the social scientific project.

Indeed, we think it too easy (and too common) to emphasize the differences that separate the historical method (as outlined in Chapter 6), and the approaches described here. We worry that the reader might walk away from this chapter thinking that constructivists only offer a critique of the naturalists' use of history. While this critique is an important and central part of the constructivist project, the project is not limited to a defensive or critical strategy. Constructivists have also written excellent historical studies and introduced new and inventive approaches and research questions. Michel Foucault's *Madness and Civilization*, Edward Said's *Orientalism* and Bent Flyvbjerg's *Rationality and Power* are three cases in point.

Indeed, both methodological traditions share a healthy scepticism of naïve inductivism, and both embrace the importance of mastering accurate empirical detail. In historical scholarship, of either methodological persuasion, there is no substitute for an analyst's familiarity with a data set or set of sources. Historians still spend their lives in archives; constructivists are no exception. For example, few researchers have dug as painstakingly and systematically into national archives as Michel Foucault.

Where the approaches differ is in ontological and epistemological terms: about the source of the patterns they seek to describe, and the epistemological approaches that can uncover and understand these patterns. Constructivists accept multiple stories; indeed, they hold that multiple stories are better (and more honest) than those which hold firmly to a master narrative. For the constructivist it is important to celebrate this difference in perspective: granting a given perspective a privileged position is more of an exercise in power than a question of truth. As a result, the focus of this chapter has been on describing the different ways that analysts come to see and understand the patterns that they study. This – more than inserting historical studies into larger social scientific projects – is what constructivism is all about.

Because knowledge and meaning are context dependent, constructivists favour approaches that allow them to interrogate and appreciate the details of a particular story. In doing, so, however, constructivists are not suggesting that behaviour is determined in some (extremely) complex manner by those contexts that they study. Rather, constructivists recognize that meanings are open-ended – they are contingent products of contexts, actions and interpretations, and their complex interactions. After all, '[t]he rules of a ritual are not the ritual, a grammar is not a language, the rules for chess are not chess, and traditions are not actual social behavior' (Flyvbjerg, 2001, p. 43).

As a result of their differences with naturalists, constructivists believe that there can be no neutral science. To the contrary, social science has an active and liberating role to play. History must be considered as a social science to the extent that it can be applied as a consciousness-raising and politically motivating discipline. For this reason, constructivists tend to cast the social scientist and/or the historian in the role of liberators. They can conduct research that serves the cause of freedom, fairness, justice and peace. They can undertake research to improve the plight of those social groups that need it the most. They can give voice to the voiceless. They can assist the downtrodden and the marginalized. Last, but not least, they can ask: which group's history is most in need of being heard?

Recommended Further Reading

E. H. Carr's *What is History?* [1961] provides a masterful example of the constructivist approach to history. To learn more about the role of emplotment, read White's *Tropics of Discourse* (1978) and his *The Content of the Form* (1987). Likewise, Foucault's *The Order of Things* (1970) and his *The Archaeology of Knowledge and the Discourse on Language* (1972) provide much of the philosophical weight to an archaeological approach to social science. Finally, Hammond's *Sociologists at Work* (1964) provides interesting examples of sociologists at work.

Chapter 10

Comparing Interpretations

In the last chapter we saw how constructivists are committed to understanding the uniqueness of social phenomena. To do this, they favour storytelling techniques that provide insight into complex social contexts. With the realization that the patterns they study are largely of our own making, constructivists prefer to climb into a particular problem and examine it from the inside out. Like Miss Marple, they exploit their familiarity with contexts to arrive at understandings that are consistent with those of the subjects they study.

The constructivist's preference for particular stories and narratives does not imply that she avoids comparisons. Rather, constructivists and naturalists use comparisons in different ways, and these differences stem from their disparate ontological and epistemological positions. Indeed, as we shall see, comparison (as association) plays a central role in the constructivist project. But when constructivists employ comparisons, they do so in a way that is designed to preserve the qualities associated with thickly descriptive narratives. More to the point, constructivists regularly use comparisons to develop associations along two related fronts: in hermeneutic exchanges between the particular and the general and in their interrogations of simplistic dichotomies used to separate Them from Us.

Like the storytelling approaches described in the preceding chapter, many constructivists use comparisons to criticize the naturalist project. For this reason, we begin with a critical discussion of comparisons in social science, based largely on the work of Alasdair MacIntyre. MacIntyre doubts the entire project of a comparative political science – in other words, he questions whether it is possible to have a political *science* that formulates 'cross-cultural, law-like causal generalizations which may in turn be explained by theories' (MacIntyre, 1972, p. 9).

In the second section we examine some of the fundamental, background issues associated with the constructivist approach. In particular, we introduce the different ways in which constructivists address their data, choose their cases, and relate to generalization. This section helps us distinguish between naturalist and constructivist approaches, but it doesn't give us a very clear idea of the promise of constructivist comparisons (in their own right). To illustrate this point, the closing part of this chapter examines how constructivists use comparisons to develop associations that facilitate better understanding in two related areas: hermeneutics and studies of the 'Other'.

We conclude by arguing that comparisons are almost as central to the constructivist project as they are to the naturalist project. Once we are cognizant of how comparisons are used in different ways – to question the mechanistic way that naturalists interpret the world, to protect and draw out contextual features, to celebrate diversity and uniqueness, and so on – then it is relatively easy to extend this reasoning to the other comparison-based methods (such as statistics and experiments). Consequently, this chapter functions as a bridge to the next two chapters by introducing the important (but different) role that comparisons play in constructivist scholarship.

Temptations of Similitude

Constructivists do not use comparisons to uncover law-like generalities in the social world. Particularity and context are the banners under which constructivists gather: they march towards meaning rather than laws, and they search for meaning by examining individual cases closely (and the contexts within which that meaning is situated).

While most social scientists believe in the utility of comparisons, there are sceptics – in both the naturalist and constructivist camps. Some naturalists are acutely aware of the ontological problems associated with a comparison-based social science. J. S. Mill, as noted earlier, was particularly sceptical of attempts to assume enough likeness in the social world to exploit his comparative methods. But most social scientists conveniently ignore Mill's caveats, and proceed with social scientific comparisons. Most, but not all, throw caution to the wind.

Arguably, the most provocative argument against the use of comparisons in social science is Alasdair MacIntyre's (1972) influential piece, 'Is a Science of Comparative Politics Possible?' MacIntyre takes Mill's criticism very seriously, and shows us how many of the apparent similarities in comparative social science are superficial and misleading. To illustrate this point we can visit two of his more entertaining examples.

MacIntyre's first example builds on a critique of Almond and Verba's [1963] influential book *The Civic Culture*. As we saw in Chapter 5, *Civic Culture* compares concepts of 'pride' to argue that some cultures identify less with their government than do others. MacIntyre doubts that the notion of pride means the same thing in different countries. He then shows how Almond and Verba simply assume that the notion of pride is constant, using it to gauge levels of identity across cultures. In contrast, MacIntyre argues that pride has different meanings – and plays different roles – in various cultures. 'Pride' in England is not the same as 'pride' in Italy:

> The notion of taking pride in Italian culture is still inexorably linked . . . to the notion of honour. What one takes pride in is what touches on one's honour. If asked to list the subjects which touched their honour, many Italians would spontaneously place the chastity of their immediate female relatives high on the list – a connection that it would occur to very few Englishman to make.   (MacIntyre, 1972, pp. 10–11)

If pride means different things in different cultures, it becomes difficult to use it as a standard for cross-national comparisons.

It is an inherent temptation in comparative scholarship to assume that things with the same names are similar. The dangers of this assumption may seem fairly straightforward when discussing something as amorphous as human 'pride'. But are these dangers any less real when we compare more concrete institutions that share the same name? For example, is it meaningful to compare political parties across countries, cultures or time? Is the Swedish Social Democratic Party (SAP) the same thing as the Social Democratic Party in The Philippines (PDSP)? For that matter, is the Swedish Social Democratic Party in 2006 really comparable to the SAP from 1935?

MacIntyre doubts the utility of such comparisons and points to the example of Ruth Schachter's description of political parties in some African nations. African party members 'were interested in everything from the cradle to the grave – in birth, initiation, religion, marriage, divorce, dancing, song, plays, feuds, debts, land, migration, death, public order – and not only electoral success' (MacIntyre, 1972, p. 14). He then wonders why Western political scientists think of these social formations as political parties rather than, say, churches. Their likeness to European or American political parties is clearly questionable. Comparing North American and African political parties is hardly as straightforward as comparing the boiling point of water on each continent. 'Where the environment and where culture is radically different the phenomenon is viewed so differently by those who participate in it that it is an entirely different phenomenon' (MacIntyre, 1972, p. 14).

At one level, MacIntyre is simply repeating the obvious (and, for that matter, Mill). As social analysts we have to be very careful in describing the relative similarity (or not) of the phenomena we wish to compare across cultures and time. Here, clearly, definitions matter. But it is quite possible that in criticizing all attempts at scientific comparison, MacIntyre throws his baby out with the bathwater.

For us, it is important to emphasize that comparisons *are* possible; indeed, they are instructive and important, even in the absence of similarities. Indeed, similarities should not be the sole focus of comparisons:

> let us beware of a misunderstanding from which the comparative method has only too frequently suffered. Too often people have believed or affected to believe that its only aim is to search for similarities . . . On the contrary, the comparative method, rightly conceived, should involve specially lively interest in the perception of the differences, whether original or resulting for the different developments from the same starting point.   (Bloch, 1967, p. 58)

MacIntyre, himself, provides the proof for this pudding. In the act of criticizing the use of rigid comparisons across different contexts, MacIntyre relies on comparisons (albeit implicitly). As reasonable as MacIntyre's argument may be, we simply cannot know that English and Italian conceptions of pride are different without actually comparing them! In criticizing the way that others use comparisons, MacIntyre actually provides us with a useful glimpse into the way that comparisons are used by constructivists: often implicitly, and with little explicit methodological reflection.

Perhaps it is easier to think about this other type of comparison if we return to Wittgenstein's notions of family resemblances. In trying to find resemblances in a family photograph, we need to look closely at patterns that may not reveal themselves in every individual – we jump back and forth between the individual and the group to try and find deeper, underlying, similarities. The resulting process of comparing and contrasting is difficult to formalize or explicate, but all of us have some experience of it. More importantly, this type of comparison does not lend itself to the sort of tests/controls that naturalists employ (for example, under conditions like these, falsification does not provide a very satisfying standard of proof). For these reasons, constructivists tend to have a rather relaxed or commonsense attitude towards comparisons.

In the Shade of the Old Mill

This chapter examines the way in which comparisons are used in constructivist efforts with the aim to understand (rather than generalize). This is no easy task, as constructivists often use their comparisons implicitly (as the MacIntyre examples suggest). Our job is to flush these comparisons out, and we do this in two stages. First, we introduce three fundamental concerns that constructivists often use to distance themselves from the naturalist project. As we mentioned in Chapter 8, a common discomfort with the methodological rigours of naturalism is one of the things that unite constructivists in a common methodological tradition. In the section that follows, we then examine the ways in which constructivists actively employ comparisons to better understand their subject of study.

Because many constructivists steer away from explicit references to method and methodological issues, it is often necessary to look for signs of deviation from the hegemonic (naturalist) methodological approach. In order to identify the methodological perspective of a given author, we have found it useful to look at three fundamental points of departure: (1) the author's commitment to generalization; (2) the author's approach to case selection; and (3) the nature of the data employed by the author. Each of these points can be used to help position a given comparativist, methodologically.

On Laws and Patterns

In David Lodge's whimsical novel *Changing Places*, we learn that Persse McGarrigle intends to write his Ph.D. thesis on T. S. Eliot's influence on Shakespeare. One reason for choosing this topic is that it serves as an excellent conversation starter and pick-up line in academic pubs. For whenever Persse tells a stranger the topic of his dissertation, they invariably seek to correct him: 'You mean to say that you are studying Shakespeare's influence on T. S. Eliot.'

> 'But my thesis isn't about that,' said Persse. 'It's about the influence of T. S. Eliot on Shakespeare.'
> 'That sounds rather Irish, if I may say so,' said Dempsey, with a loud guffaw. His little eyes looked anxiously around for support.
> 'Well, what I try to show,' says Persse, 'is that we can't avoid reading Shakespeare through the lens of T. S. Eliot's poetry. I mean, who can read *Hamlet* today without thinking of "Prufrock"? Who can hear the speeches of Ferdinand in *The Tempest* without being reminded of "The Fire Sermon" section of *The Waste Land*?'
> (Lodge, 1993, p. 280)

Lodge's example illustrates one irreverent way that constructivists employ comparisons. In a similar fashion, we could note Kenneth Waltz's influence on Jean-Jacques Rousseau – not on Rousseau himself, of course, but on the way we now read Rousseau's analysis of war and peace. Many of today's students of International Relations see Rousseau as a realist, in light of Waltz's (1959) reading. But Rousseau might just as easily be depicted as an early, and extremely influential, radical (for example, see Knutsen, 1997). In a similar fashion, we think that Theda Skocpol has had an enormous influence on Barrington Moore. This claim addresses the methods of comparison directly, and requires a closer examination.

Barrington Moore's (1966) *Social Origins of Dictatorship and Democracy* is perhaps the most influential comparative piece of historical sociology in the twentieth century. The work is commonly associated with the naturalist approach, and it is often used as a model for social scientific comparison. This rubric, however, has been placed on him by others; it is not of his own doing. In particular, his students and disciples are the ones responsible for squeezing Moore into the naturalist mould. Thus, it is Skocpol and Somers (1994, pp. 79–80) who refer to his application of Mill's Methods of Agreement and Difference.

Indeed, a methodologically innocent reading of his text reveals a remarkably casual and implicit methodology: Moore is extremely careful about how he frames his question, how he approaches his data, and the role that he gives to human understanding and agency. It is tempting to conclude, after a second or third reading of this influential book, that Moore effectively straddles our two methodological approaches. He seems to want to have his methodological cake and eat it too. This, and his strong (explicit) moral commitments, may offer a far better explanation (rather than his Millian brilliance and his methodological orthodoxy) for Moore's enduring importance and influence.

Like many constructivists, Moore was reluctant to formalize his approach. In particular, Moore did not explicate his theoretical and comparative framework: there is no concrete methodological depiction of his theory, his choice of cases, or the nature of his data. Instead of an explicit research design we find a constant emphasis on the importance of the particular at the expense of the general, and an implicit recognition of agency in social history. This relaxed attitude to methodological conformism is already evident in the opening paragraph of the book. Moore advertises his *Social Origins* as 'an attempt to discover the *range of historical conditions* under which peasants and landed lords have become important forces behind the emergence of the modern Western world – both the parliamentary versions of democracy as well as dictatorships of the right and left, that is, fascists and communist regimes' (Moore, 1966, p. xi, our emphasis).

The history of the twentieth century is often cast as a triangular contest between three modern regime types: liberal democracy, fascism and communism. Barrington Moore's ambition is to explore the advent of modernity and the historical preconditions for its three major regime types. His method hardly conforms to the principles laid out by John Stuart Mill; it is more akin to that of William Whewell. On closer inspection, *Social Origins* is not an attempt to use comparisons to capture underlying (and fixed) patterns of social reality. Rather, Moore points to a range of concrete historical circumstances that can be understood as so many preconditions for understanding the advent of modernity itself (in its three variations). Moore's discussion stresses variation and range of possibilities; it lacks the claim to sufficiency (and predictability), which is the hallmark of the naturalist approach.

Indeed, the closest Moore comes to a law-like generalization (and it is the one most often used to summarize his work) is the slogan-like claim: 'No bourgeois, no democracy' (1966, p. 418). But on closer examination, this too is used to examine the range of historical conditions. Moore is clearly not forwarding a law of social action. Worse, Moore's reference to the bourgeoisie is almost always taken out of context; his point is to emphasize the role of other agents in democracy (in particular, the agrarian sector). The bourgeoisie is seen to be the principal actor, but not the only actor. The rest of the paragraph reads as follows:

> No bourgeois, no democracy. The principal actor would not appear on the stage if we confined our attention strictly to the agrarian sector. Still the actors in the countryside have played a sufficiently important part to deserve careful inquiry. And if one wishes to write history with heroes and villains, a position the present writer repudiates, the totalitarian villain sometimes has lived in the country, and the democratic hero of the towns has had important allies there.   (1966, p. 418)

So why is Moore so often presented as a strong candidate for sainthood in the naturalist church? We think it is largely because influential reviewers of his work have represented him as such. First among these is Theda Skocpol, who read and re-presented Moore's argument in a naturalist light. Skocpol demonstrated the complex interconnections of Moore's variables and she exposed the logical design of his comparative argument – all in the light of Mill's naturalist design.

Once we are aware of Skocpol's influence on Moore, however, we can free ourselves from its naturalist representations and find in Moore a number of references to the particular, at the expense of the grand. Indeed, in his very readable introduction, Moore warns that 'too strong a devotion to theory always carries the danger that one may overemphasize facts that fit a theory beyond their importance in the history of individual countries'. He elaborates:

> In the effort to understand the history of a specific country a comparative perspective can lead to asking very useful and sometimes new questions. There are further advantages. Comparison can serve as a

rough negative check on accepted historical explanations. And a comparative approach may lead to new historical generalizations. In practice, these features constitute a single intellectual process and make such a study more than a disparate collection of interesting cases ... *That comparative analysis is no substitute for detailed investigation of specific cases is obvious.*   (Moore, 1966, pp. xiii–xiv, our emphasis).

In short, Barrington Moore suggests that comparisons can be used to ask new questions; to check/test existing hypotheses; and to produce new historical generalizations. Moore is not saying that his comparisons should be used to construct firm, law-like, generalizations about human behaviour. Rather, Moore compares in order to problematize the nature of theory in social science; comparisons are used to rejoice in the particular. Moore wants to discover the *range* of historical conditions, not elaborate on the causal variables that lead to specific outcomes.

In this respect, Moore has much in common with other important scholars in tangential fields. Marc Bloch – one of the most influential comparative historians before the Second World War – also avoided strong theoretical commitments. Daniel Chirot (1984, p. 41) has captured Bloch's uneasy relationship to theory (and his 'exceptionally lucid and colorful writing style') in the following terms: 'His theoretical models were frail constructions and disintegrated even as they sailed; by its nature change destroyed the validity of the model explaining it. To launch them at all and keep them floating for a while took great linguistic as well as scientific skill.'

Other comparative historians (or history-oriented social scientists) use comparisons in ways that first appear like structured, controlled tests of causal arguments. But closer examination shows how they tend to focus on 'concepts', 'issues' or 'themes' rather than theories or models. More importantly, their comparisons are used to highlight the particular, not bury these unique qualities under a heavy theoretical edifice. For these people – and for Barrington Moore – theory is a means, not an end, to social inquiry.

Reinhardt Bendix's *Kings or People* provides a good example of comparisons that are used in this way. Bendix shares much in common with naturalist approaches: he wants to observe the world and identify patterns in it, and he wants to establish causal relationships in those patterns. Yet his comparisons are not confined to causal analyses:

Comparative analysis should sharpen our understanding of the contexts in which more detailed causal influences can be drawn. Without a knowledge of contexts, causal inference may pretend to a level of generality to which it is not entitled. On the other hand, comparative studies should not attempt to replace causal analysis, because they can deal only with a few cases and cannot easily isolate the variables (as causal analysis must).

In order to preserve a sense of historical particularity while comparing different countries, I ask the same or at least similar questions of very different contexts and thus allow for divergent answers. Structures of authority in different countries do vary; societies have responded differently to challenges prompted by advances from abroad. The value of this study depends on the illumination obtained from the questions asked and from a sustained comparative perspective.   (Bendix, 1978, p. 15)

Note that Bendix does not rule out the possibility of causal analysis. He seems to regard this as a reasonable – if somewhat distant – possibility. But his attempt to explain the rise of royal authority in the early development of five countries is aimed at elaborating and preserving historical particularity. Indeed, Gabriel Almond, on the paperback version's cover, embraces the book on just this account: 'This affirmation of the unique is a useful corrective to the oversimplified model building which has characterized recent work in the field of development and modernization.'

In the work of Michel Foucault, we find a most explicit dedication to understanding the diversity of human action and the importance of the particular. For Foucault, Rabinow writes,

there is no external position of certainty, no universal understanding that is beyond history and society. His strategy is to proceed as far as possible in his analyses without recourse to universals. His main tactic is to historicize such supposedly universal categories as human nature each time he encounters them. Foucault's aim is to understand the plurality of roles that reason, for example, has taken as a social practice in our civilization not to use it as a yardstick against which these practices can be measured. This position does not entail any preconceived reduction of knowledge to social conditions. Rather, there is a consistent imperative, played out with varying emphases, which runs through Foucault's historical studies: to discover the relations of specific disciplines and particular social practices.   (Rabinow, 1984, pp. 4–5)

This attempt to discover the relations of specific disciplines and particular social practices is most famously expressed in Foucault's *The Order of Things* (1970), a book already introduced in Chapter 9. Since this book has had such an enormous influence – and since it is a comparative study – it merits a second glance.

The book's first chapter, entitled 'Las Meninas', is unusual for a comparative social science study: it offers a long and difficult analysis of Velázquez' famous painting of the same name from 1656, a picture which depicts the painter (Velázquez) at work. In the picture, we don't see what he is painting; we see only the back of his vast canvas. The canvas dominates the left edge of the picture and partly obscures the artist himself; he is leaning out to see his motive, brush and palette in hand. But what is his motive? We don't know and we can only guess. However, a small mirror hangs on the wall behind the painter (and to his left); it reflects two faces – these could be the painter's motive, in which case the painter is painting a double portrait of the two. The mirror could, of course, also reflect his spectators; it could reflect an audience of two people who are looking at the painting. Could the audience be the objects being painted by Velázquez?

Despite all appearances (and the energy and attention exerted), Foucault's intent is not to analyse Velázquez' painting. Rather, Foucault is hinting at the utility and playfulness of multiple understandings and plural perspectives. This, in itself, is a central quality of constructivist scholarship.

If *The Order of Things* is a comparative study, what does Foucault compare? First, he compares three fields of study: nature, language and wealth. From a synchronic comparison of these three fields of study he concludes that each obeys the same basic discourse of science. Before 1620, for example, the three fields coexisted within the larger framework of the Renaissance system of thought; they all observed the world and established meaning in their observations on the basis of the principle of similitude. After 1620, they coexisted within the larger framework of the classical system of thought; they established meaning in their observations, in light of mechanical principles of order. Foucault argued that scholars who studied language around 1610 thought very differently from those who studied language some 30 or 40 years later. This is because the two sets of scholars were affected by very different systems of thought. Likewise, Foucault argued that scholars who studied language around 1610 thought in very similar ways to their contemporaries who studied natural history or wealth. Although they studied different objects, they did so within the same system of thought.

This section has suggested that an author's attitude towards generalization can be one of the most obvious tell-tales of that author's methodological vantage point. Constructivists tend to shun a strong or explicit devotion to general explanations. Instead, constructivists celebrate in the particulars of an investigation. They tend to emphasize the differences and variations of the world, rather than the similarities, and employ comparisons as a way of thinking differently about a given subject. After all, for the constructivists it is these different perspectives, as much as the object being viewed, which call out for explanation.

On Case Selection

As we saw in Chapter 5, case selection is an important way by which naturalist comparativists control for explanatory purposes. Unable to exploit experimental or statistical controls, the comparativist tries to choose cases with an eye towards exploring variation on the dependent variable. Case selection is also intricately linked to the naturalist's admiration of statistical techniques: cases must be chosen to avoid selection and/or sampling bias. These concerns – most of which are borrowed from a statistician's world view – are irrelevant for the constructivist. For these reasons, attention to case selection is an important means for distinguishing the methodological priors of a given comparativist.

Barrington Moore's choice of cases is perhaps the main reason that he is so often seen as a contributor to the naturalist tradition. Although he does not explain the reasons behind his choice of cases (and this, itself, is noteworthy), and he does not give equal attention to all of his cases (again, worthy of note) it is difficult to argue that his choices are accidental or whimsical. He seems to be choosing cases by sampling on the dependent variable – Britain, the USA and France are offered as cases of the democratic route to modernization; Japan and China are the main cases of the fascist and communist routes, respectively. More significantly, the discussion of the Indian case (the most careful case study in the book), is used to show how India differed from the other cases of democratic transition.

By contrast, constructivists tend to be more causal in their choice of cases. In his (1978) *Kings or People*, unlike his earlier *Nation Building and Citizenship* (1964), Reinhardt Bendix provides a clear, if very brief, justification for his choice of cases. If the reader wonders why Bendix relies on (mostly) the same cases in both works (England, France, Germany, Russia and Japan), the reason is explained in terms of personal interest: 'The countries included in this book are those which I have studied for a number of years' (1978, p. 14). In his brief discussion of cases, Bendix recognizes that these countries are among the most industrialized and that they have experienced some of the world's great revolutions. More importantly, Bendix recognizes that his choice of cases is not exclusive – and that there are important omissions. However, in a book that has 692 pages, Bendix focuses the limitations of his study to a discussion of other potential cases in a paragraph that straddles pages 14 and 15.

This might be contrasted with the chapter-length methodological discussion in books that fit more comfortably in the naturalist approach. Bendix is simply not interested in justifying his choice of cases in terms of proving (or disproving) a theory.

Foucault, once again, can be used as an example in this regard. When discussing his choice of cases in *The Order of Things*, Foucault explicitly rejects the privileging argument that usually underlies case selection. When he asks himself rhetorically why he has chosen to privilege Grammar, Economics and Natural History in his comparison (and the consequences of this choice), Foucault responds that he had not sought to privilege any academic field or discipline:

> if, in fact, one took General Grammar, and tried to define its relations with the historical disciplines and textual criticism, one would certainly see the emergence of a quite different system of relations; and a description would reveal an interdiscursive network that was not identical with the first, but which would overlap at certain points. Similarity, the taxonomy of the naturalists might be compared not with grammar and economics, but with physiology and pathology: there, too, new interpositivities would emerge (one only has to compare the taxonomy/grammar/economics relations analysed in *The Order of Things* with the taxonomy/pathology relations studied in *Naissance de la clinique*). The number of such networks is not, therefore, defined in advance; only the test of analysis can show whether they exist, and which of them exist (that is, which can be described). Moreover, every discursive formation does not belong (necessarily, at least) to only one of these systems, but enters simultaneously into several fields of relations, in which it does not occupy the same place, or exercise the same function (the taxonomy/pathology relations are not isomorphic with the taxonomy/grammar relations; the grammar/Analysis of Wealth relations are not isomorphic with the grammar/exegesis relations). (Foucault, 1972, p. 159)

From this perspective, cases are not selected to try and uncover the hidden and universal patterns of the social world. Indeed, the constructivist's selection of cases is not made in light of larger theoretical or methodological designs, nor are the chosen juxtapositions privileged against others. Here too, as in the previous section, we find a celebration of the particular, at the expense of the general. In the case of Foucault's analysis, the problem of case selection is really non-existent. For if his argument is correct, and the discourse of the age pervades academic discourse in general, it does not matter which disciplines he chooses as cases. Theology, Geography, Political Philosophy, Alchemy or Military

Science . . . the discourse of the age would have made its mark on all of them. Foucault can choose a small number of disciplines to investigate (lest his entire project grow far too big to manage reasonably), because it simply doesn't matter which cases he selects.

We might add in closing that constructivists are equally nonchalant about the 'problem' of selection and/or sampling bias. These concerns come from the naturalist affinity for statistical inference. As a consequence, they tend to hold little sway for constructivists. As with the tendency to generalize, an author's level of attention to questions of case selection and sampling does not need to signal poor scholarship or methodological ineptitude. It is quite possible that an author's lack of attention to these concerns reflects her underlying methodological position. For most constructivists, issues of sampling and case selection are simply not methodologically relevant or interesting.

On Data Selection

This brings us to our final fundamental point of contrast: data selection. Scholars in the naturalist tradition aim to provide public, firm and reproducible accounts of the universal patterns they aim to uncover. For this reason, great emphasis is placed on quantification, source authority and replication. For the constructivist, however, these types of sources may not be very useful for understanding the way in which meaning is embodied in agency. As a result, a broader spectrum of data and evidence is required; the constructivist draws freely from less orthodox sources and on data generally frowned upon by scholars in the naturalist tradition. She might, for example, use private insights (intuition), subjective information (empathy) or even imagined examples, events or characters (for example, from novels or plays).

The problem with data is perhaps most glaring when we think of how someone might capture the sort of constitutive meanings that are the focus of many constructivist accounts. Anthropologists have always struggled with this problem. In the classic instance of anthropological fieldwork, a highly educated Westerner travels to a remote society – in the geographical as well as the cultural sense – in order to observe, understand, and communicate their understanding in texts and pictures.

J. Donald Moon captures the dilemma of anthropological fieldwork in his description of Edward Banfield's (1958) *The Moral Basis of a Backward Society*. Moon notes how Banfield's study is an obvious interpretation of the society in which the author lived; it is an interpretation of what members of the Montegranesi society say and do. Then he adds:

We cannot simply *ask* members of a society to explain the basic assumptions and orientations underlying their actions, since it is in terms of these constitutive meanings that people understand themselves and their own actions. Even if our informant understood the question, his answer would not be privileged, since we are concerned, for example, not with what would be the proper thing to do in some context but with understanding the concepts and the presuppositions in terms of which something can be said to be what is 'done' or 'appropriate.' Understanding actions, in this respect, is analogous to understanding a language; a native speaker's intuitions may be decisive when it comes to determining whether a given statement is properly formed, but he may be totally ignorant of the rules according to which proper utterances can be formed or of the logical and other presuppositions of a given utterance.   (Moon, 1975, p. 170)

The same can be said of Åsne Seierstad's (2002) celebrated account of war-torn Afghanistan. Seierstad lived briefly with an Afghan family in Kabul when Western powers invaded in November 2001. She witnessed how the Taliban regime was toppled, and experienced the bubbly optimism of Kabul's citizens during the spring of 2002. She converted her unique experiences into an insightful bestseller, *The Bookseller of Kabul*, which encases the life of a particular Afghan family in these dramatic world events. Seirstad appears to have done what Moon says we should not: she simply asked Afghans to explain the basic assumptions and orientations underlying their actions, without realizing or grasping the constitutive meanings within which Afghans understand themselves and their actions.

One needn't travel as far as Banfield and Seierstad to experience novel cultural insights. Michael Shapiro (1992) compares radically different strategies for describing the complexity of American culture. On the one hand, he notes the utility of investigations that rely on in-depth interviews of the kind that are familiar to naturalist social scientists (as exemplified by Robert Bellah et al.'s highly acclaimed *Habits of the Heart*). Against this scientific description of American culture he juxtaposes Don DeLillo's *Libra* – a 'true life novel' about Lee Harvey Oswald and the others who may (or may not) have been involved in the murder of the US President, John F. Kennedy. For Shapiro, both types of 'data' are legitimate and insightful. More importantly, by juxtaposing the novel and interview accounts, Shapiro is able to reveal the normative undercurrent in the latter. For Shapiro, *Habits of the Heart* reveals a 'mythic plot', despite the fact that it is an investigation that purports to be controlled by its 'non-fictional' dimensions – for example, systematic interviews and objective definitions, concepts and data (Shapiro, 1992, pp. 68–9).

By contrasting radically different types of data, Shapiro shows us the methodological limitations of both the data and the approach of traditional naturalist approaches to social phenomena. In doing so, he reminds us of something that Sigmund Freud recognized: that writers are 'valuable allies . . . [who in] their knowledge of the mind . . . are far in advance of us everyday people, for they draw upon sources which have not yet opened up for science'.[1] In short, constructivists tend to realize that art, literature and narrative often help us comprehend the world in which we live.

As Shapiro hints, popular culture can provide a key to understanding society: analysing popular culture can help us say something about the society in which the culture in question is popular. This sort of analysis begins by assuming that the fads and fashions revealed in books, films or popular music reflect more basic concerns – the norms and values but also the uncertainties and fears – of the society that sustains them. On this logic, an analysis of the runaway international success of the Harry Potter books can serve as a gateway into the main strands of international youth culture and globalization (for example, Nexon and Neumann, 2006). Similarly, Edward Said's influential study of Western representations of 'the Orient' is not based on sources concerning military might or economic prowess; its empirical basis is, ultimately, a selection of British novels (Said, 1978).

In this section we have shown how naturalist and constructivist scholars differ in their approaches to three fundamental issues: their view of generalization; case selection; and choice of data. These differences can be traced to the disparate ontological and epistemological beliefs associated with each tradition. Our objective has been to provide a few simple indicators or signifiers of an author's methodological commitment.

Constructing Comparisons

If comparisons aren't used as a control measure to test arguments about the patterns and regularities of the social world, what role do they play in constructivist accounts? In this section we introduce three different ways in which comparisons can be used by constructivists. As we saw in the preceding chapter, and with the examples provided by Alasdair MacIntyre in the introduction to this chapter, much constructivism aims to dispel the mechanical and generalizing tendencies of naturalist scholarship. For this reason, we start by looking at how comparisons can be used in a less formal way to explore possibilities and to challenge existing (more rigid) explanations.

In addition, and in a more positive vein, constructivists use comparisons to establish associations. Traditionally, these associations have taken two related forms. First, comparisons are used in a hermeneutical fashion to uncover meanings by juxtaposing the particular against the general. Second, comparisons are used to investigate the way in which our particular biases often alienate us from the object of our study. To illustrate this second type of comparison, we introduce Roxanne Euben's (1999) *Enemy in the Mirror*. Constructivists use both types of comparisons to emphasize the uniqueness, particularity and complexity of social and political phenomena.

Challenging the Old and Constructing the New

Unstructured comparisons can be used as a way to challenge existing hypotheses (derived from more rigid social theories), and generate new frameworks for historical or social study. By using comparisons in this way, the constructivist does not aim to replace one explanatory variable with another (in hopes, for example, of increasing an argument's R^2); rather, she is using comparisons to challenge the notion of rigid explanatory structures. This is best done with a firm empirical grasp on the details of particular stories.

Marc Bloch, for example, used a rather superficial comparison when he discussed the role of gold in the European economy in the Middle Ages. His aim was to challenge the dominant historical argument about why medieval Florence and Genoa were the first to issue gold-based coins. The traditional argument held that the vast wealth and rapid economic growth of these two cities could explain their issuance of gold coins. Bloch pointed out that Venice was just as wealthy as the other provinces, but – in contrast to them – relied on silver-based coinage. This enabled him to question traditional analyses and open up the possibility of an alternative explanation. In particular, Bloch turned to examine the nature of each city's wealth and found that Florence and Genoa grew rich on Asian trade (which was paid for in gold), whereas Venice grew rich on more traditional trade with the Levant (which was paid for in silver). Because Venice's wealth was accumulated in silver, it was neither interested in, nor able to issue, gold coins.

Thus, Bloch used comparisons to demonstrate the insufficiency of an existing theory. At the same time, his comparisons provided a clue as to where new explanations might be uncovered. In 'Toward a Comparative History of European Societies', Bloch (1953) emphasized this 'discovery' aspect of comparisons to explain how rough comparisons led him to discover the enclosure movements in southern France of the fifteenth to seventeenth centuries. Given his familiarity with research on contemporary English enclosure movements, Bloch wondered if something similar hadn't happened in France. The implicit comparison produced a new research question – indeed, it opened up an entirely new field of research for French economic historians (Sewell, 1976, p. 209).

Again, we would be remiss if we didn't refer to the way in which Foucault uses comparisons to challenge our presuppositions about historical patterns and generalizations. In *Discipline and Punish*, Foucault (1977) uses comparisons in a masterfully implicit way. The opening pages of the book begin with a presentation of Damiens, who has murdered a member of the royal family, and a morbid description of the French disciplinary regime in the mid-eighteenth century:

> On 2 March 1757 Damiens, the regicide, was condemned 'to make the *amende honorable* before the main door of the Church of Paris', where he was to be 'taken and conveyed in a cart, wearing nothing but a shirt, holding a torch of burning wax weighing two pounds'; then, 'in the said cart, to the Place de Grève, where, on a scaffold that will be erected there, the flesh will be torn from his breasts, arms, thighs and calves with red-hot pincers, his right hand, holding the knife with which he committed the said parricide, burnt with sulphur, and, on those places where the flesh will be torn away, poured molten lead, boiling oil, burning resin, wax and sulphur melted together and then his body drawn and quartered by four horses and his limbs and body consumed by fire, reduced to ashes and his ashes thrown to the winds'. (Foucault, 1977, p. 3)

Foucault's description continues in this gruesome detail for another three pages, when the reader is thrown, unexpectedly, into a new (but subsequent) punishment regime 80 years later. Then he introduces Léon Faucher, drawing up rules 'for the House of young prisoners in Paris':

> **Art. 17.**   The prisoners' day will begin at six in the morning in winter and five in summer. They will work for nine hours a day throughout the year. Two hours a day will be devoted to instruction. Work and the day will end at nine o'clock in winter and at eight in summer.

> **Art. 18.**   *Rising.* At the first drum-roll, the prisoners must rise and dress in silence, as the supervisor opens the cell doors. At the second drum-roll, they must be dressed and make their beds. At the third, they must line up and proceed to the chapel for morning prayer. There is a five-minute interval between each drum-roll.

> **Art. 19** . . .   (Foucault, 1977, p. 6)

Foucault is toying with our expectations. He does not coach us to compare, or tell us how to interpret the contrast. He is confident that the reader will compare these two regimes herself and draw conclusions about the changes that have taken place since March 1757, when Damiens was condemned to partake in a bestial spectacle in front of the Church of Paris. Foucault knew that by doing this we, his readers, will think of the first regime in terms of medieval barbarianism and the latter as modern civility. In short, Foucault is forcing us to see how we are, in effect, pre-programmed to think in comparative, historically progressive terms. He then uses the rest of the book to challenge and criticize this notion of linear progress. In doing so, he offers a critique of the Enlightenment project as an unambiguously progressive era in the history of the social sciences.

More than anybody else, Foucault exploits comparisons to illustrate complexity. In the 'Foreword' to the English edition of his *Order of Things*, Foucault is quite explicit about the comparative nature of his project. Yet, his understanding of the nature and the purpose of comparisons is a far cry from the naturalist 'method of testing hypothesized empirical relationships among variables on the basis of the same logic that guides the statistical method' (Lijphart, 1975, p. 164). Foucault wants to compare in order to illustrate the wondrous ways in which things can be related to one another. His aim is not to produce some universal pattern of social action. Rather, he compares in order to produce:

> results that are often strikingly different from those to be found in single-discipline studies. (So the reader must not expect to find here a history of biology juxtaposed with a history of linguistics, a history of political economy, and a history of philosophy.) There are shifts of emphasis: the calendar of saints and heroes is somewhat altered. . . . Frontiers are redrawn and things usually far apart are brought closer, and vice versa: instead of relating the biological taxonomies to other knowledge of the living being . . ., I have compared them with what might have been said at the same time about linguistic signs, the formation of general ideas, the language of action, the hierarchy of needs, and the exchange of goods. (Foucault, 1970, p. x)

Comparisons allow Foucault to shine his spotlight on what he calls a *positive unconscious* of knowledge: namely, a kind of innate knowledge that eludes the consciousness of the scientist who possesses it and yet is part of scientific discourse. He explains:

> What was common to the natural history, the economics, and the grammar of the Classical period was certainly not present to the consciousness of the scientist; or that part of it that was conscious was superficial, limited, and almost fanciful . . .; but, unknown to

themselves, the naturalists, economists, and grammarians employed the same rules to define the objects proper to their own study, to form their concepts, to build their theories. It is these rules of formation, which were never formulated in their own right, but are to be found only in widely differing theories, concepts, and objects of study, that I have tried to reveal, by isolation, as their specific locus, a level that I have called, somewhat arbitrarily perhaps, archaeological. (Foucault, 1970, p. xi)

In these ways, comparisons can be used to emphasize the superficiality of existing causal arguments, while proposing new arguments that emphasize the complexity of history and the possibilities of agency. Rather than using comparisons to test general theories, constructivists tend to use comparisons to prise open our imagination – to consider the possibilities and to encourage new readings and understandings of the empirical literature.

Hermeneutic Understanding

One of the ways in which constructivists encourage new interpretations is by employing hermeneutic approaches – approaches which are inherently comparative. Although we have already introduced the hermeneutic approach in Chapter 8, we can use this section to introduce some examples to show how it works in practice. As the careful reader will recall, hermeneutic understanding is produced by juxtaposing the particular with the general, the local with the distant. In hermeneutic studies, the comparisons are often implicit, but the contrast between particular events and general norms helps us to understand the event as something more than just particular, or local.

Clifford Geertz provides several examples of this type of comparison. His book *Islam Observed* (1971) compares two very different Muslim societies. Yet his aim is not to generalize about religious life. Rather, his aim is to investigate local cases in order to become more specific and more concrete. He hopes 'to find in the little what eludes us in the large; to stumble upon general truths while sorting through special cases' (Geertz, 1971, p. 4). At the same time, he wants to show us how different these two societies are in order to shake the commonplace notion that Muslim societies are alike.

Geertz's (1972) article on Balinese cockfights provides another example of the same attitude. The article begins by introducing the author and describing his (and his wife's) first encounter with Bali and a Balinese cockfight. What at first seems like a remarkably local event (a large cockfight held in the public square to raise money for a new school) is casually compared and contrasted with larger social symbols, institutions and practices in Bali. Again, he finds 'in the little what eludes us in the large'. The study helps Geertz (and his reader) to develop an eventual understanding of the cockfight as something more than a local or particular event: 'In the cockfight, then, the Balinese forms and discovers his temperament and his society's temper at the same time. Or, more exactly, he forms and discovers a particular face of them' (1972, p. 28). This purpose is reflected in the main title of the piece: 'Deep Play: Notes on the Balinese Cockfight'.

In another piece, Geertz (1975) applies thick descriptions to Java, Bali and Morocco. After presenting three parallel interpretations of the way in which the Javanese, the Balinese and Moroccans view their sense of self, Geertz explains his method, thus:

> notice the characteristic intellectual movement, the inward conceptual rhythm, in each of these analyses, and indeed in all similar analyses . . . a continuous dialectical tacking between the most local of local detail and the most global of global structure in such a way as to bring both into view simultaneously. In seeking to uncover the Javanese, Balinese, or Moroccan sense of self, one oscillates restlessly between the sort of exotic minutiae (lexical antitheses, categorical schemes, morphophonemic transformations) that make even the best ethnographies a trial to read and the sort of sweeping cauterizations ('quietism,' 'dramatism,' 'contextualism') that makes all but the most pedestrian of them somewhat implausible. Hopping back and forth between the whole conceived through the parts which actualize it and the parts conceived through the whole which motivates them, we seek to turn them, by a sort of intellectual perpetual motion, into explications of one another.   (1975, pp. 52–3)

In this moment of explicit methodological reflection, Geertz shows us the central role played by comparison in his interpretation. But even here, at his most explicit, Geertz avoids the word 'compare': the analyst *moves*, *tacks*, *oscillates* and *hops* to interpret.

Geertz uses comparisons the way Marc Bloch advised it – and the way Michel Foucault, Edward Said and many others practised it: to appreciate the local significance of knowledge. Rather than using comparisons to produce larger generalizations about the nature of the social world, constructivists use comparisons to interpret particular events with frequent contrasts to larger contextual settings. It is these contexts that provide the constitutive meaning to the particular events.

In practice, hermeneutic studies often require two levels of comparison. The first level juxtaposes particular events with general forms/norms. Here the cockfight is positioned against a more general Balinese culture. The second level of comparison is necessary to determine the nature of these general norms. At this level, comparisons are made across general forms in order to distinguish the unique characteristics of each form. Thus Geertz studies cockfights to further a hermeneutic dialogue within other cases – Java, Bali and Morocco – in his 1975 article. Here the three cases are clearly juxtaposed against each other in parallel and enclosed depictions: 'Making the self "smooth"' (Java); 'A theater of status' (Bali); and 'A public context for a private life' (Morocco). Although Geertz does not point our attention to it, the 'global structure' inherent in each (unique) case is provided by the implicit comparison of the three cases. Not only are we 'hopping back and forth' between the whole and the parts; but we are hopping back and forth between the three cases. In other words, to know what is 'Balinese', we need to know what is 'not Balinese'.

Contrasting Us with Them

As hinted at in the previous section, comparisons are often used by constructivists to show how our approach to an object of study can actually hinder our access to it. In today's political climate, this problem is perhaps most evident in Western attitudes towards Islam, and 'fundamentalist Islam' in particular. For this reason, we use this closing section to describe one recent attempt at understanding 'Islamic Fundamentalism and the Limits of Modern Rationalism' (Euben, 1999). Roxanne Euben holds that the methods and categories employed in Western social scientific explanations actively distort fundamentalist ideas, making it difficult for us to understand how these ideas could be so appealing for so many.

Euben compares Islamic fundamentalism with various Western critiques of rationalism to illustrate unexpected similarities shared by the two theoretical traditions. She begins by noting how political Islam is commonly depicted as a threat to modern, legitimate politics, dividing the world into two antagonistic blocs (the Islamic World vs. the West). We have come to see Islamic fundamentalism as the irrational Other to our intelligible Self – a negative mirror reflecting back on Western life (ibid., pp. 43, 44). A gulf separates these two blocs, if only because 'social scientific explanations portray the Islamic fundamentalist as the paradigmatic irrational rational actor; that is, the actor apparently rational enough to gravitate toward an ideology that is an effective and therefore appealing vehicle for essentially pathological reactionary sentiment' (ibid., p. 24). Under these conditions, and for the sake of understanding what fundamentalism is about, Euben says that we must 'strive against our own moral impulses and intellectual reflexes, to hear voices critical of our own deeply held convictions about the way the world does, or should work' (ibid., p. 16).

For those of you who aren't old enough to remember the Cold War, the same thing could be said about mindsets on both sides of the Iron Curtain. The Western image of the Soviet state was so saturated with negative images – indeed, straight inversions of the West's own political values – that it was simply impossible for many denizens of the West to understand why Soviet communism could have been embraced by so many, for so long. (Of course, the same thing could be said of Soviet depictions of the West.) Today the Red Menace has been replaced by a Green Menace (green being the colour of Islam), but the threat to our cherished political values is seen to be just as ominous.

Euben employs comparisons, at two levels, to break down these barriers to understanding. On the one hand, she wishes to help us understand Islamic fundamentalist thought on its own terms: 'to provide a window into fundamentalists' own understandings of the movements' meaning and purpose' (ibid., p. 8). To do this, she examines the work of one representative and influential thinker in that tradition, Sayyid Qutb (1906–66), to show how it is a complex reaction to a cacophony of sources (for example, Western imperialism and colonialism, corrupt regimes in the Middle East, Arab secularist power, modern forms of power and sovereignty, and the Western rationality that justifies them).

She then compares Qutb's writing with those of important predecessors in the same tradition: namely Jamal al-Din al-Afghani [al-Asadabadi] (1839–97) and Muhammad 'Abduh (1849–1905). This is done to place Qutb's argument in its own context (to better understand its message, on its own terms), but also to challenge commonplace arguments that portray fundamentalism as the inevitable return of an Islamic 'essence', or as some sort of 'natural' reaction of archaism against modernity (ibid., p. 117).

Against this home-grown depiction of Islamic fundamentalism, Euben then compares Qutb's writings with a handful of more recent Western critics of modernity to show how Qutb's argument is neither pathological nor unfamiliar. By examining Hannah Arendt's analysis of modern authority, Alasdair MacIntyre's, Charles Taylor's and Richard John Neuhaus's discussion of modern moral discourse and Robert Bellah's and Daniel Bell's arguments regarding the decline of modern community, Euben shows us how Qutb's basic argument (where modernity is depicted as a crisis defined by a degeneration of common meanings) is not antimodern – but rather another perspective on, and an attempt to redefine, what it means to live in the modern world (ibid., p. 87).

In short, Euben does not use comparisons to develop universal truths. Rather, she uses comparisons to emphasize dilemmas and questions that straddle across cultures and time. In so doing, she creates room for the radical notion that there is humanly significant knowledge that lies outside the confines of Western political thought. Euben's comparisons allow her to depict Islamic fundamentalism as something understandable – something that would be recognizable to Islamic fundamentalists themselves. Her intention is not to proselytize, or paint a sympathetic picture of fundamentalists; Euben is far too sceptical of universal truths to play that role. Rather, she recognizes that *understanding* Islamic fundamentalism requires that we must bring its followers in from beyond the pale – allow them access to the realm of rational discourse. In other words, Euben's use of comparisons allows us to understand what naturalism hides: naturalist science defines discursive practices in ways that tend to obscure the very theoretical and transcultural aspects of fundamentalist thought that are central to the meaning of Islamic fundamentalism (ibid., p. 156). A constructivist approach employs comparisons that allow us access to those important theoretical and transcultural aspects.

Conclusion

This chapter has aimed to generalize about those who avoid generalization. Consequently, our objectives have been rather modest. We have aimed to help the inquisitive reader recognize constructivist scholars by the disparate ways in which they employ comparisons. In particular, we have shown how constructivists tend to distance themselves from naturalist norms when it comes to embracing generalization; how they choose their cases; and the nature of the data or evidence they employ. It is in opposition to the naturalist Other that constructivists have come to define and understand themselves.

We hasten to note, however, that the constructivist's use of comparison entails more than just a critique of naturalism. Comparisons, as associations, are a central means for constructivists to understand complex social phenomena. Indeed, the hermeneutic or dialectical approach to understanding is inherently comparative, and can be employed on a remarkably broad set of phenomena. Thus, constructivists tend to compare in a way that is consistent with their method of choice – as an extension of the narrative approaches described in the previous chapter.

By comparing thick, in-depth and informed stories, constructivists are able to see things that are easily obscured by the naturalist approach. As they are not limited to using reason or observation, constructivists draw from a much broader set of experiences. They compare contexts, judgements, practices, trials and errors, experiences, intuitions and bodily sensations to learn and understand. The result is a fuller understanding of particular phenomena – an understanding where comparison plays a central, if often hidden, role.

Recommended Further Reading

As is noted in the text, we think it is useful to begin with MacIntyre's 'Is a Science of Comparative Politics Possible?' (1972) as it provides a critique of naturalist comparisons. We also recommend Sztompka's 'Conceptual Frameworks in Comparative Inquiry' (1988). For a detailed application of constructivist comparison we recommend Foucault's remarkable *The Order of Things* (1970). Shapiro's collection *Reading the Postmodern Polity* (1992) provides another vantage point for the constructivist approach.

Chapter 11

Contextualizing Statistics

It is relatively rare to find constructivist authors of statistical studies. This, in itself, should not surprise us. After all, the traditional objective of the statistical method is to remove the subject matter from its constitutive context in order to probe its nature in terms of correlational patterns. For the constructivist, where meaning and context are prioritized above all else, this method can do more damage than good; it contributes to a twofold distancing: between the data and their context, and between these and the analyst.

As we discovered in the previous chapters, constructivists tend to shy away from a strong demarcation principle for ranking methods (and data) in terms of their reliability; their choice of methods tend along more aesthetic and ad hoc lines. For this reason, the focus of this chapter is somewhat different from the others that precede it. Statistical techniques are designed to identify co-relational patterns. As constructivist scientists are discussing patterns no less than their naturalist colleagues, it would be odd and short-sighted if they were simply to exclude or ignore such a powerful technique of inquiry.

Our intent is to show how statistics might be interpreted and even used by inquisitive constructivists. Although the statistical method, in itself, may not appear to be particularly well suited for constructivist projects, it is our argument that appearances can sometimes be deceiving. Indeed, when we delve into the historical contexts where many of these techniques were developed, it is easy to understand why constructivists have distanced themselves from them. But more recent developments, in both graphic displays and Bayesian logic, have made some statistical approaches more relevant and attractive to the constructivist scholar. These developments could allow constructivists to find patterns, associations and meanings that are not entirely obvious in narrative approaches. Thus, in the same way that case studies fit rather uncomfortably under the naturalist rubric, statistical studies can be made to fit into the constructivist's framework.

This chapter is divided into two parts. The first part uses history to suggest a reason for why constructivists hold such a critical view of statistical approaches. The second part introduces three different statistical approaches that are consistent with constructivist beliefs about our world and how we come to understand it. These statistical approaches might be embraced by constructivists as they aim to capture and maintain the contextual integrity of the things they study.

The Dark Side of Statistics

As we saw in Chapter 4, statistics emerged as a tool for social analysis rather late in the game: it was only with the advent of the nineteenth century that statistics was embraced (and at first, hesitantly) by the scientific community. One reason for this late début was the rise of an entirely new approach to society and social issues.

During the age of absolutism, society was ordered in terms of a steep and fixed hierarchy of natural endowments. Under such an order, it made little sense to record key characteristics of all citizens – to lump them together, and analyse them all in the same way – as if they were all equal units. An enormous gulf separated the king, the aristocrat and the common peasant. This difference made it obvious that the king could not be discussed in the same way as the common butcher or baker (or candlestick maker); he was different, better and above the others. In an autocratic and many-layered society such as that of the *ancien régime*, it was inconceivable to convert all members of society into numbers of equal value and treat them all in the same, standard fashion. In other words, it was as practically impossible to be a modern statistician in sixteenth-century France as it was to be a freethinker (Febvre, 1983). This contextual bias is reflected in the two ways in which statistics were first gathered and applied: people were first counted as soldiers and taxpayers.

The Enlightenment changed all of this. Knowledge is power, wrote Bacon, and in knowledge 'the soverignty of man lieth hid'. Through systematic knowledge about the world, man could take control of his own destiny, and fashion a world that was good, orderly and peaceful (Adorno and Horkheimer, 1979, p. 42). Treating citizens as units of equal worth – be it as statistical units, or as voters whose ballots count equally at the polls – began to make sense once thinkers came to embrace the essential equality of men. The rise of statistics, then, is intricately associated with the rise of a new perspective on man – it coincides, in fact, with the advent of what Foucault calls 'the modern system of thought'. For this reason, it makes good sense to discuss its rise in light of Foucault's concepts of governmentality and bio-power.

The initial establishment of the Statistical Society of London (in 1834) reflected the renewed growth of interest in statistical approaches among governing groups. Indeed, the Society was founded after a presentation by Adolphe Quetelet. The Belgian scientist was invited to the British

Association for the Advancement of Science (BAAS) to present a paper on the relationship between the statistics of crime and age in France and Belgium. As the hosting BAAS did not have a formal statistics section, Quetelet was asked to present his ideas privately to a smaller audience, which included Thomas Malthus and Charles Babbage. Apparently, Babbage was so intrigued by the talk that he suggested a new section be formed to deal expressly with statistics. As we saw in Chapter 4, the general assembly of the BAAS was not entirely happy about this, and required that the new statistical group, Section F, should deal in facts and stay away from opinion and interpretation. Many of the subjects to which statistical techniques were being applied (such as crime, social conditions and medicine) had broad political and social implications, and the last thing that the association wanted was to become mired in politics.

Over time it would prove remarkably difficult to separate politics and statistics. Indeed, statistical techniques came to play a very important role in developing and assessing the new ambitions of government such as combating pauperism, vagrancy, unemployment and crime (to name just a few examples).

Sir Francis Galton

As we have already noted, few individuals played a more important role than Sir Francis Galton in the resurgence that followed. Galton and his students sharpened the techniques of Graunt and honed them into powerful tools in his many scientific projects. In our earlier introduction of him – in Chapter 4 – we painted a picture of a polymath, with a remarkably broad interest and scope of engagement. But in introducing Galton, we purposely neglected to mention another side of Galton's influence: his development of statistical techniques as tools for social Darwinistic projects. This is the more seamy side of modern statistics – a historical and political context that statisticians tend to forget or ignore.

Francis Galton was a man of his times and a half-cousin of Charles Darwin. Galton eagerly collected material in order to garner evidence for his cousin's arguments and to apply them to human society. Although Galton made important contributions to several fields, he concentrated his efforts on socio-biological questions. In particular, Galton worked for most of the last quarter of the nineteenth century to establish the science that he named: *eugenics,* the study of how to improve the human race by means of genetic manipulation. When he died, Galton bequeathed the University College, London with enough money to endow a chair of Eugenics.

As we saw in Chapter 4, Galton's initial work (on peas and human height) showed that big parents tend to yield big offspring. From there it was a short step to an argument concerning human reasoning: Galton argued that intelligence, like height, is distributed unevenly, and that the intelligence of children regresses towards the mean. Consequently, unintelligent parents tend to have children who are more intelligent than themselves (but not necessarily more intelligent than the average), and very intelligent parents tend to have children who are less intelligent than themselves (but more intelligent than the average). For Galton, this had clear policy consequences that could be exploited for the greater good: since intelligent parents would have intelligent children (and stupid parents would have stupid children), then intelligent people should be encouraged to procreate (whereas truly stupid people should be barred from doing so); for if stupid people procreated at a greater rate than intelligent people, then the entire race would suffer as a result (Dean, 1999, pp. 136ff).

Galton didn't stop there. In his book *Hereditary Genius* (1869) Galton argued that a system of arranged marriages between men of distinction and women of wealth would eventually produce a gifted race. Later, in a lengthy letter to the editor of *The Times*, Galton (1873) advocates the transfer of property in Africa from its traditional residents ('negroes possess too little intellect, self-reliance, and self-control to make it possible for them to sustain the burden of any respectable form of civilization without a large measure of external guidance and support . . .') to the more industrious and numerous Chinese (who 'possess an extraordinary instinct for political and social organization' and 'are good-tempered, frugal, industrious, saving, commercially inclined, and extraordinarily prolific'). In both cases, Galton thinks like an engineer, for whom no problem is too large: 'No very serious obstacle seems to stand in the way' of eradicating an entire race and moving another from one continent to another (ibid.). As a statistician, Galton conceives of the world in terms of independent variables: he has no difficulty in removing his subject matter from its original constitutive context and tossing it around in different combinations.

Of course, Galton was a product of his times, and it is perhaps understandable that he held these views in 1873 (although a rejoinder to Galton's letter by Gilbert Malcolm Sproat suggests otherwise). Eugenics only became controversial in the early decades of the twentieth century, after the Second World War. In the wake of Nazi Germany's race experiments, Galton's eugenics projects were allowed to fade quietly into infamy, and students of statistics today seldom hear of their method's eugenic roots.

Galton himself is an example of his method's main shortcomings. His approach and arguments are flawless and impressive feats of logic. But it is beneath these strengths that we find the method's weaknesses buried.

The statistical approach is foreign to the human and the humane; it is in itself insensitive to ethics, morality and politics. In the same way that students of statistics are sheltered from Galton's eugenic past, the statistical method shields its analyst from her own human context.

Statistics Lack a Sense of Context

Our second caveat is related to the first: namely, that the statistical approach requires the analyst to distance herself from the context of the study. This distancing makes it difficult for the scholar to immerse herself in the constitutive meanings of the data. Indeed, this problem is clearly evident in the apparent difficulty of modern social statisticians to distinguish between actual and statistical significance (see, for example, McCloskey and Ziliack, 1996 and 2004).

This distance, itself, is a product of two factors. First, quantification necessitates abbreviation. The very process of quantification requires that much meaning is lost as descriptive characteristics become indexed onto five-point scales (for example). Thus, the first casualties of quantification are interpretation and context. Interpretation is jettisoned because it is assumed to conflict with the scientist's need for dispassionate objectivity; context is shunned because it problematizes the analysis, as is clear from the definition for 'data' in the *Dictionary of Statistics and Methodology*:

> Data are often thought of as statistical or quantitative, but they may take many other forms as well – such as transcripts of interviews or videotapes of social interactions. Nonquantitative data such as transcripts or videotapes are often coded or translated into the numbers *to make them easier to analyze.*   (Vogt, 1993, p. 59, our emphasis).

Another reason for this distancing of researcher and data results from the way in which larger statistical projects often depend on the compilation of figures by numerous observers – each with her own background, presuppositions and conceptual schemes. Barry Hindess makes this point eloquently:

> [The sociologist or some other interpreter] cannot assume a uniform interpretation of these categories in terms of observable objects and events. Such interpretation would be legitimate only if it could be demonstrated that the initial observers and the compilers of the statistics in questions used the same rules of categorization, and that these rules were sufficient to eliminate classification by fiat in every case. (Hindess, 1973, p. 21)

Anybody who has ever worked on a large statistics-gathering project (and we speak from experience) ends up with an attitude not unlike that of a butcher's to sausages (or Bismarck's to laws): once you are made aware of their ingredients, you are likely to lose your appetite for them.

In today's large data-mining projects, graduate students are often employed to 'code' descriptions of a given social phenomenon into numerical indexes (which themselves are the product of a researcher's presuppositions of the sort of variation she expects to find). Quite often these indexes are modelled after 'classic cases' of the phenomenon in question. Imagine, for example, a project aimed at collecting data and coding the 'degree of corporatism' for a large, cross-national, cross-temporal database. To gather this enormous amount of data, a lead researcher (or several) begins by employing a number of graduate students with enough proficiency (language and otherwise) to collect the relevant data over a number of disparate countries. This data would be collected by way of a code book, which encourages the students to mill through the case study literature in search of specific, standardized responses for the country in question. We can expect that most of the student researchers would not be able to answer all of the relevant questions in a large code book, but would do their best to provide reasonable answers, in light of what they have read. In other words, there will be much interpretive give-and-take as the students try to fit the histories of various labour movements into distinct and inflexible numerical depictions.

But the interpretive distancing doesn't stop there. As the data collection part of the project approaches its end, the head researcher(s) will need to somehow bridge the interpretive divide that exists between the different nations and cultures in the study: to try and make the data comparable across states. For the constructivist, there is simply too much room for interpretive slippage in the gap that exists between (1) the historical and conceptual context, and (2) the end data collected in matrix form.

The Statistical Worldview

The third major drawback to statistics from a constructivist point of view concerns the exportability of what McKeown (1999) calls the 'Statistical Worldview'. In response to King et al.'s (1994) influential methods primer (which draws from a statistical approach to the world), McKeown argues that the logic of statistical study is not hegemonic to social phenomena, and that trying to apply it to different types of studies (in particular, case studies), is both misleading and problematic. By referring to the lack of statistical inference in most of scientific history, and by showing how alternative logics are quite successful in finding solutions,

McKeown shows how the statistical world view is different from other world views. Indeed, the statistician's view of the world, as well as the statistician's view of her own role in it, is often un-selfconscious and vague – to the point of inaccurate and misleading:

> [R]esearchers almost never begin from the starting point envisioned by Descartes or Hume – their thought experiments involving radical doubt radically misstate the situation facing the researcher. Typically, the research task is not how to move from a position of ignorance to one of certainty regarding the truth of a single proposition. Rather, it is how to learn something new about a world that one already knows to some degree. Framed in this fashion, the basic tasks of research are then (1) to devise ways of leveraging existing understanding in order to extend our knowledge, and (2) to decide what are sensible revisions of prior understanding in light of the knowledge just acquired. (McKeown, 1999, p. 187)

As we shall see below, Bayesian statistics is one way to address these issues.

This problem is particularly pronounced in the case of regression analyses. The reader should recall from Chapter 4 that regression analysis is used to manipulate, conceptually, partial correlations in a design that holds other variables constant. In doing this, statistical projects are about constructing a new version of reality, one that is insensitive to the ways in which the social world has meaning. The statistician is explicitly reconstructing the world to better investigate it. Her method is not so much about discovering facts of social life, but – rather – about constructing a different (new) version of that life, through statistical manipulation. The lessons we learn from this new, constructed reality can only be transferred to the social world by granting a series of very demanding and controversial assumptions.

On the Bright Side

So far we have endeavoured to show why constructivists are largely sceptical of statistical approaches. We are somewhat reluctant to do this, as there is already a tendency to link constructivist approaches with 'qualitative' approaches and the fear of hard numbers. Our depiction is also somewhat misleading, as some of the most sophisticated, advanced and technical of today's statistical approaches are those aimed at maintaining and protecting the very sort of context that constructivists embrace. In short, there is no clear or necessary relationship between constructivism, technophobia and/or the fear of large numbers. In the remaining part of the chapter we would like to paint a more nuanced picture. Here we introduce three distinct types of statistical approaches – descriptive, Bayesian, and what we call Statistic Narratives – and suggest that each of them offers useful means for constructivists to find and understand new associations, grounded in context.

Descriptive Statistics and Quantitative Graphics

Done properly, statistics can present a large amount of information in various patterns that allow us to better understand the role of individual pieces of information. To the extent that statistics-based graphics allow us to see the role of the particular in larger patterns, their use is consistent with the constructivist approach: in effect, quantitative graphics can facilitate a hermeneutical tacking between the general and the particular.

To understand this potential, we can begin by considering the role of an 'outlier' in statistical analyses. An outlier is defined in terms of its relation to the normal distribution of a population (recall the role and influence of Thandeka in Figure 4.3). To capture and understand an outlier, the researcher must first define the 'inliers'. With just a little reflection we can see how this process is not altogether different from the way in which constructivists (recall Geertz and Bendix) use implicit comparisons with other cases in order to define the uniqueness of a case (from which we can proceed to understand the role of the particulars, given that case). This process is clearly demonstrated with Anscombe's (1973) celebrated contrast of data in tabular and bivariate scatter plots.

As illustrated in Table 11.1, Anscombe begins by providing four columns of (apparently) similar data: A, B, C and D. We are then told that a single linear description fits all four rows of data: $Y = 3 - 0.5X$ (before the residuals are examined). So far, the quantification has not provided any greater understanding of the phenomenon (whatever it is), as the reader is lost in the particulars, unable to see any larger pattern. It is only when the numbers are presented in two-dimensional Cartesian space (as is done in Figure 11.1) that we begin to understand how radically different each row of data actually is, and the patterns (or unique logic) that is associated with each. At this point, and only at this point, is it possible to reveal the outlier(s) – or even if there are outliers – and to come to see the unique differences that separate the columns (A, B, C and D) of data.

This example should please (and appeal to) the constructivist, for constructivists tend to shun the standard, the simple and the average. In other words, constructivists tend to be holists. As such, they are likely to embrace the methodological assumption that social phenomena must be

Table 11.1 *Four columns of data*

A		B		C		D	
X	Y	X	Y	X	Y	X	Y
10.0	8.04	10.0	9.14	10.0	7.46	8.0	6.58
8.0	6.95	8.0	8.14	8.0	6.77	8.0	5.76
13.0	7.58	13.0	8.74	13.0	12.74	8.0	7.71
9.0	8.81	9.0	8.77	9.0	7.11	8.0	8.84
11.0	8.33	11.0	9.26	11.0	7.81	8.0	8.47
14.0	9.96	14.0	8.10	14.0	8.84	8.0	7.04
6.0	7.24	6.0	6.13	6.0	6.08	8.0	5.25
4.0	4.26	4.0	3.10	4.0	5.39	19.0	12.50
12.0	10.84	12.0	9.13	12.0	8.15	8.0	5.56
7.0	4.82	7.0	7.26	7.0	6.42	8.0	7.91
5.0	5.68	5.0	4.74	5.0	5.73	8.0	6.89

$N = 11$

Mean of Xs = 9.0

Mean of Ys = 7.5

Equation of regression line: $Y = 3 - 0.5X$

Standard error of estimate of slope = 0.118

$\tau = 4.24$

Sum of squares $x - \bar{x} = 110$

Regression sum of squares = 27.50

Residual sum of squares of Y = 13.75

Correlation coefficient = 0.82

$\tau^2 = 0.67$

Source: Anscombe (1973).

Figure 11.1   *Four rows plotted*

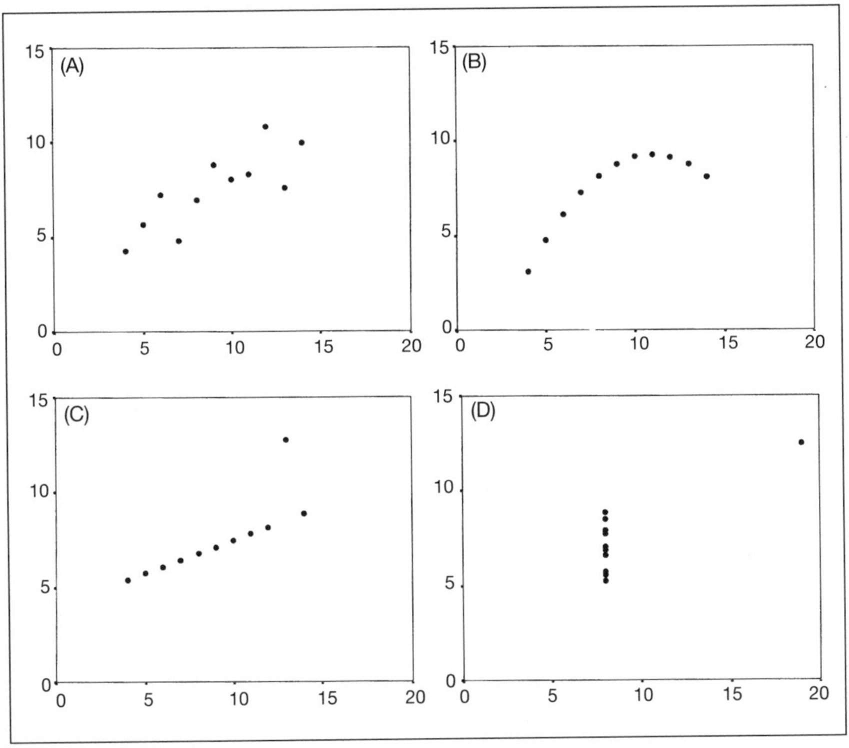

Source: Anscombe (1973).

grasped as complex units – as 'systems' and/or 'structures'. On the basis of this assumption, the properties of a social system cannot be determined or explained simply by the sum of its component parts.

It is often assumed that statistics can only capture simple aggregations of parts. If this were true, statistics could not play a very useful role in holistic analyses. But this assumption is not true: Edward Tufte, a statistician who also champions holism, has worked hard to show how descriptive statistics can be a very useful tool for conveying the whole picture, or the larger story. In particular, Tufte's work on visual displays (1983, 1997) provides us with several illustrations of how graphical depictions can help us better understand the nature of a situation by placing particular pieces of information in a useful, interpretive context or pattern. But this work began long before Tufte.

We can begin by considering a classic example of descriptive statistics: Dr John Snow's 1855 plotting of the location of cholera deaths in central

Figure 11.2   *Dr Snow's cholera map of London*

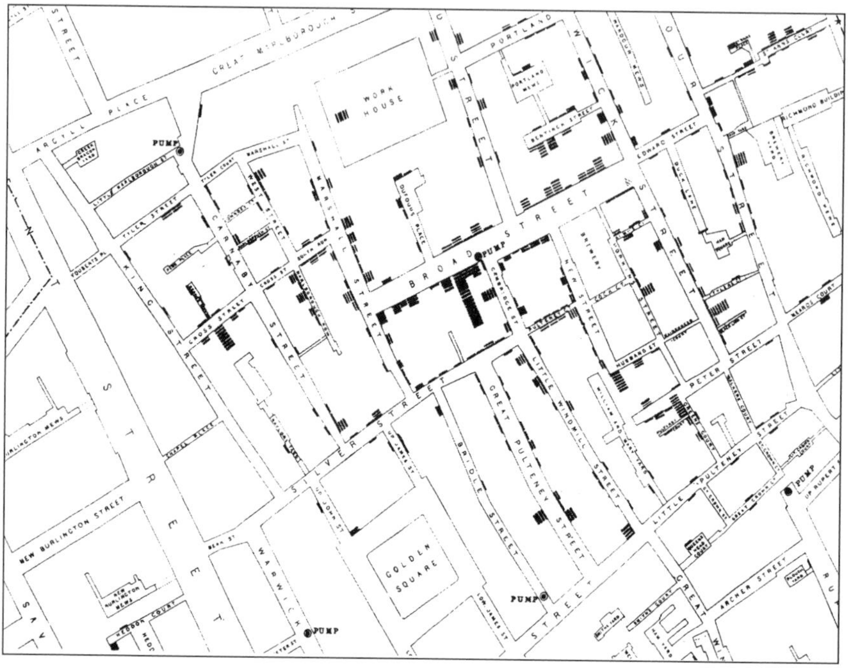

Source: Snow (1855).

London. Dr Snow collected cholera data and superimposed a tally of the number of deaths onto a city map of London, as shown in Figure 11.2. In so doing, he was able to show how most of the deaths were located in the vicinity of a common water pump on Broad Street. Consequently, Snow had the handle of the contaminated pump removed, and was credited with ending an epidemic that had already claimed more than 500 lives (see Snow (1855) and Gilbert (1958). Though there are several ways that this information could have been conveyed to help determine the cause of the cholera outbreak, this graphical depiction provides strong inner-ocular (it hits you right between the eyes) support for the water-pump hypothesis.

Étienne Jules Marey's remarkable (1878) *La Métode graphique* provides a phenomenal selection of graphs, two or which have become especially noteworthy. The first of these is a train schedule for the Paris to Lyon route in the 1880s, which is usually attributed to the French engineer Ibry. In this schedule, reproduced as Figure 11.3, we see arrivals and departures from a station along the horizontal axes, and the length of a stop at a given station is shown by the length of the horizontal line. Individual stations are separated in proportion to their actual distance apart. As a consequence, the slope of the line reflects the speed of the train (in other words, faster trains have lines that are more vertical). When two trains pass each other in opposite directions, this is indicated by the intersection of two lines, providing the time and place of the intersection.

Marey's graphical display provided the traveller with an enormous amount of information about the relationship of particular pieces of information in one simple drawing (for example, the time of departure of any given train, at any stop), in light of the general pattern of rail connections between these cities. It is difficult to think of a more efficient way of capturing the complexity of detail that is exhibited in this graphic design. A verbal depiction of this display is almost entirely useless, as the reader would be overwhelmed by the particulars and blinded from the general pattern (for example, which is the fastest train from Paris to Lyon).

Another example from Marey is provided by Minard's famous depiction of the fate of Napoleon's army in Russia, as shown in Figure 11.4. For Tufte (1983, p. 40), this 'may well be the best statistical graphic ever drawn'. Minard combines data maps and time series to depict Napoleon's costly campaign for Moscow. He includes information on a number of important variables, including diminishing troop sizes, troop movement over time, temperature and important dates. With one glance the viewer gets a remarkable overview of the relationship between some of the most relevant factors for understanding Napoleon's march on (and retreat from) Moscow. With the next glimpse the viewer can focus on a particular factor (for example, temperature) to see how changes in it are related to the size of the retreating army. Minard's figure is an excellent example of the old saying that a picture tells a thousand words.

Finally, consider a more recent example. Michael Ward and John O'Laughlin's shockwave film *The Spread of Democracy*[1] shows the variation, year to year, in the number of democratic states (narrowly defined). The brief film depicts the pulsating movements of democratic zones in the geography of the world. This picture, moving through time, allows the viewer to see complex patterns as they develop – pictures that were difficult (if not impossible) to see in the more traditional way in which these data have been presented (tables, data matrixes, comparative static maps, regression equations, and so on). On first viewing this film on the internet, we marvelled at the presentation: we played it over and over again, and saw developments that were much more rapid and startling than the literature (to date) had described. With apologies to

Figure 11.3 *Ibry's Paris–Lyon train schedule*

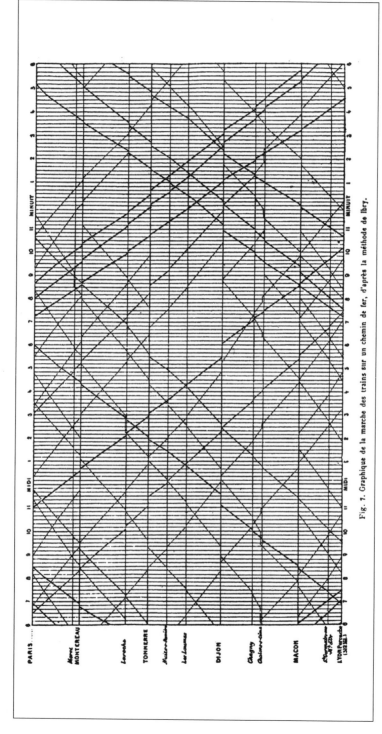

Fig. 7. Graphique de la marche des trains sur un chemin de fer, d'après la méthode de Ibry.

Source: Marey (1878, p. 20).

Figure 11.4   *Minard's depiction of the fate of Napoleon's army in Russia*

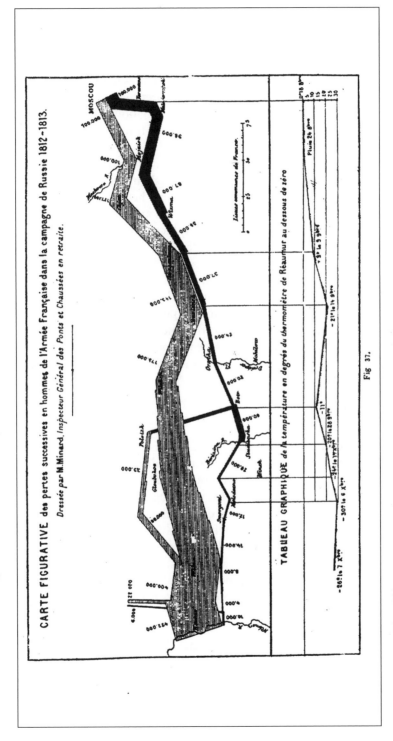

Source: Marey (1878, p. 72).

Fukuyama (1992), the film provides no sense of the world's inevitable march of history towards liberal democracy. Here, instead, is a much more nuanced picture, capturing the ebbs and flows of the democratic tide (à la Huntington, 1991).

All of these examples use descriptive statistics in the form of graphs or illustrations to allow the reader to interpret and digest a great deal of information. The nature of the presentation allows the critical reader to examine particular pieces of information (the location of individual cholera deaths, the time of departure from Lyon, the size of Napoleon's troops on a given date, whether a given state was democratic in 1978) in light of the larger pattern that the graphics' authors wish to convey. The graphs encourage us to tack back and forth between the individual data and the general patterns, of which they are an integral part.

It is also worth noting that each graphical presentation is unique. Each graph was designed with an understanding of the particular problem in mind. These are not off-the-shelf graphical depictions, and it is not certain that any of these presentations would work equally well for telling a different story. The authors' understanding of the phenomena in question provided them with a unique perspective from which to design a new form of presentation. It was their nearness to the phenomenon that allowed each author/designer to see that a graphical presentation would be more useful than, say, a verbal (or algebraic) depiction of the problem at hand.

Bayesian Statistics

The Reverend Thomas Bayes (1702–61) is credited with developing a method that has become increasingly popular in a wide variety of fields, ranging from archaeology to computing. The essence of his approach is to provide a mathematical rule for updating existing beliefs in the light of new evidence – or combing new data with existing knowledge or exper-tise. Constructivist scholars might find this approach useful as it allows them to incorporate prior knowledge about the subject (the whole) when first examining the particulars. This is quite unlike the statistics employed in a naturalist methodological approach (which can help to explain why there has been so much resistance to Bayesian statistics from naturalist scientists).

Bayes used the example of a newborn baby who works out the proba-bility of the sun rising with each passing day (apparently babies were more intelligent in the 1700s . . .). In the beginning, the baby assumes that the chance of the sun rising the following day is 50:50. To signify this, she puts two marbles, one white and one black, into a bag. The following day, the sun rises again, and the child puts a white marble in the bag. The probability of picking a white marble (the chance the sun will rise) increases from one half to two-thirds, on the basis of the new information. As the baby grows up, the number of white marbles in the bag increases. By the time the infant is a woman, she can be nearly certain that the sun will rise every day. Bayes's point is simple – by mixing experience with prior expectations we are able to produce better predictions about the probability of future events occurring. Although the focus here is on prediction, it is also possible to say that the woman has generated a better understanding of the likelihood of the sun rising tomorrow (than she did when she was just a baby).

Consider another example, from the realm of opinion studies. Opinion polling is often described to students in terms of a simple 'urn' model. The student is asked to imagine an urn filled with balls of two distinct colours. Red balls can be said to represent voters for the Red Party, and green balls represent voters for the Green Party. Choosing a sample from the electorate and asking them about their preferences (red ball or green ball?) is akin to choosing a ball, randomly, from the urn. In theory, the practice is repeatable, and the composition of the urn is uncertain. If, however, we can use information about how voters have tended to vote in other elections, this can give us important information about the 'contents of the urn'. (Remember, the urn is not filled randomly with balls, we simply don't know its content.) In the same way that the baby girl could incorporate new information to improve her predictions about future sunrises, opinion researchers can use prior information to make better predictions about the urn's likely content. In particular, the Bayesian scholar can incorporate this prior information into an *a priori* distribution about the electorate. This *a priori* distribution is combined (via Bayes's theorem) with the outcome of the sample. We can then produce what is called an '*a posteriori*' distribution – which provides us with a firmer foundation from which to make predictions.

Bayesian logic (or what some people call folk-Bayesianism) is increasingly being used by strategists and intelligence analysts whose job it is to assess threats to a nation's security. This was evident in a recent example from international affairs. During the late 1990s, America's government was constantly frustrated by the Iraqi president, Saddam Hussein, who had played cat and mouse with international weapons inspectors and successfully exploited UN sanctions for his own political advantage. When President George W. Bush assumed the reins of US foreign policy in early 2001, he held the firm opinion that his country's policy towards Saddam Hussein was untenable: not only had containment proved a failure, but Saddam Hussein had undermined America's prestige and destabilized a volatile region. In time, the Bush administration concluded that the Iraqi dictator must somehow be removed, and sought support among its allies to do so.

As most of you will be aware, many of America's European allies were not so eager. France, in particular, was reluctant to embrace a policy that aimed at toppling an established government in a terror-prone region. Besides, the French wanted to make sure that Saddam Hussein did, indeed, represent a threat to his neighbours. In order to do this, the French intelligence services adopted a two-step assessment programme. The first step was to gain access to information about Iraqi weapons programmes. This was done by traditional diplomatic means: France made it clear (to both Bush and Saddam) that it would support the US policy if Saddam refused to admit UN weapons inspectors into the country. Thus, France pressured Saddam to allow inspectors into Iraq.

The second step was analytical and based on information gleaned from the reports of the UN weapons inspectors. The inspectors travelled around Iraq and visited military installations, before delivering a series of largely negative reports. In one case after another, the inspectors found no obvious indication of nuclear weapons programmes and, more surprisingly, they found no indication of biological or chemical weapons production either. Members of the UN Security Council had access to these reports, but they read them very differently. Analysts from the Bush administration trusted neither Saddam nor the UN; they read the reports in pigheaded ways, insisting that Saddam Hussein had been toying with uncommonly naïve inspectors.

The French analysts read the reports in a different way: they applied a Bayesian logic of probability and continually upgraded their overall threat assessment. In other words, every time the French received a report of an inspection at a particular site that had failed to turn up any suspicious materials, the French analysts reduced their threat assessment by a small amount – they added another white ball to the jar, so to speak. After having read several negative reports from a substantial number of weapons sites, the French threat assessment had been so significantly reduced that they no longer believed the American assessments to be accurate.

We can now begin to appreciate how a Bayesian approach might be useful to a constructivist. By incorporating new information, the analyst's picture of the 'whole' is continually evolving. This understanding of the whole is used to update interpretations of the (new) particular data that are always coming in. McKeown (1999, p. 180), referring to Gooding (1992), describes Bayesianism in terms of the researcher who 'move[s] back and forth between theory and data, rather than taking a single pass through the data'. This process is very similar to the hermeneutic approach, as described in previous chapters, and is quite different from traditional statistical approaches.

Bayesian inference is different from traditional (statistical) inference in at least two ways. First, Bayesian inference is built on the concept of subjective probabilities. By introducing subjective probability, the analyst is allowed to enter her own degree of belief about an uncertain event into the estimation – it is not a fact describing the real world, but rather a personal statement about the analyst's level of certainty or confidence. These subjective probabilities are then added to the sample data to produce 'posterior probability' statements about the parameters of a statistical model. In so doing, we blur the solid line that usually separates the naturalist's facts from his values. These posterior probability statements express the researcher's degree of belief in the parameters (given the data and the prior subjective probabilities). By limiting the variation in parameters in this way, the analysis can focus on areas where there is disagreement or less understanding.

Second, Bayesian inference allows for the introduction of prior information (in addition to the sample) when making inferences. Both of these differences present radical challenges to the way in which naturalists assume that we should approach our subject matter (though it is not at all unlike the way much statistical work is actually done). More to the point: an awareness of the fact that analysts approach their research with preconditions (influenced by normative positions as well as *a priori* knowledge), and that these preconditions frame our understanding of the world under study, are two central characteristics of constructivism.

Bruce Western and Simon Jackman (1994) show how Bayesian inference can address some of the most common problems of statistical inference in comparative political research. They do this by applying a Bayesian approach to evaluate the competing claims of two comparative statisticians (Michael Wallerstein and John Stephens) – in a context characterized by the relative absence of information. Using Bayesian inference, Western and Jackman replace the regression coefficients estimated from Wallerstein and Stephens' data set with a set of regression coefficients that Western and Jackman believe are most probable (*a priori*). They then use this *a priori* information, combine it with the sample information, and produce a multivariate normal posterior distribution for the coefficients.

Such *a priori* beliefs can be developed on the basis of information that is not easily quantifiable. For example, Western and Jackman suggest that Stephens' deep historical grasp of the Swedish conditions allow him to generate realistic priors. Indeed, '[t]he Bayesian approach allows the information informally introduced into the analysis by Stephens and Wallerstein to enter formally through a prior distribution' (Western and Jackman, 1994, p. 417). This has radical methodological consequences. By allowing for this sort of interpretive variation, we can expect that no two researchers will prefer one prior probability distribution to another. In other words, the analyst no longer needs to try and understand a (singular) Real World – the world itself is allowed to vary in line with these *a priori* expectations. In effect, Bayesian statistics allow individual interpretations to re-enter the statistical project. In addition, the emphasis on prior information encourages Bayesian statisticians to familiarize themselves with local contexts before setting off on any statistical journey.

It is important to emphasize that Bayesianism is not a panacea, either for the naturalist or for the constructivist. For the constructivist, Bayesian approaches suffer from many of the shortcomings that are common to other statistical projects. Not only do many Bayesians strive for stronger predictions and application to causal analysis, but the approach suffers from a number of operational and philosophical short-comings. Primary among these is the distance necessarily created between the researcher and the context that she studies. To most constructivists, Bayesian statistics are still a long way from the serendipitous storytellers described in Chapter 9.

For the naturalist, however, the integration of subjective priors spoils the scientific credentials of the Bayesian approach. In this context it is important to recall that the renowned statistician Ronald Fisher held that an experiment interpreted with prior information 'would carry with it the serious disadvantage that it would no longer be self-contained, but would depend for its interpretation from experience previously gathered. It could no longer be expected to carry conviction to others lacking this supplementary experience' (1953, p. 69). Similarly, Leamer (1994, p. xi) finds the Bayesian approach less attractive because '[i]t may in fact increase the burden by requiring analysts to think consciously about their "priors" ' [!!].

Thinking consciously about one's priors, or one's presuppositions, is – of course – a foundational component of the constructivist approach. Applying a Bayesian statistical approach forces the analyst to be explicit about her normative and epistemological priors, and requires her to consider the general nature of the phenomenon when studying its particular parts. This, in turn, allows for the possibility of having various, even competing, interpretations of a given event.

Statistic Narratives

We have one final illustration of how statistics might be used by constructivist scholars: one that can be called Statistic Narratives. The motivation for this approach is an influential book by Bates et al. (1998), entitled *Analytic Narratives*. The novelty and influence of this collection can be found in the authors' attempt to use rational choice and game theoretic approaches to generate empirically testable general hypotheses from particular cases. In short, *Analytic Narratives* is an attempt to combine rational choice approaches with detailed case studies.

In a similar vein it is possible to imagine statistical studies that are used to formulate general hypotheses that can then be studied in detail with thick narratives. Obviously, as long as the focus of this sort of study remains on generating testable laws about real-world events, then the constructivist will show little interest in the potential of Statistic Narratives. But a more modest approach may offer more promise. Such an approach can use estimated (statistical) parameters to explore the historical development of associations between variables – but not in a strict theory-testing framework based on unwarranted assumptions, like sample representativeness or coefficient stability; see, for example, Kittel (1999, pp. 238–42) and Kittel and Obinger (2003, pp. 32–6).

Perhaps it is easier to consider this argument if we reflect again about how the constructivist employs comparisons. In the same way that we saw constructivists using comparison as a way to foil established theories in the previous chapter, we might expect that constructivist scholars would be interested in a Statistic Narrative approach that uses sophisticated regression analyses to generate hypotheses, which are then problematized or nuanced by the use of applied or focused narratives.

Conclusion

We have come a long way from the stories told by the Princes of Serendip. As a consequence, most constructivists don't feel very comfortable in the foreign world inhabited (and created!) by statisticians. For this reason, we have tried to illustrate how some forms of statistics can be employed in a way that is consistent with constructivists' core beliefs about how the social world is, and how it can be understood. By extending the way that constructivists use comparisons – in particular, by using them to establish associations and patterns for further enquiry, and by recognizing explicitly the source of these patterns – we can begin to recognize how some statistical projects can be employed by constructivists. After a brief attempt at contextualizing the history of statistics, our discussion has focused on three examples – quantitative graphics, Bayesian statistical approaches and Statistic Narratives – as natural extensions of the way in which comparisons can be used by constructivists. In the next chapter we take one step further away from constructivists' home territory to look at how experiments can be used to further our understanding of social phenomena.

Recommended Further Reading

For those who can read French, we recommend returning to the original source of much modern graphical study: Marey's impressive *La Méthode graphique* (1878). Edward Tufte's *The Visual Display of Quantitative Information* (1983) and his *Visual Explanations* (1997) provide access to the English reader, and more contemporary examples. For criticisms of the statistical world view and its influence in social science, read McKeown's 'Case Studies and the Statistical Worldview' (1999). As mentioned in the text, Western and Jackman's 'Bayesian Inference for Comparative Research' (1994) provides a nice glimpse of the power of a Bayesian approach. Similarly, Bates et al.'s *Analytic Narratives* (1998) illustrates the potential of our proposed Statistics Narratives approach.

Chapter 12

Interpretive Experiments

As with statistical approaches, it is – at first – difficult to imagine how constructivists might employ experiments. After all, in an experiment researchers control the conditions under which the study takes place and the variables being studied. As we saw in Chapter 3, it is this type of control that allows researchers greater certainty about the nature of the causal relationships being tested. This, in turn, produces firm predictions about the nature of the Real World. As Kathleen McGraw (1996, p. 770) notes: 'Structurally, experiments are marked by a deliberate intervention in the natural, ongoing state of affairs.'

This willingness to deliberately intervene and manipulate the empirical context of a given social phenomenon is a hallmark of naturalist science. The constructivist, by contrast, wants to avoid it. When an experimenter manipulates the contexts surrounding a phenomenon, she undermines the very ground in which interpretation and meaning are anchored. Thus, on the surface, it would seem rather preposterous to consider experimental methods from a constructivist perspective.

In this chapter we show that much of the actual process of ground-breaking science occurs in the form of thought experiments. These experiments are different from the ones introduced in Chapter 3, as they encourage the researcher to think in hermeneutic ways, immersed in context. More to the point: the new ground being broken by these thought experiments is not the terra firma of the Real World – it is fanciful: a product of the researcher's imagination. However, it is upon this ground that we can begin to see how constructivists might embrace experiments. Thought experiments allow the researcher to explicitly create and imagine alternative worlds – imagine different patterns in a counterfactual world. By examining a number of different thought experiments – from both worlds (that of the natural sciences and that of the social sciences) – we find ourselves straddling a remarkably large piece of common ground.

We do this by mapping out that ground in three distinct (but tangential) territories. The first section looks at the role of thought experiments in a number of actual scientific endeavours. The second section moves quickly to the terrain of social theory to illustrate the similarity of their endeavours. The third section examines one modern variant of this deductive tradition, rational choice theory, to show how thought experiments might attract the interest of both constructivists and naturalists alike, in rather unexpected ways.

As naturalist scientists from many disciplines rely on thought experiments (as will be evident below), it is rather uncommon to claim this important piece of territory in the name of constructivism. More controversial yet will be our attempt to place rational choice theorists in the constructivist camp. After all, rational choice theorists like to think of themselves (and their work) as being at the forefront of modern (read natural) social science. We close on such a controversial note because we believe that it can shake our common perceptions of the scientific landscape and allow us to see possibilities in a place where none existed before.

Experiments in Science

We can end where we began: with Galileo Galilei throwing things off the tower of Pisa. Galileo's experiment is one of the most famous in the history of science, yet doubts have always been raised about the veracity of Galileo's account of the stunt. These doubts provide us with our point of departure, as they raise a number of important questions. For example, does it matter if Galileo didn't actually perform his famous experiment? If he didn't, how should we assess the soundness of his argument? What happens to modern physics if Galileo actually lied about his procedures? In raising these questions we begin to shift the terrain of our inquiry from empirical to more imaginary ground.

It is difficult to provide anything but hazy answers to these questions. What we can say is this: if Galileo lied about his experiment, it was a brilliant lie. Generations of subsequent scientists have not held the fib against him – nor have they doubted the soundness of his argument. One reason for this may be that the story itself rests firmly on the logic of the experiment and the experiment itself (true or false) is dressed in a vivid and convincing imagery. This is the stuff of convictions. Besides, Galileo's account employed such simple means and he described such a simple procedure that any doubter could easily repeat the experiment for herself.

Throughout this book we have maintained that experimentation is the basic method of naturalist science, and we have used Galileo as its poster boy – such is the imagery of science, and it is a powerful image at that. Still, we mustn't forget that images are nothing more than illusions or constructions in our mind.

Indeed, much scientific discovery begins in the thin air of imagery. This seems to have been evident to the famous mathematician Jules Henri Poincaré (1854–1912), who noted in his 1904 *Mathematical Definition in Education*: 'It is by logic we prove, it is by intuition that we invent.' While we cannot be certain whether Galileo's experiment was real or fictitious, we can be certain that other great scientists employed imaginary experiments. Clearly Charles Darwin – one of the most influential scientists in history – couldn't use the experimental method to claim (or prove) that the evolution of species resulted from natural selection. Neither could Charles Lyell (on whom Darwin relied heavily) employ experiments to conclude that the world was millions of years old and that whole mountains have grown and eroded several times over the course of the earth's natural history. Alfred Wegener could not employ experiments to prove his claim that the surface of the earth consists of vast, tectonic plates in constant motion. Neither could George Lemaître or Edwin Hubble, when they asserted that the universe originated with a 'big bang'. These men – Darwin, Lyell, Wegener, Lemaître and Hubble – have all contributed greatly to our knowledge of the world. All of them are giants in the history of natural science, but none of them could rely on the experimental method.

That is to say, none of them relied on the type of experiment we described in Chapter 3. None of these great scientists could afford to tinker in the laboratory! The objects of their investigations were far too big, or too time-consuming, to fit in laboratory conditions. To compensate, they relied on the *imagery* of the experiment – on deductive arguments to fashion a convincing case in the abstract.

Well, not entirely in the abstract, for they included bits and pieces of empirical evidence in their argument – but only bits and pieces. Darwin, for example, was a breeder of pigeons and he studded his argument with real-world, pigeon-breeding evidence. But this evidence merely served as illustration; his larger case did not rest on it. Of course, he supported his theory of adaptation on empirical evidence wherever such evidence was obtainable – but this was remarkably infrequent. As a result, Darwin's argument was necessarily speculative. Indeed, in its first and most famous formulation, in *On the Origin of Species*, the argument is remarkably anecdotal and woefully incomplete – as his many detractors were quick to point out (Hull, 1973).

Scholars who work in evolutionary biology, geology or astrophysics often find themselves in the same boat as Darwin. They all observe objects that are too big, or take too long, for experimental set-ups. Charles Darwin, for example, operated with a time scale that covered millions of years. Charles Lyell's argument about the growth and erosion of mountains operated with a time frame that covered hundreds of millions of years. Alfred Wegener thought in terms of billions of years.

The continental drift that he hypothesized was so enormous and so slow that he could not possibly observe or measure it directly (although he pretended that he did).

In short, scientists like Darwin, Lyell, Wegener and Hubble could not depend on observations derived from physical experiments to form their theories. Instead, they had to imagine another world. In this imagined world they developed scenarios and asked what was necessary to support them. Finally, they searched for elemental knowledge and related it systematically to their various imagined scenarios, all the time asking which scenario was best supported by the observations collected. In short, much of the progress of science occurs in the minds of great scientists.

It is in this basic, methodological maxim that constructivists can find distant relatives. Benedetto Croce stressed it when he claimed that all history is contemporary history. R. G. Collingwood emphasized it when he argued that the historian's past is inseparable from his present. The point is simple: when we run mental experiments – and all scientists do – the laboratory is situated close to home. It is coloured by the world that the scientist knows best. It is informed by the experiences that the scientist has accumulated during the course of her life.

Two examples can illustrate this point in more detail: the first is provided by a Norwegian lawyer and fur-trapper, who became one of the most controversial archaeologists of Norse history; the second is a Texan cowboy and banker who became a contentious archaeologist of Mayan affairs. It is to these two examples that we now turn.

Imaginary Journeys

For decades, Norwegians were convinced that Vikings had crossed the Atlantic Ocean and landed in North America. Indeed, by some of the more enthusiastic accounts, the Vikings had sailed along America's east coast all the way down to Florida and the Bahamas (Prytz, 1991). These claims had one main source: the Viking sagas – which were read with extreme care, and where every sentence was carefully gleaned for suggestions and clues. However, as many critics pointed out, the saga texts were too general to support the claims made by Scandinavian historians. Most significantly, no archaeological evidence had been found in the Americas to substantiate the claim that the Vikings had ever been there.

Helge and Anne Stine Ingstad set out to search for such evidence. While Anne Stine's background was in archaeology (she had turned to it rather late in life), Helge's background was less orthodox: he had originally studied to become a lawyer, but instead struck out across the North Atlantic to try his hand as a trapper, polar explorer and historian.

Undoubtedly, this singular combination of life experiences provided the Ingstads with a unique vision of scholarly endeavour.

In the 1950s, the Ingstads began to map the Norse settlements on Greenland. While participating in the archaeological digs there, Helge Ingstad was in the habit of sitting on the front step of an old Viking stone house, looking out over the ocean. From that doorstep he would wonder how the sea and the landscape might have looked a thousand years earlier, when the house was built and its front step laid. In short, Ingstad tried to imagine himself in a Viking settlement a thousand years earlier. In this imagined context, he came to wonder where *he* would have set sail, had he been Leif Eiriksson at the end of the first millennium.

After two years of such imaginings, Helge Ingstad came to draw a probable sea route from Greenland to America – to L'Anse aux Meadows, on an island off the east coast of Canada. Ingstad felt that the North Newfoundland landscape and scenery suited the few geographical descriptions that can be found in the sagas.

> I looked out over the plains towards the islands, and north over the ocean, where Belle Isle looked like a fairy-tale castle, towards the distant blue coast of Labrador, along which the Vinland voyagers of old had sailed south. It was almost a *déjà-vu*, so much was reminiscent of what I had seen in the Norse settlements of Greenland, and on the west coast of Norway – the houses built on ground higher than the surrounding land, with a view of the ocean, the green fields and meadows, the rippling brook in the open landscape, and perhaps also something else, less easily grasped. People from Greenland must have felt at home here.   (Ingstad and Ingstad, 2001, pp. 126–7)

Thus, by reading the ancient Norse sagas about Vinland, by studying Viking culture and technology, by considering other prominent theories of Vinland's location, the Ingstads came to form an idea of where the Vikings might have settled in the New World. But a very important piece of this intellectual puzzle was an effort by Helge Ingstad to *imagine* how the Vikings would have evaluated different landing sites in America. In the early 1960s, the couple arrived at L'Anse aux Meadows, after marvelling over how well it fitted the sagas' description of Vinland.

It must have been difficult for the couple to raise funds for a research expedition on the basis of such flimsy evidence. (Just imagine the exasperated reply of a potential funding agent: '*What?!!* You *imagined* that the Vikings would have liked to settle there?'). Anne Stine and Helge Ingstad persevered, however, and they managed to fund an archaeological expedition to the site. Counter to the forecasts of many sceptics, who saw this as yet another wild goose chase, they soon made important discoveries. Before long, their archaeological team uncovered conclusive evidence in the shape of a soapstone spindle-whorl, a Viking ring pin and the remains of a dozen Viking buildings.

By Ingstad's account, the site at L'Anse aux Meadows is, in all probability, the Viking camp mentioned in Leif Eiriksson's *Saga*. It was here, Ingstad claims, that sailors from an Icelandic trading ship landed around 985, and were the first to describe these new lands to the west. Fifteen years later, Leif Eiriksson had sailed from Greenland, and wintered at a settlement which the saga refers to as Straumfjord. In the years following, members of his family and a group of colonists visited the camp. They built timber and sod longhouses and several smaller buildings – in one of which they made the first iron tools in the New World. It was the remnants of these houses and activities that the Ingstads believed they had found.

Ingstad argued that members of the camp ventured as far southwest as New Brunswick. But it would seem that conflict with the indigenous population obliged them to withdraw from the area and they returned to Greenland within a decade. Norse contacts with the New World continued and knowledge of the new lands likely remained with European sailors, facilitating the reopening of the Atlantic sea lanes in the 1490s.

Which methods did Helge Ingstad use to find Straumfjord? It would be grossly unfair to say that he made a wild stab in the dark. He guessed; but his was an educated guess. In effect, Ingstad's thought process is akin to the one described by Whewell, or by Peirce's retroduction, as introduced in Chapter 8. Similarly, Popper might have claimed that Ingstad made a 'conjecture', informed by deep knowledge of his subject. After all, Ingstad was a trapper and a sailor: he knew the winds and the waters of the Arctic, and drew on his own expert knowledge when he made his conjecture. He was assisted by the realization that the Vikings would have given much thought about where to settle – and he could tap into that thinking/reflective process. Ingstad's conjecture was, in a sense, the result of a series of mental experiments that he had run over and over in his mind, over the course of several years.

At this point of imagined truth, the archaeologist, the historian, the evolutionary biologist, the geologist and the astrophysicist might join in methodological agreement. Ingstad started with a few surviving artefacts – the Norse sagas and the stone remnants of Viking settlements in Greenland. He then retroduced a series of probable events that could have produced them. Then, on the basis of the properties that marked this process, Ingstad ran mental experiments with the aid of knowledge, logic and a good deal of imagination.

A similar process appears to have guided Richardson B. Gill. When he visited the Mayan ruins of Southern Mexico in 1968, Gill was deeply affected by the people and the place. As a result, he resolved to find the reason behind the collapse of Mayan civilization.

Mayan society had flourished for more than 2000 years, evolving into an empire before disaster struck around AD 800. Rather abruptly, the construction of pyramids halted and whole cities were abandoned. The most advanced civilization of the Western hemisphere suddenly unravelled, allowing the jungle to reclaim its cities and fields. Like the ancient city of Troy, the sudden collapse of Mayan civilization presented a tantalizing mystery for generations of archaeologists.

Prevailing theories ascribed the decline of major civilizations to human error. Accordingly, historians and archaeologists tended to blame the Mayas themselves for their destiny – laying the blame, for example, on slash-and-burn agricultural techniques, religious doctrines, invasion and warfare, rebellions, diseases, foolish administrative practices, and so on. Gill believed none of them. He resolved that climate, not the Indians, was to blame: drought might have caused the Mayan civilization to topple.

At this point, of course, the critical reader will note how Gill's perception of the problem is remarkably similar to the one that dogs his own, late twentieth century context. Is it really just coincidence that the Mayans were struggling with the same sort of problems as are we? Gill was aware of this uncomfortable parallel and wrestled with his bias face to face, turning it to his favour. In so doing, Gill's eventual explanation resulted less from books or careful study, and more from his own personal history: it came from recollecting the devastating droughts in the 1950s, when Texan farmland was parched and fires raged. 'Being a Texan,' he explained later, 'I'm very aware of drought. It's something we deal with on an annual basis; we never know from one year or the next if we'll have enough rain' (Wong, 2001).

In the early 1980s, Texas was hit by a financial crisis and Gill's family bank collapsed. Dick Gill went back to college to study anthropology and archaeology so that he could study Mayan history more systematically. He studied fragments of pottery and counted Mayan farmsteads in order to estimate the demographic trends of the region. From these he drew a dramatic conclusion: Mayan society could have counted as many as 15 million inhabitants around AD 800, but this number had dropped to less than 1.5 million by AD 900. In other words, more than 90 per cent of the Mayan population simply disappeared during the course of the ninth century. Although Gill was aware that several factors could account for such an enormous drop in population, he was convinced that drought was among them.

In order to make his case, Gill needed to reconstruct the climate of ninth-century Yucatan. Since the Maya weren't in the habit of recording exact rainfall and temperature, Gill had to use whatever evidence he could find. First he turned to the national archives in Mexico City. They revealed that a severe, three-year-long drought had devastated Mayan society between 1902 and 1904. This suggested that his basic proposition was reasonable: droughts *had* occurred in the Yucatan at least once in the past. If it had occurred a hundred years ago, Gill reasoned, it *could* have occurred a thousand years ago. But had it?

Searching further, Gill investigated older, colonial records from Spanish authorities in the Yucatan province of Mexico. Here he found evidence of repeated droughts. For example, a particularly bad drought had destroyed the harvests in 1795, and a document from that year contained a plea to Spain for help: the region was running out of grain and they feared the consequences. Now Gill had proof that devastating droughts had occurred more than once in the Yucatan's past. This increased the likelihood of his argument. But he was unable to find any archival sources with enough detail to allow him to reconstruct the peninsula's weather patterns accurately. Nor did he find any evidence that a great drought actually had occurred during the ninth century.

To reconstruct the weather patterns and provide evidence of his hypothesized drought, Gill began – Miss Marple-like – to pursue new sources. He turned from archives to trees. Tree trunks grow fast in warm, wet weather; their growth is arrested in arid weather. Thus, by measuring the width of the rings in Yucatan tree trunks, Gill hoped to reconstruct the peninsula's precipitation pattern. On the basis of tree-ring records, Gill could identify the droughts of the Yucatan peninsula over the last few centuries. However, to support his case, he needed to analyse 1200-year-old tree trunks – of which there were none to be found.

In search of a solution, Gill began to read meteorology papers. After ploughing through hundreds of dead-end sources, he finally stumbled across a paper on 'Dendrochronology, Mass Balance and Glacier Front Fluctuations in Northern Sweden' (Karlén, 1984). This paper allowed him to count the rings in a 1200-year-old pine tree from Arctic Sweden. In this process of counting he made an astonishing discovery: that the pattern in the outer part of the old Swedish pine trunk matched exactly the 200-year-old record he had made of drought and disaster in the Yucatan! Not only did the Yucatan droughts (of 1902–4 and 1795) match perfectly with severe cold snaps in Sweden; every time there had been a drought in the Maya lowlands, there had also been severe cold in Sweden!

Meteorologists could inform Gill that he had tapped into the effects of a well-known weather system called the North Atlantic High. The term refers to an area of high pressure that travels annually, eastwards across the Atlantic – from the Caribbean towards northern Europe – and back again. When the high pressure moves towards Europe, it brings balmy temperatures to Sweden and pulls moist air in over Central America. However, every once in a while, the North Atlantic High – for reasons that are unclear – doesn't fully complete its eastward journey; it stops a bit short of Europe. In these years, Sweden turns bitterly cold and the Yucatan suffers a drought.

Because it connected Scandinavian and Central American weather patterns with clocklike regularity, the North Atlantic High allowed Gill to use old Swedish tree trunks (as operational indicators) for reconstructing ancient weather patterns in the Yucatan. As he patiently inspected Swedish wood, and filled in the missing centuries of his ancient weather charts, he found indications of a string of cold winters in ninth-century Sweden – which would indicate a similar string of dry years in Central America. Gill's proposition thus graduated from plausible to highly possible.

The circumstantial evidence was growing stronger. But Gill still lacked direct proof of a devastating drought in ninth-century Yucatan. He finally got this evidence from a team of American researchers who collected mud samples from the Yucatan lake Chichancanab. The research team drove long hollow tubes deep into the bottom of the lake and collected samples of mud from thousands of years back – the deeper the mud, the older the sediments (and the seeds and shells that were trapped in it). The surfaces of shells from times of high rainfall are dominated by a particular type of light oxygen. If the rainfall is sparse, the water in the lake will evaporate and produce a dominance of heavy oxygen in the shells. Core samples from the ninth century showed an exceptional surge of heavy oxygen, indicating that it was an exceptionally dry period. Indeed, comparative analyses showed that it was the driest century in the region for over 7000 years (Gill, 2000).

Like Ingstad and the other scientists described above, Gill retroduced or conjectured a series of probable events that were consistent with his hunch about the decline of the Mayas. Through a long and tenacious period of exploration, Gill juggled a number of mental experiments. Experiments fuelled by knowledge, logic, detective work and a good deal of imagination. These experiments led him to search for particular pieces of a vast puzzle. The patterns that constituted the entire puzzle existed first in Gill's mind; he then tried to locate individual pieces in the real world. Like the others, Gill could not hope to find all of the missing puzzle pieces – he searched for individual pieces, here and there, to anchor his dream in terra firma.

Social Thought Experiments

In the examples above we have shown the important (if under-appreciated) role that thought experiments can play in scientific discovery. We have then shown how scientists employ retroduction to anchor these thought experiments to their empirical foundations. Social theorists also employ thought experiments to construct imagined communities or contexts which can then be juxtaposed against the real world (at certain empirical points of tangency), or used as ideal types. As such, the thought experiments used in traditional social theory are remarkably similar to the examples above. To illustrate this we can consider three prominent examples from Western social thought: Plato, Hobbes and Rousseau.

When Plato is asked to describe his ideal state, he begins with a discussion about human nature. 'Society originates,' we are told, 'because the individual is not self-sufficient, but has many needs which he can't supply himself' (Plato, 1987 [*c.*360 BC], p. 59, *369b*). In addition, Plato adds that 'no two of us are born exactly alike. We have different natural aptitudes, which fit us for different jobs' (ibid., p. 59, *370b*). Thus, Plato shows us how the construction of a social community can be imagined on the basis of the (interrelated) needs of its inhabitants (such as to provide food, shelter and clothing).

Indeed, it is quite clear (implicit, but clear) from Plato's Book II of *The Republic* that Plato's community did not exist historically; it was devised (imagined) to help us understand the nature of the individual citizens who might inhabit it, and the justice that will characterize both. When Glaucon criticizes Socrates' first attempt as 'founding a community of pigs' (ibid., p. 63, *372d*), Plato imagines an even more complex social arrangement. But this second, grander, community remains nothing more than a mental construct.

A similar argument was developed some 2000 years later by Thomas Hobbes. In his *Leviathan,* Hobbes writes that it is possible (if not very attractive) to consider human beings divorced from their community, in an imagined state of nature. In contrast to Plato, Hobbes begins by assuming that humans are – on balance – equal, and that each man is driven by a number of *passions*, including a powerful lust for power: 'a perpetual and restless desire of power after power that ceases only in death' (Hobbes, 1958 [1651], p. 86). This lust for power among equals, in the context of a hypothesized state of nature, produces lives that are (most famously) 'solitary, poor, nasty, brutish and short' (Hobbes, 1958, p. 107). For Hobbes, the solution to this living hell is escape to an imagined sovereign community: the *Leviathan* – a fanciful creature on loan from the Bible.

In the same way that Plato imagines an ideal state (*The Republic*) as a just solution to the purported nature of man, Hobbes offers an imagined community (governed by an almighty *Leviathan*) to liberate man from the state of nature (also imagined). The attractiveness of the *Leviathan* or the *Republic* can only be understood by knowing how each author hypothesized the nature of man.

Rousseau provides yet another take on the same theme. When addressing the *Origin and Foundations of Inequality among Men*, he begins by:

> setting all the facts aside, for they do not affect the question. The researches which can be undertaken concerning this subject must not be taken for historical truths, but only for hypothetical and conditional reasonings better suited to clarify the nature of things than to show their true origin. (Rousseau, 1964 [1755], p. 103)

Rousseau is explicitly critical of Hobbes's depiction of human nature, and the more timid pictures painted by Cumberland and Pufendorf. Rousseau has a different conception of human nature, which he introduces by placing his imagined man in a state of nature (like Hobbes, only very different). Unlike Plato (but like Hobbes), Rousseau has no difficulty in imagining a pre-social man. But unlike Hobbes, Rousseau's man in the state of nature is a noble savage: 'most of our ills are our own work, and . . . we would have avoided almost all of them by preserving the simple, uniform, and solitary life prescribed to us by nature' (Rousseau, 1964, p. 110).

For Rousseau, it is society that is corrupt – not man. He illustrates this argument in the same way as the other authors: by having his readers imagine man in a state of nature and contrasting that imagined creature with the one more familiar to us from everyday experience. In doing so, Rousseau reminds us to be careful 'not to confuse savage man with the men we have before our own eyes' (ibid., p. 111). For Rousseau as for Hobbes, the state of nature is an imagined condition – a condition 'which no longer exists, which perhaps never existed, which probably never will exist, and about which it is nevertheless necessary to have precise notions in order to judge our present state correctly' (ibid., p. 93).

Drawing from authors as different as Plato, Hobbes and Rousseau, we have aimed to illustrate the way in which thought experiments in social theory share several traits with constructivism, as described in the preceding chapters. In particular, there are two points worthy of note.

First, none of these authors, regardless of their point of departure, used thought experiments to justify a fixed ontological perspective (a Real World). We are asked to imagine that man is equal (or unequal), cooperative (or competitive), and reasoned (or not) in a world – a state of nature

– that is otherworldly. Similarly, we are asked to imagine these fictional characters in a society that is also a product of the author's imagination. This sort of ontological flexibility is one of the hallmarks of the constructivist perspective.

Second, the very question being asked lends itself to a hermeneutic approach. Simply asking the reader to imagine mankind in the state of nature requires that we imagine: (1) man, (2) society and (3) their interaction/juxtaposition. Plato cannot imagine man prior to the community. Hobbes can (imagine the unimaginable), but it is not very attractive: humans in the state of nature were a desperate lot. Finally, Rousseau not only imagines, but he dreams of a man uncorrupted by society. By frequently hopping back and forth between the imagined individual and the imagined community, we come to understand each in light of the other.

We hasten to end this section with a word of caution: one woman's dream is another's nightmare. As many authors, over the centuries, have noted with respect to some of social theory's grander castles in the sky: attempts to build real copies of masterful thought experiments often end in disaster. Thought experiments, we note with despair, have the same potential for social engineering as do Galton's statistics.

Rational Thought Experiments

On the flip side of this danger lies hope. In social theory, thought experiments are used to understand the nature of cooperation and community, and the individual's relationship to these. Like most constructivists, Rousseau believed that the key to human behaviour lies in its context. Humans are malleable creatures. If individuals are to behave in an orderly manner, and live moral lives, it is crucially important that they are brought up in an orderly and moral society – that they are moulded by the protective framework of a tender, just and nourishing state. Within the ordering presence of the state, the inculcation of public feeling imparts to each citizen a spirit of devotion to the welfare of the whole, and equality prevents the development of partial interests which may be fatal to civic order and the unity of the state.[1]

Thus, if people are treated firmly and fairly, society will be unified (and conflict can be eliminated):

> If children are brought up in common in the bosom of equality; if they are imbued with the laws of the State . . .; if they are taught to respect these above all things; if they are surrounded by examples and objects which constantly remind them of the tender mother who nourishes

them . . ., we cannot doubt that they will learn to cherish one another mutually as brothers.   (Rousseau, 1950 [1755], p. 309)

On the other hand, if individuals live in a corrupt society, they will become corrupt themselves. In the absence of an ordering and moral state, individuals cannot develop the skills and social graces that order a community. In the early state of nature, Rousseau argues, individuals were egotistical, they thought only of themselves and their own advantage. They did this not out of malice, but out of ignorance. Under such conditions, human behaviour is governed by the two principles that humans possess before society endows them with reason: well-being and self-preservation. Under these primitive conditions, humans do not associate, let alone cooperate, very easily. Indeed, cooperation is possible only in the most dire and peculiar of circumstances. Rousseau imagines a situation in which natural men have been driven into cooperation by a common threat of hunger:

> That is how men could imperceptibly acquire some crude idea of mutual engagements and of the advantages of fulfilling them, but only insofar as present and perceptible interest could require; for foresight meant nothing to them, and far from being concerned about a distant future, they did not even think of the next day. Was it a matter of catching a deer, everyone clearly felt that of this purpose he ought faithfully to keep his post; but if a hare happened to pass within reach of one of them, there can be no doubt that he pursued it without scruple, and that having obtained his prey, he cared very little about having caused his companions to miss theirs.   (Rousseau, 1964, p. 145)

The hunger of all can be satisfied if they cooperate together in hunting down a deer (a deer is difficult to catch alone, but it yields good meat for many). At the same time, the hunger of each can be satisfied with a hare (a hare can be caught alone, providing poor – but sufficient – meat for one). Thus, individuals have to decide which is better: to trust and cooperate with others in hope of a nice venison dinner; or defect and secure a rabbit for oneself. In effect, the story of the stag hunt is the story of the social contract; it surveys the groundwork for community.

Rousseau's point is that no individual is strong enough to subdue a deer by herself, whereas it takes only one hunter to catch a hare. Everyone prefers deer to a hare, and a hare to nothing at all (which is what the hunting party will end up with if too many members run off chasing hares). Modern game theorists, such as William Poundstone (1992, pp. 218ff.), envision Rousseau's deer hunt as a game between two rational people – let's call them Robinson and Friday. Poundstone then

Figure 12.1   *Stag hunt payoff matrix*

		Robinson	
		Hunt deer	Chase hare
Friday	Hunt deer	3,3	0,2
	Chase hare	2,0	1,1

adds that the value (or payoff) of catching a deer is 3, the value of catching a hare is 1, and there is no value (0) in catching nothing at all. The outcome of the game is summarized in Figure 12.1. To clarify, the conditions in the upper right corner can be described thus: Friday chooses to hunt the deer, while Robinson chooses to chase a hare, with the corresponding payoffs: 0 for Friday; 2 for Robinson.

In modern game theory, a stag hunt game is one which describes a choice between safety and social cooperation. Hunting deer (large and very tasty) represents social cooperation; chasing hares (small, but hits the spot) is the safe bet.[2] Because Friday and Robinson don't trust or talk to one another, they don't really know what the other is going to do. Under these conditions, each has to find out what makes most sense under different possible scenarios.

Thus, Friday might begin by assuming that Robinson will hunt deer. He then has to decide if it makes more sense for him to cooperate (and hunt deer) or to defect (and chase bunnies). In the first case (cooperate), he can expect a reward of 3; in the latter (defect), he can expect a 2 – it is clear that it is best for Friday to also hunt deer. However, when Friday begins by assuming that Robinson might chase rabbits, he finds that it is now more rational for him to also chase rabbits.

In this game, what is rational for Friday depends on his belief of what Robinson will do (this is, by the way, quite different from a Prisoner's Dilemma). Both stag hunting and bunny chasing represent *equilibria* (in other words, that it is best for Friday to hunt deer if Robinson hunts deer and it is best for Friday to chase bunnies if Robinson does so). If Friday chooses to hunt deer, he takes a bigger chance of going hungry (as he takes a chance that Robinson will not join in the deer hunt).

Alternatively, if Friday chooses to chase bunnies, he runs no such risk, since his payoff does not depend on Robinson's choice of action. Weighed against all these considerations is the realization that everyone prefers venison to bunny stew. In this game, rational players are pulled in two different directions: at one end is a consideration of mutual benefit; at the other is a consideration of personal risk.

This is the essence of Rousseau's dilemma for natural men. Also, as Poundstone (1992) makes clear, it is a dilemma for all rational actors who live outside of an ordered society, or who think exclusively of themselves.

An Afterthought

We're moving fast here, so hold on tight. From thought experiments in natural science, we have moved to thought experiments in social theory, from which we have migrated to theories of rational choice. From the view of constructivists, it might seem that we have moved from the frying pan and into the fire: surely rational choice theory can have nothing to do with constructivism?! If this should be the case, it is time to remind constructivists of some of their own methodological assumptions: perceptions (and observations) can be deceiving, and methodological biases can sometimes blind us from seeing things in a useful and nuanced light.

The roots of rational choice approaches can be traced back to René Descartes, and his role in (re)legitimizing deduction, in the form of mathematical expression, for the scientific community. In effect, Descartes planted an intellectual seed that lay dormant for a century and a half, while remaining fertile all the while. Then, with the protection and sustenance offered by David Ricardo (1772–1823), a deductive approach began to take root in the modern study of economics. From Ricardo (and the modern study of economics) grew rational choice approaches, which have spread rapidly to neighbouring fields of social science.

Rational choice theorists formulate their argument on the basis of axioms. An axiom is a statement for which no proof is required. Because of this, axioms form an important premise to an argument – but they don't, themselves, furnish a conclusion. Common axioms in rational choice approaches include perfect rationality, transitivity and non-satiety – axioms that are necessary for deriving inference curves that are convex to the origin.

Upon these axiomatic premises lies the logic imbedded in mathematics. It is these rules of logic that allow the modeller/analyst to deduce consequences. In short, the method involves establishing basic axioms that are either true by definition or 'self-evident', and using deductive logic to derive theorems which are not self-evident. In other words, the main role of deductive approaches is to guarantee consistency. The use of logic, the set of rules that preserve the truth of an argument, guarantees that an argument is consistent.

Rational choice theorists aim to explain collective outcomes with reference to the maximizing actions of individuals. Thus, the stag hunt game is an example of a rational choice model. It builds on a number of implicit assumptions (for example, that both Friday and Robinson will choose a strategy with the highest payoff, *ceteris paribus*). It then outlines the different strategic choices that these individuals face, and the expected outcomes that result from these individually rational actions.

In effect, rational choice theorists are imagining alternative worlds. They create a highly structured thought experiment, where imagined individuals act in a fabricated or fanciful context to help the analyst interpret and understand real world situations. Rational choice theorists are consciously constructing their own mental patterns – the games they play are mental constructs. Indeed, it is because of this obvious lack of contact with the Real World that rational choice theorists are often criticized by their colleagues. Consider the critique of two political scientists, Donald Green and Ian Shapiro:

> We contend that much of the fanfare with which the rational choice approach has been heralded in political science must be seen as premature once the question is asked: What has this literature contributed to our understanding of politics? We do not dispute the theoretical models of immense and increasing sophistication that have been produced by practitioners of rational choice theory, but in our view the case has yet to be made that these models have advanced our understanding of how politics works in the real world. To date, a large proportion of the theoretical conjectures of rational choice theorists have not been tested empirically. Those tests that have been undertaken have either failed on their own terms or garnered theoretical support for propositions that, on reflection, can only be characterized as banal: they do little more than restate existing knowledge in rational choice terminology.   (1994, p. 6)

We can conclude this section by noting that the techniques employed by rational choice theorists are not foreign to the constructivist (as we expect many constructivists will be surprised to learn). After all, there is a hermeneutical edge to rational choice theorizing that is not unlike the techniques employed by constructivists. In the same way that the constructivist *tacks* back and forth between her implicit comparisons of the parts and its wholes, and in the same way that the social theorist *hops* back and forth between her imagined individuals and her imagined community, so too does the rational choice theorist *oscillate* back and forth between the imagined individuals in her model and the imagined collective outcome.

Even more to the point, however, we must recognize and acknowledge the central role played by context in thought experiments. Even though this context is largely imagined, the whole point of rational choice models and thought experiments is to consider alternative and reasonable parallel worlds, where imagined institutions and imagined contexts are imposed on individuals to consider how these individuals can be expected to react under different conditions.

Conclusion

True experiments, where contexts are manipulated in order to control for expected outcomes, are surely the least attractive method available to constructivists. Experiments are simply too destructive to the contexts that give meaning in the storytellers' stories. Neither do experiments play an absolutely central role in the actual practice of naturalist science – they have certainly not played a necessary part of ground-breaking scholarship in that tradition. Indeed, as we have hoped to show in this chapter, much of what the world's most innovative scientists actually do is quite close to the constructivist's heart. Employing thought experiments has helped scientists overcome some of the practical difficulties in assuming that there is only one Real World out there, and that we can get best access to it by empirical observation and/or experience. When we understand this, and allow for a somewhat broader definition of experiment, it becomes possible to see how scientists (of all shapes and colours) have used thought experiments to leverage our understanding of the human condition.

In finding this common ground, we have shown how thought experiments – with their fictionalized accounts – rely on contexts and employ hermeneutical approaches. In so doing, we find ourselves among the great canons of political and social theory, not far from traditional constructivist territory. At the same time, thought experiments deliver us to the back door of the naturalist tradition. Deductive models, such as those employed by rational choice theorists, return us unwittingly to Descartes and the important role that he (and others) played in providing naturalist science with an approach that relies on both deductive and inductive techniques.

This chapter leaves us in an odd place, straddling our two methodologies. Despite the central role that thought experiments have played in real scientific discoveries, they are quite alien to naturalism's methodology. The patterns inherent to thought experiments are created in the scientist's mind, and only touch down to the Real World at precise (and rather minute) points of tangency (for example, in finding a Viking ring pin at L'Anse aux Meadows; or in Darwin's pigeon-breeding evidence). The criterion for evaluating thought experiments is not empirical veracity, but logic and reason. Indeed, some of the most vocal critics of rational choice do so by pointing to the remarkable paucity of studies that substantiate rational choice's theoretical claims in the empirical world.

Because the patterned reality in thought experiments exists first and foremost in the mind of the researcher, we might expect this approach to be more attractive to constructivists. But there are important tensions here as well. Much of the strength of constructivism lies in the analyst's closeness to and familiarity with the particular parts (and the way they come together, hermeneutically, as a whole). Thought experiments exist in the ether that is Plato's *noesis* or *epistēmē*; they are far removed from commonsense understandings based on familiarity and experience (Plato's *pistis*). Although the objective of knowledge in thought experiments can be explicitly normative (as is clearly seen in the social theory tradition) there is also a strong commitment to an implicit demarcation principle of sorts (based on consistencies and context): there are right and wrong ways to solving the problems being considered.

Thought experiments encourage us to imagine a social science that is big enough and accommodating enough to embrace both naturalist and constructivist approaches to understanding the world. Our concluding chapter is used to elaborate on this observation.

Recommended Further Reading

Interested readers can follow up on the thought experiments literature by turning to Sorenson's *Thought Experiments* (1992). Social scientists interested in game theory are encouraged to read Gates and Humes' *Games, Information and Politics* (1997). For an overview of the rational choice controversy in social science, see Green and Shapiro's *Pathologies of Rational Choice Theory* (1994) and Friedman's *The Rational Choice Controversy* (1996).

Chapter 13

Conclusion

Detectives, such as Sherlock Holmes and Miss Marple, have played an important and recurring role in this book on social science methods and methodologies. There is a reason for this (as there are for so many things we do). Popper once noted that science is about solving mysteries, and we tend to agree. Science is all about solving problems and answering riddles; and scientific riddles are often derived from some observed regularity. Realizing this provides the key to opening our text: all scientists are concerned with patterns or regularities, but some social scientists argue that these patterns are part of the social world, whereas others argue that they are contingent.

On Design

The design of this book reveals much of our intent. It depicts two wondrously different manners of studying social phenomena: one half of the book is dedicated to naturalist approaches; the other to constructivist approaches. In each part we have described the different roles played by similar methods. More to the point, we have noted a strong methods hierarchy in the naturalist approach, as scholars in this tradition tend to prioritize experiments, statistics, comparisons and case studies (in that order). Naturalists are willing to subscribe to a strong demarcation principle that can be used to establish such a hierarchy.

The constructivist part of the book is more circular – at least, not linear – in design. Lacking a clear demarcation principle, constructivists tend to be less catholic with regard to questions of method. Not only are decisions regarding method usually left implicit, they are seldom used in a way that limits opinion or voice. Personally, we find this lack of a demarcation principle somewhat worrisome as we have no clear-cut measure for distinguishing between good and bad constructivist designs. This lack of a clear standard can easily lead to the (unfortunate) impression that 'anything goes' in the name of constructivism. This is clearly not the case; there is a point at which an analysis can lose both utility and credibility – for example, where deconstructing a text becomes more of a playful act than any sort of useful analytical device.[1] The problem is that

285

this demarcation line is a delicate one and its location seems to differ for each one of us: we have different sensibilities with respect to these things.

Even if they avoid an explicit demarcation principle, constructivists do find some methods more dependable than others. Most obviously, constructivists tend to rely on thick narratives, or storytelling techniques. This emphasis on narration and the importance of context and contingency is extended to the way in which constructivists employ comparisons: as a tool for developing associations that can leverage meaning. Consequently, comparisons play a central role in constructivist studies (as they do in naturalist studies). As statistical and experimental studies are seen to violate the very context that constructivists hold dear, these methods are seldom used by scholars in this methodological tradition. We think this is a mistake and a shame, so we have used the preceding two chapters to show how statistical and experimental approaches can be designed and used in ways that should appeal to constructivists.

As is common in social scientific endeavours, we can contrast the two approaches in a table, which outlines some of the most basic differences. In providing this table, however, we hasten to note that it cannot possibly capture the diversity and complexity that is each approach. This is why we have saved such a table for the concluding chapter. Like the constructivist's attitude towards numerical data, we fear that too much important information is lost when we try to distil a whole methodological tradition down to a number of simple table entries. Like the naturalist, however, we value the utility of having simple, concrete points of comparison. Table 13.1 is our attempt to balance these different concerns and provide a summary.

In introducing this type of methodological divide we hasten to reiterate that we employ the naturalist/constructivist dichotomy with at least two reservations. First, we are concerned that any dichotomy has the potential to solidify scholars into two disparate (and autonomous) camps. As we note below, we began writing this book because we were concerned about the effect of another divide on our students: we wanted to bridge what was commonly seen as a divide that separated quantitative from qualitative approaches. With this caveat in mind, we have proceeded with caution, as we believe there can be much utility in re-surveying any terrain, with a changed parallax. New perspectives – even if they result in new divisions – can be useful if they challenge our presuppositions and make us think anew about old problems.

Our second reservation concerns simple typologies: in dividing social phenomena into two groups we risk dividing some research projects down the middle. We also risk marginalizing different research traditions or particular authors. To resolve this potential dilemma we have tried to emphasize how these two approaches needn't be seen as exclusive or

Table 13.1 *Comparing approaches*

	Naturalism	*Constructivism*
View of the world	Objectively real/permanent	Human construction/changeable
View of man	Man is similar to material objects (e.g., man has mass and extension), but with a capacity to reason. Man can be seen as meaningless (literally), as will/agency is generally downplayed. Constant and predictable.	Like naturalists, but more. Greater focus on will, agency, reason and empathy: men and women are creatures of their context, and help to create it. Malleable.
View of knowledge	Cumulative and based on sensual experience (primarily observation).	Knowledge is overlapping: it advances, retreats and moves sideways. Willingness to embrace a much larger epistemological field: observation, authority, reason, empathy, etc.
View of theory	Theory is an aid to explaining and is used to reveal patterns in world. Theories are clusters of objective laws.	Theory is an aid to understanding and is used to reveal contingent phenomena. Theories are products of the human imagination.
View of truth	Subscribes to the correspondence theory: a statement is true when it corresponds to the facts in the Real World. Fixed.	Truth is derived from changing constellations of power and perspectives. Fleeting.
View of objectivity	Following Hume: normative studies should be banished from scientific study.	Normative framing is important, unavoidable, and should be brought out into the open.
View of language	Instrumental and objective. Language is an unbiased conduit for transmitting experience.	Language is saturated with meaning and is an important part of the social scientific project. Language helps to frame the way we understand the world.
View of context	Context is not important in itself: the world can be manipulated in a mechanical fashion to reveal causal relationships.	Context is central and must be protected in order to access meaning.

exclusionary. As we noted in the introductory chapter, this attitude is probably most familiar to students of International Relations – a sub-discipline in Political Science that has developed around a recognition of the utility in maintaining different ideological perspectives. For generations, students have been taught to understand the world in terms of wearing different-coloured lenses – that different perspectives provide different understandings of the international context, and that each is legitimate. It is in this embracing spirit that we think about the different methodological approaches to social science.

On Methodological Pluralism

The most important lesson that a student can take away from reading this text is a willingness to recognize and distinguish between the different methodological traditions used to understand social phenomena. Our intention in providing this methodological smorgasbord is to emphasize the need for students to be able to read, critically, contributions from both traditions. The social science literature (in general), and our own experiences (in particular), provides ample evidence of methodological misunderstanding. Worse, much contemporary social science straddles an uncomfortable chasm between the analysts' implied methodology and the methods they use.

In short, we hope to encourage students to understand social science in a way that is sensitive to the methodological presuppositions of the authors they read. Only in this light can we truly appreciate the way in which methods are used in such disparate ways. We also hope to encourage readers to consider their own methodological priors before beginning any research project. We fear that both objectives are discounted or ignored in traditional introductions to social science methods: ergo this book.

We encourage methodological pluralism with respect to the social sciences generally, and for individual authors in particular. The second position is, by far, the most contentious. After all, it is one thing to recognize that different approaches by different authors need to be evaluated differently. It is another thing altogether to suggest that individual authors might choose freely from this methodological potlatch.

After all: social analysts tend to see the social world as fixed and patterned; or they don't. But in the decade-long process of writing this book, and teaching the course that inspired it, we have begun to consider a less orthodox, and more difficult, position. In particular, by reading a wide variety of texts on the ontology of both natural and social sciences, we have come to accept the possibility of embracing more than one ontological (and hence methodological) perspective. How could this be? Perhaps analysts simply tend towards one ontological view (or the other) because they are brought up to see the world in these terms. Perhaps this, too, is a convention that can be relaxed. We regret that there are few easy answers to this difficult question (here too!).

We have come to this position from the simple recognition that we gain something useful and important from both approaches. Sometimes we can better understand the world through the lenses of naturalism. Sometimes, however, these same lenses tend to obscure more than they clarify. It seems to us that recent developments in the natural sciences are opening up the possibility of a sort of methodological rapprochement between naturalist and constructivist methodologies. It is becoming increasingly acceptable to recognize, like Roscoe (1995, p. 500), that because:

> the physical world is neither wholly deterministic nor wholly regular or recurrent in its action, natural scientists get on with analyzing those aspects of the physical world that do seem to exhibit regularity or recurrence.

The same sort of distinction is clearly evident in the social world as well. Indeed, scientific realism is spearheading many of these developments on both fronts. The social world is not wholly determinist nor wholly regular or recurrent in its action. Consequently, social scientists shouldn't be afraid to impose naturalist (and dependable) frameworks to get on with analysing those aspects of the social world that do seem to exhibit regularity or recurrence. After all, we have learned a great deal about the social world by employing approaches that are based on these ontological and epistemological foundations. At the same time, we should be open-minded enough to recognize that much of social life doesn't fit into this pattern, at least not comfortably. As in the natural sciences, understanding certain parts of the social world might require that we loosen the naturalist's grip, encouraging different methodological approaches and attitudes.

It is this embrace of methodological pluralism that distinguishes our approach from that of the scientific realists. While scientific realists seek a new synthesis – one that can draw on the best that naturalism and constructivism have to offer – we think it is more helpful to separate the different methodological positions to help illustrate the different and complicated ways that ontological, epistemological and methodological choices can influence a researcher's choice and application of methods. Sometimes compromise is useful; at other times compromise is costly. Because of this we are sceptical of any attempt to create a new hegemonic vision of science.

In short, we have come to the conclusion that it is possible for the individual to choose and change her methodology. This means that designing a research strategy requires the consideration of several preliminary steps. First of all, before an analyst decides upon and applies a given method or methodological approach to a problem, she needs to consider the nature of the phenomenon in question. At this point, analysts might choose between a naturalist and a constructivist methodology – whichever is best suited for the phenomenon and question under consideration. Once this issue is resolved, the analyst can proceed in choosing the appropriate method and apply it according to the requirements and sensitivities of the chosen methodology.

At this point we can return to Joan Robinson's toolbox metaphor from the introductory chapter. Like a good craftsperson, we can let the problem at hand determine which toolbox and tool is best suited for the job. As social scientists, then, it is possible to be a handyperson (or general practitioner) – somebody who owns a number of different toolboxes (or medicine bags), and can solve any number of different (but usually relatively simple and/or common) problems. Indeed, we tend to think of ourselves in this way: methodological jacks-of-all-trades; masters of none.

We believe that by embracing methodological pluralism we can best pursue one of the central objectives that we share with scientific realists: the need to encourage problem-driven (not methods-driven) science. Synthesizing diverse methodological positions does not always make sense, as each particular methodological perspective brings something unique to our understanding of complex social phenomena. Attempts at compromise can risk jeopardizing the value that each perspective brings to the compromise. Rather than trying to unify different ontological and epistemological positions, we might follow Richard Rorty's recommendation (with respect to reconciling different traditions in liberal thought) to look at the relations between these two methodologies 'as being like the relations between two types of tools – as little in need of synthesis as paintbrushes and crowbars' (Rorty, 1989, p. xv).

But it is also possible for social scientists to become specialists: experts in wielding hammers (even a particular type of hammer, say a framing hammer) or screwdrivers; stethoscopes or crystals. The point of this metaphor, however, is to remind the reader that specialists have their own limitations, because of the narrow scope of their work. Specialists should avoid playing the role of the general practitioner, and vice versa; like Plato's citizens in *The Republic*, each of us should be aware of our limitations, and be satisfied with our contribution to the bigger picture. This requires that the specialist recognize the limited scope of her expertise, as well as the legitimate utility of generalists and specialists working in other areas.

Over the course of writing this text we have come around to a position that recognizes individual methodological pluralism. This realization is not meant to affect the student's own use or interpretation of our text. We are not looking for methodological converts. We mention our own personal conversion in closing, because we feel that readers of this book deserve an honest answer to a very difficult question raised by the nature of the text itself.

On Methodological Rapprochement

In encouraging students to be aware of methodological pluralism, we do not aim to incite methodological warfare or secession. To the contrary, our objective is to draw together the disparate trends in today's analyses of social phenomena. Our hope is that by introducing new social science students to the wide array of methods and methodological choices that are available to them, we can contribute to a sort of methodological rapprochement. Obviously, this type of rapprochement will require some flexibility from scholars in both the naturalist and constructivist camps. Luckily, both camps have much to gain and learn from one another.

For example, naturalists need to come to terms with the important role of narratives and constitutive contexts; they need to recognize more explicitly the biases associated with their own narrow definition of data and authority; and they need to stop trying to monopolize scientific discourse.

As we have hinted at throughout the book, the natural sciences have already come to recognize the utility of alternative approaches. It can only be sheer stubbornness and inflexibility that keeps this sort of suppleness out of the social sciences (a realm where arguably the role of agency and reflexivity should be more pronounced). 'Even if humans could, in theory, act to subvert all regularity in their behavior, it is unlikely that they would do so in practice if for no other reason than cultural reproduction – indeed, human reproduction and survival – would become impossible' (Roscoe, 1995, p. 500). In fact, it is possible to see a weakening of the naturalist's grip in all the fields of social science.

For constructivists, on the other hand, rapprochement will require a willingness to be more open (indeed, honest) about the methods and methodological choices that lie behind (or beneath) their research projects. To our mind, constructivist scholars have most to gain by engaging in dialogue with the hegemonic camp. In particular, we note two related gains that might attract constructivists to the promise of rapprochement.

First, like MacIntyre (1972), constructivists risk throwing out the baby with the bathwater. By dwelling on the problematic way in which naturalists employ their methods, constructivists can miss out on important methodological developments that could improve their own interpretations and understandings of the world. Rapprochement can allow constructivists to jettison their (unfounded) reputation of being methodologically unsophisticated or their uncomfortable tendency to lean heavily on a single, serendipitous method.

Second, constructivists tend to drive an artificial wedge between their own activities and those of science (Holy, 1987). By refusing to engage in mainstream social science, constructivists risk getting caught in an academic tide pool. Without the circulation of new influences and methods, such tide pools can easily become stagnant. Constructivists, most of all, need an infusion of new methods for maintaining and protecting the context that is so central to their project.

Finally, this sort of rapprochement might contribute to a broader, more encompassing definition of science. Instead of subscribing to a narrow and exclusionary demarcation principle, a methodological rapprochement can encourage us to define science in much more flexible terms. Already in 1913, Theodore Roosevelt worried about the increasing specialization of knowledge that was distancing the study of history from that of science. He wrote: 'Because history, science, and literature have become specialized, the theory now is that science is definitely severed from literature and that history must follow suit. Not only do I refuse to accept this as true for history but I do not even accept it as true for science' (Roosevelt, 1913, p. 475). For Roosevelt – reminiscing about a time 'when history was distinguished neither from poetry, from mythology, nor from the first dim beginnings of science' (ibid., p. 473) – history, science and literature were fruitful allies in the battle for understanding.

This type of rapprochement might allow us to embrace Collingwood's (1962, pp. 22–3) distinction between:

> the desultory and casual thinking of our unscientific consciousness and the orderly and systematic thinking we call science. In unscientific thinking our thoughts are coagulated into knots and tangles; we fish up a thought out of our minds like an anchor foul of its own cable, hanging upside-down and draped in seaweed with shellfish sticking to it, and dump the whole thing on deck quite pleased with ourselves for having got it up at all. Thinking scientifically means disentangling all this mess, and reducing a knot of thoughts in which everything sticks together anyhow to a system or series of thoughts in which thinking the thoughts is at the same time thinking the connexions between them.

Such a broad and embracing definition of science can make it easier to encourage collaboration across the methodological divide.

The recent growth and popularity of scientific realism is, we think, evidence of a changing attitude and willingness to find common ground. This is the most important part of methodological rapprochement. But it is also important to emphasize that rapprochement implies 'tension' and the development of cordial relationships between previously antagonistic camps. In short, rapprochement is an explicit recognition of the equal worth of each part in a contentious relationship – not an attempt to overcome them by imposing a new hegemonic order. We fear that scientific realism harbours these sorts of imperial ambitions.

On the Numerology Divide

We wish to close by pointing to a hiatus. The alert reader has probably noticed that, throughout the text, we have avoided any reference to 'quantitative' and 'qualitative' methods. It is important for us to conclude by emphasizing that the dichotomy delineated in this book (naturalist/constructivist) *does not* dovetail or harmonize with this older, counterproductive, divide.

The quantitative/qualitative divide, if it ever existed, is a relic of the past. Worse, it is a remarkably offensive relic: after all, this divide implies that quantitative work lacks quality. By continually harping on a division between quantitative and qualitative methods, we end up doing more harm than good: we reproduce this detestable division, keep a useless debate artificially alive, and undermine attempts to build bridges across what has become a divide (even if it is an imagined one). Indeed, by dwelling on the qualitative/quantitative divide we are doing just the opposite: rather than bridge building, we facilitate trench digging among social scientists. This quantitative/qualitative schism has been the incubus of social science for almost 100 years. We can live with it no more.

In today's field of research one can find new methods and techniques that have already wiped out any meaningful differences between quantitative and qualitative studies. The growing appeal and sophistication of Qualitative Comparative Analysis (QCA), as described in Chapter 5, is evidence of this trend. Likewise, as we have endeavoured to show in Chapter 11, constructivists can now employ some of the most sophisticated empirical tools on the market to help them approach and understand the patterns they study. At the same time, naturalist social scientists are increasingly aware of the importance of employing narrative and context-supporting approaches when uncovering their own (different) patterns. It is high time for methods teachers to take heed and relegate concepts like 'qualitative research methods' to the dustbins of history. All of us, on both sides of an imposed methodological divide, can produce quality research.

It is remarkable (and frightening) to see how many of our students enrol in a class on historical and comparative methods because they are intimidated by numbers. In encouraging students to think in these terms we are encouraging them to limit themselves to very narrow views of the world. In the same way that some statisticians – having learned to use a hammer – see the whole world as a nail, social scientists suffering from numberphobia risk seeing the whole world as a screw.

To erase this false distinction, we have emphasized the way in which few-N studies actually require more methodological reflection and sophistication than large-N studies (as there is less analytical leeway, fewer degrees of freedom, and more problems to face). In addition, we have used the last couple of chapters to show that some of the most sophisticated 'quantitative' strategies can be associated with the constructivist methodology.

There is no reason to encourage students to consider research projects in terms of a qualitative/quantitative divide. Similarly, we caution against making too much of the difference between the naturalist and constructivist approaches introduced above. Our hope is that readers of this text will take us seriously when we encourage them to embrace methodological pluralism. It is in choosing this path that we can best exploit the manifold ways of knowing.

Notes

Chapter 1 Introduction

1. In a review for the science magazine, *Nature*, Pimm and Harvey (2001, p. 149) suggested that Lomborg 'employs the strategy of those who argue that . . . Jews weren't singled out by the Nazis'. Allegations of the Antichrist are found in Browne (2002).
2. Lomborg was eventually (17 December 2003) cleared of 'scientific dishonesty' by Denmark's Ministry of Science, Technology and Innovation.
3. McCloskey (1986, p. 26) hints that this depiction should be attributed to the economist Joan Robinson, but we are not aware of any direct reference.
4. For those who would like to learn more about scientific realism, influential social science introductions to it include Sayer (2000); Shapiro and Wendt (2005); Lane (1996); and Somers (1998). See also Archer et al. (1998).
5. We hasten to note that there is a difference between 'empiricism' and 'empirical'. Both of the methodological traditions covered in this book embrace empirical descriptions of the world. Empiricism, by contrast, is an approach to research that relies heavily on observation and experiment, and a belief that only such an approach can yield true knowledge about the world. Consequently, the terms 'empiricism' and 'positivism' can be understood as close siblings to our naturalist methodology.

Chapter 2 Philosophy of Naturalist Science

1. Karl Popper also had many contacts with the Vienna Circle, though he did not formally belong. Wittgenstein's *Tractatus* was discussed in the Circle, and there were several meetings between Wittgenstein, Schlick, Waismann and Carnap. The Circle members published a de facto manifesto: Hahn et al.'s (1929) *Wissenschaftliche Weltauffassung. Der Wiener Kreis* [A Scientific World View. The Vienna Circle].

Chapter 3 The Experimental Method

1. In the fuller version of the argument, Galileo explained that all objects fall with the same speed *in principle*. He did not expect that all bodies should fall with the same speed in practice, for the simple reason that small and large bodies have different surface areas and that large surface areas would involve greater air resistance – and such resistance would slow the fall of the larger-surfaced bodies.

2. Donald Campbell is the author most associated with the concepts of internal and external validity. For Campbell, internal validity is the 'appropriate validity with which we infer a relationship between two variables is causal', while external validity refers to 'the approximate validity with which we can infer that the presumed casual relationship can be generalized to and across alternate measures of the cause and effects as well as across different types of persons, settings and times' (Cook and Campbell, 1979, p. 37). Subsequent controversy led Campbell (1986) to devise new labels (internal validity became 'local molar causal validity'; external validity became 'proximal validity'), but the concepts have become so common in the vocabulary of the social scientist, we think it is useful to keep them.

3. Extrinsic factors are those that occur prior to the experiment (such as selection effects); intrinsic factors include those that occur during the study period, changes in the measuring instrument, or the reactive effect of the observation itself. See Frankfort-Nachmias and Nachmias (1996, pp. 106ff.) for a more detailed discussion and examples.

4. For one group of rats, Maier would hide the food behind the same symbol, but would change the symbol's location – sometimes it would be on one door, sometimes on the other – in order to map the *symbol–reward responses* of the animals. For another group of rats, Maier would keep the location of the food constant, but he would move the symbol between the two doors, in order to test the *position–reward responses* (Maier, 1949, p. 26). Although the jumping sessions were interrupted by 'vacations' of up to 4 months, Maier laconically comments that 'out of 31 rats, 21 survived this period of testing' (ibid., p. 44).

Chapter 4   The Statistical Method

1. As an illustration of the continued strength of this cleavage between statistics and science, we refer to a letter by Mark Lynas to the editors of *The Economist* (16 February 2002), in response to their glowing review of Lomborg's *The Skeptical Environmentalist*. Mr Lynas's letter begins: 'Mr Lomborg is not a scientist, he is a statistician.'

2. Of course, this example is hypothetical. Actual data were used in a regression study by Romer (1993) to show that attendance may substantially affect (economics) learning.

3. Galton's first formulation used the word 'reversion', by which he meant 'the tendency of that ideal mean type to depart from the parent type, "reverting" towards what may be roughly and perhaps fairly described as the average ancestral type' (Galton, 1877, p. 513). Later, he changed his reference of the 'coefficient of reversion' to the 'coefficient of regression'. See Gillham (2001, p. 203).

4. For a critique of this position, see McKeown (1999) and Brady and Collier (2004).

5. For example, if we do not set the constant to zero, and let it float freely, the equation becomes: $GRADES = -0.7051 + .7726\ ATTENDANCE$; with an

R^2 of .939. Note how the slope to this equation is steeper, and the strength of the explanatory model increases (from .9224 to .939). But interpreting the constant term forces us to suggest that a student who hadn't attended any classes would get a negative number (–0.7051) of good grades. This hardly makes sense.

6. A spurious relation is one in which two or more variables are found to be statistically related (they co-vary), but they are not in fact causally linked – usually because the variable is caused by a third (lurking) variable. Sometimes spurious relations are referred to as 'illusory correlations'; this refers to a special case when a correlation is not present in the original observations, but is an artefact of the way in which the data are handled.

7. For a deeper discussion of developments along these lines, see Jackson (1996).

Chapter 5   The Comparative Method

1. MVQCA can be performed using software programs such as TOSMANA (Tool for Small-N Analysis, see http://www.tosmana.org) and/or Charles Ragin's 'Fuzzy Sets' (fs/QCA software – see Ragin (2000, 2004)). For more information on developments in this exciting field, see the COMPASSS homepage (COMParative methods for the Advance of Systematic cross-case analysis and Small-n Studies) at http://www.compassss.org.

2. In addition, Mill had a fifth: the Method of Residues. Following Durkheim (1964, p. 129), however, we do not think that this method has any special utility in the study of social phenomena. Social phenomena are too complex for us to eliminate the effect of all causes, save one.

3. Each of Mill's four definitions that follow was presented in italics in the original text. The italics have been dropped in our presentation.

4. It is not, however, the same as the statistical approach, in that statistical methods rely on probabilistic relationships; the comparative method establishes patterns of invariance. See Ragin (1987, pp. 39–40).

Chapter 6   History and Case Studies

1. Hobsbawm (1997, p. 11) sees this exploitation of history for patriotic purposes as a major threat to serious historiography in the new nations of Eastern Europe. He warned, in a speech to the students of the Central European University in Budapest, that 'we cannot wait for the generations to pass. We must resist the *formation* of national, ethnic and other myths, as they are being formed. It will not make us [the historians] popular. Thomas Masaryk, founder of the Czechoslovak Republic, was not popular when he entered politics as the man who proved, with regret but without hesitation, that the medieval manuscripts on which the Czech national myth was based were fakes. But it has to be done, and I hope those of you who are historians will do it.'

2. Tuchman may concede that this is, of course, true in principle. But it does not affect the mechanics of writing. She (1981, p. 22) explains how she wrote her critically acclaimed book *The Guns of August*, about the outbreak of the First World War: 'Though it may seem absurd, I even cut references to the ultimate defeat of Germany. I wrote as if I didn't know who would win, and I can only tell you that the method worked. I used to become tense with anxiety myself, as the moments of crisis approached . . .'
3. Judge Grey's 300-page long discussion of Mr Irving's works is found at: http://www.pixunlimited.co.uk/news/rtf/irvingjudgment.rtf.

Chapter 7   Sowing Doubts and the Naturalist Methodology

1. In short, this principle in quantum mechanics holds that increasing the accuracy of measurement of one observable quantity increases the uncertainty with which another conjugate quantity may be known. To this we should add that Heisenberg recognized there are quantitative bounds on these uncertainties.
2. Although it is important to recognize that Huntington's civilizations are remarkably amorphous. Huntington himself is not sure whether Africa should be categorized as a civilization – in other words, his definition of civilization is so diffuse that the author can't even decide whether it applies to a given case. This very amorphousness is probably one of the reasons for Huntington's broad appeal – but pursuing this argument will lead us too far astray from the issues at hand.
3. The authors are careful to note that the explanation is incomplete, in that the probability of a French worker, 24, employed in a large factory, and voting Communist is still far from 1.00. There are, of course, several other factors that can explain his vote.

Chapter 8   A Constructivist Philosophy of Science

1. Indeed, when Kant learnt that some critics had confused his argument with that of George Berkeley, he immediately distanced himself from Berkeley and tried to express himself more clearly. Berkeley, an Irish clergyman, wrote a *Treatise Concerning the Principles of Human Knowledge* [1710], in which he rejected material substance altogether. Berkeley argued that the world as presented to our senses depends for its existence on being perceived. In the second edition of his *Critique of Pure Reason*, Kant added a section where he referred to Berkeley's view as 'empirical idealism' and refuted it. To distinguish his view from Berkeley's, he then labelled his own argument 'empirical realism' and defended it.
2. We should note that Kant provides intellectual support for many contemporary academic traditions, not all of which could be called constructivist. This is a result of Kant's intellectual breadth and scope of influence. Our

focus is on Kant's ontological stance: his willingness to separate our knowledge of *phenoumena* from our (lack of) knowledge about *noumena*. By contrast, and for example, the search by neo-Kantian political theorists for substantive principles of social organization and ethics (that are deontological in form) does not necessarily lend itself to a constructivist methodology. For a discussion along these lines, see Shapiro (1990, pp. 3–18).

3. In 1840, Whewell wrote, 'we need very much a name to describe a cultivator of science in general. I should incline to call him a scientist' (quoted in Williams, 1976, p. 279).

4. The 'Frankfurt School' aimed to develop a new, interdisciplinary and critical theory of contemporary society, by drawing on the works of Hegel, Marx, Nietzsche, Freud and Weber. The Frankfurt School included, among others, Herbert Marcuse, Max Horkheimer, Theodor Adorno, Erich Fromm, Leo Lowenthal and Jürgen Habermas. See Jay (1973) and Wiggenhaus (1995) for overviews.

5. Note that the first title is a play on the title of Emile Durkheim's famous *Elementary Forms of Religious Life*. The latter title is a pun. It is known in English as *The Savage Mind* – the author's own title, *Pansies for Thought*, was turned down by the American publisher. The translated title, however, fails to capture the multiple meanings of the original. In French '*pensée*' means both 'thought' and a particular flower ('pansy'); '*sauvage*' means both 'primitive', 'savage' and 'wild'. This book, which presents Lévi-Strauss's theory of culture and mind, seeks to identify the most basic (or 'primitive' or 'wild') or universal forms of human thought – forms which we all use. The French edition retains to this day a picture of a pansy on its cover.

Chapter 9 From Story Telling to Telling Histories

1. For an elaboration of this argument, see Knutsen (2002).

2. Foucault's definition of this key term is influenced by structuralist arguments and is related to Kuhn's concept of a paradigm. Foucault explains that the concept of the episteme refers to:

> the total set of relations that unite, at a given period, the discursive practices that give rise to epistemological figures, sciences, and possibly formalized systems . . . The episteme is not a form of knowledge [*connaissance*] or type of rationality which, crossing the boundaries of the most varied sciences, manifests the sovereign unity of the subject, a spirit, or a period; it is the totality of relations that can be discovered for a given period, between the sciences when one analyses them at the level of discursive regularities.   (Foucault, 1972, p. 191)

3. For more, see the recent biographies by Jones (1998) and Haslam (2000). Consider, also, some of Carr's own work. For example: Carr [1939], *The Twenty-Years' Crisis* or his *magnum opus* on Russia.

4.　In particular, Carr (1987) saw history as a dialectic between the historian and his facts (Chapter 1) and between society and the individual (Chapter 2). As we have already broached the difficulties that analysts face with their data, this section will elaborate on the relationship between the analyst and her context.

Chapter 10　Comparing Interpretations

1.　Sigmund Freud, 'Delusions and Dreams in Jensen's *Gradiva*', in *The Standard Edition of the Complete Psychological Works of Sigmund Freud*, vol. IX (London: Hogarth Press, 1907), p. 8. Here quoted from Flyvbjerg (2001, p. 18).

Chapter 11　Contextualising Statistics

1.　This video can be downloaded from: http://www.colorado.edu/IBS/GAD/spacetime.html.

Chapter 12　Interpretive Experiments

1.　On the importance of building patriotism, see Rousseau's *Considerations sur le government du Pologne*, II: 437. On the importance of equality, see his *Projet de Constituion pour la Corse* and extracts from *Emile*.
2.　Formally, a stag hunt is defined by a game with two pure strategy equilibriums. Both players prefer one equilibrium to the other – it is both Pareto optimal and Hicks optimal. However, the inefficient equilibrium is less risky as the payoff variance over the other player's strategies is lower. Specifically, one equilibrium is payoff-dominant, while the other is risk-dominant. Other names for the same game include 'assurance game', 'coordination game', and 'trust dilemma'.

Chapter 13　Conclusion

1.　This may be illustrated by adding a third detective. Where Sherlock Holmes represents the naturalist approach to mysteries, and Jane Marple the constructivist approach, Thursday Next is a postmodernist, deconstructivist sleuth. She is a LiteraTec – that is, an agent in section 27 (the literary section) of the British Special Operations Network. Her first major case – a series of kidnappings (related in Fforde, 2003) – is triggered, first by the removal of a minor character in *Martin Chuzzlewit* and then by the disappearance of the heroine in Bronte's *Jane Eyre*. Literary detective Thursday Next finds that villain Acheron Hades is behind these evil acts (although, he is not precisely evil, he's more, 'like . . . well differently moralled'). Hades is set on destroying the British identity, either by kidnapping the protagonists of the nation's famous novels or by introducing devious clones to stage hostile takeovers of famous plots. Having proven herself as a clever sleuth, Ms. Next is transferred to the section of Jurisfiction – first as an ordinary Prose Resource Operative; later she advances to become its director.

References

Acton, Lord Emerich Edward Dalberg (1907) *The Cambridge Modern History: Its Origins, Authorship and Production* (Cambridge: Cambridge University Press).

Acton, Lord Emerich Edward Dalberg (1906a) 'Inaugural Lecture on the Study of History'. [1895] In his *Lectures on Modern History*, edited by John Neville Figgis and Reginald Vere Laurence (New York: Macmillan), pp. 1–30. Available online at <http://oll.libertyfund.org/ToC/0028.php>. Accessed 14 December 2005.

Acton, Lord Emerich Edward Dalberg (1906b) 'Letters to Contributors to the Cambridge Modern History'. [1898] In his *Lectures on Modern History*, edited by John Neville Figgis and Reginald Vere Laurence (New York: Macmillan), pp. 315–19.

Adorno, Theodore and Max Horkheimer (1979) *Dialectic of the Enlightenment* (London: Verso) [1944].

Almond, Gabriel A. and Sidney Verba (1965) *The Civic Culture: Political Attitudes and Democracy in Five Nations* (Boston, MA: Little Brown and Company) [1963].

Anscombe, F. J. (1973) 'Graphs in Statistical Analysis', *American Statistician* 27 (February): 17–21.

Archer, Margaret, Roy Bhaskar, Andrew Collier, Tony Lawson and Alan Norrie (eds) (1998) *Critical Realism: Essential Readings* (London: Routledge).

Ayer, Alfred J. (1952) *Language, Truth and Logic* (New York: Dover) [1936].

Bacon, Francis (1627) *Sylva Sylvarum, or a Naturall Historie in Ten Centuries* (London: William Rawley).

Bacon, Francis (1994) *Novum Organum* (Chicago, IL: Open Court) [1620].

Ball, Terence (1987) 'Introduction'. In Terence Ball (ed.), *Idioms of Inquiry: Critique and Renewal in Political Science* (Albany, NY: SUNY Press), pp. 1–12.

Banfield, Edward C. (1958) *The Moral Basis of a Backward Society* (New York: Free Press).

Bates, Robert H., Avner Greif, Margaret Levi, Jean-Laurent Rosenthal and Barry R. Weingast (1998) *Analytic Narratives* (Princeton, NJ: Princeton University Press).

Becker, H. S. (1968) 'Observation: Social Observation and Social Case Studies'. In D. L. Sills (ed.), *International Encyclopaedia of the Social Sciences*, vol. 2 (New York: Macmillan).

Bellah, Robert, Richard Madsen, William M. Sullivan, Ann Swidler and Steven M. Tipton (1986) *Habits of the Heart* (New York: Harper and Row).

Bendix, Reinhardt (1964) *Nation Building and Citizenship. Studies of Our Changing Social Order* (London/New Brunswick: Transaction Publishers).

Bendix, Reinhardt (1978) *Kings or People* (Berkeley, CA: University of California Press).

Berger, Peter L. and Thomas Luckmann (1966) *The Social Construction of Reality* (New York: Doubleday).

Berkeley, George (1998) *Treatise Concerning the Principles of Human Knowledge,* edited by Jonathan Dancy (Oxford: Oxford University Press) [1710].

Berlin, Isaiah (1954) *Historical Inevitability* (London: Oxford University Press).

Best, Joel (2001) *Damned Lies and Statistics* (Berkeley, CA: University of California Press).

Bloch, Marc (1953) 'Toward a Comparative History of European Societies [*Pour une histoire comparée des sociétés européenes*]'. In Fredric C. Lane and Jelle C. Riemersma (eds), *Enterprise and Secular Change* (London: Allen and Unwin), pp. 494–521.

Bloch, Marc (1967) *Land and Work in Medieval Europe. Selected Papers by Marc Bloch,* translated by J. E. Anderson (Berkeley, CA: University of California Press).

Bloch, Marc (1973) *The Royal Touch: Sacred Monarchy and Scrofula in England and France* (London: Routledge and Kegan Paul). Originally published as *Les rois thaumathurges* [1924].

Bourdieu, Pierre (1977) *Outline of a Theory of Practice* (Cambridge: Cambridge University Press).

Brady, Henry E. and David Collier (eds) (2004) *Rethinking Social Inquiry. Diverse Tools, Shared Standards* (Oxford: Rowman and Littlefield).

Braudel, Fernand (1977) *Afterthoughts on Material Civilization and Capitalism* (Baltimore, MD: The Johns Hopkins University Press).

Browne, Anthony (2002) 'Glum Greens vs Eco-optimists in Global Mudfight', *The Observer,* 10 March.

Bryson, Bill (2003) *A Short History of Nearly Everything* (New York: Broadway).

Burke, James (1985) *The Day the Universe Changed* (Boston, MA: Back Bay Books).

Burton, Dawn (2000) 'The Use of Case Studies in Social Science Research'. In Dawn Burton (ed.), *Research Training for Social Scientists* (London: Sage), pp. 215–25.

Campbell, Donald T. (1975) ' "Degrees of Freedom" and the Case Study', *Comparative Political Studies* 8(2): 178–93.

Campbell, Donald T. (1986) 'Relabeling Internal and External Validity for Applied Social Scientists'. In W. Trochim (ed.), *Advances in Quasi-Experimental Design Analysis: New Directions for Program Evaluation* (San Francisco, CA: Jossey-Bass), pp. 67–77.

Campbell, Donald and Julian Stanley (1966) *Experimental and Quasi-Experimental Designs for Research* (Chicago, IL: Rand McNally).

Cantor, Norman F. (1991) *Inventing the Middle Ages: The Lives, Works and Ideas of the Great Medievalists of the Twentieth Century* (New York: W. Morrow).

Capra, Fritjof (1982) *The Turning Point: Science, Society and the Rising Culture* (New York: Simon and Schuster).

Carr, Edward Hallett (1987) *What is History?*, 2nd edn (Harmondsworth: Penguin) [1961].

Carr, Edward Hallett (2001) *The Twenty Years' Crisis, 1919–1939* (Basingstoke: Palgrave Macmillan) [1939].

Chaffee, Steven H. (1989) 'Review of *News That Matters: Television and American Opinion*', *Public Opinion Quarterly* 53(2): 277–78.

Chirot, Daniel (1984) 'The Social and Historical Landscape of Marc Bloch'. In Theda Skocopol (ed.), *Vision and Method in Historical Sociology* (Cambridge: Cambridge University Press), pp. 22–46.

Christensen, Larry (2001) *Experimental Methodology* (Boston, MA: Allyn and Bacon).

Christie, Agatha (2000) *A Pocket Full of Rye* (New York: Signet) [1953].

Cochran, William G. (1976) 'Early Development of Techniques in Comparative Experimentation'. In D. B. Owen (ed.), *On the History of Statistics and Probability* (New York and Basle: Marcel Dekker), pp. 1–26.

Collingwood, R. G. (1956) *The Idea of History* (New York: Galaxy) [1946].

Collingwood, R. G. (1962) *An Essay on Metaphysics* (Oxford: Clarendon Press) [1940].

Collins, Randall (1980) 'Book Review: *States and Social Revolutions*', *Theory and Society* 9(4): 647–51.

Comte, Auguste (1949) *Cours de philosophie positive: (première et deuxième leçons): Discours sur l'esprit positif* (Paris: Garnier Frères) [1830–42].

Converse, Philip E. (1964) 'The Nature of Belief Systems in Mass Politics'. In D. E. Apter (ed.), *Ideology and Discontent* (New York: Free Press), pp. 206–62.

Converse, Philip E. (1970) 'Attitudes and Non-attitudes: Continuation of a Dialogue'. In Edward R. Tufte (ed.), *The Quantitative Analysis of Social Problems* (Reading, MA: Addison-Wesley).

Cook, T. D. and Donald T. Campbell (1979) *Quasi-Experimentation* (Chicago, MA: Rand McNally).

Dahl, Robert (1971) *Polyarchy: Participation and Opposition* (New Haven, CT: Yale University Press).

DCSD (Danish Committees on Scientific Dishonesty) (2002) 'Decision Regarding Complaints against Bjørn Lomborg'. Available online at <http://www.forsk.dk/uvvu/nyt/udtaldebat/bl_decision.htm>. Accessed 5 May 2003.

Dean, Mitchell (1999) *Governmentality: Power and Rule in Modern Society* (London: Sage).

DeLillo, Don (1988) *Libra* (New York: Viking).

Descartes, René (1973) *Discours de la Methode* (Osnabruck: Editio Simile) [1637].

Descartes, René (1993) *Mediations on the First Philosophy*, edited and with an introduction by Stanley Tweyman (London: Routledge) [1641].

Dewey, John (1910) *How We Think* (London/Boston: Heath).

Diesing, Paul (1992) *How Does Social Science Work? Reflections on Practice* (Pittsburgh, PA: University of Pittsburgh Press).

Downs, Anthony (1957) *An Economic Theory of Democracy* (New York: Harper and Brothers) [1950].

Doyle, Sir Arthur Conan (1927) 'Silver Blaze'. In Sir Arthur Conan Doyle, *The Complete Sherlock Holmes* (New York: Doubleday and Company), pp. 335–50.

Doyle, Sir Arthur Conan (1930) *The Sign of Four* (London: Longman) [1890].

Dunn, John (2005) *Setting the People Free: The Story of Democracy* (London: Atlantic).

Durkheim, Emile (1952) *Suicide: A Study in Sociology* (London: Routledge & Kegan Paul).

Durkheim, Emile (1964) *The Rules of Sociological Method and Selected Texts on Sociology and Its Method*, translated by Sarah A. Solovay and John H. Mueller; edited by George E. G. Catlin (New York: The Free Press) [1895].

Eckstein, Harry (1975) 'Case Study and Theory in Political Science'. In Fred I. Greenstein and Nelson W. Polsby (eds), *Strategies of Inquiry*. Handbook of Political Science, vol. 7 (Reading, MA: Addison-Wesley), pp. 79–137.

Einstein, Albert (1953) 'Aphorisms for Leo Baeck'. Reprinted in *Ideas and Opinions* (New York: Dell).

Einstein, Albert (1905) 'On the Electrodynamics of Moving Bodies'. English translation of Einstein's original 1905 German-language paper (published as 'Zur Elektrodynamik bewegter Körper' in *Annalen der Physik* 17: 891). An electronic (English) version is available online at <http://www.fourmilab.ch/etexts/einstein/specrel/specrel.pdf>. Accessed 3 December 2005.

Elton, G. R. (1967) *The Practice of History* (London: Fontana).

Euben, Roxanne L. (1999) *Enemy in the Mirror. Islamic Fundamentalism and the Limits of Modern Rationality* (Princeton, NJ: Princeton University Press).

Evans, Richard J. (1997) *In Defence of History* (London: Granta).

Fearon, James (1991) 'Counterfactuals and Hypothesis Testing in Political Science'. *World Politics* 42 (January): 169–95.

Febvre, Lucian (1983) *The Problem of Unbelief in the Sixteenth Century* (Cambridge, MA: Harvard University Press). Originally published as *Le problème de incroyance au XVIe siècle: la Religion de Rabelais* [1942].

Feyerabend, Paul (1975) *Against Method* (London: Verso).

Feyerabend, Paul (1978) *Science in a Free Society* (London: New Left Books).

Fforde, Jasper (2003) *The Eyre Affair* (London: Penguin).

Fish, Stanley (1987) 'Dennis Martinez and the Uses of Theory', *Yale Law Review* 96: 1773–1800.

Fisher, Ronald A. (1953) *The Design of Experiments*, 6th edn (London: Oliver and Boyd) [1935].

Flyvbjerg, Bent (1998) *Rationality and Power. Democracy in Practice* (Chicago, IL: University of Chicago Press).

Flyvbjerg, Bent (2001) *Making Social Science Matter* (Cambridge: Cambridge University Press).

Fogel, Robert William (1964) *Railroads and American Economic Growth: Essays in Economic History* (Baltimore, MD: Johns Hopkins Press).

Fogel, Robert William and Stanley L. Engerman (1974) *Time on the Cross: The Economics of American Negro Slavery* (Boston, MA: Little, Brown and Company).

Foucault, Michel (1965) *Madness and Civilization: A History of Insanity in the Age of Reason*, translated by Richard Howard (London: Tavistock).

Foucault, Michel (1970) *The Order of Things* (London: Routledge).

Foucault, Michel (1972) *The Archaeology of Knowledge and the Discourse on Language*, translated by A. M. Sheridan Smith (New York: Pantheon).

Foucault, Michel (1977) *Discipline and Punish: The Birth of the Prison*, translated by Alan Sheridan (New York: Vintage) [1975].

Foucault, Michel (1978) *The History of Sexuality*, vol. 1: *An Introduction* (New York: Vintage).

Foucault, Michel (1984) 'The Order of Discourse'. In Michael J. Shapiro's (ed.), *Language and Politics* (Oxford: Basil Blackwell), pp. 108–39.

Frankfort-Nachmias, Chava and David Nachmias (1996) *Research Methods in the Social Sciences*, 5th edn (New York: St. Martins).

Freedom House (2000) 'Democracy's Century'. Available online at: <http://www.freedomhouse.org/reports/century.pdf>. Accessed 21 December 2005.

Freedom House (2005) 'Freedom in the World 2005: Tables & Charts'. Available online at <http://www.freedomhouse.org/research/freeworld/2005/tables.htm>. Accessed 21 December 2005.

Freud, Sigmund (1996) *The Interpretation of Dreams*, translated by A. A. Brill (New York: Gramercy Books) [1900].

Friedman, Jeffrey (1996) 'Introduction: Economic Approaches to Politics'. In Jeffrey Friedman (ed.), *The Rational Choice Controversy* (New Haven, CT: Yale University Press), pp. 1–24.

Froude, J. A. (1963) *Short Studies on Great Subjects* (London: Fontana) [1867].

Frye, Northrop (1957) *Anatomy of Criticism* (Princeton, NJ: Princeton University Press).

Fukuyama, Francis (1992) *The End of History and the Last Man* (New York: Free Press).

Furet, François (1999) *The Passing of an Illusion*, translated by Deborah Furet (Chicago, IL: University of Chicago Press) [1995].

Gadamer, Hans-Georg (1984) 'The Hermeneutics of Suspicion'. In Gary Shapiro and Alan Sica (eds), *Hermeneutics* (Amherst, MA: University of Massachusetts Press), pp. 54–65.

Galileo, Galilei (1957) 'The Starry Messenger'. [1610] In *Discoveries and Opinions of Galileo* (New York: Doubleday), pp. 21–59.

Galton, Francis (1869) *Hereditary Genius* (London: Macmillan).

Galton, Francis (1873) 'Africa for the Chinese'. Letter to the Editor of *The Times*, 5 June. Available online at: <http://galton.org/letters/africa-for-chinese/AfricaForTheChinese.htm>. Accessed 21 July 2006.

Galton, Francis (1877) 'Typical Laws of Heredity'. *Nature* 15 (5 April): 492–5, 512–14, 532–3.

Galton, Francis (1886) 'Regression towards Mediocrity in Hereditary Stature'. *Journal of the Anthropological Institute* 15: 246–63.

Galton, Francis (1889) *Natural Inheritance* (London: Macmillan). Available online at <http://galton.org/books/natural-inheritance/pdf/galton-nat-inh-1up-clean.pdf>. Accessed 6 December 2005.

Galton, Francis (1904) 'Eugenics: Its Definition, Scope and Aims'. *The American Journal of Sociology* 10(1). Available online at <http://galton.org/essays/1900-1911/galton-1904-am-journ-soc-eugenics-scope-aims.htm>. Accessed 10 January 2005.

Galton, Francis (1908) *Memories of My Life* (London: Methuen).

Garfinkel, Harold (1984) *Studies in Ethnomethodology*, 2nd edn (Cambridge: Polity) [1967].

Gates, Scott and Brian D. Humes (1997) *Games, Information and Politics* (Ann Arbor, MI: University of Michigan Press).

Geddes, Barbara (1990) 'How the Cases You Choose Affect the Answers You Get', *Political Analysis* 2: 131–50.

Geddes, Barbara (2003) *Paradigms and Sand Castles* (Ann Arbor, MI: Michigan University Press).

Geertz, Clifford (1971) *Islam Observed: Religious Development in Morocco and* Indonesia (Chicago, IL: University of Chicago Press).

Geertz, Clifford (1972) 'Deep Play: Notes on the Balinese Cockfight', *Dædalus* 101(1): 1–37.

Geertz, Clifford (1975) 'On the Nature of Anthropological Understanding', *American Scientist* 63 (January–February): 47–53.

Geertz, Clifford (1993) *The Interpretation of Cultures* (London: Fontana Press) [1973].

Giavazzi, Francesco and M. Pagano (1988) 'The Advantage of Tying One's Hands: EMS Discipline and Central Bank Credibility', *European Economic Review* 32: 1055–82.

Giddens, Anthony (1982) 'Hermeneutics and Social Theory'. In Anthony Giddens, *Profiles and Critiques in Social Theory* (Berkeley, CA: University of California Press), pp. 1–17.

Gilbert, E. W. (1958) 'Pioneer Maps of Health and Disease in England', *Geographical* Journal 124: 172–83.

Gill, Richardson B. (2000) *The Great Maya Droughts: Water, Life and Death* (Albuquerque, NM: University of New Mexico Press).

Gillham, Nicholas Wright (2001) *A Life of Sir Francis Galton* (Oxford: Oxford University Press).

Ginzburg, Carlo (1980) *The Cheese and the Worms: The Cosmos of a Sixteenth-Century Miller* (New York: Penguin).

Goldstein, Leon (1976) *Historical Knowing* (Austin, TX: University of Texas Press).

Gooding, David (1992) 'The Procedural Turn; or, Why Do Thought Experiments Work?' In Robert N. Giere (ed.), *Minnesota Studies in the Philosophy of Science*, vol. 15: *Cognitive Models of Science* (Minneapolis, MN: University of Minnesota Press), pp. 45–76.

Graff, Gerald (1979) *Literature against Itself* (Chicago, IL: University of Chicago Press).

Graunt, John (1996) *Natural and Political Observations . . . upon the Bills of Mortality*, rendered into HTML format by Ed Stephan, 25 January 1996. Available online at <http://www.ac.wwu.edu/~stephan/Graunt/0.html>. Accessed 5 December 2005 [1662].

Green, Donald P. and Ian Shapiro (1994) *Pathologies of Rational Choice Theory* (New Haven, CT: Yale University Press).

Gunnell, John G. (1982) 'Interpretation and the History of Political Theory: Apology and Epistemology', *American Political Science Review* 76: 317–27.

Gurr, Ted R. (1970) *Why Men Rebel* (Princeton, NJ: Princeton University Press).

Hague, Rod, Martin Harrop and Shaun Breslin (1998) *Comparative Government and Politics*, 4th edn (Basingstoke, Palgrave Macmillan).

Hahn, Hans, Otto Neurath, Rudolf Carnap and Moritz Schlick (1929) *Wissenschaftliche Weltauffassung. Der Wiener Kreis* (Vienna: A. Wolf).

Hall, Peter (2003) 'Aligning Ontology and Methodology in Comparative Research'. In James Mahoney and Dietrich Rueschemeyer (eds), *Comparative Historical Analysis in the Social Sciences* (Cambridge: Cambridge University Press), pp. 373–404.

Hammond, Phillip (ed.) (1964) *Sociologists at Work* (New York: Basic Books).

Hanson, Norwood Russell (1961) *Patterns of Discovery* (Cambridge: Cambridge University Press).

Hanushek, E. and J. Jackson (1977) *Statistical Methods for Social Scientists* (New York: Academic).

Haslam, Jonathan (2000) *The Vices of Integrity* (London: Verso).

Hempel, Carl G. (1942) 'The Function of General Laws in History', *Journal of Philosophy* 39: 35–48.

Hempel, Carl G. (1969) 'Explanation in Science and History'. [1962] In Robert H. Nash (ed.), *Ideas of History*, vol. II (New York: E. P. Dutton), pp. 79–105. Originally published in R. G. Colodny (ed.) (1962) *Frontiers of Science and Philosophy* (Pittsburgh: University of Pittsburgh Press), pp. 9–33.

Hindess, Barry (1973) *The Use of Official Statistics in Sociology* (Basingstoke: Palgrave Macmillan).

Hobbes, Thomas (1958) *Leviathan* (New York: Bobbs-Merill Company) [1651].

Hobsbawm, Eric (1962) *The Age of Revolution, 1789–1848* (New York: New American Library).

Hobsbawm, Eric (1989) *The Age of Empire, 1875–1914* (London: Cardinal) [1987].

Hobsbawm, Eric (1994) *The Age of Extremes* (London: Michael Joseph).

Hobsbawm, Eric (1996) *The Age of Capital, 1848–1875* (New York: Vintage) [1975].

Hobsbawm, Eric (1997) 'Outside and Inside History'. In Eric Hobsbawm, *On History* (London: Little Brown), pp. 1–13.

Hollis, Martin (1994) *The Philosophy of Social Science* (Cambridge: Cambridge University Press).

Holy, Ladislav (1987) 'Introduction: Description, Generalization and Comparison: Two Paradigms'. In Ladislav Holy (ed.), *Comparative Anthropology* (Oxford: Basil Blackwell), pp. 1–21.

Homer (1999) *The Odyssey*, translated by Samuel Butler. Project Guttenberg e-text. Available online at: <http://www.gutenberg.org/etext/1727>. Accessed 4 October 2006.

Hughes, John (1990) *The Philosophy of Social Research*, 2nd edn (London: Longman).

Hull, David (1973) *Darwin and His Critics: The Reception of Darwin's Theory of Evolution by the Scientific Community* (Cambridge, MA: Harvard University Press).

Hume, David (1983) *An Inquiry Concerning Human Understanding*, 8th edn (Indianapolis, IN: Bobbs-Merrill) [1748].

Huntington, Samuel P. (1991) *The Third Wave: Democratization in the Late Twentieth Century* (Norman, OK: University of Oklahoma Press).

Huntington, Samuel P. (1993) 'The Clash of Civilizations?' *Foreign Affairs* 72(3): 22–49.

Huntington, Samuel P. (1996) *The Clash of Civilizations* (New York: Touchstone).

Hyman, Ray (1989) 'The Psychology of Deception', *Annual Review of Psychology* 40: 133–54.

Ingstad, Helge and Anne Stine Ingstad (2001) *The Viking Discovery of America* (New York: Checkmark Books).

Iyengar, Shanto (1991) *Is Anyone Responsible?* (Chicago, IL: University of Chicago Press).

Iyengar, Shanto and D. R. Kinder (1987) *News that Matters* (Chicago, IL: University of Chicago Press).

Jackson, John E. (1996) 'Political Methodology: An Overview'. In Robert E. Goodin and Hans-Dieter Klingeman (eds), *A New Handbook of Political Science* (Oxford: Oxford University Press), pp. 717–48.

Jay, Martin (1973) *The Dialectical Imagination: A History of the Frankfurt School and the Institute of Social Research, 1923–1950* (Boston, MA: Little, Brown).

Jones, Charles (1998) *E. H. Carr and International Relations: A Duty to Lie* (Cambridge: Cambridge University Press).

Kant, Immanuel (1929) *Critique of Pure Reason*, translated by Norman Kemp Smith (London: Macmillan) [1787].

Kant, Immanuel (1942) 'Notizen zur Beantwortung einer Preisfrage der Berliner Akademie über die Fortschritte der Metaphysik'. In *Gesammelten Werken* Akademie-Ausgabe, vol. 20: 253–332. Available online at <http://www.ikp.uni-bonn.de/kant/aa20/>. Accessed 12 January 2005.

Kant, Immanuel (1969) 'Prolegomena to any Future Metaphysics' [1783]. In Robert P. Wolf (ed.), *Ten Great Works of Philosophy* (New York: New American Library), pp. 298–400.

Kant, Immanuel (1991) 'Perpetual Peace' [1795]. In Immanuel Kant, *Political Writings*, edited by Hans Reiss (Cambridge: Cambridge University Press), pp. 93–130.

Karlén, W. (1984) 'Dendrochronology, Mass Balance and Glacier Front Fluctuations in Northern Sweden'. In N.-A. Morner and W. Karlen (eds), *Climatic Changes on a Yearly to Millennial Basis* (Dordrecht: D. Reidel Publishing), pp. 263–71.

King, Gary, Robert O. Keohane and Sidney Verba (1994) *Designing Social Inquiry* (Princeton, NJ: Princeton University Press).

Kittel, Bernhard (1999) 'Sense and Sensitivity in Pooled Analysis of Political Data', *European Journal of Political Research* 35(2): 225–53.

Kittel, Bernhard and Herbert Obinger (2003) 'Political Parties, Institutions, and the Dynamics of Social Expenditures in Times of Austerity', *Journal of European Public Policy* 10(1): 20–45.

Knapp, T. R. (1996) *Learning Statistics through Playing Cards* (Thousand Oaks, CA: Sage).

Knutsen, Torbjørn L. (1997) *A History of International Relations Theory* (Manchester: Manchester University Press).

Knutsen, Torbjørn L. (2002) 'Twentieth-Century Stories', *Journal of Peace Research* 39(1): 119–27.

Kuhn, Thomas S. (1957) *The Copernican Revolution* (Cambridge, MA: Harvard University Press).

Kuhn, Thomas S. (1970) *The Structure of Scientific Revolutions* (Chicago, IL: University of Chicago Press) [1962].

Landman, Todd (2000) *Issues and Methods in Comparative Politics* (London: Routledge).

Lane, Ruth (1996) 'Positivism, Scientific Realism and Political Science', *Journal of Theoretical Politics* 8(3): 361–82.

Leamer, Edward E. (1994) *Sturdy Econometrics* (Brookfield, VT: Edward Elgar).

Le Roy Ladurie, Emmanuel (1966) *Les Paysans des Langedoc* (Paris: Mouton).

Lévi-Strauss, Claude (1962) *La pensée sauvage* (Paris: Plon).

Lévi-Strauss, Claude (1964–71) *Mythologiques*, 4 vols (Paris: Plon).

Lévi-Strauss, Claude (1969) *The Elementary Structures of Kinship*, translated from the French by James Harle Bell, John Richard von Sturmer and Rodney Needham (Boston, MA: Beacon) [1949].

Lévi-Strauss, Claude (1973) *From Honey to Ashes*, translated from the French by John and Doreen Weightman (New York: Harper and Row) [1967].

Lévi-Strauss, Claude (1979) *The Raw and the Cooked: Introduction to a Science of Mythology*, translated from the French by John and Doreen Weightman (New York: Octagon) [1964].

Levy, Jack S. (1989) 'The Causes of War: A Review of Theories and Evidence'. In Philip E. Tetlock, Jo L. Husbands, Robert Jervis, Paul C. Stern and Charles Tilly (eds), *Behavior, Society and Nuclear War*, vol. 1 (New York: Oxford University Press), pp. 209–313.

Lewis-Beck, Michael S. (1980) *Applied Regression. An Introduction.* Quantitative Applications in the Social Sciences, No. 22 (London: Sage).

Lieberson, Stanley (1991) 'Small Ns and Big Conclusions: An Examination of the Reasoning in Comparative Studies', *Social Forces* 70: 307–20.

Lijphart, Arend (1971) 'Comparative Politics and the Comparative Method', *American Political Science Review* 65(3): 682–93.

Lijphart, Arend (1975) 'The Comparable-Case Strategy in Comparative Research', *Comparative Political Studies* 8(2): 158–77.

Locke, John (1984) *An Essay Concerning Human Understanding* (Glasgow: Collins) [1690].

Locke, John (2004) 'On the Conduct of the Understanding'. In *Collected Works of John Locke*, vol. II (Liberty Fund Edition).

Lodge, David (1993) 'Changing Places'. In David Lodge, *A David Lodge Trilogy: Changing Places; Small World; Nice Work* (London: Penguin), pp. 219–578.

Lomborg, Bjørn (2001) *The Skeptical Environmentalist. Measuring the Real State of the World* (Cambridge: Cambridge University Press).

Lomborg, Bjørn (2002) 'Bjørn Lomborg's Comments to the 11-page Critique in January 2002 *Scientific American*'. Available online at <http://www.lomborg.com/files/SABLnoInf2.pdf>. Accessed 5 May 2003.

Lundberg, George A. (1926) 'Case Work and the Statistical Method', *Social Forces* 5: 60–3.

Lustick, Ian S. (1996) 'History, Historiography, and Political Science: Multiple Historical Records and the Problem of Selection Bias', *American Political Science Review* 90(3): 605–18.

MacIntyre, Alasdair (1972) 'Is a Science of Comparative Politics Possible?' In Peter Laslett, W. G. Runciman and Quentin Skinner (eds), *Philosophy, Politics and Society*, 4th series (Oxford: Basil Blackwell), pp. 8–26.

Mahoney, James and Gary Goertz (2004) 'The Possibility Principle: Choosing Negative Cases in Comparative Research', *American Political Science Review* 98(4): 653–69.

Maier, Norman (1949) *Frustration: The Study of Behavior Without a Goal* (Ann Arbor, MI: University of Michigan Press).

Mannheim, Karl (1936) *Ideology and Utopia* (London: Routledge & Kegan Paul).

Marey, Étienne Jules (1878) *La métode graphique dans les sciences expérimentales et principalement en physiologie et en médicine* (Paris: G. Masson). Online at Virtual Library at the Max Planck Institute for the History of Science (Berlin): <http://vlp.mpiwg-berlin.mpg.de/library/data/lit3585>. Accessed 4 October 2006.

Marsh, David and Paul Furlong (2002) 'A Skin Not a Sweater: Ontology and Epistemology in Political Science'. In David Marsh and Gerry Stoker (eds), *Theory and Methods in Political Science*, 2nd edn (Basingstoke: Palgrave Macmillan), 17–43.

Marx, Karl (1844) 'Private Property and Communism', *Economic & Philosophical Manuscripts of 1844* (third manuscript). Available online at <http://www.marxists.org/archive/marx/works/1844/manuscripts/comm.htm>. Accessed on 21 December 2005.

Mason, Stephen F. (1962) *A History of the Sciences* (New York: Macmillan).

Mazower, Mark (1998) *Dark Continent* (Harmondsworth: Penguin).

McCloskey, Donald (1986) *The Rhetoric of Economics* (Brighton: Harvester Press).

McCloskey, Deirdre and Stephen Ziliak (1996) 'The Standard Error of Regressions', *The Journal of Economic Literature* (March): 97–114.

McCloskey, Deirdre and Stephen Ziliak (2004) 'Size Matters: The Standard Error of Regressions in the *American Economic Review*.' Available online at <http://www.econ.mq.edu.au/seminars/McCloskey.pdf>. Accessed 18 March 2004.

McGraw, Kathleen M. (1996) 'Political Methodology: Research Design and Experimental Methods'. In Robert E. Goodin and Hans-Dieter Klingemann (eds), *A New Handbook of Political Science* (Oxford: Oxford University Press), pp. 769–86.

McKeown, Timothy J. (1999) 'Case Studies and the Statistical Worldview: Review of King, Keohane and Verba's *Designing Social Inquiry: Scientific Inference in Qualitative Research*', *International Organization* 53(2): 161–90.

Mill, John Stuart (2002) *A System of Logic* (Honolulu: University Press of the Pacific) [1891].

Miller, Richard W. (1987) *Fact and Method: Explanation, Confirmation, and Reality in the Natural and Social Sciences* (Princeton, NJ: Princeton University Press).

Moon, J. Donald (1975) 'The Logic of Political Inquiry: A Synthesis of Opposed Perspectives'. In Fred I. Greenstein and Nelson W. Polsby (eds), *Political Science: Scope and Theory*, vol. 1 (London: Addison-Wesley), pp. 131–228.

Moore, Barrington, Jr. (1966) *Social Origins of Dictatorship and Democracy* (Boston, MA: Beacon Press).

Moses, Jonathon W., Benoît Rihoux and Bernhard Kittel (2005) 'Mapping Political Methodology: Reflections on a European Perspective', *European Political Studies* 4: 55–68.

Nagel, Ernest (1961) *The Structure of Science* (New York: Harcourt, Brace and World).

Neurath, Otto (1959 [1932/33]) 'Protocol Sentences'. In A. J. Ayer (ed.), *Logical Positivism* (New York: Free Press).

Newton, Sir Isaac (1968) *Mathematical Principles of Natural Philosophy* (London: Dawsons of Pall Mall) [1687].

Nexon, Daniel and Iver Neumann (eds) (2006) *Harry Potter and International Relations* (London: Rowman & Littefield).

Nietzsche, Friedrich (1967) *On the Genealogy of Morals and Ecce Homo*, edited by Walter Kaufman (New York: Vintage).

North, Douglass C. (2005) *Understanding the Process of Economic Change* (Princeton, NJ: Princeton University Press).

Oakeshott, Michael (1933) *Experience and Its Modes* (Cambridge: Cambridge University Press).

Outhwaite, William (1975) *Understanding Social Life. The Method Called Verstehen* (London: George Allen and Unwin).

Parsons, Talcott (1949) *The Structure of Social Action*, 2nd edn (New York: Free Press).

Passmore, John (1987) 'Hume: Dialogue with John Passmore'. In Bryan Magee, *The Great Philosophers* (Oxford: Oxford University Press), pp. 144–67.

Pearson, Karl (1892) *The Grammar of Science* (London).

Pearson, Karl (1930) *The Life, Letters and Labors of Francis Galton* (Cambridge: Cambridge University Press).

Pearson, Karl (1978) *The History of Statistics in the 17th and 18th Centuries*, edited by E. S. Pearson (London: Charles Griffin).

Peceny, Mark (1997) 'A Constructivist Interpretation of the Liberal Peace', *Journal of Peace Research* 34(4): 415–30.

Peters, Thomas J. and Robert H. Waterman Jr. (2004) *In Search of Excellence* (New York: HarperCollins).

Pheby, John (1988) *Methodology and Economics. A Critical Introduction* (Armonk, NY: M. E. Sharpe).

Pimm, Stuart and Jeff Harvey (2001) 'No Need to Worry about the Future', *Nature* 414 (8 November): 149–50.

Plato (1987) *The Republic*, translated by Desmond Lee, 2nd edn (Harmondsworth: Penguin Books).

Poincaré, Henri (1904) 'Les définitions en mathématiques', *L'Enseignement Mathématique* 6: 255–383. English translation in *Science and Method* by Henri Poincaré (1914).

Polity IV (2005) 'Political Regime Characteristics and Transitions, 1800–2003'. 10 August version. Available online at <http://www.cidcm. umd.edu/inscr/polity/>. Accessed 21 December 2005.

Popper, Karl R. (1989) *Conjectures and Refutations: The Growth of Scientific Knowledge* (London: Routledge) [1953].

Popper, Karl R. (1994) 'Knowledge and the Shaping of Reality'. In Karl R. Popper, *Search of a Better World* (London: Routledge), pp. 3–30.

Popper, Karl R. (2002) *The Poverty of Historicism* (London: Routledge) [1957].

Poundstone, William (1992) *Prisoner's Dilemma* (New York: Doubleday).

Preston, Larry (1995) 'Theorizing Difference: Voices from the Margins', *American Political Science Review* 89(4): 941–53.

Prytz, Kåre (1991) *Westward before Columbus* (Oslo: Norsk maritimt forlag).

Przeworski, Adam and Henry Teune (1970) *The Logic of Comparative Social Inquiry* (New York: John Wiley and Sons).

Rabinow, Paul (1984) 'Introduction'. In Paul Rabinow (ed.), *The Foucault Reader* (New York: Pantheon), pp. 3–30.

Ragin, Charles C. (1987) *The Comparative Method* (Berkeley, CA: University of California Press).

Ragin, Charles C. (2000) *Fuzzy-Set Social Science* (Chicago, IL: Chicago University Press).

Ragin, Charles C. (2004) 'From Fuzzy Sets to Crisp Truth Tables'. COMPASSS Working Paper WP 2004–26. Available online at <http://www.compasss.org/WP.htm>. Accessed 10 January 2006.

Ragin, Charles C. and Howard S. Becker (eds) (1992) *What is a Case?* (Cambridge: Cambridge University Press).

Rampolla, Mary Lynn (2002) *A Pocket Guide to Writing in History* (New York: St. Martin's).

Ranke, Leopold von (1956) 'Preface' to *Histories of the Latin and German Nations from 1494 to 1514*. In Fritz Stern (ed.), *The Varieties of History* (New York: Random House), pp. 54–60.

Ringdal, Kristen (2001) *Enhet og Mangfold* (Bergen: Fagbokforlaget).

Romer, David (1993) 'Do Students Go to Class? Should They?' *Journal of Economic Perspectives* 7(3): 167–74.

Roosevelt, Theodore (1913) 'History as Literature', *The American Historical Review* 18(3): 473–89.

Rorty, Richard (ed.) (1967) *The Linguistic Turn: Essays in Philosophical Method* (Chicago, IL: University of Chicago Press).

Rorty, Richard (1979) *Philosophy and the Mirror of Nature* (Princeton, NJ: Princeton University Press).

Rorty, Richard (1982) *Consequences of Pragmatism* (Minneapolis, MN: University of Minnesota Press).

Rorty, Richard (1989) *Contingency, Irony and Solidarity* (New York: Cambridge University Press).

Roscoe, Paul B. (1995) 'The Perils of "Positivism" in Cultural Anthropology', *American Anthropologist* 97(3): 492–504.

Rousseau, Jean-Jacques (1950) 'Discourse of Political Economy' [1755]. In G. D. H. Cole (ed.), *The Social Contract and Discourses* (London: Dutton), pp. 283–330.

Rousseau, Jean-Jacques (1964) *The First and Second Discourses*, translated by Roger D. and Judith R. Masters (New York: St. Martin's).

Rousseau, Jean-Jacques (1971a) 'Projet de Constituion pour la Corse.' *Oeuvres complétes*, vol. III (Paris: Edition du Seuil), pp. 492–516.

Rousseau, Jean-Jacques (1971b) 'Considerations sur le government du Pologne.' *Oeuvres complétes*, vol. III (Paris: Edition du Seuil), pp. 527–70.

Rousseau, Jean-Jacques (1979) *Emile, or On Education* (New York: Basic Books) [1762].

Russett, Bruce (1993) *Grasping the Democratic Peace* (Princeton, NJ: Princeton University Press).

Russett, Bruce and John Oneal (2001) *Triangulating Peace* (New York: W.W. Norton).

Said, Edward W. (1978) *Orientalism: Western Conceptions of the Orient* (London: Routledge & Kegan Paul).

Saussure, Ferdinand de (1986) *Course in General Linguistics* (La Salle, IL: Open Court) [1916].

Sayer, Andrew (1992) *Method in Social Science*, 2nd edn (London: Routledge).

Sayer, Andrew (2000) *Realism and Social Science* (London: Sage).

Schelling, Thomas (1978) *Microfoundations and Macrobehavior* (New York: W.W. Norton and Co).

Schumpeter, Joseph. A. (1950) *Capitalism, Socialism and Democracy*, 3rd edn (New York: Harper and Row) [1942].

Searle, John. R. (1995) *The Construction of Social Reality* (New York: Free Press).

Seierstad, Åsne (2002) *Bokhandleren i Kabul: et familiedrama* (Oslo: Cappelen).

Sewell, William H. Jr. (1976) 'Marc Bloch and the Logic of Comparative History', *History and Theory* 6: 208–18.

Shapiro, Ian (1990) *Political Criticism* (Berkeley, CA: University of California Press).

Shapiro, Ian (2005) *The Flight from Reality in the Human Sciences* (Princeton, NJ: Princeton University Press).

Shapiro, Ian and Alexander Wendt (2005) 'The Difference that Realism Makes: Social Science and the Politics of Consent'. In Ian Shapiro, *The Flight from Reality in the Human Sciences* (Princeton, NJ: Princeton University Press), pp. 19–50.

Shapiro, Michael J. (1988) *The Politics of Representation. Writing Practices in Biography, Photography and Policy Analysis* (Madison, WI: University of Wisconsin Press).

Shapiro, Michael J. (1992) *Reading the Postmodern Polity* (Minneapolis, MN: University of Minnesota Press).

Skinner, Quentin (1975) 'Hermeneutics and the Role of History', *New Literary History* 7(1): 209–32.

Skocpol, Theda (1979) *States and Social Revolutions: A Comparative Analysis of France, Russia and China* (Cambridge: Cambridge University Press).

Skocpol, Theda (1984) 'Emerging Agendas and Recurrent Strategies'. In Theda Skocpol (ed.), *Vision and Method in Historical Sociology* (Cambridge: Cambridge University Press), pp. 356–91.

Skocpol, Theda (1994) 'A Critical Review of Barrington Moore's *Social Origins of Dictatorship and Democracy*'. In Theda Skocopol (ed.), *Social Revolutions in the Modern World* (Cambridge: Cambridge University Press), pp. 25–54.

Skocpol, Theda and Margaret Somers (1994) 'The Use of Comparative History in Macrosocial Inquiry'. In Theda Skocopol (ed.), *Social Revolutions in the Modern World* (Cambridge: Cambridge University Press), pp. 72–98.

Smelser, Neil (1973) 'The Methodology of Comparative Analysis'. In Donald Warwick and Samuel Osherson (eds), *Comparative Research Methods* (Englewood Cliffs, NJ: Prentice-Hall), pp. 45–52.

Snow, John (1855) *On the Mode of Communication of Cholera* (London).

Soboul, Albert (1958) *Les Sans-Culottes parisiens de l'An II* (La Roche-sur-Yon: H. Poitier).

Soboul, Albert (1962) *La Révolution française*, 2 vols (Paris: Gallimard).

Somers, Margaret R. (1998) ' "We're no Angels:" Realism, Rational Choice and Relationality in Social Science', *American Journal of Sociology* 104(3): 722–84.

Sorensen, R. (1992) *Thought Experiments* (Oxford: Oxford University Press).

Stigler, Stephen M. (1986) *The History of Statistics: The Measurement of Uncertainty before 1900* (Cambridge, MA: Belknap).

Stinchcombe, Arthur L. (1978) *Theoretical Methods in Social History* (New York: Academic Press).

Sullivan, J. L., J. E. Piereson and G. E. Marcus (1978) 'Ideological Constraint in the Mass Public: A Methodological Critique and Some New Findings', *American Journal of Political Science* 2: 233–49.

Sztompka, Piotr (1988) 'Conceptual Frameworks in Comparative Inquiry: Divergent or Convergent?' *International Sociology* 3(3): 207–18.

Tuchman, Barbara W (1962) *The Guns of August* (New York: Macmillan).

Tuchman, Barbara W (1966) *The Zimmerman Telegram* (New York: Macmillan).

Tuchman, Barbara W. (1981) 'In Search of History.' In Barbara W. Tuchman, *Practicing History* (New York: Ballantine Books), pp. 13–25.

Tufte, Edward R. (1983) *The Visual Display of Quantitative Information* (Cheshire, CT: Graphics Press).

Tufte, Edward R. (1997) *Visual Explanations* (Cheshire, CT: Graphics Press).

Vidal, Gore (2000) *The Golden Age* (New York: Doubleday).

Vogt, Paul W. (1993) *Dictionary of Statistics and Methodology* (London: Sage).

Waltz, Kenneth (1959) *Man, State and War* (New York: Columbia University Press).

Waltz, Kenneth N. (1979) *Theory of International Politics* (Reading, MA: Addison-Wesley).

Ward, Michael and John O'Laughlin. 'The Spread of Democracy'. Shockwave film available online at: <http://www.colorado.edu/IBS/GAD/spacetime.html>. Accessed 5 January 2006.

Weber, Max (1949) 'Objectivity in Social Science and Social Policy'. In Max Weber, *The Methodology of the Social Sciences*, translated and edited by Edward A. Shils and Henry A. Finch (Glencoe, IL: Free Press), pp. 50–112 [1904].

Western, Bruce and Simon Jackman (1994) 'Bayesian Inference for Comparative Research', *American Political Science Review* 88(2): 412–23.

Whewell, William (1967) *History of the Inductive Sciences*, 3 vols (London: Frank Cass) [1837].

Whewell, William (1996) *Philosophy of the Inductive Sciences*, 2 vols (London: Routledge/Thoemmes Press) [1840].

White, Hayden (1973) *Metahistory: The Historical Imagination in Nineteenth-Century Europe* (Baltimore, MD: Johns Hopkins University Press).

White, Hayden (1978) *Tropics of Discourse* (Baltimore, MD: Johns Hopkins University Press).

White, Hayden (1987) *The Content of the Form: Narrative Discourse and Historical Representation* (Baltimore, MD: Johns Hopkins University Press).

Wiggenhaus, Rolf (1995) *The Frankfurt School: Its History, Theories and Political Significance* (Cambridge, MA: MIT Press).

Williams, Raymond (1976) *Keywords* (London: Fontana).

Wilson, Edward O. (2003) *Consilience* (New York: Vintage).

Winch, Peter (1958) *The Idea of a Social Science and Its Relation to Philosophy* (London: Routledge and Kegan Paul).

Wittgenstein, Ludwig (1999) *Philosophical Investigations*, translated by G. E. M. Anscombe, 3rd edn (New York: Prentice Hall) [1953].

Wolf, Eric (1968) *Peasant Wars in the Twentieth Century* (New York: Harper Torchbooks).

Wong, Kathleen M. (2001) 'Too Warm for the Maya', in *California Wild* 53(2).

Wood, Michael (1986) *In Search of the Trojan War* (London: BBC).

Yin, Robert K. (1994) *Case Study Research: Designs and Methods*, 2nd edn (London: Sage).

Zimeny, G. H. (1961) *Method in Experimental Psychology* (New York: Ronald Press).

Index